# NATIVE AMERICANS, CRIME, AND JUSTICE

# NATIVE AMERICANS, CRIME, AND JUSTICE

*edited by*
## Marianne O. Nielsen
Northern Arizona University

## *and Robert A. Silverman*
Queen's University

A Division of HarperCollins*Publishers*

*For Harry and Grethe Nielsen, my parents, with love, and to*
*Dr. Chester Cunningham, my counsellor and guide,*
*with great appreciation*

**M.O.N.**

*For Dr. Gwynne Nettler, a wise man, whom I am fortunate to*
*count as friend, colleague, and mentor, and for Herb Goldstein and*
*Mack Gordon, native guides of a different sort*

**R.A.S.**

Published in 1996 in the United States of America by Westview Press, 5500 Central Avenue, Boulder, Colorado 80301-2877, and in the United Kingdom by Westview Press, 12 Hid's Copse Road, Cumnor Hill, Oxford OX2 9JJ

Library of Congress Cataloging-in-Publication Data
Native Americans, crime, and justice / edited by Marianne O. Nielsen
and Robert A. Silverman.
    p.   cm.
  Includes bibliographical references.
  ISBN 0-8133-2988-4 (hardcover). — ISBN 0-8133-2989-2 (pbk.)
  1. Indians of North America—Social conditions.   2. Crime—United
States.   3. Criminal justice, Administration of—United States.
I. Silverman, Robert A., 1943–   .
E98.C87N37   1996
364.3'497—dc20                                                     96-20809
                                                                   CIP

The paper used in this publication meets the requirements of the American National Standard for Permanence of Paper for Printed Library Materials Z39.48-1984.

10     9     8     7     6     5     4     3     2     1

# CONTENTS

# FOREWORD

## THE HONORABLE ROBERT YAZZIE
### *Chief Justice of the Navajo Nation*

We live in a postcolonial world. There have been five decades of efforts to end
alien control of distinct peoples in colonies. Most often, Native Americans and
other indigenous peoples are left out of the process. The picture is changing.
Around the world, there is a new awareness that indigenous peoples are still here.
Rather than assimilate or enter the mainstream of national (and nationalist) society, they keep their languages, cultures, and religions. One aspect of culture is law,
and there is still traditional law and government. Its use may be open, as with
Navajo Nation efforts to consciously use Navajo common law as the law of preference. There are subtle efforts to keep community justice, as with Canadian
Indians hiding offenses or child neglect cases from non-Native officials to handle
them locally.

States attempt two general approaches to indigenous law. Some take an integrationist approach to respond to high numbers of indigenous prison inmates
and the obvious failure of state law in dealing with social problems. That is, justice planners assume that if Native Americans are brought into the state system as
justices of the peace, judges, lawyers, police, or social workers, that will resolve the
problem. It does not. The law used by Native American actors in justice systems is
an alien law that does not respond to local needs and indigenous thinking about
justice. Native Americans are still subject to control by legislatures, attorneys general, or non–Native American program heads or police commanders.

The other approach is one of recognition. It assumes that communities are capable of handling their own problems and that a local decision is superior to an
imposed one. Colonial police and judges can attempt to watch and enforce, but
that works only so long as someone is watching. Native American leaders, including women, were stripped of their traditional positions as peacemakers, and social
disruption followed. The Courts of the Navajo Nation are conscious that even
they must address the issue of community empowerment. Accordingly, they use
Navajo common law as the law of preference in a national (that is, Navajo Nation)
court system, but they nourish the return of responsibility for justice to commu-

nities through peacemaking. Our courts recognize and enforce decisions made on a local level by the participants in a dispute and return justice competence to communities.

This book reviews the nature and sources of social disruption to clarify the issues. It outlines indigenous institutions and thinking to show Native American responses to contemporary justice problems. It clearly outlines the contrasts of "integrationist" and "recognition" approaches to crime so readers can form their own conclusions. This is a policy sourcebook that shows that effective justice comes from the people, from traditional leadership patterns, informed by the values of Native American languages, cultures, and religions. What is "crime"? It is an illness and the negation of traditional Native American values in modern life. The answer is not more power, force, and control by outsiders but the use of indigenous knowledge in community institutions under local control. This book offers important approaches to that process.

# Preface and Acknowledgments

The articles in this book were brought together because there is a growing interest about the involvement of Native peoples in the criminal justice system. *Native Americans, Crime, and Justice* is intended to introduce students to issues in this area and, therefore, should be of use to students of criminal justice, criminology, Native studies (Native American or American Indian studies), law, sociology, and anthropology. It will also provide resource materials for practitioners in the various criminal justice fields and in private agencies providing services to Native peoples.

It is a collection of edited articles by academic faculty and practitioners, a number of whom, we are happy to say, are of Native ancestry. The authors come from a wide range of disciplines and occupations, as can be seen from our list of contributors at the back of the book. Because this is an edited volume, there is no overall theoretical framework within which the articles are presented, although the issues are put into an overall context in Chapters 3 and 37. There are newspaper and other informal articles at the beginning of each section to give topical illustrations of the issues being discussed. Because this is an introductory book, we thought it desirable to expose the students to as wide a range of voices as possible. The writing levels and styles vary from chapter to chapter for the same reason, although the general level of writing should be comfortable for an introductory student.

The chapters are excerpts or edited versions of papers originally published in journals or other books, with the exception of five chapters that were especially written for this volume. A full reference is given for readers who wish to peruse the complete version of a paper. A combined reference section is given at the back of the book for the convenience of readers, which should be a rich source of materials for students who wish to pursue some of the topics presented in their term or research papers. The combined reference section represents a very contemporary overview of issues involving Natives and justice. However, we should apologize for one aspect of the reference section: Because our selections came from varied sources, the bibliographic styles varied enormously. We made every effort to provide complete references in the style of most criminal justice literature, but in a few cases we simply could not locate the complete reference. We have provided as much information as was available for those citations.

In putting together this volume, we discovered that empirical research on Native peoples was relatively scarce in the crime and criminal justice literature. We also learned that research into some of the areas of concern was more thorough in Canada than it has been in the United States. In fact, it is reasonable to say that Native issues of crime and justice have been neglected in U.S. research. In trying to present as broad a picture as possible of the past, present, and future of Native involvement, we issued a call for papers to U.S. universities with Native studies and criminal justice (and related) programs. We wish to thank all those who responded. Although the primary focus of this book is the United States, there are great similarities in the criminal justice issues faced by Native peoples in Canada and the United States. As a result we thought it appropriate to incorporate papers that discussed related issues and initiatives in Canada.[1] Despite all these efforts, we still feel the book is not as comprehensive as it could be. While we do have one article dealing with justice issues in Alaska, the issues specific to Inuit and Aleut are noticeably underrepresented, as are those specific to Native Hawaiians.

Unfortunately, in our society "law and order" is a growth industry, and stereotypes of Native involvement in the criminal justice system abound. Criminal justice system members make decisions based on inadequate or inaccurate information—decisions about new laws; new facilities; the life or death of service programs; the allotment of funding and resources for policing, courts, and corrections; even the freedom and fate of individuals. The distribution of knowledge is an important step in alleviating this situation. More educational courses are an important part of the process, but there is also a great deal of research waiting to be done. We encourage graduate students, especially Native graduate students, to give serious consideration to pursuing this area of study.

This book is organized in such a way that the reader is taken through the criminal justice system starting with the social and historical context of Native involvement in the criminal justice system. The differences in Native and non-Native culture and values are discussed so that the reader can get an awareness of these as sources of conflict within the criminal justice system. The theme is repeated often in the book. The section on law points out that Native peoples had well-functioning "legal" systems long before the non-Native system was imposed on them. This section also gives an overview of some of the major pieces of non-Native legislation that define the criminal justice powers of American Native nations today. The section on Native criminal behavior gives an overview of trends in crime statistics and highlights several categories of crime that are of particular importance to Native communities, including juvenile crime and family violence.

The sections on policing, courts and sentencing, and corrections describe some of the most important issues, including the effectiveness of Native police forces, the overrepresentation of Native offenders in jails, the lack of favorable parole decisions for Native offenders, and the need for Native spirituality programs in correctional institutions. The final section addresses the future of Native involvement in crime and in the criminal justice system. Initiatives based in traditional justice practices are discussed, along with the issues that surround them.

We believe the book that follows is a balanced collection that will introduce students to the major issues involved in Native American crime and justice. We could not have done it without the cooperation of many people. We are grateful to colleagues across the United States and Canada for allowing us to review their work. We are particularly indebted to those who allowed us to include and edit their articles and papers.

The Department of Criminal Justice at Northern Arizona University and the Department of Sociology at University of Alberta provided the atmosphere and tools that allowed us to complete the task. At Northern Arizona University, we are indebted to Arlene Bauer, the Department of Criminal Justice's administrative assistant, for patient assistance with the multitude of production details that putting together a book entails; to the students of CJ 415 (Native Americans and Criminal Justice) for their frequently creative feedback on earlier versions of the manuscript; to Pat Stetson of the Art Barn for her liaison work with Benson Halwood, our cover artist; and to Benson Halwood, a talented young Navajo artist who not only provided us with a beautiful cover but was very understanding about the limitations of color reproduction. At the University of Alberta we appreciate the work of Jana Grekul, Francis Donkor, and Avi Goldberg, who all participated in the tedious task of compiling the references. In the end, Jana put it all together in a most user-friendly form.

At Westview Press, we thank Jill Rothenberg, who was our contact person and supporter from the beginning. She was enthusiastic about the topic and its potential as a useful book and provided us with both the personal and institutional support necessary to bring this project to completion.

We welcome your comments and suggestions about this book. The path we walk is shared.

*Marianne O. Nielsen*
*Flagstaff, Arizona*

*Robert A. Silverman*
*Edmonton, Alberta*

# NOTES

1. In Canada Native peoples are referred to as Aboriginal Peoples or First Nations. We have kept this terminology when it occurred in the Canadian articles.

PART ONE

---

*Context*

# 1

*The New York Times*

# YEARNING TO BREATHE FREE

## Urban Indians Long for Lives Left Behind

BY N. R. KLEINFIELD

Without being dour, Lorraine Canoe makes do with life in New York City, but it is not the same. You can find all kinds of things, but the supermarkets do not stock deer meat or boiled corn bread. In no borough are regular Mohawk ceremonies held for each of the year's 13 moons.

"And it's not easy trying to find someone I can talk Mohawk with," she said.

This is why, after living in Brooklyn for more than 35 years, Ms. Canoe considers her real home to be Akwesasne, the Mohawk reservation that straddles

*The New York Times*, "Yearning to Breathe Free: Urban Indians Long for Lives Left Behind," N. R. Kleinfield, Tuesday, January 3, 1995: B1, B3. Copyright © 1995 by The New York Times Company. Reprinted by permission.

the border between New York and Canada. She was raised there, and it is only a matter of time before she returns for good to the place where everyone knows her as Kanaratitake, her given and preferred name.

Worshipful of Mohawk traditions but needing to work, the tough-spirited Ms. Canoe, 62, leads the split life of many American Indians transplanted to New York City. She savors the manic dazzle but finds her most resonant pleasure during occasional excursions, and frequent phone calls, back to the reservation.

Thousands of American Indians have moved off reservations into cities and towns across the United States to find jobs. And while many have spent years as high-rise Indians, they often suffer from a culture clash that causes them to yearn for the extended family, open spaces and time-honored ceremonies of their reservations. Those who have chosen New York have found the liabilities particularly pronounced.

"Most tribal customs are to take place on the earth," said Rosemary Richmond, the director of the American Indian Community House, a center that provides services and sponsors cultural events for Indians in New York and is currently marking its 25th year. "There is very little earth in New York City. And most of it is public and restricted. Catholics can go to a Catholic church in any city they move to. Indians have their own ways of worshiping that they can't find anywhere else."

According to the 1990 census, more than 26,000 American Indians live in New York City, nearly triple the number in 1980, making them one of the fastest-growing minorities in the city. And Indian organizations think the census figures undercount the actual population, and estimate it to be about 35,000, with the heaviest concentration in Brooklyn and Queens. New York City's Indians, thought to belong to more than 60 different nations, converge from as far away as Alaska. More Indians live in New York than on any reservation except the Oklahoma land areas and the Navajo reservation, which sprawls across Arizona, Utah and New Mexico. Among cities, only Los Angeles and Oklahoma City have higher Indian populations.

There has not been a true Indian neighborhood in New York since the 1950's and 1960's, when many Indians, principally Mohawks, congregated in downtown Brooklyn because they worked in construction and this was near the union hall. There was also a bar called the Wigwam where many of them drank. Indians have long been strongly represented in the construction industry; while most have a healthy respect for heights, they have a reputation for having little fear. A fair number of New York's Indians still work in construction, though far more are in artistic fields.

Many who come to New York today face difficulty finding work and decent housing. Indian organizations say they have a group unemployment rate of more than 45 percent, and many families live below the poverty level.

The American Indian Community House, in Greenwich Village, hopes to open a hotel within the next few years that will devote a sizable share of its space to housing Indians. The group also offers job counseling and substance abuse counseling, and it serves as a central meeting place where on any given day one is apt to find Senecas and Hopis and Shinnecocks.

Even if gainfully employed, many urban Indians wrestle with their connection to their past. Some want nothing to do with it. The children of one transplant did not even know they were Indians. Others keep up a superficial connection.

But there are many others who are attentive to their traditional customs, and for them, New York can be a lonely and constricting place. They miss the rituals. They are accustomed to open spaces. Animals are a vital part of their way of life. The simple act of going outdoors each day is starkly different from what it is on the reservation.

"People have done ceremonies in Central Park," said Ingrid Washinawatok, who came to New York in 1981 but intends to eventually move back to the Menominee Reservation in Wisconsin. "But Central Park is not truly clean so far as energy. Ceremonies aren't events. They are communications between you and whatever you want to call the creator. That should be done on the reservation."

In many ways, Ms. Canoe is typical of the urban Indian whose heart remains on the reservation. At her second-floor apartment in Sunset Park, Ms. Canoe was cooking and talking and cooing to her 7-month-old grandson—and she was happy. That was because her daughter, Monica, was visiting from the reservation.

Ms. Canoe, who teaches a course on conquered peoples in America at Hunter College, was especially upbeat because a few weeks earlier she had been to the reservation for the Harvest Ceremony, when the last food is removed from the earth. All boys born during the year are formally named at the ceremony, and her grandson had his name announced: Kaientatiesa.

"New York is very exciting," she said. "But the reservation is my home. The belief system is not the same. My belief system is the ceremonies in the longhouse. Here they go to church or synagogue. It's not the same."

In order to worship, she tries to get to the reservation for as many ceremonies as she can. There, traditional celebrations are held in a large building known as the longhouse. They require a Mohawk water drum with a deerskin top and rattles. On ceremonial occasions, Ms. Canoe puts on fringed and beaded clothes and moccasins. Men wear headdresses boasting three eagle feathers.

Although many Indians on the reservations have assimilated into mainstream American culture and attend Christian churches rather than longhouse ceremonies, Ms. Canoe is fervidly traditional. "That genocidal thought of religion has gotten into their heads," she said of nontraditionalist Indians. "The church is a crutch. It's a white man's religion. They brought it here to conquer us and civilize us."

Ms. Canoe takes the nine-hour bus trip to the reservation for about half of the 13 annual ceremonies, and spends her summer breaks from Hunter there. She owns a house on the reservation, where her two daughters—Monica, 26, and Sara, 23—live. Though both daughters were raised in New York, they moved to the reservation when they became adults. Ms. Canoe intends to retire in four years and settle there, as well.

She accompanied her husband, an ironworker, when he came to Brooklyn to work on the Verrazano-Narrows Bridge in 1958. The marriage eventually dissolved, but she stayed in the city and married Frank Montoia, a Mexican Indian. He is a window washer.

Not all of New York's food offerings are to Ms. Canoe's tastes, but she improvises. The three "sisters"—beans, corn and squash—are the sacred foods that are her staples. She makes her own boiled corn bread. She is not supposed to eat meat, like pork, that comes from an animal that would eat another animal.

She brings one of her favorites—deer meat—back from the reservation. She finds that Mexican restaurants serve dishes close to what she customarily eats.

Alcohol, she has come to believe, is something "the white man brought here to make us crazy." Thus she swore off drinking 20 years ago. She even refuses to use wine vinegar or to cook with any form of alcohol.

Another difficulty for urban Indians is that the public perception of them is rarely to their liking. Too often, in their view, it is an erroneous, simple-minded conception of warring heathens. "People say stupid things to us," Ms. Richmond said. "Like, 'Hey, chief,' or 'Do you live in a tepee?' You're always treated as a savage or an alcoholic."

Monica said she moved to the reservation three years ago because she felt incomplete in New York. Her husband, Ron LaFrance, is an audiovisual technician and teaches song and dance on the reservation.

"I've tried being in the city and it wasn't for me," he said. "I just feel more freer. It's not like we're living in a rain forest. But anywhere you go on the reservation, there are trees. I like to look for hawks. That's a little hard in the city."

And life on the reservation is more relaxed. "We have a thing that we call Indian time," Mr. LaFrance said. "If you set a meeting for 8, people will show up at 8:30 or a quarter to 9. It's not a fast-paced life."

# 2

*Albuquerque (New Mexico) Tribune*

## URBAN REFUGE

BY TINA GRIEGO

There's a tiny stucco office building, almost hidden in a row of apartments and auto body shops in the Southeast Heights, where there are stories, in hundreds of variations, as familiar as the hum of passing traffic.

They are stories from what's been half-jokingly called New Mexico's second-largest reservation: Albuquerque. They are told by the so-called urban Indians, a term disliked by some American Indians, but then again, that's the least of their worries.

\*     \*     \*

A young woman stops at a discount store. She can't find what she needs and leaves, pushing her daughter ahead of her in the shopping cart. The store manager and a security guard run after her. She is a Navajo with a law degree. "Can I sign your receipt?" the manager

*Albuquerque Tribune,* "Urban Refuge," Tina Griego, July 6, 1994: B5–6. Reprinted with permission of the *Albuquerque Tribune.*

asks. "I didn't buy anything," she replies. "Did you check out with the customer service desk before you left?" "I didn't buy anything," she repeats. "Well, can I search your diaper bag?" She doesn't have a diaper bag.

\*     \*     \*

A woman and her family were in trouble. They'd been away from the reservation too long, didn't want to go back. Everyone told them the same thing. "You're Indian, why don't you just go to the Bureau of Indian Affairs? Why don't you just go to Indian Health Services? You're Indian, why don't you just go home?"

\*     \*     \*

In a way these stories are the Albuquerque Indian Center, which, like the people it serves, is misunderstood by many, supported by few and until recently, was ignored by the city it calls home.

Last week, at a symposium he sponsored to develop the city's first urban

Indian policy, Mayor Martin Chavez said he would urge the City Council to help fund the center, which now runs on donations and state funds.

If that happens, Indian Center board members say, it could become a central gathering place for the city's Indian residents, it could be something Indians in town haven't had for a long time: a familiar doorway to a strange city, a place to meet, to learn, to joke, a little slice of home.

"Roughly 30,000 Native Americans are living here and many come from rural areas or reservations and it's really a culture shock for them," said board member Nate Mayfield, a Cherokee/Osage Indian who has lived in cities all his life. "The center is a place they can go and socialize with people of the same background, where they can make that transition to urban life in a sane fashion."

And, board members say, they want to bring attention to a population of thousands that seems invisible.

"UNM has never had an Indian on its Board of Regents, there's never been an Indian on the County Commission or on the City Council," said artist Sam English, a Chippewa who has his own art gallery in Old Town. "Yet in terms of the dollars we bring to the city, the taxes we pay, we get nothing in return. We talk about equality in our country, about democracy and jobs and we are not getting it."

If you are Indian and you live in Albuquerque, you are three times as likely to be refused a bank loan. You are twice as likely to be unemployed as anyone else in the county, and more likely to be living in poverty.

A quarter of your children never graduate from high school, and of those who make it to college, eight out of 10 will drop out after the first year.

If you are a male, you have a one in three chance of dying before your 36th birthday.

But if you survive all that, if you become a lawyer or a teacher, if you have two master's degrees, if people from New York are paying $2,000 for one of your paintings, it still doesn't mean that someday some security manager won't demand your receipt.

"I think in general a lot of people think Indian people don't pay taxes, or we are all on welfare, that we get some kind of subsidy either from the federal government or the tribes," said Angelita Benally, the executive director of the center and the woman who was stopped outside the discount center. "They see us only in stereotypes."

\*     \*     \*

In the earliest days, when everyone would listen and nod politely but no one would give them any money, the Albuquerque Indian Center was just a name they called themselves.

There was no center. Starved for money, it closed in the early 1980s.

In those days, Tony Jojola, now a businessman, worked for Albuquerque Public Schools Indian Education Program as a home/school liaison. It gave him and his colleagues a firsthand look at how Indians in the city were living, and that convinced them that an Indian Center must be resurrected.

"There were things like finding families living in cars and still sending their children to school, families living in campgrounds, things like finding absolutely nothing in the house to eat," Jojola recalled. "And actually, those were pretty routine."

The problems of urban Indians have been blamed in part on the 1950s' federal policy of forced assimilation. During that time, Indians were encouraged, through financial aid, to leave reservations.

"I've been sucked out of my culture, introduced to another way of life that I am supposed to accept and I can't do that," said Indian Center board president English, who was sent to an Oakland, Calif., electronics school.

At least 60 percent of the nation's Indian population live off the reservation, according to the 1990 census. Albuquerque has either 12,000 American Indian residents (1990 census) or closer to 35,000 (numbers used by Indian Center and other agencies based upon school population.)

It's a population scattered throughout the city, though many live in the Southeast Heights, according to census data. Many are single-mother households.

It's a diverse population, representing more than 100 tribes, different socioeconomic backgrounds, different generations. There are American Indians who were born in the city and would be lost on a reservation, Indians who live in the city and work on the reservations, and vice versa.

Many of those who were not born here came here for the same reasons: education and employment.

\*     \*     \*

LaFrenda Frank sits at a computer in the front office of the center. She's working on her résumé. The 26-year-old Navajo has been in the city three weeks and has been coming to the center almost every day.

"I'm looking for a job," she says. "I needed a computer and it's expensive to rent one someplace, and I couldn't use the one at UNM because I'm not a student. I did my résumé here, my cover letter. I've used the phone. I come here daily to check my messages."

Down the hall, through the tiny kitchen, and in the conference room, Frannie Loretto, an Albuquerque resident from Jemez Pueblo, is teaching three Navajo children to mold storyteller figures from clay.

The number of programs are expanding, but there are still gaps. With an annual budget of $115,000, the center is rarely able to offer what many of its clients seek: emergency money.

"I've come here a few times in the last three years and never really got any assistance," said Gilbert Chee, a Navajo from Arizona who stopped in to use the phone. "But you know how it is for Indians in the city, we have to pay for everything. I'm going home. Forget city life."

The center has been quietly criticized by Indians in other agencies for having little to offer the Indian community, for lack of organization, public relations and constant staff turnover. The critics point to more well-established, comprehensive urban Indian centers in Phoenix and Los Angeles as examples of what Albuquerque's should become.

Board member Mayfield responds that the center is not quite four years old, and says that the basic elements are in place. Given time, the center will become the one-stop shop for social services, information and cultural resources, he said.

Executive director Benally said they want to expand the cultural programs, provide computer training, move into a larger building, continue voter registration drives so that urban Indians begin to assume more power in the city.

But the people in the tiny stucco office know that no matter what they do, some problems can't be solved. Nothing they can do will end discrimination, but they can teach Albuquerque's Indian residents to challenge the system.

"For this Indian community to enter all these arenas is a big, big step for us," English said. "Overcoming the intimidation and fear, becoming part of the community of Albuquerque is a major step. . . . What we want to do is help people survive in society here without forgetting who they are."

# 3

# CONTEXTUALIZATION FOR NATIVE AMERICAN CRIME AND CRIMINAL JUSTICE INVOLVEMENT

MARIANNE O. NIELSEN

*When the white man first seen us, when they first said, "Well, there's something wrong with these people here. They don't have no religion. They have no judicial system. We have to do something for these people." I guess that must have been what they thought because they totally screwed up what we already had.*

*They introduced new religion and there was nothing wrong with our old religion. They just didn't understand it. We had our own ways of teaching our children, like the Elders and everything. There was nothing wrong with that way of teaching children. They just didn't understand it.*

*The same thing with our judicial system. We had that judicial system and the white people, when they come here, they didn't see that. They said, "These guys have nothing. We have to introduce all these different things to them so they can be one of us." That's exactly the problem that we have.*

> —Chief Philip Michel Brochet, quoted by Hamilton
> and Sinclair (1991:17)

This book is about Native peoples and their involvement in the criminal justice systems of the United States and, to a lesser extent, Canada. This issue cannot be understood without recognizing that it is just one of many interrelated issues that face Native peoples today. Political power, land, economic development, individual despair—these and other issues must be considered in exploring Native involvement in the criminal justice system.

Native peoples are the original inhabitants of what we now think of as North America. Morse (1985:1) defines Native peoples as "people who trace their ancestors in these lands to time immemorial." This definition encompasses all Native peoples, including those of half-Native ancestry such as the Metis of Canada, and is an excellent general definition. Native peoples are referred to by a variety of names, depending on which country their modern-day lands are found within and on their political and legal status in that country. In the United States Native peoples are most commonly called Indians, Native Americans, or American Indians. This group includes Inuit, Aleuts, and Native Hawaiians. In Canada Native peoples are called Aboriginal peoples, Native peoples, Indigenous peoples, and First Nations. They include more specifically the legal categories of Status Indians and non-Status Indians (or Registered Indians and non-Registered Indians), Bill C-36 Indians, Metis, and Inuit.[1] In this book all of these terms will be used at one point or another; "Native peoples" will be used when referring to the peoples of both countries.

The legal category in which Native individuals find themselves is very important because some categories have certain rights, obligations, and benefits associated with them. Registered members of many tribes in both countries, for example, have the right to housing on a reservation (called "reserves" in Canada); or, for example, they are not allowed to have alcohol in their home if they live on a "dry" reservation. It is important to realize that the legal categories imposed on Native peoples by the governments of the dominant, colonizing societies and the different rights and obligations that accompany each category more often than not serve to divide the interests of Native peoples and sometimes prevent them from working together.

In terms of group identity, many Native American groups are called by names that are not their own; that is, the name they have now may be based on an inaccurate description (like the word "Indian" itself) or may even be an insult because the European explorers learned the name from a neighboring unfriendly tribe. The Inuit, for example, were called Esquimaux and Eskimo, meaning "eaters of raw meat," a name given to them by neighboring Abenaki (Algonquin) tribes, who thought of raw meat as a questionable dinner item. "Inuit" means "people." Similarly, the Navajo call themselves "Dine," which also means "people." In fact, the names that many Native American groups have for themselves mean "people." In specific situations the most appropriate and respectful response to this confusion of names is to find out what the Native people in question call themselves and to use that name.

Because the issues that arise when Native peoples are involved with the criminal justice system are very similar in the United States and Canada and because unique program initiatives are being tried in both countries, articles about both countries are included in this book. Issues involving the Native peoples of Mexico are not included primarily because of the many important differences in the political and social situation of the Native peoples of Mexico.

Native peoples are of interest to the study of law, crime, and criminal justice for a number of important reasons. Expanding on Snipp (1989:2–3), these reasons are first, that Native peoples have a special historical and political status. They are the first peoples of this continent, and in order to understand the legal and justice-related history of the countries of North America, it is necessary to understand the important contributions that Native peoples have made to the social and political histories of these countries.

Second, both the United States and Canada have ideals of equality of opportunity and justice, but the history of Native peoples and the past and present conditions of Native peoples' lives are in complete contradiction to these ideals. Native peoples are among the poorest members of both countries.

Third, Native peoples have a special legal status. There is a body of law in both the United States and Canada that applies only to them. They are the only minority group mentioned specifically in the U.S. Constitution, and their rights are specially protected by the Canadian Constitution. In both countries special branches of government have been set up to regulate and administer Native peoples.

Fourth, Native peoples are central to the mythology of North America. Stereotypes of Indians continue to influence the way Native people are treated, not just on an individual basis but politically, socially, and bureaucratically. This discriminatory treatment extends to the criminal justice system (see Chapter 29 in this volume).

Fifth, the welfare of Native peoples is of interest to a large proportion of the public. Nearly 7 million Americans and over 1 million Canadians[2] identify themselves as Native or part Native (Snipp, 1989; Statistics Canada, 1993).

Sixth, Native cultures and lifestyles were historically different from European-based North American cultures. Native societies are still in the process of adapting to the cataclysmic changes that colonization by Europeans produced. As part of this adaptation, Native peoples are developing innovative criminal justice (and other) services from which the dominant society could learn a great deal. Several of these services are described in this book.

Seventh and last is the factor that particularly galvanizes the interest of criminal justice scholars: Native peoples are overrepresented in the criminal justice system statistics in the United States and Canada. To illustrate: If Native people make up 4 percent of the population of a state, one would expect that they would also make up 4 percent of the prison population. As it is, however, Native people, who make up 15.6 percent of the population of the state of Alaska, for example, actually make up 31 percent of that state's prison population (U.S. Department of Justice, 1993), which means that they are an overrepresented population in the criminal justice system of that state. In other states, the overrepresentation is less dramatic, being concentrated in specific categories such as substance abuse–related crime (see Chapter 10 in this volume). Furthermore, in some states Native offenders are not only overrepresented in terms of their numbers in prison but receive longer sentences and serve more of their sentence than any other group (see

Chapter 25 in this volume). This situation is even more pronounced in Canada, where Native peoples are the largest minority group (about 4 percent of the total population). Native peoples make up about 8 percent of the federal prison population and make up an average of 20 percent of provincial prison populations (Frideres, 1993:214). It should be noted that in Canada Native offenders and Native criminal justice issues are a major focus for both scholars and administrators, but in the United States Native issues and offenders receive comparatively little attention because they are overshadowed by the large numbers of African American and Hispanic offenders in the system.

*country interest level by pop. type*

This same trend of overrepresentation is found in every country in which an indigenous population has been overrun by an invading group. It is found, for example, among the Aborigines of Australia, the Maoris of New Zealand, and the indigenous peoples of Papua New Guinea, Scandinavia, Japan, Russia, and many African countries. With few exceptions, it seems that the processes of invasion and colonization produce conditions that increase the involvement of the original inhabitants in the criminal justice system of the dominant (colonizing) society.

*colonization crime ↑*

In order to understand how this overrepresentation in the United States and Canada came about and what is being done about it, it is necessary to understand the impact that the colonization of Native lands by Europeans has had on Native peoples and how Native people have become active in the criminal justice system in more roles than just that of offender.

## THE IMPACT OF COLONIZATION

Before European contact, the Native peoples of North America had their own cultures, economic systems, societal structures, laws, and methods of enforcing good behavior (see, for example, Chapters 4 and 7). The arrival of the Europeans severely damaged these institutions over a relatively short period of time.[3] Some of this destruction was the result of deliberate government policy; some of it was unintentional. The changes brought by the Europeans affected Native American demographics, technology, economic systems, ecology, culture, law, and politics. Indian Nations were affected by these agents at different times because of the differential rate of European settlement.

The most significant agent of change brought by the Europeans was probably disease. They brought smallpox, yellow fever, measles, chicken pox, bubonic plague, influenza, and many more diseases—against which Native peoples had no natural immunities. Because of the extensive trade networks among Native tribal groups, it was not necessary for a group to have direct contact with Europeans to be exposed to the disease. It is estimated that the numbers of Native people in North America fell from somewhere between 2 and 5 million inhabitants pre-contact to a low of about 228,000 inhabitants in 1890 (Snipp, 1989:6–11, 13). Some tribal groups became nearly extinct; some tribes were so diminished that they

*Europeans brought diseases millions of natives died*

joined other Native groups to survive. European settlers found some Indian lands nearly deserted and found many Native groups trying to reestablish their economy, social structure, and culture after the collapse of their society. Most Native groups, as a result, found themselves unable to defend themselves and their lands against the ever-increasing advance of the European settlers.

Disease was not the only agent of population decrease; after contact other factors included "military conflict, mistreatment, starvation or malnutrition, depression and loss of vigor or will to live, and exportation into slavery" (Utter, 1993: 24).

The impact of European technology was not limited to the edge that the guns used during the "pacification of the Indians" gave the European settlers. European technology introduced changes in the economies of most Native groups. The Dine (Navajo), for example, adopted the newly reintroduced horses and sheep, and many Native groups traded for iron to use in knives and other tools. Guns were also a popular trade item and contributed to heightened warfare between rival Native groups. Because of the popularity of fur in European fashion at the time, Europeans encouraged the development of a continent-wide fur trade that drew many Native groups away from their traditional economies (horticulture, hunting, fishing, and so on). European hunting, for sport and food, of animals such as the buffalo changed the ecology of whole regions of the continent and depleted Native resources. This led to a dependence on European foods. The removal of Indians to reservations changed Native economic systems as well, since reservations were usually placed on land inappropriate for traditional economic activities and too poor to farm, even if the group in question wished to. The combination of these factors led to an economic dependence on the colonial governments.

Europeans (including Canadian and American colonists) used ideologies based on Social Darwinism and paternalism to justify their treatment of Native peoples. Social Darwinism was the belief that humans were the pinnacle of evolution and that Europeans were the pinnacle of human evolution (Trigger, 1985). Because of their "obvious" superiority, many Europeans believed that they had the right to impose their culture, economy, laws, and religion on "inferior" peoples. In gratitude, the "inferior" peoples were expected to give up their land, economy, beliefs, and occasionally their lives. In the interests of making Native peoples adopt the "superior" European culture, laws were passed forbidding the practice of Native beliefs and ceremonies and children were taken from their families and communities and placed in European-run schools in which they were forbidden to speak their own language, to eat the food they were used to, or to practice their own spirituality. Missionaries played an important role in many parts of North America in these efforts to assimilate Native peoples.

Because Native peoples were considered to be "like children," reservations and laws were also designed to protect Native peoples from unscrupulous Whites and from themselves. Remnants of this paternalism are still found in government policies that refuse Native peoples the right to make decisions about the use of their lands and funds or the right to provide services for themselves.

Native peoples have managed to preserve a great deal of their culture, which is now being revitalized, sometimes rediscovered, and taught to current generations. It is important to note that there are no single entities that can be called "the Native culture" or "the Native community." Native cultures are not homogeneous; nor are they static. There are differences between Nations based on historical developments, economic pursuits, geography, spiritual views, and so on. There are also differences among the individuals within communities. Not all Native person believe in or practice traditional culture. They differ in how acculturated they are (Gerber, 1980), so that Native individuals and communities can be described as varying from very traditionally oriented to completely assimilated into the dominant non-Native society. In between are communities and individuals who are integrated into both societies.

Treaties were made between the colonizing powers and Indian tribes. These were legal contracts between nations agreeing to terms of peace, trade, and exchange. Because of differences in conceptualizations of very basic things, such as the ownership of land (the Europeans wanted to own it; Native peoples believed it could not be owned, only protected), and because of the greed of speculators, most of the treaties were broken almost immediately by the Europeans.

Indian Nations in the United States are domestic dependent nations, which means that they have the right, within limits set by U.S. law, to control their own internal affairs, including the administration of justice. In Canada Indian Nations are not recognized in the same way, that is, as semiautonomous nations, but their "existing Aboriginal rights" are entrenched in the Canadian Constitution, which means that they can negotiate some degree of self-determination from the Canadian government. As a result, some groups in Canada also have their own criminal justice programs. In both countries, Native peoples are trying to gain more power to develop and control more of their own social institutions—not just criminal justice, but education, health care, social services, and others. This is what is meant by "self-determination initiatives." It should be noted that the terms "self-determination," "sovereignty," and "self-government" are sometimes used interchangeably. "Self-determination" usually refers to the ability to make decisions about one's own community. "Sovereignty" and "self-government" refer more specifically to the right to govern one's own political affairs.

The process of colonization has led to Native peoples becoming marginalized; that is, they have been placed at the economic and political edges of society. A large proportion of Native peoples live in poverty. It has been said that Canadian society is "a vertical mosaic, a totem pole, with native people at the bottom" (Vallee, 1978:333). Native peoples have been excluded from U.S. and Canadian society, which contradicts the policy of assimilation mentioned earlier. A number of examples of their marginalization can be cited: Politically marginalized, Native peoples only received the right to vote in national elections in the United States in 1920 and did not win that right until 1960 in Canada. Economically marginalized, about 23 percent of Native Americans live below the poverty line, compared to 7 percent of Whites (and 26.5 percent of Blacks). Seventeen percent of Native men are unemployed, compared to about 6 percent of the White male population. Native American men are less likely to finish school and are more likely to work in lower-income jobs such as manual labor. Partly as a result of economic marginalization, Native Americans are more likely to suffer from ill health than are White North Americans. This is not to say that all Native Americans are disadvantaged, but a greater proportion of them are disadvantaged than in the White population of the United States, and a smaller proportion than in its Black population (see Snipp, 1989). Figures follow a very similar trend in Canada, where, for example, the Native unemployment rate is three times as high as the national average and the average Native income is half the national average (Frideres, 1993:170, 160). Discrimination and stereotyping by members of the dominant society also increase marginalization.

The socioeconomic conditions described above, along with language barriers, cultural conflicts, and continuing paternalistic government policies, are conducive to the development of alcoholism, violent behavior, suicide, and, of course, crime (see Chapters 7, 10, 11, 12, and 13 for discussions of a variety of Native American crimes and their antecedents).

## NATIVE PEOPLES' ROLES IN THE CRIMINAL JUSTICE SYSTEM

Native offenders face special problems in dealing with the criminal justice system because of isolation from the dominant society. They may not be familiar with European-based laws and justice; they may lack education about the criminal justice system; they may have language difficulties; they may not know about legal assistance; they may lack money to pay lawyers, fines, or bail; they may lack knowledge of resources to help with criminogenic conditions such as alcoholism and unemployment; or they may be discriminated against.

But Native peoples are not just offenders. Native people are also victims of crime. Unfortunately, very little research has been done on this aspect of Native involvement with criminal justice.

Nor are Native people passive observers of the criminal justice system; they are active service providers working not only to improve the effectiveness of the criminal justice system services to Native victims and offenders but also to improve the socioeconomic conditions that lead to crime. As they do this, they are also working to increase self-determination for Native peoples. Native Americans are active in four criminal justice administration roles: as service providers within the dominant system, as operators of reservation-based services, as designers and operators of urban "pan-Indian" services, and as designers and operators of traditional justice-based services. These categories are not mutually exclusive.

Native peoples who work within the dominant society's criminal justice system may be police officers, probation supervisors, correctional officers, lawyers, or judges; that is, they may fill any of the roles normally found within the system. Native people are, on the whole, underrepresented as service providers and decisionmakers in the criminal justice system. A study carried out in Canada found that in one province, in which Native peoples made up 30 percent of the inmate population, Native people were only 2 percent of the people working in the criminal justice system (Cawsey, 1991:8.41; see also Hamilton and Sinclair, 1991:106–107). No similar studies have been done in the United States.

The second role is that of operators of reservation-based services. In the United States there are reservation-based courts, police forces, juvenile delinquency services, and a number of other programs. In Canada there are all of these except tribal courts. Most of these programs are based on some modification of the dominant society's services. Not all reservations are large enough or well-funded enough to operate their own criminal justice systems. In Canada some tribes have cooperated to form, for example, regional police forces as a solution. Also, not all reservations want to operate their own services.

In both countries the dominant society's government places limitations on the Native services. The Dine (Navajo) courts, for example, can hear only misdemeanor cases and cases involving infractions of tribal law. The two Native-run correctional institutions in Alberta, Canada, can house only minimum-security level prisoners. Some Native police forces in Canada have the right to carry arms, some do not. Most Native American police forces do (see Chapters 15 and 16 for more issues dealing with Native policing.)

The third role is that of designers and operators of urban criminal justice services for Native people. In both countries a significant proportion of Native peoples live in urban areas. In the United States that proportion is estimated to be over 50 percent; in Canada it is estimated to be somewhat lower. These people face many of the same social problems as do Native Americans living on reservations, but they do not have the assistance of reservation-based services. In Canada there are well-developed networks of urban services operated by courtworker agencies and friendship centers. These organizations provide a wide variety of free services to all people of Native ancestry, services that include providing assistance in courts and prisons, operating crime-prevention and legal-education programs, and operating correctional facilities and community corrections programs. Both countries have Native Elders providing spiritual counseling in correctional centers (see Chapter 30 in this volume). There are also Native organizations operating alcohol and substance-abuse treatment centers (see Chapter 34 in this volume). In the United States more service organizations are appearing. Furtaw (1993) lists dozens of national, regional, state, and local service organizations. One example is Native Americans for Community Action in Arizona, which offers substance-abuse counseling and mental health programs among its other services.

The fourth role is that of designers and operators of traditional justice-based services. This is both the oldest and the newest area of service provision. Many of the traditional justice practices of Native groups were driven underground by the assimilationist laws mentioned earlier, but they were not forgotten (see Chapter 6). The traditional mechanisms included counseling and mediation by community Elders and leaders, enforcement of good behavior by police societies, and informal control mechanisms such as gossip, teasing, and banishment (see Chapters 4 and 33). In recent years there have been a number of "new" initiatives developed that are based on some of these strategies. The Navajo Peacemaker Courts, for example, use community members to settle disputes and arrive at peaceful resolutions (see Chapters 13 and 22). In Canada sentencing circles and youth justice committees involve respected community members in developing sentencing recommendations for offending community members.

The involvement of Native persons as service providers in the criminal justice system is important because Native service providers have a better understanding of the issues and problems faced by their Native "clients" (see Chapter 20 in this volume). They understand the socioeconomic conditions that may contribute to their clients' personal problems. They are aware of the resources, Native and non-Native, that are available to their clients in the community. They know that there are minority groups within Native groups. Native women, Native young offenders, and members of small tribal groups may have different needs from those of other Native groups (see Chapters 7, 11, and 26).

The potential that these programs have for contributing to the welfare of the entire population of both countries is profound. There is a movement in the dominant criminal justice system toward developing new services that are more effective in preventing offenses and in keeping offenders from re-offending. The "new" concepts being used by non-Native society—diversion, community ownership, community responsibility—are old ideas in Native communities. In reviving and modifying their traditional services to fit contemporary problems, Native peoples are working in the same direction as the dominant society's leading-edge reformers. Undoubtedly, Native communities and the dominant society alike have a great deal to gain from these ground-breaking Native programs.

## NOTES

1. The Inuit are Native peoples who live in the circumpolar parts of the United States and Canada. They were formerly called "Eskimos." Aleuts are inhabitants of the western Alaska peninsula, the Pribilof Islands, and the Aleutian Islands. Alaskan Inuit, Aleuts, and Indians together are sometimes refered to as "Alaska Natives." Native Hawaiians have ancestors who include the indigenous people of Hawaii. In Canada, the terms "Aboriginal peoples," "Native peoples," "Indigenous peoples," and "First Nations" are used more or less interchangeably, although each term has slightly different connotations; for example, "First

Nations" implies sovereign political status. "Status Indian," "Registered Indian," and "legal Indian" are used interchangeably and refer to a person who is registered with the Canadian federal government as being an Indian under the provisions of the Indian Act. Registered Indians whose ancestors signed a treaty are called "Treaty Indians." Those whose ancestors did not are "non-Treaty Indians." "Non-Registered Indians," also called "non-Status Indians," are those individuals whose ancestors refused or were not allowed to make agreements with the Canadian federal government. They may also be individuals who voluntarily or involuntarily gave up their Indian rights (a process called "enfranchisement"). Both Registered and non-Registered Indians may be members of Indian Bands. "Bill C-36 Indians" are enfranchised Indians who have recovered some of their Indian rights. Metis are people of mixed Native and European ancestry and have a special legal status in some Canadian provinces (Utter, 1993:67, 68; Frideres, 1993:24–44).

2. American and Canadian figures cannot be directly compared. Seven million Americans identify themselves as having at least one Native American ancestor, according to Snipp (1989). However, over 1 million Canadians identified themselves in the 1991 census as having one or more Native ancestors (Statistics Canada, 1993). Conceivably, the Canadian number would be a great deal larger if it included all Canadians who consider themselves as belonging to another ethnic group but who have one Native ancestor.

3. This overview of the colonization process is, of necessity, superficial. Recommended as excellent surveys of the major change agents on Native American life over the five hundred years from contact to the present day are Hagan, 1993; Wright, 1992; Miller, 1989; and Trigger, 1985.

# 4

# JUSTICE AND NATIVE PEOPLES

JAMES DUMONT

## CULTURAL EMERGENCE OF
## TWO DISTINCT JUSTICE SYSTEMS

Menno Boldt and T. Anthony Long, in their discussion of the fundamentally different concepts of sovereignty in European-Western development and Aboriginal North American tradition, identify such concepts as authority, hierarchy, and ruling entity in Western thought, as opposed to spiritual compact, tribal will, and custom/tradition in the Aboriginal world view (Boldt and Long, 1984:537–547). Menno Boldt and Anthony Long point out that the Euro-Western concept of authority stems from a background of belief in the inherent inequality of men and the European system of feudalism. Where individual autonomy was regarded as the key to the successful acquisition of private property and for achievement in competitive pursuit, authority was deemed necessary to protect society against rampant individual self-interest (Boldt and Long, 1984:541). The sovereign authority vested in a person (e.g., a monarch) or an impersonal entity (a constitution or government) serves to guarantee efficient distribution of wealth, property, and (with enlightenment) the equal benefit of accumulation of wealth and the exercise of power along with the development of more egalitarian and humane political structures. Authoritative power is essential to maintain the integrity of a sovereign society from within, and, its hierarchical power arrangements are necessary to ensure the distribution of privileges and the maintenance of order in society from the most authoritative to the most powerless.

The evolution of authority, hierarchy and the concept of a ruling power is fundamentally different from either the Aboriginal concept of sovereignty or the

Edited version of James Dumont, "Justice and Aboriginal People," from *Aboriginal Peoples and the Justice System*, Royal Commission on Aboriginal Peoples. Ottawa: Ministry of Supply and Services, 1993. Reprinted by permission of Ministry of Supply and Services Canada, 1995, and the author.

Aboriginal experience of the emergence of responsible and egalitarian government. Boldt and Long note that, in Aboriginal society, self-interest was inextricably intertwined with the tribal interest; that is, the general good and the individual good were taken to be virtually identical (Boldt and Long, 1984:541). In Western-European society the ideal of a social contract evolved as a result of a more enlightened concept of how authorities might more humanely exercise the right to govern others and devise egalitarian methods of extending authoritative rule from the ruler to the ruled. In Aboriginal society, it was recognized as inherent that no human being was deemed to have control over the life of another (Boldt and Long, 1984:543).

In the Aboriginal belief good government was viewed as a "spiritual compact" (541), "equality was derived from the Creator's founding prescription" (542), and, the good order that promoted harmony had a "source and sanction outside the individual and the tribe. It was the handiwork of the Creator". In the Aboriginal experience "the organizing and regulating force for group order and endeavour . . . was custom and tradition." "Customs were derived from the Creator", and because they were spiritually endowed and through history had withstood the test of time, they "represented the Creator's sacred blueprint for the survival of the tribe" (Boldt and Long, 1984:543).

Personal authority, hierarchical relationship, and the concept of a separate ruling entity is based in European thought and evolved from Western-European experience, then applied to the North American political and legal landscape. The absence of these prerequisites which evoke an allegiance to Western authoritative law and order, has profound implications for the relationship of Aboriginal people to the present justice system imposed upon them. Equally, the evolution of a unique and fundamentally different mode of government and style of decision making in the North American experience, has important ramifications for the development of culturally meaningful justice systems and the creation of appropriate mechanisms of litigation and enforcement.

Boldt and Long point out that "key ideas contained in the European-Western doctrine of sovereignty are incompatible with core values comprising traditional Indian culture" (540). Further, if, psychologically, these core values have a sufficient degree of persistence (as studies continue to affirm), and if cultural beliefs and structures are highly resistant to change over time (as both history and research bear out), then the approach to the most appropriate development of constructs and mechanisms of justice among Aboriginal people would appear to be best derived from a culture-based approach. Such a development of Aboriginal-appropriate, culture-based approaches would hinge upon a thorough knowledge of traditional culture and a proper understanding of the core values. The purpose of this present chapter is to identify these core values, follow their persistence capacity over time and compare them with the same evolution of the dominant Western contemporary behavioural orientations from Western-European core values. Such a study would be foundational for any consideration of the development of appropriate contemporary but Aboriginally based approaches to justice as well as for assessing Aboriginal peoples' response to the justice system.

## The Principal Traditional Values of the Aboriginal People

An underlying premise of this document, at the outset, is the basic assumption that there is a degree to which certain key Aboriginal values can be universalized to be representative of most Aboriginal cultures in North America. Another assumption is that these values that are most representative of Aboriginal people are sufficiently resistant to acculturation so as to persist over time and through various assimilative forces that have been at work since the time of contact (i.e., about 500 years).

[Editors' note: The author goes on to compare in detail the cultural values of a number of North American Indian Nations, paying particular attention to Siouan, Cheyenne, Ojibwa, Navajo, and Apache traditions (Banai, 1979; Bryde, 1971; Walker, 1917; Chisholm, 1983; Basso, 1970; Hoebel, 1960). He also surveys a number of other studies that examine Aboriginal values (Brown, 1982; Hendry, 1969; McNickle, 1973; Miller, 1979; Couture, 1978) and suggests "from these studies it soon becomes obvious that there emerge certain prevalent values that are consistent across various Aboriginal cultures." These prevalent values are summarized in the remainder of this chapter.]

From a consideration of the persistent values from various cultures of North America can be generalized certain traditionally-based Aboriginal values that appear to be consistent across cultures and across time changes. To view these we

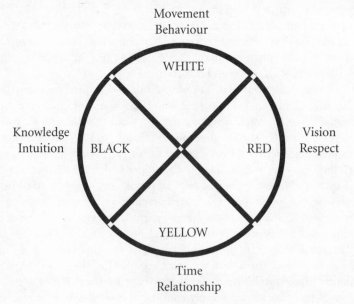

FIGURE 4.1

FIGURE 4.2

will go to the values of the Ojibwa Anishinabe in order to consider these persistent general and primary values in that framework.

First, let us look at the original design of the four colours of man as seen in Figure 4.1.

From this original placement of the four colours of man, the Red Man (Anishinabe) or Aboriginal person is gifted with the unique quality of vision. This is both his special way of seeing the world as an Aboriginal person, and, the capacity for holistic or total vision. With this ability to see beyond the boundaries of the physical and the capacity for all-around, circular vision comes respect: respect for creation, respect for knowledge and wisdom, respect for the dignity and freedom of others, respect for the quality of life and spirit in all things, respect for the mysterious.

Now, when the foundational four directional principles and the seven values are placed around this central capacity for vision, the design looks like Figure 4.2.

Vision, in this design, is the primary generator of the Ojibwa value system. Vision is wholeness; it recognizes the interconnectedness of all things and the totality of its interrelatedness. Because of this, vision generates respect. Respect conditions all other values, thus engendering a unique value system with a unique interpretation and prioritizing of each value. Values such as wisdom, honesty, humility, kindness and strength, may be claimed equally by other peoples and cultures. However, what makes for the uniqueness of Aboriginal values is the perception and understanding of these values because of the primal gift of vision/wholeness and the primary motivator, respect.

The primary Aboriginal values influenced from this core vision and attitude of respect can be interpreted as:

- Kindness: The capacity for caring and the desire for harmony and well-being in interpersonal relations.
- Honesty: To act with the utmost honesty and integrity in all relationships recognizing the inviolable and inherent autonomy, dignity and freedom of oneself and others.
- Sharing: Recognizing interdependence and interrelatedness of all of life, to relate with one another with an ethic of sharing, generosity, and collective/communal consciousness and co-operation.
- Strength: Conscious of the need for kindness and respecting the integrity of oneself and others, to exercise strength of character, fortitude and self-mastery in order to generate and maintain peace, harmony and well-being within oneself and in the total collective community.
- Bravery: The exercise of courage and bravery on the part of the individual so that the quality of life and inherent autonomy of oneself and others can be exercised in an atmosphere of security, peace, dignity and freedom.
- Wisdom: The respect for that quality of knowing and gift of vision in others (striving for the same within oneself) that encompasses the holistic view, possesses spiritual quality, and is expressed in the experiential breadth and depth of life. A person who embodies these qualities and actualizes them in others deserves respect as an elder.
- Humility: The recognition of yourself as a sacred and equal part of the Creation, and the honouring of all of life which is endowed with the same inherent autonomy, dignity, freedom, and equality. This leads to a sensitivity toward others, a posture of non-interference and a desire for good relations and balance with all of life.

These values, defined by the primary motivators of the Native personality (the capacity for vision and the quality of respect), can be presented as the original traditional Aboriginal values. They appear to be characteristic of Native people generally and seem to have persisted into the present time where they act as foundational to the patterns of behaviour of the contemporary Aboriginal person.

## ABORIGINAL VALUES IN AN ALIEN SOCIAL, CULTURAL ENVIRONMENT

Where the "Redman" is governed in all things by the primary motivators of vision and respect, the "Whiteman's" primary motivators are movement and behaviour. Because of this, the "White Brother" will interpret and rank major values differently from the Aboriginal person. This will, in turn, make a difference in how each one will function in the community and how each will generate institutions, structures or codes to foster and maintain harmony and well-being.

In the most positive view of the dominant society's fundamental values, it can be said that this society believes in permitting the maximum freedom in active personal pursuit, while guaranteeing the greatest good to the greatest number. In order to regulate this primary goal, society must institute laws or rules so that men and women are able to achieve the greatest personal success while assuring the collective well-being. By these rules society must seek the most generalized norm to which all must be encouraged to conform. Rules or laws are made therefore to guarantee individual freedom of pursuit (protecting the individual's right to the benefits of personal achievement), and to ensure the greatest good for the greatest number.

Being motivated by a primary drive of movement and behavioural activity, the white person understands the values of autonomy and freedom of the person as the freedom of active personal pursuit and sharing as the equal right to well-being. However, he must ensure these are acted upon; so, rules or laws are established whereby benefits gained through freedom of active personal pursuit will also accrue to those not fortunate to excel in personal pursuit. Usually the surplus goes to be shared with those less fortunate, or systems of taxation are implemented in order to fulfil the obligation of equal opportunity or right to well-being of the greatest number.

Aboriginal society believes, however, that while the individual must be permitted and encouraged to express his/her potentiality with the greatest possible freedom and autonomy, the freedom and autonomy of others must also be respected. It was not by imposing rules and laws to guarantee the personal freedom and autonomy of the individual, but rather the value of respect was engendered (inculcated) in the individual person from birth and reinforced throughout individual and community life. Thus, by the building of an individually internalized conscience (or internalized law of desirable behaviour) the person can exercise personal freedom of pursuit of development, while respecting the same in others— leading to the greatest harmony in interpersonal relations and socialization and to the building of the collective or common good. Personal autonomy and freedom and individual pursuit of achievement and success are always conditioned by respect.

By understanding the values of Aboriginal and non-Aboriginal people in terms of the core or primary motivators, we can see that there are fundamental differences in the way each expresses commonly held values.

## Contrasting Values

Contemporary Aboriginal behaviour is rooted in traditional perceptions of reality, Aboriginal values, and a belief system that is grounded in prolonged cultural practice and centuries of Aboriginal experience. This Aboriginal perceptual, psychological and epistemological rootedness is the foundation that the contemporary Aboriginal personality is built upon, and thus in an essential way, influences modern behaviour as well as conditions present day adaptive behaviour. Often these values and resulting behavioural preferences contrast or conflict in fundamental ways with the values and behavioural tendencies of the non-Aboriginal dominant society.

Table 4.1   Value Comparisons Between Aboriginal and Non-Aboriginal Societies

| Aboriginal | Non-Aboriginal |
|---|---|
| Fostering of individual autonomy by providing foundations for the individual's responsibility for survival; inculcating attitude of individual responsibility and respect; providing a knowledge base in terms of information and awareness of process for decision making. | Motivating individual autonomy by fostering assertiveness, by engendering competitiveness, by providing education base for future work; by training person in attitudes of persistence, individual creativity; success through punishment and reward method by demanding adherence to rules and acceptable goals. |
| Sharing as generosity which respects the personhood of all living beings who contribute cooperatively to the well-being of life; striving to bring about the greatest harmony and collective good while honouring the freedom and autonomy of oneself and others. | Sharing as an obligation, to guarantee the right to well-being of all and the right to equal opportunity, while maximizing individual achievement and success in active personal pursuit. |
| Wholeness as the perception of the undivided entirely of things and the visioning of the interconnectedness of all things. | Totality as the summation of all the parts that make up the whole and the quantifying and objectifying of parts to calculate the connections leading to the total picture. |
| Kindness, as the desire for harmony and a preference for amiability in all inter-personal relations, human and other-than-human. | Charity as an admonition to exercise compassion and benevolence in acceptance of the common humanity of all, acknowledging a primary motivation of personal pursuit of individual development, success and private gain |
| Honour as an essential attitude of respect for the freedom and autonomy of other persons, towards other-than-human persons, for Elders, for wisdom, and for the kinship with nature and the forces of life, both known and unknown. | Consideration as courtesy and fair play toward peers and equal achievers, and stewardship toward the less fortunate and the things upon which survival and well-being depend, e.g. good order, law and nature. |
| Respect for the freedom and autonomy of oneself and others and for the inherent dignity of the human person as well as for the maintenance of the collective harmony and well-being. | Respect for the personal and private property of others and oneself, along with the right to pursue private enterprise, personal achievement and gain, concurrent with a moral duty to recognize the equality of human persons. |
| Bravery as strength of character that requires great inner strength and fortitude in situations of great difficulty or personal danger, while maintaining self-mastery, control, and the rightful dignity of others. | Bravery as courage and valour, that requires one to place, even over one's own life and principles, a nobler cause or ideal or higher authority— even if this infringes upon others' rights and freedoms. |
| Honesty as truthfulness and integrity, i.e., to act with the utmost honesty and integrity in all relationships recognizing the inviolable and inherent autonomy, dignity and freedom of oneself and others. | Honesty as truthfulness and respectability; i.e., acting in accordance with defined laws and principles in an upright and creditable manner, with the expectation of the same from others. |

Tables 4.1 and 4.2 compare and contrast some of the essential values and behavioral patterns of Aboriginal and non-Aboriginal people. Table 4.1 on value comparison takes similar value-categories and contrasts the different ways that each of the values are expressed in the two different societies. Table 4.2 shows how the contemporary expression of the original values of each group leads to a zone of conflict where the two come together in the modern experience.

Table 4.2, which follows, begins from the original values as they are expressed in each of the Euro-Western original culture and the North American Aboriginal culture. As the reader moves from the primary Aboriginal value expression (Aboriginal—far left, and Euro-Western—far right) toward the centre of the table, these value expressions change as they adapt to changing environments and historical circumstances. Though, as can be seen, these values are still expressions of the original values in their Aboriginal intent, nevertheless, they become modified by time and the context of expression. As these values approach their contemporary mode of behavioral expression, it becomes much more apparent that persons operating from their own cultural position, being motivated by their own value expressions, will come into conflict with one another in situations where they must relate to each other in achieving common ends.

Differences in value orientation cause significant differences in behaviour, and, where Aboriginal people come into the legal context of the dominant society, the situation appears to foster behavioral conflicts within the courtroom as well as with enforcers of the law.

Besides the particular differences in behavioral preferences, there does appear to be an overall difference in the approach to determining a just solution to acts of deviance or anti-social behaviour. Table 4.3 explains that for the Aboriginal community and for the individual, the over-riding motivation for achieving justice in situations of conflict or deviance was that of restoring the peace and equilibrium within the community and reconciling the accused with his/her own conscience and with the individual family that is wronged. This is a primary difference. It is a difference that significantly challenges the appropriateness of the present legal and justice system for Aboriginal people in resolution of conflict, reconciliation and maintaining community harmony and good order.

## CONCLUSION

A justice system that is based in Aboriginal culture would presumably speak more appropriately to Aboriginal people and be responsive to culture-based values and behaviour. Further, such an Aboriginal justice system would restore the integrity of the Aboriginal community and reduce the conflict Aboriginal persons and communities have with the shortcomings and unsuitability of the present justice system in dealing with the Aboriginal people.

Table 4.2   Value Differences Leading to Contemporary Conflict

| | Aboriginal Values and Behaviour | | | |
|---|---|---|---|---|
| Value | Meaning | Resulting Behaviour | Modern Behaviour | Z |
| Wholeness | Perception of the undivided entirety of things. A vision of the interconnected-ness, and interde-pendence within life. | Prefers to see the whole picture before acting. Has a capac-ity for seeing totality of things. Reflective, careful, considering all sides before de-ciding to move on something. | Exhibits behavioural preferences for what can be termed "motionless alert-ness"; i.e., will wait until she/he feels confident, knowl-edgeable or adept before speaking, making decisions, or acting on it. Con-siderate of other side and the sensitivities and rights of others when facing a diffi-cult situation. Time is relative and judge-ment flexible and qualified by respect and circumstances. The part is only understood in rela-tion to the whole. | O N E O F |
| Respect | Regard for auton-omy and the free-dom of oneself and of others, as well as the inherent dignity of the human person and of the collective. | Respect of others and for one's own personal integrity, which engenders an attitude of friend-liness and trust; characterized by a preference for ano-nymity, modesty and sensitivity toward others; predisposed toward a posture of noninterference. | A sensitivity toward others; tendency toward non-inter-ference and non-intrusiveness in interrelating; a non-manipulative beha-viour; a tendency toward compliance; shows patience and self-restraint. | |

| | | | | |
|---|---|---|---|---|
| | *Euro-Canadian Values and Behaviour* | | | |
| C | *Modern Behaviour* | *Resulting Behaviour* | *Meaning* | *Value* |
| O<br>N<br>F<br>L<br>I<br>C<br>T | Active experimenting disposition; objective, analytical approach in problem solving; assertive and manipulative behaviour in acting on it; must act on a situation from its beginning point to reach successful conclusion; achievement and goal oriented; order is externally maintained and the truth of any situation depends on objective analysis of the facts and detached judgement of its verifiability and its credibility. | The objectifying, the quantifying and analyzing of things to determine interconnections that make up the total picture; assertive and persistent in moving from the beginning to successful completion; proven and defined fundamental components leads to understanding the interconnections which sum up the total picture—a fundamentally linear approach that is analytical and critical. | Perception of wholeness as a totality where the sum of all the parts make the total picture; must determine and define parts to build the total picture. Must create the total picture by manipulating the parts. | Movement |
| | Activity oriented; assertive, persistent task oriented—if at first you don't succeed try and try again; tendency toward coercive and intrusive behaviour with preference for confrontational approach to problem solving; employing a forward, direct strategy in social and interpersonal relations; expectation of self-assurance, assertiveness in others. | Assertion of the right to pursuit of private enterprise, acquisition of personal achievement, and individual gain; success, personal attainment and progress are seen as measures of personal integrity and acceptance; posture of confrontational, intrusive behaviour, with predisposition toward disciplined, conscientious, and forceful behaviour. | Movement, being the primary motivating pre-disposition governs all behaviour and causes it to be active and intense. Active behaviour is fundamental and dominant trait. | Behaviour |

*(continues)*

Table 4.2 *continued*

| | | | | Z |
|---|---|---|---|---|
| | | *Aboriginal Values and Behaviour* | | |
| *Value* | *Meaning* | *Resulting Behaviour* | *Modern Behaviour* | |
| Kindness | Harmony in inter-personal relations, and the capacity for caring. | Friendship, caring, amiability, mild-ness, compliance and acquiescence. Prefers peaceful resolution rather than con-frontation. | One's actions and expressions must affirm the dignity and self-worth of others; desires ami-able and peaceful interactions; avoids confrontation. | O N E O F |
| Honesty | Truthfulness and integrity. Honesty conditioned by respect. | Tolerance and equa-nimity; respect for the inviolable and inherent dignity of the individual; a highly internalized conscience and trust-worthiness; honour-able and loyal. | Careful, considered responses are more reliable and more truthful. After reflec-tion, answers with honesty and candour rather than carefully worded responses to avoid incrimination. | |
| Sharing | Generosity, co-operativeness, desir-ing harmony and collective well-being. | Assertion of one's freedom and auto-nomy is balanced by responsibility to assure harmony and collective well-being; i.e., sharing of wealth acquired through individual pursuit for the col-lective good and general well-being. | Generosity engen-ders respect. Fru-gality is more like avarice than a virtue. Care/co-operation are preferred beha-viours. Sense of responsibility/respect for others' well-being. Won't demand reciprocation but feel the need to share. | |
| Strength | Strength of charac-ter, fortitude, self-mastery—for peace, harmony and well-being in oneself and others. | Bravery is thus defined as fortitude and inner strength required for difficult situations; maintain-ing self-mastery and control, while res-pecting the inherent dignity of others. | Prefers self-disci-pline over restraint imposed from with-out; favours self-control and guidance over adherence to impersonal goals or authority; shows quiet self-assurance. | |

| | *Euro-Canadian Values and Behaviour* | | | |
|---|---|---|---|---|
| **C** | *Modern Behaviour* | *Resulting Behaviour* | *Meaning* | *Value* |
| O N F L I | While favouring the competitive spirit and the right to pursue private gain, benevolence and compassion are to be shown to the meek by correcting inequality. | Compassion/sympathy for less fortunate and those unable to succeed. Confronts inequality by applying charitable and remedial solution. | Kindness as charity as it is shown especially to the unfortunate and the helpless. | Kindness |
| C T | Makes hasty, precipitous judgements based on assumption of knowing what's best for other people. Obedience to law prevails over tolerance, fairness and respect for others. | Respectability, uprightness and obedience to defined law and norms of society. External restraint and modification of behaviour and freedom are sanctioned when law is contravened. | Truthfulness and respectability. Abiding by defined laws in an upright and creditable manner. | Honesty |
| | Sharing as charitable act ensures equal opportunity and as obligation secures equitable distribution of wealth and benefits. Otherwise, attainment is the worthy goal and frugality the greater virtue. Individual competitive spirit vs. the collective. | While maximizing individual achievment and success in active personal pursuit, the successful individual is obliged to share fruits of success to guarantee the welfare of the general masses and the underprivileged. | Sharing as an obligation rather than unconditional generosity. Obligation to share for the wellbeing of all. | Sharing |
| | Rugged individualism; aggressive and competitive behaviour upheld; superiority of the person based on keenness to get ahead; individual rights along with obedience to higher authority. | Strength is ability to place ideal over sentiment or compassion, for a nobler cause or higher authority. Mastery and control are determined by dispassionate use of power and forthrightness. | Control, confidence, determination, persistence and forthrightness are all needed to gain mastery of a situation. | Strength |

Table 4.3   Zone of Conflict in the Justice Arena

| Aboriginal Response to the Law | Expectation of Legal System |
| --- | --- |
| • regular teaching of community values by Elders and others who are respected in the community; | • everyone under obligation to obey set laws as determined by superior state authorities; |
| • warning and counselling of particular offenders by leaders or by councils representing the community as whole; | • society reserves the right to protect itself from individual who threatens to harm its members or its property; |
| • mediation and negotiation by Elders, community members, by clan leaders, aimed at resolving disputes and reconciling offenders with the victims of the misconduct; | • retributive punishment: justice requires that a man should suffer because of and in proportion to, his moral wrong-doing. Punishment is set by legislation; judgement is imposed; |
| • payment of compensation by the offenders (of their clan) to their victims or victims' kin, even in cases as serious as murder; | • the perpetrator is the object of sentencing; retributive incarceration and rehabilitation are means to deter and punish offenders; |
| • in court, a front that appears silent, uncommunicative, unresponsive and withdrawn—based on noninterference and learn-by-observation preference of behavior and on desire to maintain personal dignity and integrity; | • expected behaviour in court: defendant must give appearance of being willing to confront his/her situation and voice admittance to error and show remorse and willingness to change; must express desired motivation for change; |
| • reluctance to testify for or against others or him/herself, based on a general avoidance of confrontation and imposition of opinion or testimony; | • obligated to testify and defend oneself in order to get at the facts based on an adversarial mode of dealing with legal challenges; |
| • often pleads guilty on the basis of honesty or non-confrontational acquiescence. | • expected to plead not guilty on the basis that one is innocent until proven guilty. |

On the Canadian legal landscape, as in the experiences of other countries' dealings with Aboriginal peoples, various forms of indigenization of the justice system have been experimented with. On the whole these have produced models that use the process of indigenization as ways of injecting Aboriginally appropriate concepts and mechanisms into (or more likely adhering Aboriginal adjudicative mechanisms onto) the existing legal concepts and the prevailing justice system. Though some of these have been an improvement on the basically ethnocentric approach previously administered by the Canadian justice system, they have not addressed the problems Aboriginal people face in their disproportionate representation in prison. Nor have they responded to the foundational distinctiveness of Aboriginal culture, ways of law or social institutions.

After reviewing the approaches taken in the United States, Australia and in Canada, Professor Michael Jackson concludes that, though these are an improvement on what was there before, and though such efforts should be encouraged, they do not go far enough. We must look for more far reaching models, he asserts.

This is what the present situation calls for, and is indeed what Aboriginal people themselves seek:

> As we have seen from a review of the experience with tribal and Aboriginal courts in the United States and Australia and Canada, the development of native justice systems has been one directional in the sense that these systems have been an adaptation of our common law concept or a court applying our law and our sanctions. What is now being sought by native people is the right to revitalize their indigenous institutions and develop and adapt them to respond to the contemporary problems which their communities face. (1988:43)

In conclusion, the Euro-Canadian justice system that has been applied to the Aboriginal people of Canada is one that has evolved out of a context and history that is very different than the cultural and historical context of North American Aboriginal people. Euro-Western concepts of sovereignty, authority, hierarchy and ruling entity appears diametrically opposed to the concepts of spiritual compact, tribal will, custom/tradition, and respect for the inherent equality and integrity of the individual of the Aboriginal worldview. Where it has almost universally been applied to Aboriginal people, it has been a system imposed upon them and found to be basically incompatible with the concepts and values of persisting Aboriginal culture and world view.

Psychologically, the core values of Aboriginal people, as well as the cultural beliefs and structures, have been highly resistant to change. The values and the behaviour generated by these values have persisted through time and acculturational forces. This being so, the difficulties arising from an imposed system of justice which is based on a very different value system and core principles would still persist in the courtrooms of today. A study of these core values, with their ensuing behaviours, comparing them with that of the Euro-Canadian culture, shows that continuing difficulties for Aboriginal people in conflict with the law and in relating to the justice system can be directly traced to the unsuccessful meeting of two distinctive cultures and traditions.

# PART TWO

---

# *Law*

# 5

*Ann Arbor (Michigan) News*

# CONFLICTING CULTURES

## Casino Growth Reveals Differences
## Between Indian Law, State Law

*As Indians and non-Indians have increased contact, role of tribal law causes confusion.*

BY FEDERICO MARTINEZ

LANSING—Growing tourism on American Indian reservations in Michigan is prompting a rise in the number of legal disputes between Indians and non-Indians.

More and more visitors and businesses are finding out that the state's seven Indian tribes have their own laws, and that they are subject to them when they're on the reservations.

Tribal sovereignty in civil cases sometimes comes as a surprise to non-Indians, said Kathryn Tierney, a tribal

Edited version of *Ann Arbor News*, "Conflicting Cultures: Casino Growth Reveals Differences Between Indian Law, State Law," Federico Martinez, July 27, 1994:E13–14. Booth News Service.

attorney for the Bay Mills Indian Community, near Brimley in the Upper Peninsula.

"They say we're all Americans, why should we have different laws?" said Tierney, who has been a tribal law attorney for 20 years. "They don't understand there are people living every day on reservations who are subject to their tribal court."

Tribal courts went largely ignored by state and federal courts until about 1972, when reservations began setting up gambling casinos and other tourist attractions, said Houghton County Circuit Court Judge Garfield Hood.

"The systems have been operating parallel with each other for a long time but not with each other," said Hood. "It all seemed to work in the 1940s and '50s, but that is now changing as tribes become more active in business and commerce."

Casino gambling is bringing Indians and non-Indians together as never before, Hood said. The growing industry has also brought more companies— construction firms, convenience stores, gas stations—to the reservation.

"Twenty years ago there was virtually no interaction," said Hood.

Now, if a company fails to complete a job at a casino as specified, for instance, the tribe can be in a quandary.

"The tribal member files suit and wins but the tribal court doesn't have authority to enforce the ruling," Hood explained.

The Michigan Bar Association recently formed a committee to try to clarify jurisdiction issues, said Hood, co-chairman of the group's Standing Committee on Indian Law.

"The state and tribal courts need to reach an agreement to work together," said Hood.

Seven American Indian reservations in Michigan are recognized as individual sovereign nations by the federal government and operate under their own laws and ordinances, Tierney said. Tribal courts have jurisdiction only over civil issues—criminal issues are subject to state law—and their power applies to both Indians and non-Indians. [Editors' note: Native American criminal offenses committed on-reservation are under federal jurisdiction in Michigan; Native offenses committed off-reservation are under state jurisdiction.]

One frequent problem is collecting child support in cases where one parent is an Indian and the other is not, said Hood. The tribe is not required to honor a circuit court ruling for child support, he said, even though he says most do.

Other common problems between Indians and non-Indians involve child custody disputes that are under the jurisdiction of tribal courts, but which are sometimes ignored or challenged by state courts, said Brad Dakota, chief tribal judge for the Keweenaw Bay Indian Community near Baraga in the Upper Peninsula.

The seven federally recognized Michigan tribes include, in the Lower Peninsula, the Grand Traverse Band of Ottawa and Chippewa Indians near Traverse City and the Saginaw Chippewa Indian Tribe in Mount Pleasant. In the Upper Peninsula tribes include the Lac Vieux Desert Band of Lake Superior Chippewa Indians near Watersmeet, the Keweenaw Bay Indian Community, the Hannahville Indian Community near Escanaba, the Sault Ste. Marie Tribe of Chippewa Indians and the Bay Mills Indian Community.

# 6

# SELF-DETERMINATION AND AMERICAN INDIAN JUSTICE

## Tribal Versus Federal Jurisdiction on Indian Lands

ZOANN K. SNYDER-JOY

The intervention of the United States government into American Indian tribal justice systems has resulted in a substantial loss of sovereignty for the Indian nations.[1] In particular, the federal government has substantially narrowed the authority of Indian tribes to maintain jurisdiction over many criminal activities in their communities. Which government maintains jurisdiction is not always clear. Deloria and Lytle (1983:178) liken the contemporary American Indian justice system to a *jurisdictional maze* wherein the federal government, the state governments, or the tribal governments retain authority over certain criminal acts.[2]

Given the complex nature of American Indian criminal justice, questions must be raised regarding the impact this arrangement has had on the American Indian people. Current research indicates that one of the possible outcomes of the alterations of American Indian criminal justice systems is the disproportionate over-representation of American Indian defendants reported in the non-Indian criminal justice process.

This chapter addresses some of the statutes and case laws that the federal government has used to alter American Indian legal systems and structure American Indian law in the United States. This chapter also proposes future research con-

Edited version of Zoann K. Snyder-Joy, "Self-Determination and American Indian Justice: Tribal Versus Federal Jurisdiction on Indian Lands," in *Ethnicity, Race and Crime: Perspectives Across Time and Place,* ed. D. Hawkins, 310–320. Albany: SUNY Press. Reprinted by permission of the State University of New York Press and the author.

siderations as a means of arriving at more equitable American Indian justice processes both on and off reservations.

The historical relationships between the federal government and American Indians were founded on the government's trust responsibility for American Indians. Hall (1980) provides a comprehensive definition of the federal trust responsibility. He defines the relationship as "the unique legal and moral duty of the United States to assist Indian tribes in the protection of their property and rights." He notes that the trust responsibility is based on treaties, court decisions, and laws.

Criminal laws and jurisdiction over crimes on Indian lands, while not part of the initial trust responsibility, have been defined and redefined over the course of the last two hundred years. Both laws and court decisions have greatly narrowed tribes' criminal jurisdictions over offenses committed on reservations. I review several of these decisions and laws as a means of depicting the encroachment of the federal government into the sovereignty of American Indian tribes, especially their inherent rights to maintain social control on their own lands. For a more comprehensive overview of Indian law, see Canby, 1988; Cohen, 1982; Shattuck and Norgren, 1991; and Strickland, 1975.

## SOVEREIGNTY AND THE CHEROKEE NATION CASES

During the first third of the nineteenth century, a series of Supreme Court decisions were made regarding federal/Indian relations. These cases have had a profound impact on Indian legal systems and continue to influence decisions regarding tribal sovereignty and self-determination (Canby, 1988). These rulings, often referred to as the Cherokee Nation cases (see Deloria and Lytle, 1983), are Cherokee Nation v. Georgia, 30 U.S. (5 Pet.) 1 (1831); and Worcester v. Georgia, 31 U.S. (6 Pet.) 575 (1832). In delivering its opinions, the Supreme Court recognized Indian tribes as distinct political entities with some rights to sovereignty.

In Worcester v. Georgia (1832), the Supreme Court decided that state laws were not enforceable in Indian country. The court, in recognizing the Cherokee nation as a state, noted:

> The Cherokee nation, then, is a distinct community, occupying its own territory, with boundaries accurately described, in which the laws of Georgia can have no force, and which the citizens of Georgia have no right to enter, but with the acts of Congress. The whole intercourse between the United States and this nation, is, but our Constitution and laws, vested in the government of the United States. (31 U.S. [6 Pet.] 515 [1832], 561).

Although the Supreme Court decided in support of American Indian sovereignty and self-government to the exclusion of state laws, this decision did not set a precedent for the federal Indian policies that followed. The expansion of white settlers into the territories west of the Mississippi River resulted in renewed efforts to dislocate American Indian claims to their lands. The intrusion of white settlers on Indian land was accompanied by federal encroachment into Indian land ways (Deloria and Lytle, 1983; Shattuck and Norgren, 1991). An incident in 1881 was used by the federal government to establish greater federal control over American Indian legal systems.

## The Crow Dog Case
## and the Major Crimes Act

On August 5, 1881, Crow Dog shot and killed Chief Spotted Tail. Both the victim and assailant were Brule Sioux and Brule law required that Crow Dog make reparations to Spotted Tail's family, thus providing justice for the victim's family (Shattuck and Norgren, 1991). While justice was served under Brule law, non-Indian society was not satisfied with the outcome. Crow Dog was arrested and brought forward for a new trial, supposedly at the instigation of local whites who were not satisfied with the tribal resolution of the matter (Shattuck and Norgren, 1991). In his second trial, Crow Dog was found guilty of murder and sentenced to hang. An appeal was filed and the Supreme Court upheld the Sioux's treaty rights. The court maintained that the Sioux justice system was sovereign and exempt from outside interference (Shattuck and Norgren, 1991). However, the opportunity for federal intervention into Indian justice systems was also established in the Supreme Court's decision:

> Justice Matthew's opinion in Ex Parte Crow Dog (109 U.S. 556 [1883]) rejected the government's reading of the disputed Sioux treaties, arguing instead that Indian sovereignty, as described by Marshall in the 1830s Cherokee cases and as recognized by the United States when it entered into these treaties was binding. There should be no repeal of a treaty right by implication, and any new criminal jurisdiction policy on the part of the United States government would require "*a clear expression of the intention of Congress.*" (Shattuck and Norgren, 1991: 93; emphasis added)

Soon after the Crow Dog decision, the Major Crimes Act (18 U.S.C.A. 1153) was passed in 1885, providing "federal jurisdiction over seven crimes committed by Indians in Indian country" (Canby, 1988: 105). The crimes covered by the Major Crimes Act were murder, manslaughter, rape, assault with intent to kill, arson, burglary, and larceny. Subsequent additions to the Major Crimes Act read:

> Any Indian who commits against the person or property of another Indian or other person any of the following offenses, namely, murder, manslaughter, kidnaping, rape, carnal knowledge of any female, not his wife, who has not attained the age of sixteen years, assault with intent to commit rape, incest, assault with intent to commit murder, assault with a dangerous weapon, assault resulting in serious bodily injury, arson,

burglary, robbery, and larceny within Indian country, shall be subject to the same laws and penalties as all other persons committing any of the above offenses, within the exclusive jurisdiction of the United States. (18 U.S.C.A. 1153)

The Major Crimes Act made substantial inroads into American Indian sovereignty to define and enforce criminal law on their own lands. The imposition of federal jurisdiction over Indian country was further expanded to include state authority in some areas.

Public Law 280 (67 Stat. 588), passed in 1953, granted some states criminal and civil jurisdiction over Indian lands. The states affected by the legislation were California, Minnesota (except the Red Lake Reservation), Nebraska, Oregon (except the Warm Springs Reservation), and Wisconsin (except the Menominee Reservation). Public Law 280 also provided that any states that wished to gain jurisdiction over tribes could do so by state law or by amending the state constitution. This latter activity could be done *without* the consent of the affected tribes. The passage of the Indian Civil Rights Act of 1968 modified state jurisdiction on Indian lands.

## INDIAN CIVIL RIGHTS ACT OF 1968 (82 STAT. 77)

The Indian Civil Rights Act of 1968 (ICRA) amended Public Law 280 such that Indians must vote to approve the extension of state civil and criminal jurisdiction over Indian land. The change in Public Law 280 is reported to have been widely approved by American Indians (Canby, 1988; Shattuck and Norgren, 1991).

The ICRA also extended most of the provisions of the Bill of Rights to the tribes. While some people criticized it as a further encroachment on tribal rights by the federal government (Shattuck and Norgren, 1991), others (Canby, 1988) praised this action as a means of upholding Indians' individual rights.

Shattuck and Norgren (1991:169) assert:

> From a tribal perspective, the imposition of constitutional rights and liberties standards on tribes was in direct conflict with principles of Indian sovereignty and tribal self-determination. Meaningful self-determination must preclude appeal to external authorities by reference to rules not congruent with traditional tribal concepts of authority and justice.

Canby (1988) suggests that while further federal intrusion into Indian internal matters does lessen the sovereignty of tribes, it could also be indicative of further support for tribal governments. He notes:

> On the other hand, congressional action to require constitutional procedures by tribal governments seemed to contemplate the continued existence of those governments, rather than their withering away. (Canby, 1988:29)

The impact of external authority on tribal self-determination and sovereignty was put to the test a few years later. The Oliphant decision brought about further restrictions for tribal sovereignty.

## OLIPHANT V. SUQUAMISH INDIAN TRIBE
## (435 U.S. 191 [1978])

Mark Oliphant, a non-Indian living on the Port Madison Reservation (Washington), was arrested by tribal police and brought to trial for resisting arrest and assault of a police officer. In his appeal, Oliphant claimed that he could not be subject to Indian jurisdiction, because he was not an Indian.

The Supreme Court upheld Oliphant's claim and ruled that the tribe, due to its domestic, dependent status, does not have jurisdiction over non-Indians unless such power is granted by Congress.[3] In a subsequent decision, the Supreme Court further defined the power of tribes as that which "is necessary to protect tribal self-government or to control internal relations" (Montana v. United States, 450 U.S. 544 [1981]). The move to further restrict tribal criminal jurisdiction culminated with the Duro decision in 1990.

## DURO V. REINA (110 S.CT. 2053 [1990])

Perhaps one of the most debilitating decisions with respect to tribal sovereignty was passed down by the Supreme Court in Duro v. Reina. Albert Duro, an enrolled member of the Torres-Martinez Band of the Cahuilla Mission Indians (California), was living and working in the Salt River Pima-Maricopa Indian Community in Arizona. On June 15, 1984, Duro allegedly shot and killed a 14-year-old boy from the Gila River Indian Tribe while both parties were in the Salt River Pima-Maricopa Indian Community.

Duro was arrested by Salt River tribal police and held for trial in the Salt River Community. The tribe was to prosecute for discharging a firearm on the reservation. (The Indian Civil Rights Act of 1968 limited the criminal jurisdiction of tribes to misdemeanors, while the murder was under federal jurisdiction.) Duro filed a petition for habeas corpus in the United States district court. The writ was granted, for the district court maintained that the Indian Civil Rights Act of 1968 prohibits tribes from prosecuting non-Indians. The district court noted that "to subject a nonmember Indian to tribal jurisdiction where non-Indians are exempt would constitute discrimination based on race" (110 S.Ct. 2053 [1990], 2058).

The court of appeals reversed the decision and did not uphold the equal protection clause of the Indian Civil Rights Act of 1968. The court responded:

> It justified tribal jurisdiction over petitioner by his significant contacts with the Pima-Maricopa Community, such as residing with a member of the Tribe on the reservation and his employment with the Tribe's construction company. A need for effective

law enforcement on the reservation provided a rational basis for the classification. (110 S.Ct. 2053 [1990], 2058)

The Supreme Court reviewed the case and determined that the Salt River community did not have jurisdiction over nonmember Indians. The majority decision was based on the fact that there was diversity among tribal social and cultural structures, and that the assumption should not be made that all tribes are alike. A second point presented in the court's decision maintained that enrolled membership in a tribal community constitutes consent to the authority of the tribe.

The dissenting opinion issued by Justices William Brennan and Thurgood Marshall criticized the logic of the court's decision. They noted:

> That the Court finds irrelevant the fact that we have long held that the term "Indian" in these statutes does not differentiate between members and nonmembers of a tribe. . . . Rather, the Court concludes that the federal definition of "Indian" is relevant only to *federal jurisdiction and is "not dispositive of a question of tribal power"*. . . . But this conclusion is at odds with the analysis in Oliphant in which the congressional enactments served as evidence of a "commonly shared presumption" that tribes had ceded their power over non-Indians. Similarly, these enactments reflect the congressional presumption that tribes had power over all disputes between Indians regardless of tribal membership.
>
> By refusing to draw this inference from repeated congressional actions, the Court today creates a jurisdictional void in which neither federal nor tribal jurisdiction exists over nonmember Indians who commit minor crimes against another Indian. (110 S.Ct. 2053 [1990], 2069–70)

Brennan and Marshall's conclusion substantiates the concerns expressed by American Indians that the federal government had been employing contradictory approaches to Indian issues for some time and ignoring the mandates of Congress.

In response to the Duro v. Reina decision, Congress established a one-year reinstatement of the power of tribes to exercise criminal jurisdiction over Indians. On October 28, 1991, Congress passed Public Law 102–137 (105 Stat. 616, 1), "to make permanent the legislative reinstatement, following the decision of Duro against Reina, of the power of Indian tribes to exercise criminal jurisdiction over Indians." Given the conflicting actions taken by Congress and the Supreme Court, future actions regarding federal Indian law are anticipated with both hope and trepidation.

From the brief historical overview presented, it is clear that the federal government has greatly restricted the authority of American Indians to formally address crime in their on-reservation communities. What is not as clear is what impact this loss of power has had on American Indian criminality. The extant literature addresses the effects of the loss of sovereignty for American Indians and their tribal cultures (Deloria and Lytle, 1983, 1984; Green, 1991; Prucha, 1984, 1985; Snipp, 1986; Szasz, 1977, 1990).

I suggest that the American Indians' lack of representation in the legislation and enforcement of the law may result in the overrepresentation of American Indian defendants in the non-Indian criminal justice process. If American Indian cultures are not recognized in the policy-making process, it is possible that their norms and values may be viewed as deviant and subject to greater scrutiny by the dominant society's agents of social control.

## SUMMARY AND CONCLUSIONS

American Indians in the U.S.A. have disproportionately high rates of arrest and incarceration, and possibly longer prison terms than whites due to discretionary actions by criminal justice decision-makers. Further empirical research remains a necessity in order to determine the extent to which discrimination is a factor as opposed to variables such as a prior criminal record and types of behavior while incarcerated (Bynum and Paternoster, 1984; Pommersheim and Wise, 1989; Zatz, Lujan, and Snyder-Joy, 1991). Future research must examine the entire criminal justice process to better understand how decisions made at the various stages in the process affect the outcome for American Indian defendants (Green, 1991; Zatz, Lujan, and Snyder-Joy, 1991). Discrimination may be cumulative rather than occurring at only one stage, such as arrest or sentencing.

If the research findings indicate the possibility of discriminatory behavior against American Indians at specific stages of the criminal justice system, administrative policies and practices need to target criminal justice professionals in those stages. Multicultural training for all criminal justice workers may be required to create greater awareness of diversity among employees. Intraagency task forces may be needed to formally sanction discriminatory practices among personnel.

In addition to systemic discrimination, future studies also need to focus on the social, economic, and political factors that may contribute to increased alcoholism and violence by American Indians and non-Indians alike. It is important to generate policy changes to alleviate the social problems prevalent in American Indian communities and for American Indians in off-reservation society.

Research on American Indian social problems (Bachman, 1992; Deloria and Lytle, 1983, 1984; Green, 1991; Szasz, 1977) has noted the need for greater American Indian self-determination and local control of programs and policies, reducing economic barriers, and providing for greater recognition of Indian cultures as a means of reducing social ills. More attention should focus on local control as a means of ameliorating the reservations' social problems, including violence and alcohol-related abuses among American Indians. American Indian–operated diversion and treatment programs must be examined to chart their impact on American Indian crime and social problems. Local control should also extend to tribal criminal jurisdiction on Indian lands. In this way, social control relevant to Indian cultures and concerns might be used to better address the social problems in Indian country.

# Notes

1. This chapter addresses issues for American Indians in the United States. Native peoples living in other parts of the Americas are not included in the discussion due to variation in the legal and political organizations among these peoples and the federal governments of their countries.

2. I deliberately refer to American Indian justice *systems* in the first sentence in recognition of the tribal and cultural diversity among American Indian peoples, while referring to the postintervention structure in the singular form. The actions taken by the federal and state governments often do not recognize the diversity of American Indian cultures and their related law ways.

3. In the Cherokee Nation v. Georgia decision of 1831, Chief Justice John Marshall referred to American Indian tribes as *domestic dependent nations.* He noted:

> They occupy a territory to which we assert a title independent of their will, which must take effect in point of possession when their right of possession ceases. Meanwhile, they are in a state of pupilage. Their relation to the United States resembles that of a ward to his guardian. (30 U.S. [5 Pet.] 1, 16 [1831])

# 7
# TRADITIONAL APPROACHES
# TO TRIBAL JUSTICE

## History and Current Practice

TROY L. ARMSTRONG
MICHAEL H. GUILFOYLE
ADA PECOS MELTON

In the face of continuing federal efforts to expand the use of tribal courts and impose a Western system of jurisprudence in Indian Country, tribes are increasingly experimenting with more flexible and inclusive approaches that combine customary Native American sanctioning philosophy and practice with elements of the Western legal system. These developments have resulted in a major reexamination and revitalization by numerous tribes across the entirety of the United States of their traditional justice systems. The following discussion provides a description of the range and nature of customary approaches to justice among a number of these tribes. The underlying beliefs, as well as the approaches through which social control was justified and exercised prior to contact with European society, varied considerably from tribe to tribe. Yet, certain basic themes tended to characterize the ways used to constrain and respond to anti-social behavior. Authority for decision making as it is related to social deviance was grounded in the wider social group, and approval to pursue any particular course of action against violative behavior was achieved through a process of attaining tribal consensus. Further, it should be kept in mind that violations of tribal beliefs were

Excerpted and revised from T. Armstrong, M. H. Guilfoyle, and Ada Pecos Melton, "Native American Delinquency." Office of Juvenile Justice and Delinquency Prevention, U.S. Department of Justice, 1992.

overwhelmingly the exception rather than the rule in the daily lives of these groups. Conformity to the norms of tribal values was strongly instilled among all members and were constantly reinforced by one's kinsmen. Quite simply, violative behavior was relatively rare in traditional Native American communities.

When misconduct did occur, there was often a tendency to generalize this behavior across the wider kin group to which the individual offender belonged. This mode of social control led to a situation in which there was a lesser sense of individual guilt, and instead a wider sharing of shame by kinsmen. When individuals were targeted for sanctioning, the form taken by the reprimands was verbal shaming. For example, on the Plains, where ridicule was frequently used to rebuke misconduct, the guilty party was chided by his/her "joking relative" (Driver, 1969). Further, even when individual stigma and censure were utilized, every effort was made to retain the offender as an integral part of the social order. Consequently, customary penalties were used for the purpose of helping the offender make amends and to restore self-respect with a sense of dignity (Melton, 1989). Generally, punishment was not a tribal technique; rather, the focus and purpose of customary justice was atonement by the offending party to the entire social group. Prime consideration was given to the "purification" of offenders and the restoration of balance and tribal harmony.

In spite of the widespread reliance upon a generally more benign approach to crime and misconduct, it is essential to realize in assessing customary Indian justice that tribes were not without some tradition of physical punishment—often quite extreme in nature—being imposed upon perpetrators of serious crime. The possibility of and actual resort to vengeance was a reality underlying the justice practices of many tribes. Among the Cherokee, for example, vengeance was employed in response to the occurrence of certain heinous crimes (Traisman, 1981). However, the practice was structured by a set of customary rules so that punishment for a violent crime such as homicide was the functional responsibility of the victim's clan (Reid, 1970). In this situation, only the victim's and the offender's clans played any role in administering justice. In fact, the offender's clan often aided the avenging clan in the execution of the guilty individual. For less serious offenses, this tribe utilized a wide variety of sanctioning techniques including ostracism, sarcasm, and ridicule. Such interventions were far more commonly used than blood vengeance for maintaining order.

Perhaps as a safeguard against the possible outbreak of blood vengeance between kin groups, customary practice widely utilized by tribes was the imposition of reparative sanctions (i.e., various forms of restitution and community service). This approach had considerable value for reducing the hostility that could result from violent crimes since it restored a sense of equity to the aggrieved parties. A particularly interesting account of the kind of practice involves the Yurok Indians of California, a tribe studied by Kroeber (1925) in great detail in the 1920s, where a very elaborate scaling of offenses for purposes of making restitution had been developed.

Kroeber's account makes it clear that among these Northern California Indians "it was well understood that every possession and privilege, and every injury and offense, could be exactly valued in terms of property; and that every invasion of privilege and property must be exactly compensated" (Kroeber 1925, quoted in Bohannon 1967:9). Restitution took the form of various types of wealth and service, and the amount of restitution was dependent upon the harm done to the victim, rather than the economic status of the offender. In fact it was the harm done to the victim, plus the status of the victim, that served to determine the amount of compensation in any given case.

When sanctions were imposed upon individual offenders, the actual administration of these duties was conducted by persons or groups who were designated this role by birth and/or social position within the larger society. In Iroquoian society, which was organized upon the basis of matrilineal clans, the maternal uncles within the kin groupings were assigned the responsibility of sanctioning misconduct (Driver, 1969). A similar clan-based system of administering justice existed among the Cherokee (Reid, 1970). The underlying assumption in this kinship-based system of justice was that when a member of one clan killed a member of another clan, the victim's clan was owed one life from the killer's clan (Traisman, 1981). In most Apache bands, it was the role of the Council of Patriarchs to exercise authority (French, 1982). In addition, a number of tribes, especially those located on the Great Plains, had specially designated warrior societies among whose primary roles was the responsibility to administer punishment (Walker, 1982).

A wide range of descriptive accounts of tribal justice systems and particular sanctioning techniques across different culture areas can be found in the anthropological literature. Although this body of information is far too extensive to quote here, it is worth noting several interesting examples drawn from these ethnographic descriptions of traditional tribal justice systems. William MacLead published three articles in the 1930s documenting traditional methods of social control by American Indians in different culture areas. "Aspects of the Earlier Development of Law and Punishment" (1932) provided an overview of various legal customs practiced by Northwest Coast tribes; "Law, Procedure, and Punishment in Early Bureaucracies" (1934) described traditional methods of handling social deviants, mostly by Eastern Woodland and Southeastern tribes (Hurons, Menominees, Creeks, and Choctaws); "Police and Punishment Among Native Americans of the Plains" (1937) discussed customary methods of social control, particularly the use of police societies among tribes in this culture area (Cheyenne, Crow, Ojibwa, and Sioux). Likewise, Hoebel (1954) offered a detailed description of traditional tribal judicial practices among Plains Indians (Comanche, Kiowa, and Cheyenne).

An example of this kind of ethnographic description is offered in an account of traditional justice in three Northwest Coast communities. Pre-Salish communities were structured in a way that minimized open disputing and emphasized a cooperative co-existence within the family and village. Community consensus about standards of behavior, various forms of indirect social control, rather than written regulations and sanctions, pressured individuals to control their behavior. Elders were the primary source for teaching proper behavior and attitudes. This was accomplished by example, lecture, storytelling, and recounting family history. The Council of Elders, later referred to as the "Indian Court" during post-contact times, was called upon to facilitate marital separations or deal with acts of infidelity, theft, and other types of bad behavior. It was important for the selected spokesperson from the Council to be able to speak "good words" that would "not hurt the people." Individuals who failed to comply with Council guidelines and recommendations would be "given the cold shoulder" for however long it took for them to modify their behavior (Northwest Intertribal Court System, n.d.).

Traisman (1981), in "Native Law: Law and Order Among Eighteenth-Century Cherokee, Great Plains, Central Prairie, and Woodland Indians," documents that across vast areas of the North American continent tribes utilized three basic approaches to the deterrence and punishment of crime. These practices ranged from the use of blood vengeance by the Cherokee in the Appalachian region for serious crimes and "satirical sanctions" for lesser offenses, to the Great Plains, where tribes tended to be police societies assigning the responsibility for the maintenance of law and order to specific warrior groups, and finally to tribes of the central prairie and woodlands, where restitutive gestures to repay the families of crime victims were widely utilized to avoid blood feuding between the involved kin groups.

A number of tribes throughout the U.S. have continued to rely upon certain aspects of their traditional practices for administering justice. In some instances, there is direct linkage back to a cultural period preceding the impact of European society. Other times, tribes have reformulated and reintroduced practices that were dropped following contact but that are again beginning to be explored based upon their appropriateness to the traditional values and mores of the tribes. The application of reparative sanctions is an excellent example of an approach for maintaining and reinforcing social control that was widely utilized prior to contact with White society. Certain tribes have continued to use these techniques throughout their histories while others have made the decision to revive reparative justice practices.

In one fascinating example of reintroduction, the Office of Juvenile Justice and Delinquency Prevention (1978) initiated a nationwide project to test the utility of restitution as an alternative to traditional dispositions in the juvenile court. Among the programs started under the auspices of this programming initiative was one located on the Menominee Reservation in Wisconsin and operated by the tribal court. Not only has this program been distinctive for having been developed by the Menominee Tribe and tailored to meet the specific circumstances, problems and needs of the reservation, but also it has been acclaimed for its success in intervening with severely delinquent youth and dramatically reducing the rate of incarceration for the offenders. The program was begun with an underlying philosophical commitment to the idea that delinquent youth should be held accountable for their crimes by playing an active role in compensating their victims, but at the same time these youth should also be provided with a helping hand in becoming productive members of their community. Key to the success of this program has been its ability to tie the restitution orders and activities to the traditional values and mores of the Menominee Tribe. Participants in the program are required to maintain close contact with tribal elders and to strictly observe tribal rituals. In this way, an opportunity is provided for strengthening tribal cohesion and reducing the alienation of troubled Indian youth from customary lifeways (Armstrong, n.d.).

Another example of the modern application of traditional sanctioning approaches in a tribal setting has been documented in a study of justice practices among the contemporary Navajo (Johnson, 1990). As a result of overburdened courts and demands for judicial economy, the Navajo Nation established the Navajo Peacemaker Court under its judiciary in 1982. By judicial resolution the use of customary practices in civil actions and other legal matters was institutionalized. Incorporation of the practices of mediation and arbitration was based on a study of traditional Navajo dispute resolution. This inquiry revealed that: ". . . the legal and cultural needs of Navajo people are not met solely by relief in Americanized tribal courts. Rather tribal judges and chapter officials have resorted to old customs and methods" (Johnson, 1990: 23).

The traditional methods that were reintroduced into the tribal court could be traced back to the clanship system in place prior to the United States–Navajo Treaty of 1868. Under this system tribal members selected "headmen" on the basis of age, experience, knowledge of ceremonial precepts and traditional values, oratorical skills, and wealth. The civic duties of headmen included: mediations and/or arbitration of disputes, family conflict resolution, correction of public wrongdoers, and advocacy of the tribe in relations with other communities, tribes, and governments. The dispute resolution process was non-coercive and employed traditional ethics, values and mores. The goal was to achieve social harmony by having the affected groups "talk over" an unpopular tribal decision or to negotiate an intergroup problem. The headman's role was to provide guidance and to facilitate a fair settlement. The process was structured to avoid resolutions in which there were clear winners and losers. This outcome allowed a nurturance of peace and harmony in the community in spite of ongoing disputes and conflicts.

As designed, the Peacemaker Courts are components within the larger Navajo District Courts. Their structure and procedures are intended to preserve, protect, and encourage the use of traditional methods of dispute resolution by keeping them independent and customary. As Zion (1983) has noted, the substantive content and procedural rules cover seven disputational areas and provide guidelines for the participation of the involved parties. These guidelines identify the types of disputes that can be mediated, who can mediate, what methods of mediation can be used, the nature of binding authority, etc. The Peacemaker Courts have limited jurisdiction to hear local disputes of a civil nature. However, the Navajo District

Court retains the authority to refer other matters to the Peacemaker Court for "good cause." For example, criminal matters can be handled through customary dispute resolution under the following kinds of circumstances: no personal injury occurs; all parties consent to participate; a victimless crime; and as a condition of probation. Transfer to the Peacemaker Court can also occur when a determination is made by the District Court judge that a "reasonable condition" exists for a traditional disposition of the case (Johnson, 1990).

Traditional justice among the Navajo tends to be swift, direct, personal and emphasizes the restoration of harmony and reacceptance by the community rather than punishment and ostracism. Although the court process may seem to some to be overly authoritarian, the core practices derive from a widely shared and deeply ingrained worldview, as well as from the virtual unanimity with which that approach to social control and sanctioning is held by tribal members. As Navajo Chief Justice Tom Tso also notes elsewhere in this volume, another difference in the Navajo courts is the emphasis that is placed on the traditional relationship between the tribe and nature.

The adoption of these customary practices parallels a very similar cultural tradition among Pueblo tribes, where there is also a strong ethic of community responsibility. Hoebel (1969: 98) has noted in this regard:

> The dominant integrating factor of Grand Pueblo culture is the view of the universe as an orderly phenomenon. People or things are not merely "good" or "bad". "Evil" is a disturbance in the equilibrium that exists between man and the universe, while "good" is a positive frame of mind or action that maintains harmonious balance.
>
> To keep man and universe in harmonious balance, all must work together and with "good" thoughts. Unanimous effort of body and mind is not only a key value, but it is also enforced. . . . The Cacique [the priest-chief] and the War Captains exert strict control over the activities of village members and see that all physically able members participate in a rigid calendric series of ceremonies. Among the members of a village there is a serious concern over a neighbor's behavior and a perpetual watch is maintained over his or her activities. Any action, whether physical or verbal, which is construed by Pueblo authorities to be contrary to group concerns and unanimous will of the village is promptly and severely punished. [Quoted in Alper and Nichols, 1981:198]

When translated into the contemporary tribal setting, these philosophical precepts result in the operation of a traditional court that is guided by two basic principles: a case should be settled with the minimum of persons necessary and quarrels should be avoided because they "poison the mind and interfere with the good thoughts necessary to maintain harmony in the world" (Hoebel, 1969:108). Further, the authority of this court is accepted by the tribal members whom it serves. Verdicts are accepted as just for the very fact that they are consistent with cultural values and are positively reinforced by tribal members.

# PART THREE

*Crime*

# 8

*Tulsa (Oklahoma) World*

# Tribes Find Solution to Child Abuse Law Gap

BY JULIE DELCOUR

SHANGRI-LA—In an event U.S. Attorney General Janet Reno termed historic, Oklahoma tribal leaders and government officials signed a pact Monday to fight Indian child abuse.

A crisis on another front—the Cuban refugee exodus—prevented Reno from appearing here to speak on a crisis she said cooperation can help alleviate.

Reno sent a videotaped message that was to play to 150 people, including leaders from 18 tribes, two U.S. attorneys and scores of tribal, law enforcement, health and social service officials

Edited version of *Tulsa World,* "Tribes Find Solution to Child Abuse Law Gap," Julie DelCour, August 30, 1994: B4. Reprinted by permission of *The Tulsa World.*

attending a three-day seminar on the topic.

Reno said that because of jurisdictional voids, Indian child-abuse cases often have not reached federal prosecutors' attention.

She said that a 1993 Indian Health Services report indicated that nationally, there were 32,000 cases of rape and sexual abuse reported on Indian land—4,000 involving children.

But the real number may be two to three times higher, she said.

"These are alarming figures and underscore the vital need of combining efforts to address these problems," Reno said.

The agreement and seminar are the first of their kind and were organized by Northern District U.S. Attorney

Steve Lewis, Assistant U.S. Attorney Kathleen Bliss and Eastern District U.S. Attorney John Raley.

In Arizona, interdisciplinary teams have been formed to aid Indian child victims.

Teams, including law enforcement, counselors and medical and social service workers, are planned for Oklahoma.

Monday's agreement formalizes guidelines and protocol for handling physical and sexual abuse cases involving Indian children or abusers on Indian land.

Figures for such abuse in Oklahoma were not available.

"I can't tell you if there are 25 cases or 500 cases, but in either respect, that's way too many," said Lewis, who signed the pact.

"There must be equal protection," said Oklahoma FBI Special Agent in Charge Bob Ricks.

"When you have a gap in the law, when crimes are ignored, the words of the Constitution become very hollow indeed," Ricks said. "The jurisdictional difficulties are great. But Steve Lewis decided we would put that behind us."

Cherokee Nation Principal Chief Wilma Mankiller, who signed the pact, said: "We're very happy. We have taken a very aggressive path to regroup (tribal) law enforcement and judicial systems. We've had to work with federal authorities to provide protection for our people. This formalizes what we've done already."

George Tallchief, president of the Osage Nation, said: "It is great to see how this has evolved. For years we've known of the tragedies that have occurred with young people."

Ron Grinnell, division manager of Indian Health Services, said: "The rates of this type of crime have been alarming. We'd like to minimize those and the trauma on the children."

Don Greenfeather, leader of the Loyal Shawnee Citizens, recalled a tearful phone call from a grandmother, beside herself because her grandchildren were being abused and she didn't know where to turn.

"Her grandchildren were helpless. Maybe, with this, we can help those who are helpless," Greenfeather said.

Others signing the agreement include L.W. Collier Jr., Anadarko, and Merritt E. Youngdeer, Muskogee, area directors of the Bureau of Indian Affairs; Lynda K. Arnold of the Department of Human Services; Lewis B. Ketchum, leader of the Delaware citizens; Bill Fife, Muscogee (Creek) Nation principal chief; Alex Mathews, Pawnee president; Grace Marie Goodeagle, Quapaw tribe chairwoman; Leaford Bearskin, Wyandotte chief; and George J. (Buck) Captain, Eastern Shawnee chief.

And, Terry L. Whitetree, Seneca-Cayuga chief; Floyd Leonard, Miami chief; Donald E. Giles, Peoria chief; Bill Gene Follis, Modoc chief; Charles Dawes, Ottawa chief; Bill Anoatubby, Chickasaw Nation governor; Hollis E. Roberts, Choctaw Nation chief; Jerry G. Haney, Seminole Nation principal chief; and Charley McGertt, town king, Thlopthlocco tribal town.

# 9

*Associated Press*

# More Indian Kids
# Joining Gangs

TULSA, Okla. (AP)—American Indian youths in the past have had little involvement with street gangs. But social workers and police say that is changing.

Max Benson, a youth guidance counselor at the Lloyd Rader Center in Sand Springs, said when he first began working at the juvenile detention facility, "maybe three out of all the number of young people we had were Indian."

"Now we have Indian kids in every unit," said Benson, a member of the Pawnee tribe.

Law officers also are alarmed by the apparent increase in gang activity among Indian youth, said Cpl. Al Wilson, with the Tulsa Police Department's Gang Task Force.

"Three years ago we didn't know of a Native American gang," Wilson said in

a story for Sunday's editions of the Tulsa World. "We had Native Americans in gangs, but now we have more than one gang that is strictly Native American."

Wilson said Indian gangs are similar to gangs in Los Angeles and other large metropolitan areas, where gang affiliation falls along racial lines.

"In Tulsa that's very unusual. Ours are more multicultural."

These Indian gang members often commit crimes in cities and flee to tribal land to hide, a trend Indian leaders would like to see stopped.

The Pawnee tribe last spring created a gang intervention unit that is believed to be the first in the nation geared to the problem of Indian gangs.

Through a tribal resolution, the Tribes of Oklahoma Gang Task Force was created with the purpose of educating tribes and other groups about the growing problem. Benson is a member.

Edited version of *Associated Press*, "More Indian Kids Joining Gangs," Monday, Nov. 21, 1994. Clarinet. News.

The group will talk to anyone—tribes, teachers, children or audiences at schools. They can identify potential gangs and gang problems; do assessments; look at graffiti and the way children dress and help tribal police develop strategies to identify gangs.

An Indian lawman who asked to remain anonymous said 15 Indian gangs have been identified in Oklahoma.

"Gang members from Tulsa and Oklahoma City come to Indian land and recruit and sell drugs. They're doing the same things gangs in cities are doing," he said.

Those things include drive-by shootings, burglary, development of their own language and wardrobe. Indian gangs borrow heavily from the lingo and fashion of Hispanic groups, the unidentified lawman said.

"We want the gangs to realize they may get some of our kids but they will have a fight in doing so," the lawman said. "Kids are our most valuable resource."

American Indian children are no different from other children who have turned to gangs for emotional support they're not getting elsewhere, officials have found.

"Poverty and racism and other problems typical in cities exist in Indian tribes," the lawman said. "The juveniles feel the same absence of family, of belonging, and are trying to replace the belonging with the family or the tribe with belonging to gangs."

Federal officials say the problem is not limited to tribes in Oklahoma, which has the largest Indian population in the nation.

"Indian young people in Montana don't have contact with city gangs, yet they adopt their mannerisms, customs and types of crimes," a federal agent noted. "This means they are emulating what they see on television."

"Tribes throughout the nation are experiencing the problem."

# 10

## PATTERNS OF
## NATIVE AMERICAN CRIME

ROBERT A. SILVERMAN

The object of this chapter is to describe the extent of Native American involvement in crime. Arrest rates are usually used to determine the amount of law-breaking activity engaged in by any particular ethnic group.

The measurement of Native American criminality (as indicated by arrest rates) is not a straightforward process. When reading this chapter it is important to keep a couple of things in mind. First, our measure of the criminal involvement of any ethnic or racial group is based on police records of arrests of group members, and as will be shown below, these are flawed in general and specifically with regard to the notation of "race." Second, we are dependent on two agencies to provide the data that will be used in our calculations: the Federal Bureau of Investigation (FBI) and their Uniform Crime Reports and the U.S. Bureau of the Census.

Our object is to determine Native American involvement in crime. To do so, we calculate population-based rates.

### WHAT ARE CRIME RATES?

Crime rates are simple calculations that relate the amount of crime (the numerator) to the population that can generate crime (the denominator). The equation for calculating most crime rates looks like this:

---

I would like to thank Gwynne Nettler, Anatole Romaniuc, and Edna Paisano for advice with this project. I would also like to thank Marianne Nielsen and Larry Gould for comments on an earlier draft of this chapter.

$$\frac{\text{Number of crimes x 100,000}}{\text{Population}} = \text{Crime rate}$$

For example, there were a total of 14,872,883 index crimes recorded in the FBI's Uniform Crime Reports[1] for 1991. The U.S. Bureau of the Census estimates that 252,177,000 people were living in the United States in that year. Hence, using the formula above, the total crime rate is calculated as follows:

$$\frac{14,872,883 \text{ x } 100,000}{252,177,000} = 5,897.8$$

The crime rate is expressed as the number of crimes per 100,000 population. In this example, there are about 5,898 crimes recorded in the Uniform Crime Reports for every 100,000 people estimated to have been living in the United States in 1991.

## Arrest Rates

When we are interested in determining the participation in criminal activity of members of ethnic groups, we have to calculate arrest-based rates, which include only a portion of crimes. For much crime we do not know who the offender is, so we cannot calculate a crime-based rate. But police do record the race of arrested offenders, so we can calculate an ethnically based arrest rate. It is important to keep in mind that knowing an arrest rate gives us only a part of the picture (and probably not a very accurate part). For instance, in about 90 percent of burglaries, no offender is known to the police.

The calculation for an arrest rate is shown below:

$$\frac{\text{Number of persons arrested x 100,000}}{\text{Population}} = \text{Arrest rate}$$

In 1992 there were 11,876,202 offenses charged by police as reported to the FBI Uniform Crime Reporting System. The estimate of the population for that year was 255,028,000, so the calculation would be:

$$\frac{11,876,202 \text{ x } 100,000}{255,028,000} = 4,656.8$$

This means that for every 100,000 people living in the United States, about 4,657 arrests were made.[2]

Problems can arise in either the numerator (that is, in the counting of crimes) or in the denominator (that is, in the counting of populations) of this calculation.

In fact, in the case of Native Americans, problems are encountered in both and are extensive.

**Problems of Counting Crimes**    National crime data are available from the FBI Uniform Crime Reports. Police departments across the country collect information about crimes and arrests in their jurisdictions. They file reports with the FBI, which become the basis for the Uniform Crime Reports. These are the national database for police-collected crime.

As noted above, number of arrests is actually a poor indicator of involvement in crime. It is possible that a high ratio of members of a particular group is arrested for particular types of crime or it is possible that a low proportion of a group is arrested. In any case, arrests are only made for a small proportion of crimes. Even in the case of murder, no offender is apprehended in about one-third of the cases (Silverman and Kennedy, 1995).

There is a litany of problems directly associated with the collection of crime data (Green, 1991; Green, 1993), but two have special impact on the collection of crime and arrest data as they refer to Native Americans. First, the Uniform Crime Reporting System does not have complete coverage of the United States in the reports received. When the FBI produces the statistical reports, it notes the "coverage." The coverage misses more rural areas than urban areas, and Native Americans are more likely to be living in rural areas; hence crime data about them are more likely to be missed. Harring (1982), using Bureau of Indian Affairs data, estimates that the Uniform Crime Reports could be missing up to 50 percent of Native American arrests. Second, the notation of "race" on these forms is not likely to be accurate. It is often based on observation on the part of the police officer doing the report; that is, the police officer looks at the offender and decides what race he or she is. Confounding this problem is the fact that in some jurisdictions "Native American" is not an available category on the arrest form. Hence, police would code Native Americans as "other" or White.[3]

**Problems with Counting Populations**    Population data are provided by the U.S. Bureau of the Census. A census (or count of the population) is held every ten years in the United States. Among other questions, the census asks for individuals' racial or ethnic group. In the 1990 census, 9.8 million people did not specify racial group. So the first problem is missing information. The second problem is that the classification of race or ethnicity is very troublesome. Most recent analysis has shown that the problems emanate mainly from the classification of Hispanics, but there are also many problems involving ethnic or racial mixes. (For example, if a person's mother is Hispanic and father is Cherokee, how does that person list him- or herself?). The bottom line for our calculation is that the denominator—the population—cannot be completely accurate.

Although I have only scratched the surface of the sources of errors in calculating arrest rates, it is clear that there will be real problems in interpreting results.

As we will see after examining current information about Native American arrest rates, the problems go even deeper.

## LITERATURE REVIEW AND
## ILLUSTRATION OF THE PROBLEM

There has not been a great deal of literature on Native American criminality. Because Native Americans make up such a low proportion of the American population (about 0.83 percent in 1990), their impact on the overall crime and arrest rates is very limited. Nonetheless, some of the early literature shows huge arrest rates for Native Americans. Only a few major research articles after the 1960s deal with Native American crime on a national level as delimited in the Uniform Crime Reports.[4]

Most articles compare arrest rates for African Americans (Blacks), Whites, and Native Americans. Omer Stewart (1964) was first to examine these groups using Uniform Crime Report data. Using 1960 data, he found that the Native American arrest rate was three times that of African Americans and eight times that of Whites. Anticipating virtually all future studies, Stewart found that much of the Native American crime was alcohol related.

Reasons (1972) analyzed data for seven selected years between 1950 and 1968. His calculations used Uniform Crime Report data and census figures from the 1950 and 1960 U.S. censuses. Calculations were based on populations over the age of thirteen.[5] Reasons (1972:320) echoes Stewart's earlier study in finding that "the Indians consistently have an arrest rate approximately three times that of Blacks and ten times that of whites." In his crime-specific analyses, he confirms that much Indian crime is alcohol related, but he also shows that the Indian rates are lower than those of Blacks in many crimes (for example, homicide, rape, assault, burglary, robbery, larceny). In general, for non-alcohol-related offenses, the Indian rates and the Black rates are similar during the period reviewed. For drinking-related offenses, the Indian rate (at the end of the period) is more that twenty times that of Whites and nine times that of Blacks. What is striking is the fact that Reasons does not comment on the extraordinary level of Native American crime involvement. For 1968 he reports a rate of over 27,000 per 100,000, which means that for every 100,000 Native Americans over the age of thirteen there were 27,000 arrests. Even keeping in mind that the population used makes for a higher rate, compare that figure with the sample rate (4,657) that we calculated for the U.S. population in 1992. Reasons looks for explanations for the finding in economic conditions and sociological theory. In effect, he accepts the data as accurate.

Jensen, Stauss, and Harris (1977) did a similar analysis based on the 1970 census and Uniform Crime Reports. Like Stewart, their rates were reported for whole populations. They differentiate between urban and rural rates, but they show that

Table 10.1    Selected Arrest Rates Reported in Studies of Native American Crime

|  | Native American | African American | White |
|---|---|---|---|
| 1950 (14 and over)[a] | 3,492 | 1,957 | 572 |
| 1959 (14 and over)[a] | 26,931 | 7,507 | 1,730 |
| 1960 (total pop.)[b] | 15,123 | 5,908 | 1,655 |
| 1968 (14 and over)[a] | 36,584 | 12,256 | 3,271 |
| 1970 (urban)[c] | 27,535 | 7,715 | 2,423 |
| 1985[d] | 7,859 | 10,273 | 3,896 |

[a]Reasons, 1972
[b]Stewart, 1964
[c]Jensen et al., 1977
[d]Flowers, 1988

regardless of urban or rural status, Native Americans have the highest rates for all offenses, alcohol-related offenses, and non-alcohol-related offenses. The arrest rate for alcohol-related offenses is seven times that of Blacks and twenty-two times that of Whites (findings that are very similar to Reasons's).

Flowers (1988:106) continued the examination of Native American criminality using 1985 data. He quite modestly states that his analysis "reveals a somewhat different pattern than did earlier studies." His is the first research that shows African Americans to have higher arrest rates than Native Americans. The Native American rate is about twice that of Whites but is higher than either of the other groups' rates for alcohol-related and substance-abuse offenses. For both alcohol-related and non-alcohol-related groups, the disparity between Native Americans and others is not as high as previously reported. Flowers is cautious in his conclusions and (at least indirectly) suggests that the crime data are incomplete and that discrimination in the justice system might have some influence on these results. Again, explanations for the discrepancies in rates are being sought in the crime data (the numerator of the rate calculation).

Table 10.1 summarizes some of the findings from the research studies discussed above. Even keeping in mind that none of the studies are directly comparable, one wonders what happened between 1970 and 1985 to make Native American rates drop so dramatically. It is a question that needs an answer.

## The Elements of an Arrest Rate

Given that arrest rates are calculated from only two sets of information—arrests and the enumerated population—these data merit examination. Table 10.2 shows the U.S. population and the populations for the subgroups White, African American, and Native American for all censuses between 1950 and 1990.[6] Table 10.3 shows arrest data for the same groups. According to Table 10.2, the 1990 U.S. population is 64 percent larger than the 1950 population. The White population grew 48 percent in those forty years, and the African American population doubled. The Native American 1990 population is 419 percent larger than the 1950

Table 10.2   Population (U.S. Census) for African Americans, Native Americans, Whites, and the Total United States, 1950–1990

| | | | | Population | | | | |
|---|---|---|---|---|---|---|---|---|
| Year | Total U.S. | Percent | Whites | % of total | African Americans | % of total | Native Americans[a] | % of total |
| 1950 | 151,325,798 | 100 | 135,149,629 | 89.3 | 15,044,937 | 9.9 | 377,273 | 0.25 |
| 1960 | 179,323,175 | 100 | 158,831,732 | 88.6 | 18,871,831 | 10.5 | 551,669 | 0.31 |
| 1970 | 203,211,175 | 100 | 177,748,975 | 87.5 | 22,580,289 | 11.1 | 827,268 | 0.41 |
| 1980 | 226,545,805 | 100 | 188,371,622 | 83.1 | 26,495,025 | 11.7 | 1,420,400 | 0.63 |
| 1990 | 248,709,873 | 100 | 199,686,070 | 80.3 | 29,986,060 | 12.1 | 1,959,234 | 0.79 |
| Change 1950–1990 | 97,384,075 | 64.4 | 64,536,441 | 47.8 | 14,941,123 | 99.3 | 1,581,961 | 419.3 |

[a]Includes American Indians, Eskimos, and Aleuts
Source: U.S. Department of Commerce, Bureau of the Census

Table 10.3   Arrest Rates (per 100,000) for Total U.S. Population, African Americans, Whites, Native Americans, 1950–1990

| | | | | Arrests | | | | |
|---|---|---|---|---|---|---|---|---|
| | Total U.S. | | Whites | | African Americans | | Native Americans[a] | |
| Year | N | Rate | N | Rate | N | Rate | N | Rate |
| 1950 | 794,000 | 524.7 | 576,000 | 426.19 | 206,000 | 1,369.2 | na | |
| 1960 | 3,867,541 | 2,156.7 | 2,629,224 | 1,655.35 | 1,115,015 | 5,908.4 | 79,246 | 14,364.8 |
| 1970 | 6,257,104 | 3,079.1 | 4,373,157 | 2,460.30 | 1,688,389 | 7,477.3 | 130,981 | 15,833.0 |
| 1980 | 9,683,672 | 4,274.5 | 7,145,763 | 3,793.44 | 2,375,204 | 8,964.7 | 109,480 | 7,707.7 |
| 1990 | 11,151,368 | 4,483.7 | 7,712,390 | 3,862.26 | 3,224,060 | 10,751.9 | 122,586 | 6,256.8 |
| % change 1960–1990 | 188.3 | 107.9 | 193.3 | 133.3 | 189.1 | 82.0 | 54.7 | −56.4 |

[a]Includes American Indians, Eskimos, and Aleuts
Source for crime data: Uniform Crime Reports

population. This is an annual increase of 10.5 percent, whereas the expected annual rate of natural increase is about 2 percent.

Furthermore, according to these data, the White population, as a proportion of all Americans, declined by about 9 percent. As a proportion of the whole, African Americans rose from about 10 percent to about 12 percent. The Native American proportion of the population more than tripled (even though it is still less than 1 percent of the total). Such numbers need explanation.

Table 10.3 confirms the problem. Here we deal with the thirty-year period between 1960 and 1990.[7] According to the table, the actual number of recorded arrests rose 188 percent for the U.S. population and about 190 percent for African Americans and Whites. But arrests only rose 55 percent for Native Americans. This, too, makes no sense. Adding our suspicious population figures to the mix only compounds the error by showing *increases* in crime rates for all Americans, African Americans, and Whites but a 56 percent *decline* in the rates for Native Americans.

While researchers have been examining potential problems in the numerator of the calculation, they have ignored the denominator—the demographic component of the equation. On the basis of Tables 10.1, 10.2, and 10.3, it seems that Native Americans have historically been defined and enumerated differently, with obvious implications for the calculation of arrest rates. Smaller numbers in the denominator produce larger rates. This seems to be what happened in those early studies. If researchers had estimates of the "real" Native American population (rather than the estimate produced by the censuses), they would have had larger denominators and smaller rates.

## Census Issues

In the examination of race across time, several data collection issues arise.[8] These affect all racial or ethnic groups, but between 1950 and 1990 Native Americans are particularly poorly enumerated.

In the 1950 census and, in most areas, in the 1960 census, race was assigned on the census form "by observation"; that is, the census taker looked at the respondent and decided his or her racial or ethnic origin. There are few worse ways to determine race, and one can assume that race, as an enumerated category, is simply not accurate. In 1970 a mailed questionnaire was used, and the respondent filled in his or her own race. This is an improvement, but it does not guarantee accuracy. Nettler (1989:108–109) points out the complexities in the ways people classify themselves and shows that they may identify their race or ethnicity on the basis of what seems to be good for them at any given point in time. Some demographers and sociologists have used this as an explanation for the growth in Native American population (see Passel, 1976; Passel and Berman, 1986; Harris, 1994; Green, 1993). Nagel (1995) argues that "ethnic renewal" has resulted in peoples switching their ancestry on census forms to denote that they are Native Americans, thus boosting the census count of that group.

Although ethnic switching cannot be dismissed as a source of part of the large shifts in the Native American populations (for example, a 72 percent increase between 1970 and 1980), it is unlikely that it can account for all of this extraordinary change. Most demographers and sociologists writing on the subject chose to ignore or explain away "undercounting" as an explanation. Yet until the 1980 census, the Bureau of the Census had no "working relationship" with American Indians or Alaska Natives. Whole tribes simply did not participate. Counting Native Americans was neither systematic nor complete.

In the 1980 and 1990 censuses, 90–95 percent of the country was covered. At this time the race question was put face-to-face. Furthermore, in 1990 there were more "outreach" and promotional programs directed toward Native Americans, raising both their awareness and their participation. Even so, the Bureau of the Census estimate of undercounting was 4.5 percent for Native Americans nationally and 12.2 percent on reservations and trust lands.

The issue of race as a category is itself problematic. As a genetic issue race is more or less dead. However, it is still an important social category and, in fact, drives much of the discussion of crime and inequality in the United States. In the last two censuses, race was counted by self-report. It is known that in self-reports people may change their race from one census to the next, and the census does not cope well with multiethnic origins (Nettler, 1989; Wright, 1994). Anatole Romaniuc[9] provides a fascinating example from the 1991 Canadian census: "The Census puts the figure of Native peoples at 626,000 who are registered Indians and/or who identify themselves with an Aboriginal group, and at 1,002,675 who reported having Aboriginal origins (as can be traced through ancestry). A difference of 38%!" Which one of these figures should we use?

All we can say about race in the denominator of the arrest-rate equation is that it represents the category to which individuals say they belong. In the numerator, race often simply represents a police officer's guess. It is an understatement to say that the two definitions will sometimes not correspond.

With regard to arrest rates based on Native American populations, it is likely that data generated from the 1990 census are the most accurate we have to date.[10] We should be suspicious of anything before that time, though data produced by the 1980 census are probably the next best. Estimates of arrest rates before that period require serious speculation about the actual size of the Native American population. If, for instance, it is projected that Native Americans made up about 0.7 percent of the U.S. population between 1960 and 1990, the resultant rates are similar to but a little lower than those found by Flowers (1988). However, even if we do the calculations based on that "best guess" about the Native American population, we are still forgetting about the very real problems with the numerator in the calculation. Not only are both the numerator and denominator beset by problems, but they are often incongruent—they do not always refer to the same population subset. Put simply, there are insurmountable problems with both the numerator and the denominator in calculations that rely on these historic data.

## PATTERNS OF NATIVE AMERICAN
## CRIMINALITY, 1987–1992

There is no doubt that the 1990 census gave us better estimates of the Native American population than had been available. The argument that the latest Uniform Crime Reports are more valid than earlier versions is a little more tenous. Given the problems discussed above, what can we say about contemporary Native American crime or arrest patterns? First, with regard to crime we know that crime by Native Americans is very much underreported. But we do not know the specific nature of the crimes that are missed. Second, with regard to the population base, we can only suggest that the current enumeration is more accurate than that which was used in the early studies noted above, but we also know that the current population figures are not absolutely accurate. Third, there is still a problem in identifying who is a Native American. In sum, we know that rates generated using these figures are not completely accurate and may, in fact, be quite flawed.

How can analysis using these data be justified? The data available during the time period under review are probably more accurate than anything available to date. It is likely that problems with the data are consistent during the six-year period under review. Although the rates are inaccurate, they probably give us a reasonable notion of the relative position of Native Americans with regard to arrests made.[11] With these caveats in mind, findings of the analysis of Native American arrest rates for a six-year period between 1987 and 1992 are presented. The data are from the Uniform Crime Reports and the census.

### All Reported Crime, Violence, and Property Crime

Figures 10.1, 10.2, and 10.3 show the computed arrest rates by race or ethnic group for Native Americans, African Americans, Whites, and the total U.S. population. Examining Figure 10.1, one can see that there is a certain amount of stability in the rates (for each group) during the time period but that there are clear differences between the rates for the groups. African Americans have the highest rates of crime (between 9,800 and 11,300 per 100,000 African Americans enumerated in the U.S.); the White rates are about one-third of these peaks. Native American rates fall between those of African Americans and Whites, ranging from 5,400 to 6,300 per 100,000 enumerated Native Americans. These numbers are lower than but similar to those generated by Flowers (1988) using 1985 data. Rather than being three times or ten times as high as other groups (as was reported in earlier research), the Native American rate is only about 25 percent higher than the White rate.[12]

Much that is written about Native Americans perpetuates the notion that they are violent. Certainly, built into the fabric and myth of U.S. culture is the image of the murderous Indian (see, for example, McKanna, 1993 or the old western movie *The Searchers*). But the Native American arrest rate for violent crimes (between 189 and 216 per 100,000) is just below the average for the U.S. population.

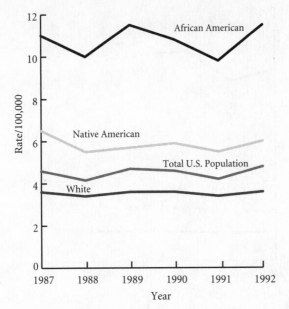

FIGURE 10.1    All Reported Crime: United States, 1987–1992, Race-Specific Arrest Rates

Although the rate is a little above the White rate (between 115 and 160 per 100,000), it is only a fraction of the African American rate (which seems to be driving the U.S. rate) (Figure 10.2).

In the case of property crimes (Figure 10.3), Native Americans generate rates (818 to 960 per 100,000) about 50 percent higher than White rates (520 to 570 per 100,000) but about one-half African American rates (1,700 to 2,000 per 100,000). The average U.S. rates are between those of Native Americans and White Americans.

Native Americans do have relatively high arrest rates for all crimes and for violent and property crimes when compared to White Americans. But their rates of arrest are nowhere near those reported by many of the earlier studies and are much closer to the arrest rates of White Americans than to the arrest rates of African Americans. In fact, their arrest rates are usually not very much higher than the average for the total U.S. population. All of the earlier work identified alcohol-related crime as a particular problem for Native Americans. The next three figures examine Native American arrests for alcohol-related offenses and compares them with the same groups as in the earlier analysis.

## Drunkenness, Driving While Intoxicated, and Liquor Violations

Patterns of arrests for drunkenness for the total U.S. population, for White Americans, and for African Americans are similar, though of those groups African Americans have the highest rates (Figure 10.4). Nonetheless, the rates for each

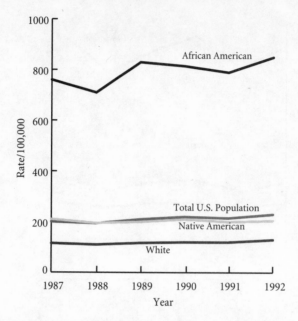

FIGURE 10.2    Violent Crime: United States, 1987–1992, Race-Specific Arrest Rates

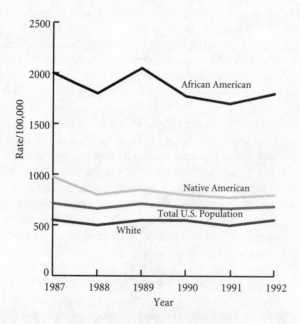

FIGURE 10.3    Property Crime: United States, 1987–1992, Race-Specific Arrest Rates

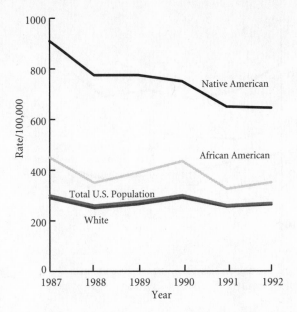

FIGURE 10.4    Drunkenness Offenses: United States, 1987–1992, Race-Specific Arrest
Rates

group are parallel, having peaks and lows in the same years. Native Americans have
much different patterns. First, their rates are substantially higher than those of any
of the other groups. In their peak year, 1987, their rate is four times that of Whites,
and even in the lowest year, 1992, they have rates two-and-a-half times those of
White Americans. The more interesting finding is that the rate has declined in six
years, from a high of 914 per 100,000 to 646. Keeping in mind all of the other data
problems, this decline means either that Native Americans are being arrested less
for drunkenness, that they are actually engaging less in illegal drunkenness, or that
the reporting of Native American drunkenness offenses has declined. We cannot
tell which of these might provide an explanation for the decline.

Unlike drunkenness arrests, arrests for driving while intoxicated reveal similar
patterns for White Americans and for the total U.S. population (driven by the rate
for White Americans) but a low and generally declining rate for African
Americans (Figure 10.5). Again, Native Americans have the highest rates (between
705 and 830 per 100,000 which is 30–40 percent higher than rates for White
Americans, which are 535 to 600 per 100,000). Native American rates decline for
a couple of years and then rise again at the end of the period (as do rates for the
other groups, but not as dramatically). I can offer no explanation for this pattern,
but it should be noted that the general findings of the earlier studies is confirmed.

Figure 10.6 shows that the Native American pattern for liquor offenses is again
quite different from the other groups. The African American rates are the lowest
(140 to 170 per 100,000) and along with White American rates decline in the last

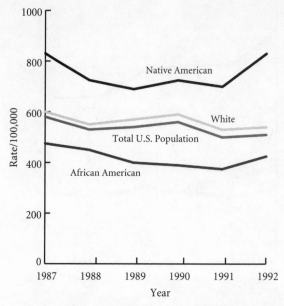

FIGURE 10.5   Driving While Intoxicated: United States, 1987–1992, Race-Specific Arrest Rates

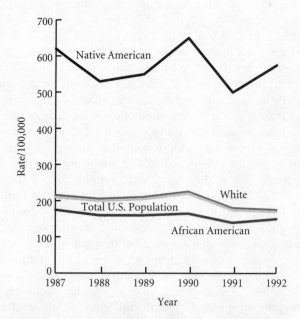

FIGURE 10.6   Liquor Offenses: United States, 1987–1992, Race-Specific Arrest Rates

FIGURE 10.7    Drug-Abuse Offenses: United States, 1987–1992, Race-Specific Arrest Rates

two years of the period. Native American rates bounce from 614 per 100,000 in 1987 to 525 in 1988, then back up to 650 in 1990, down to 503 (1991), and back up to 567 in 1992. These are rather large one-year swings and probably indicate more about reporting practices than about the actual rates of offense. Nonetheless, these rates are almost 300 percent higher than those of African Americans.

*Drugs*

In discussions of criminality, drug and alcohol offenses are often coupled. In the next figure, Figure 10.7, we observe rates of drug-abuse offenses. Native Americans have the lowest reported arrest rates for these offenses. In the peak year for African Americans (1989 generated a rate of 1,501 per 100,000) the Native American rate (170 per 100,000) was 11 percent of that for African Americans. Furthermore, the rates are relatively stable, at a very low rate, for Native Americans.

*Homicide*

Books have been written about Native American homicide (for example, Bachman, 1992). There is concern that the living conditions in which Native Americans find themselves produce violence in general (see Figure 10.2) and homicide in particular. Figure 10.8 shows that the Native American arrest rate (5–7 per 100,000) for homicide is not much different than that of the total U.S.

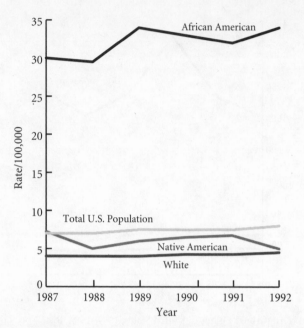

FIGURE 10.8    Homicide: United States, 1987–1992, Race-Specific Arrest Rates

population. However, it is almost 70 percent higher than the rate for White
Americans (3.5–4 per 100,000) but only about 20 percent of that for African
Americans (greater than 30 per 100,000). There is no doubt that homicide is a so-
cial problem among Native Americans that should be addressed.

## Summing Up the Data

According to the best data available, the Native American arrest rate is not as high
as has generally been believed. However, for specific offenses (that is, for alcohol-
related offenses), Native Americans have the highest rate of all the groups examined, and it is an alarming rate. Furthermore, while the rates are lower than previously believed, they tend to be somewhat higher than those for White
Americans. Crime, as measured by arrests, is a problem for Native Americans that
must be dealt with. Of course, the truth of these statements depends on the quality of the data used to analyse the situation.

## CONCLUSION

Native American criminality (as measured by arrest rates) is nowhere near as high
as it has been portrayed in the criminological literature and popular press. Those
arrest rates were calculated using faulty numbers and are wrong. Based on 1990

census data, arrest rates for Native Americans are, in fact, often similar to those for White Americans. The error in the earlier research occurred because the denominator in the equations used to calculate rates was incorrect. The questions that must be raised are: Why did this error happen? Why did it persist?

There are probably a number of reasons that the error occurred and persisted. The most obvious reason is the way we treat census data. Researchers treat the census as gospel. It is assumed that census data accurately reflect the population that the census purports to count. No one thinks to question the denominator. In fact, the census represents an "enumerated" population that is unlikely to accurately represent the actual population. The actual number of persons in the country is knowable, as it is a finite number; but it is not really known. At best, the census provides an approximation—sometimes a very good approximation but (as we see in the case of Native Americans) sometimes a poor approximation.

Population estimates become even less accurate for identifying subpopulations—especially racially and ethnically self-identified groups. A critical examination of the numbers (particularly when historical trends are being attempted) is crucial. In fact, the findings in this chapter have implications far beyond the calculation of arrest rates. Any rates based on census data generated before 1990 that claim to portray the Native American population are wrong.

The lesson to be learned from this exercise should be obvious. More attention must be paid to the components of rate calculations before we present these calculations as valid "facts" that can be used to either test our theories or create policy. Finally, social scientists, no doubt, owe Native Americans an apology for misportraying them as the most criminal population in the United States. Such a portrayal does not accurately reflect the best available information on the subject.

## Notes

1. The FBI has been collecting and reporting crime in the United States since the 1930s. Police departments across the nation send summary reports to the FBI. These provide one of the major sources of national crime data. The crime index is made up of eight specific crimes (murder and non-negligent manslaughter, forcible rape, robbery, aggravated assault, burglary, larceny-theft, and motor vehicle theft) and serves as an indicator of crime trends in the United States.

2. It is important to note that the number of arrests includes multiple arrests of the same individuals. That is, if the same person is arrested five times in one year, that counts as five arrests in this calculation.

3. Larry Gould, in a personal communication, notes that this situation exists in the Deep South of the United States.

4. Other authors have dealt with Native American crime using self-report techniques and Bureau of Indian Affairs data. Both of these techniques are limited in their applicability and cannot be generalized.

5. The argument for using populations over the age of thirteen is that children younger than that are less likely to be involved in crime and arrest and therefore should not be in-

cluded in the population. The effect is to reduce the size of the denominator. Dividing by a smaller number increases the size of the result and thus, in this case, of the crime and arrest rates.

6. The data that appear in Table 10.2 (and that are used for the rate calculations in Table 10.3) were provided by the Population Division, U.S. Bureau of the Census. These data differ somewhat from published reports.

7. In the 1950 census, Native Americans were included in a different combination than in later censuses.

8. I am indebted to Edna Paisano of the Population Division of the U.S. Census Bureau for the information contained in this section.

9. Personal communication.

10. An example of the persistence of the problem is seen in Albuquerque, N.M., which "has either 12,000 American Indian residents (1990 Census) or 35,000 (numbers used by Indian Center and other agencies based upon school population)" (Griego, 1994).

11. Every sentence in the last couple of paragraphs has qualifiers. This was done on purpose, as the author is really not sure about the quality of these data—for all the reasons delineated earlier.

12. That is, to estimate the Native American rate one adds 25 percent to the White rate (multiply by 1.25), whereas the earlier research suggests one multiply the White rate by three or by ten.

# 11

## NATIVE AMERICAN DELINQUENCY

### An Overview of Prevalence, Causes, and Correlates

TROY L. ARMSTRONG
MICHAEL H. GUILFOYLE
ADA PECOS MELTON

## INTRODUCTION

Today, American Indian youth living on reservations throughout the United States face a myriad of problems. Among the most serious of these difficulties is the disproportionate extent to which Indian adolescents are involved in criminal and delinquent activities. Available documentation suggests that with regard to racial and ethnic involvement in the juvenile justice system in this country, Indian tribal youth are vastly over-represented at all points in formal processing. This extends from perpetration and arrest to disposition and incarceration.

The development of guidelines and procedures to aid the formulation and implementation of policies for responding to these problems continues to be plagued by the relative lack of general information and specific research findings on the causes, nature, and extent of crime and delinquency among Native Americans. This situation is especially pronounced in the area of juvenile justice studies, where the existing literature is quite scanty. A complicating factor impeding efforts to conduct appropriate research and fact finding is that the diversity of culture, language, customs, and tradition among tribes has made it extremely dif-

This work was supported by Contract OJP–91-M–246 from the Office of Juvenile Justice and Delinquency Prevention, U.S. Department of Justice. Points of view are those of the authors and do not represent the opinion of the Department of Justice. An earlier version of this paper was submitted to the Office of Juvenile Justice and Delinquency Prevention as a background document for the Native American Community-Based Alternative for Adjudicated Youth (NCAAY) Project (March, 1992).

The alphabetical order of the authors' names reflects their equal contributions to this article.

ficult to carry out systematic studies providing aggregated trends and patterns of crime and delinquency for American Indian populations at a national level. Further, tribes can have vastly different relationships with federal, state, and local governments, thereby adding problems in the development of uniformity in the collection and organization of data.

To emphasize these difficulties in previous attempts to produce a valid profile of Native American delinquency is not to suggest that important steps have not been undertaken in the past to achieve this goal. The ethnographic literature extending back to the turn of this century provided occasional glimpses and accounts of social misconduct among American Indians and the ways in which tribes have administered justice. The reader is referred to Chapter 7 in this volume, "Traditional Approaches to Tribal Justice," which provides an overview of such practices, past and present.

As early as 1955, the U.S. Congress began to take steps to develop a more comprehensive sense of this problem area in terms of its causes, its extent, and primary responses. The interim report of the U.S. Senate Subcommittee to Investigate Juvenile Delinquency stated, ". . . the incidence of juvenile delinquency was found in many instances to be higher among the Indian than among the non-Indian population of the United States" (1955:45). It further pointed out that poverty, lack of education, unemployment, family disruption, and cultural conflict were among the probable causes of rising juvenile delinquency among Indian youth. Yet, in spite of all efforts over the past 35 years to describe, understand, and reduce delinquency within this population, the problem persists, and, indeed, appears to be worsening. For example, acts of violence and substance abuse appear to be escalating at a rapid pace among Indian adolescents.

The purpose of this chapter is to review the existing body of knowledge about Native American delinquency across several major topical areas. Since the documentation of this problem across its many dimensions is so scattered in the literature, both published and fugitive, we feel it is important to bring together in one review a review of much of what has been written and researched about Native American Delinquency. The following discussion is organized under two issue headings that, in each case, bear upon some essential dimension of this problem. They are: Profile of Native American Delinquency, and Causes and Correlates of Native American Delinquency.

## PROFILE OF NATIVE AMERICAN DELINQUENCY

A number of studies have noted the comparative lack of statistical information regarding crime and delinquency among Native American youth (Forslund and Meyers, 1974; Jensen, Stauss, and Harris, 1977; O'Brien, 1977; Black and Smith, 1980; Robbins, 1985). A number of reasons have been offered concerning why this difficulty exists, but regardless of the cause the result has been a situation in which it is difficult for researchers, planners, and public administrators to develop a national profile of illegal behavior for this population along any of its major dimensions: incidence, arrest, prosecution, adjudication, incarceration, or recidivism. One interesting observation, offered as a partial explanation for this problem, is that unlike any other racial or ethnic group in the U.S., Native Americans are arrested, processed, and sanctioned through three distinctively different justice systems: tribal, state, and federal jurisdiction (Black and Smith, 1980).

The extent to which information has been generated regarding Native American crime has focused largely upon the adult Indian population. One statistical pattern for which research has sporadically provided some insights about Indian juvenile offenders is the prevalence of delinquent behavior on specific reservations and their local environs. The earliest accounts of the prevalence of crime and delinquency on reservations date to the research conducted by Hayner (1942) on three reservations in the Northwest where he reported on respective rates of crime. Although he focused attention primarily on differences in the rates of offending behavior across the three tribes, he noted that for certain categories of crime, the rates were significantly higher on these reservations than the national average for the larger U.S. population. Further, he concluded that Indian crime had risen with increased Indian wealth and contact with Whites. Several years later, Von Hentig (1945) in reporting the results of a trend analysis on Indian arrest rates during the period between 1930–1940 noted that these rates were three times higher than the national average for Whites (2,510 per 100,000 as compared to 836 per 100,000). In seeking an explanation for this dramatic difference, he suggested that rapid acculturation and changing norms had contributed to the high rates of Indian crimes. Following these two studies conducted in the 1940s of rates of Indian criminality, there was roughly a 20-year lag before Stewart (1964) published his analysis of Indian arrest rates based upon the 1960 FBI Uniform Crime Reports. He found the overall arrest rate for Indians to be eight times higher than those of Whites, and three times higher than those of Blacks. Furthermore, these findings of disproportionate criminality among Native American populations held not only for alcohol-related crime but also for other crime categories as well. This particular finding has been a source of some controversy and dispute since most subsequent research has not found this pattern of disproportionate involvement across most crime categories, especially the more serious, non-drug related crimes.

Two studies examining homicide rates among Native Americans that were published during the same period as Stewart's research reaffirmed the earlier finding of Hayner, namely, there are extreme intertribal variations in crime rates. In the first of these studies of Indian homicide (Kaplan, Gans, and Kahn, 1968), the authors showed that the homicide rate in 1964 among the Sioux on the Pine Ridge Reservation in South Dakota was 16.6 per 100,000, in contrast to a national average of 5.1 per 100,000 for the general population. In the second study, Levy, Kunitz, and Everett (1969) found that the homicide rate among the Navajo for the period of 1956–1965 was stable and comparable to the national average.

The other major study from this period was a trend analysis of FBI Uniform Crime Reports conducted by Reasons (1972), but one that went far beyond previous work of this type in its longitudinal perspective—examining changes in crime rates over an 18-year period (1950–1968)—and in its delineation of rates for specific crime categories, not just the overall rate. Generally, these findings substantiated Stewart's earlier work in that Reasons's found that aggregated arrest rates for Indians are three times greater than those for Blacks and ten times greater than those for Whites. However, for specific non-alcohol related offenses (homicide, rape, assault, burglary and larceny), Reasons's findings were not consistent with Stewart's analysis that showed higher rates for Indians across virtually all crime categories. Instead, Reasons found that Blacks had the highest rates for non-alcohol related crimes, followed closely by Indians, both of whom had rates considerably above those for Whites. The one exception was auto theft, for which Indians had the highest arrest rates.

Beginning in the 1960s and continuing into the 1970s, studies for the first time began to offer some details about patterns and rates of delinquent behavior among Indian youth on specific reservations. Noteworthy among these studies was the Minnis study (1963) of rapidly increasing rates of delinquency on the Fort Hall Reservation in Idaho. Here, in the period between 1955 and 1960, it was shown that the rates for crime and delinquency nearly tripled, rising from 13 to 34 percent. It should be noted that both figures were considerably above the national average at the time. This research was followed by another study of Native American delinquency released in 1968. The Community Mental Health Services on the Pine Ridge Reservation reported upon rates of delinquency, stating that the rate was four times higher than the national average (10 percent of Indian juveniles on this reservation being adjudicated delinquent as compared to 2.2 percent for White youth) and that 39 percent of the 17-year-olds had been officially labeled delinquent sometime during their adolescence.

During the 1970s, more detailed accounts of rates of delinquency for specific crime categories became available. In addition, these studies as a whole seemed to suggest that the greatest concentration and highest rates of crime among the youths on reservations were confined to either alcohol-related or petty offenses. However, when all categories of offenders were aggregated, the overall rate of delinquent behavior was highest for Indian youth among all racial and ethnic groups in the U.S. Generally supportive of this pattern was the finding by Forslund and Meyers (1974) regarding delinquency among Wind River Reservation youth, where these authors noted that the aggregated rate of Indian adolescents is comparable to the rate found in the highest delinquency areas of America's largest cities.

A study of Native American delinquency by O'Brien (1977) focused primarily upon youth crime on the Warm Spring Reservation in Oregon. Here, the overall rate for delinquency was found to be five or six times higher than the national average for juvenile offenders. This pattern of juvenile delinquency and misconduct was characterized by a high incidence of status offenses and other "victimless" crimes, as well as a relative scarcity of serious or violent offenses. For example, O'Brien observed that during the period of time covered in the study (1972–1974), 58.1 percent of all referrals to the tribal court were confined to four offense categories: possession of alcohol, runaways, truancy, and possession of drugs. By comparison, the incidence of serious and violent crime was much higher during the same period for Oregon's total juvenile population. Further, in looking at the involvement of Native American youth in the juvenile court system statewide in Oregon, O'Brien states that in 1973, seven percent of all persons referred for juvenile offenses were Indian, while Indians constituted only .64 of one percent of the Oregon population. Thus, Indian juveniles were statistically overrepresented in the court by a factor of eleven.

These kinds of patterns closely resembled what was found in the Forslund and Meyers study (1974) of the rates and types of delinquency on the Wind River Reservation, especially the high concentration of alcohol-related and minor/status offenses among Indian youth. Likewise, research based on official records and conducted by Jensen, Stauss, and Harris (1977), profiling national patterns of delinquency among Indian youth, revealed that differences between Indian and non-Indians were greatest for alcohol-related crimes, while at the same time Indian arrest rates closely paralleled the arrest rates for Black youth for a number of non-alcohol related types of offenses.

Without question, the most detailed description of national rates of delinquency among Indian juvenile offenders on reservations can be found in a special report, *A Preliminary Assessment of the Numbers and Characteristics of Native Americans Under 18 Processed by Various Justice Systems* (Black and Smith, 1980) prepared by the National Juvenile Justice System Assessment Center of the American Justice Institute for the Office of Juvenile Justice and Delinquency Prevention, U.S. Department of Justice. This study provides a one-year snapshot of Indian juvenile crime for 1979. Two data sources were utilized to compile the statistical profile: (1) FBI Uniform Crime Reports, and (2) BIA records of juvenile cases handled by tribal courts and reported by individual reservations (the BIA publishes an annual data report detailing both major and misdemeanor offenses). The authors note that a combined statistical report for all American Indians under the age of 18 arrested for selected offenses shows a total of 28,682 offenses being reported for Indian youth for that year. Further, the overall arrest rate for Native American youth was greater, at 60.0 per 100,000 juveniles, than for either Black (52.6) or White (33.9) youth in 1979. The only offense categories where Indian juveniles did not exceed the other two groups were for serious offenses.

An analysis of individual crime categories in this report reveals that serious crimes (i.e., murder and non-negligent homicide, forcible rape, robbery, aggravated assault, burglary, larceny-theft, motor vehicle theft, and arson) constitute a smaller portion (10.8 percent) of Indian juvenile arrests than for the other two groups (White, 16.3 percent, and Black, 25.8 percent). Figure 11.1 illustrates the percentage of juvenile arrests that were attributed to these major offense categories (serious, less serious, and status). Though Indian youth were relatively low in serious crimes, they tended to be higher in the frequency of status offense cases (19.3 percent). It was apparent from the reported data that fewer Indian juveniles were arrested per capita for serious crimes (6.5 percent) and more per capita for less serious crimes (42.0 percent) and status offenses (11.6 percent) than for the other two groups. The number of arrests of Indian youth for these less serious cases in 1979 was 20,063, or 70 percent of their total of 28,682 arrests.

The report indicated that the index crime rate shows little variation for Indian youth in comparison to the other two groups. The greatest variance lies within the non-index crime categories. Here, statistics indicate that, of all non-index crimes for which the Indian juveniles were arrested, drug and alcohol offenses comprised a far higher percentage of the arrest population (40.0 percent) than for the other two groups. This relationship is evident in their arrest rate of 14.0 per 100,000 in this category compared to 6.3 per 100,000 for White youth and 2.4 per 100,000 for Black youth. In sum, Indian juveniles are not only arrested much more often for less serious crimes, but also among these less serious crimes, alcohol and drug offenses seem to be much more frequently represented than any other category of crime. At least, this was the statistical profile existing nationally at the close of the 1970s.

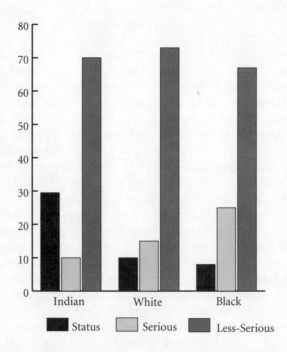

FIGURE 11.1    National Estimates of Percent of Total Arrests by Race/Ethnicity by Offense Category

The most current profiles of crime, delinquency, arrest, prosecution, and incarceration among Native American youth and adults paint an extremely grim picture. Although virtually no methodologically sound studies focusing specifically upon the rates of delinquency among Indian juvenile offenders have been published over the past decade, available information suggests an alarming trend. For example, in making recommendations to the Congress with regard to the reauthorization of the Juvenile Justice and Delinquency Prevention Act, the National Task Force on Juvenile Justice for Native Americans and Alaska Natives (1987) stated that the rates of serious crimes against persons committed by juveniles are three times higher in Indian Country than in the general juvenile population of the U.S.

With regard to adult offenders, the problem of Indian crime represents the highest rate of arrest, conviction, incarceration, and recidivism among all racial and ethnic groups in this country (Guilfoyle, 1988). Indian offenders within the criminal justice system are 15 percent less likely to be considered for deferral of sentencing and are also 15 percent less likely to receive consideration for parole. When released, Indian offenders recidivate at a rate of approximately 70 percent; further, the majority of recidivists are rearrested for drug or alcohol-related crimes. The profiling of violent crime among adult Indian offenders on reservations, especially with regard to homicide, has received increased attention recently. The results of a survey conducted and distributed by the National Clearinghouse on Alcohol Information (1985) shows that homicide accounts for 3.2 percent of all Native American deaths in comparison to 1.1 percent for the larger U.S. population. In several recent studies, Bachman (1991a, 1991b) has documented an extremely high rate of murder being perpetrated on reservations. Although data regarding Indian homicide nationwide show a rate of approximately 9.6 per 100,000, the homicide rate on reservations and their local environs are close to or are slightly more than 100 per 100,000 population. In comparison, the next highest rate of murder among any other minority group in the U.S. is Black Americans, who have a murder rate of 33 per 100,000.

This national picture of Indian crime, characterized by an extraordinarily high level of over-representation across most offense categories, is currently being contested by one scholar. In Chapter 10 in this volume Robert Silverman suggests that prior assertions of crime rates among Native Americans have been based on severely flawed information. His arguments are extremely well grounded and should provide some corrective for the ongoing debate over the historical patterns and prevalence of crime and delinquency among Native Americans nationwide. However, the key question now facing researchers in this particular arena of inquiry is how to take steps to improve both the quantity and quality of data bearing on this problem.

Although less information is available regarding the current levels of crime among Indian youth, the extent to which Native American juvenile offenders are being confined in state correctional facilities suggests a disproportionate rate of serious delinquency in this population. The most recent profile of the institu-

Table 11.1   Confinement of Native American Youth in Selected Juvenile Residential Facilities, 1990

| State | Number of Confined Youth | Number of Native American Confined Youth | Percent of Native Americans |
|---|---|---|---|
| Alaska | 190 | 62 | 32.0 |
| Arizona | 652 | 22 | 3.3 |
| Minnesota | 141 | 25 | 17.0 |
| Montana | 192 | 45 | 23.0 |
| Nebraska | 209 | 21 | 11.0 |
| New Mexico | 488 | 56 | 11.0 |
| North Dakota | 61 | 26 | 42.0 |
| Oregon | 514 | 21 | 4.0 |
| South Dakota | 170 | 53 | 30.0 |
| Washington | 848 | 48 | 6.0 |
| Wisconsin | 640 | 29 | 4.0 |

Adapted from *The Corrections Yearbook—Juvenile Corrections,* G. and C. Camp (1991).

tional confinement of Native American youth in those states that have substantial Indian populations has been provided by Camp and Camp (1991). Table 11.1 reflects these patterns of confinement. In each instance, the number of confined Indian youth is disproportionate to the total population of Native Americans in that state.

These statistics are consistent with the historical pattern of disproportionate confinement of Native American youth in training schools and other types of correctional facilities in this country. In 1955, 50 percent of the girls confined in the South Dakota Training School were Indian (Stewart, 1964). In 1969, nine percent of the youth in Minnesota's juvenile correctional facilities were Indian although Native Americans only comprised one percent of the state's total population (Patterson, 1972). In 1971, two of Montana's residential facilities for juvenile offenders had very disproportionate numbers of Indian residents: 50 percent of the population of Mountain View School were Indian and 35–40 percent of the population of the Pine Hill School for Boys were Indian (Mudd, 1972).

## CAUSES AND CORRELATES OF
## NATIVE AMERICAN DELINQUENCY

The Working Group for the Native American Community-Based Alternatives for Adjudicated Youth Initiative noted in its *Concept Paper* (1991) that a number of factors can be readily identified as contributing to the dismal legacy of crime and delinquency among American Indians on reservations. This group suggested that among the critical factors were poverty, lack of education, chronic unemployment, substance abuse, marital and family disruption and violence, loss of cultural identity, over-reliance on aggression to resolve disputes, and an inability/reluctance to assimilate into mainstream American society. This range of factors is consistent with the large set of variables identified in studies over the past 25 years attempting to provide an explanation for the disproportionate rate of crime and delinquency on American Indian reservations.

One particularly convincing argument has emerged from the field of anthropology, where studies have repeatedly linked these problems to the disruption of culture, custom and tradition following in the wake of contact and conflict with European society (Stewart, 1964; Wax, 1967; Hoebel, 1969; Robbins, 1985; Winfree, Griffiths, and Sellers, 1989). Another framework that has been presented to help explain anti-social behavior among Native Americans has been social disorganization theory. From this perspective, Bachman (1991a) has argued that this theory convincingly demonstrates how rapid social change is associated with increases in crime due to the breakdown of social controls. This author suggests that on reservations social disorganization is manifested in many forms, including the breakup of families and high rates of geographical mobility of reservation residents between urban areas and the reservation, and also between various reservations. The following discussion provides a relatively detailed description of many of these factors and their role in generating anti-social behavior; this discussion is organized under the headings of: substance abuse, socioeconomic considerations, and youth maltreatment.

## Substance Abuse

Substance abuse, especially excessive alcohol consumption, has posed special problems for Native American populations since the time of initial contact with European society. Much of the concern over excessive drinking by American Indians can be traced to the sheer scope of the problem, as well as to the strong, observed correlation between drinking and a variety of other social problems in these communities. Problems such as child abuse and neglect, automobile accidents and death, loss of jobs, ill health, crime, and the neglect and damage of property have long been linked by research to alcohol abuse (Dozier, 1966; Graves, 1967; Ferguson, 1968).

The problem of alcohol abuse appears to pose almost as severe a problem for Indian youth as it does for Indian adults. One study (Beiser and Attneave, 1982) estimated the alcoholism rate among Indian adolescents to be two to three times higher than for the overall youth population in the U.S. In the narrative of the recently enacted Public Law 99-570, Indian Alcohol and Substance Abuse Prevention and Treatment Act (1968), the scope of the overall problem is explored:

> . . . 3) alcoholism and alcohol and substance abuse is the most severe health and social problem facing Indian tribes and people today and nothing is more costly to Indian people than the consequences of alcohol and substance abuse measured in physical, mental, social, and economic terms; 4) alcohol and substance abuse is the leading genetic risk factor among Indians, and Indians die from alcoholism at over four times

the age-adjusted rates for the United States population and alcohol and substance mis-use results in a rate of years-of-potential-life lost nearly five times that of the United States; 5) four of the top ten causes of death among Indians are alcohol and drug re-lated injuries (eighteen percent of all deaths), chronic liver disease and cirrhosis (five percent), suicide (three percent), and homicide (three percent); 6) primarily, because deaths from unintentional injuries and violence occur disproportionately among young people, the age-specific death rate for Indians is approximately double the United States rate for the 15 to 24 age group; 7) Indians between the ages of 15 and 24 years of age are more than two times as likely to commit suicide as the general popu-lation and approximately 80 percent of those suicides are alcohol-related. . . .

Paradoxically, there is no evidence or history of any substance abuse in tradi-tional North American Indian societies. To the extent that alteration of con-sciousness was a culturally approved practice, it occurred within the context of re-ligious, ceremonial, or healing rituals. The ingestion of chemicals and drugs was carefully regulated by strong cultural values in these settings.

The vast majority of criminal and delinquent acts committed by both urban and rural Indians has been shown to be alcohol-related. For example, approxi-mately 90 percent of all Indian crimes are either specifically drug/alcohol offenses or somehow linked with substance abuse (Guilfoyle, 1988). The national rate of alcohol-related crimes among Indian populations is approximately eight times greater than among Black and Hispanics and twenty times greater than among Whites (French and Hornbuckle, 1982). This phenomenon was noted as early as 1955 when the Judiciary Committee of the U.S. Congress reported an inordinately high rate of alcohol-related juvenile delinquency among American Indians. Recently, Weibel-Orlando (1984) has reiterated this assertion by noting that most attempts to explain inordinately high rates of juvenile delinquency underscore the alcohol and drug-relatedness of crimes committed by Indian juvenile offenders.

The problem of substance abuse among Indian adolescents has been widely studied. The most extensive survey of adolescent substance abuse among Indians was conducted by Oetting and Goldstein (1979), who surveyed patterns of abuse in junior and senior high schools through the use of self-administered question-naires. They found the highest use rates for alcohol, with almost 90 percent of the 11th and 12th graders using alcohol. Marijuana was the next most commonly used drug, with roughly 62 percent of the 11th and 12th graders using it. Amphetamines (21 percent) and inhalants (17 percent) were the next most frequently used sub-stances by 11th and 12th graders. In summarizing a number of these surveys of adolescent substance abuse among Indian youth, McBride and Page (1980) con-cluded this population has higher rates of substance abuse for virtually all cate-gories of intoxicants than any other racial/ethnic group in this country. Further, the issue of substance abuse, especially alcohol consumption, has repeatedly appeared in the findings of assessments of problems and needs among Indian youth. For ex-ample, a needs assessment conducted by the California Youth Authority (Torres and Palmer, 1987) of Native American juveniles living on reservations in California revealed that among the four most serious unmet needs of rural youth (i.e., alcohol-abuse services, recreational activities, drug-abuse services, job training and placement services), alcohol-abuse services was listed as the top priority. Further, the report stated that increased drug abuse by adolescents was the most significant emerging problem on reservations over the past ten years.

Inhalant use represents an especially serious problem for Native American youth. A disturbing study conducted by Beauvais et al. (1985) surveyed this practice among youth on four reservations; their findings were:

- usage usually begins very early (average age of 11.5 years) and is often associated with consumption of other drugs,
- by the time these youths have reached 18 years of age, approximately 40 percent had at least tried inhalants (e.g., gasoline, glue, spray paint, etc.),
- this percentage of inhalant users appears to be increasing over time for Indian youth, and
- most of these youth indicated they might use them again if conditions were right (e.g., at a party, inhalants were available, associating with peers who were using).

This behavior has profoundly troubling implications for Indian youth, since inhaling solvents can have very damaging physiological effects. Researchers have reported damage to the brain, kidneys, and liver, as well as some indication of neurological damage (McBride and Page, 1980).

A variety of possible causes have been identified in efforts to explain why Native American youth are so vulnerable to and engage at such high rates in substance abuse. Some of this research has focused upon the cultural values and belief systems as instigating factors in a vulnerability to substance abuse. For example, Wax (1967) has noted that "self-determination," a belief in individual autonomy and laissez-faire child-rearing practices and a long-established Siouxan cultural edict, fosters parental tolerance of adolescent substance abuse. Adult Sioux assume that a person should take care of him/herself and, therefore, do not intervene even though they may personally disapprove or even deplore the drinking behavior of their adolescent kinsmen. Likewise, in a more recent study by Albaugh and Albaugh (1979), further cultural explanations are provided. They observe that several aspects of Plains Indian societies appear particularly pertinent to an understanding of the association between cultural values and the propensity to ingest mind-altering substances. The validation of important personal character traits such as egalitarianism and sharing is established by young tribal members during periods of altered consciousness, achieved through various means: self-inflicted privation (the vision quest), ingestion of hallucinogenic drugs (the peyote dream), or consumption of alcohol (getting drunk). Consequently, there is a general social acceptance of getting drunk or sniffing inhalants as appropriate activities through which self-expression and assertion of ethnic identity can be achieved. Finally from a cultural perspective, a recent test of social learning theory (Winfree, Griffiths, and Sellers, 1989) suggests that the extent to which there are major differences in the patterns of drug use (alcohol and marijuana) between White and Indian adolescents can be heavily attributed to the influence of one's cultural heritage.

Factors arising from social disorganization theory such as poverty, anomie, family dysfunction, and acculturation and cultural conflict have also been repeatedly identified as causal to substance abuse among Native Americans. Winfree, Griffiths, and Sellers (1989) have observed that acculturation is a primary focus of considerable research into factors underlying patterns of Indian substance abuse. They argue that social integration, as measured by the individual's role in the community, is a significant factor in determining substance abuse susceptibility among American Indians. The central point is that Indians with well-defined social roles in either traditional or modern society have the lowest susceptibility, whereas Indians with more confused social identifies and less well-defined social roles have the highest susceptibility. Another factor in social disorganization, family dysfunction, was identified by Longclaws et al. (1980) as a very powerful predictor of adolescent substance abuse. They repeatedly found that when Indian adolescents reported good family relationships, they were less likely than those with less satisfactory relationships to abuse alcohol and drugs. In fact, this finding about the profound effects that early socialization and positive relationships within the context of the home have upon subsequent patterns of adolescent substance abuse seems to exhibit great predictive power across cultures generally.

## Socioeconomic Considerations

In broadly defining the nature and role of socioeconomic circumstances as factors underlying Indian crime and delinquency, this discussion will include for consideration a wide range of characteristics: demographics (birth rates, median and mean ages), economic deprivation, housing, and education. The simple fact is that most reservations are plagued by high unemployment, high dropout rates, and a high percentage of females living below the poverty level; these problems are highly correlated with anti-social and destructive behavior in all of its forms.

The level of economic deprivation experienced by the Indian residents of reservations throughout this country is a subject of outrage for Native American citizens. The BIA (1974) stated that in 1970, the average per capita income for rural Indians was $1,140 on an annual basis, compared to $2,108 for urban Indians. Both figures represented income well beneath the poverty level. This report also noted that two-thirds of all rural Indians live in houses without running water, a figure eight times the national average for urban dwellers. About the same point in time, Reese (1975) concluded that single-parent households headed by Indian mothers are the lowest income group in the U.S. He further argued that extreme economic deprivation and the resulting strains it places upon intra-family relationships can have devastating effects upon the psychological development of

Indian children, especially in terms of manifesting anti-social behavior. Bachman (1991b) further argues that aggression appears to be one mechanism utilized by Indians in a number of contexts—not just domestic settings—to cope with the alienation and stress caused by poverty.

The educational experience for many Indian youth on reservations is also very troubled. A major review of psychosocial adjustment of Indian youth at school found overwhelming support for the argument that the contrast between the culture in which a child is raised and the school culture into which he/she is placed can create significant problems for that child (Saslow and Harrover, 1968). Consequently, difficulties in adjustment to these educated settings has contributed to the high dropout rate of Indian students (Latham, 1985).

Demographically, emerging population trends in Indian Country resemble the growth patterns in a number of Third World countries. As early as 1973, Price (1973) observed that despite the hardships of poverty and alcoholism, the Indian population had increased at a rate of four times greater than the national average during the 1960–1970 census period. As a result, the Native American population was becoming increasingly youthful. In this regard, O'Brien stated in his 1978 study of the Warm Springs Reservation in Oregon that 48 percent of the total Indian population was less than 18 years of age. Guilfoyle (1988) provided additional documentation of this emerging trend of a lowered age among Native Americans when he observed that in contrast to a median age of 29 years for the general population of the U.S., the median age for American Indians is slightly over 18 years. The major implication of this pattern is that substantially larger numbers of Indian youths will be at risk for possible involvement in delinquency over the foreseeable future.

## Youth Maltreatment

Child abuse and neglect are clear manifestations of family dysfunction in Indian Country and are often a prelude to Native American juvenile delinquency. A vast majority of the Indian adolescents in the juvenile justice system are the same children who were in custody proceedings involving incidents of child abuse and neglect. This problem of maltreating Indian children is being driven largely by poverty, rapid social change, and social disorganization. Cross-cultural studies have shown that societies in transition are especially susceptible to problems such as child abuse. How does the cultural/tribal context and seemingly inevitable culture change affect the incidence of child maltreatment among Indian peoples? The cultural context will determine what constitutes abuse, will define situations that excuse or medicate abuse, and will identify the types of appropriate interventions that can be applied. This assessment should take into account factors such as the individual strengths and personal resources that exist within any given community.

While, to date, no definitive research has been conducted to determine the extent of child abuse and neglect on reservations or to determine how these behaviors correlate with other forms of family violence, increased attention is being directed to the problem. The Children's Justice Act (CJA) was signed into law in 1986 to provide funding for states to establish programs to improve the investigation and prosecution of child sexual abuse cases. In 1988, the Anti-Drug Act, which amended the Victims of Crime Act (VOCA) of 1984, was passed, authorizing a portion of the CJA funds to be used to assist Indian tribes improve the handling of serious child abuse cases on Indian reservations. This legislation made a limited amount of funds available to assist Indian tribes in implementing programs and to improve the handling of child abuse cases, especially child sexual abuse cases, in a manner which limits additional trauma to child victims, and to improve the investigation and prosecution of such cases.

Another step recently taken to assist Indian tribes to respond to child abuse has been the passage of Public Law 101-630, the Indian Child Prevention and Family Violence Prevention Act (1990). The goals outlined in this federal legislation are to identify the scope of incidents of abuse of children and family violence in Indian Country and to reduce such incidents. In addition, the Act will provide funds for the mental health treatment of Indian victims of child abuse and family violence on Indian reservations.

# 12

# TRENDS IN INDIAN ADOLESCENT DRUG AND ALCOHOL USE

FRED BEAUVAIS

Alcoholism and alcohol abuse have been, historically, issues of major concern for Indians. Despite laws that until 1953 prohibited the sale of alcohol to Indian people, high rates of alcoholism continue to be observed among many tribes. Until the early 1970s, therefore, the research literature focused on the use of alcohol. Pinto (1973) was one of the first researchers to suggest that drug use might be a problem among Indian youth. But his argument was indirect, and it was based on the assumption that the same socioeconomic conditions that seemed to spawn alcohol abuse among these youth would lead to high levels of drug abuse. Only a few anecdotal reports of drug use were available at the time, and Pinto made the plea that more data were sorely needed.

Shortly after Pinto's paper appeared, Western Behavioral Studies (now the Tri-Ethnic Center for Prevention Research) at Colorado State University began to collect the first systematic data on the epidemiology of drug use among Native American youth. This project began in 1975 and continues today.

In this chapter I will attempt to provide a comprehensive picture of drug and alcohol use among American Indian adolescents. The data are drawn from our work over 17 years with thousands of Indian youth from dozens of tribes, and new data relating to Indian youth who do not live on reservations will be incorporated. The discussion will begin in this paper with the trends in drug use for reservation-based Indian youth whom we have monitored since 1975.

Edited version of Fred Beauvais, "Trends in Indian Drug and Alcohol Use," *The Journal of the National Center* 5(1) (1992). Reprinted by permission of *The Journal of the National Center* and the author.

## THE SAMPLE

For our long-standing survey of reservation Indian youth, each year we select five to seven tribes that are geographically and culturally representative of Indian youth across the country. When we report on drug use prevalence rates, we aggregate across two- or three-year periods to reduce sampling bias. We do recognize the great diversity among Indian tribes; in one sense it is not possible to obtain a sample of tribes that represent all Indian people. Indeed, if we were looking at cultural variables, we could not aggregate measures across tribes; rather we would have to deal with each tribe separately to characterize it accurately. Drug use, however, is a behavior that exists in a larger social context, and we have found in the past that there is only small variation in use rates among tribes. This situation may change in the future, however, as some tribes launch successful prevention programs that substantially reduce drug use in specific locations.

Although we attempt to contact and enlist the cooperation of all schools within each tribe, we are not always successful for logistic or administrative reasons. Once a school agrees to cooperate, all students in the 7th–12th grades are administered the self-report survey by the classroom teacher. (See Oetting and Beauvais [1990] for a discussion of reliability and validity issues related to self-report data and the instrumentation used.) Clearly these data are lacking in information about school dropouts, and any conclusions drawn must be restricted to Indian youth who remain in school. There are theoretical reasons and anecdotal reports indicating that drug use is higher among school dropouts—an important point that must be born in mind throughout this chapter.

## TRENDS IN LIFETIME PREVALENCE

Table 12.1 presents the trends in lifetime prevalence for Indian 7th–12th graders since 1975. (Lifetime prevalence is the percent of youth who respond "Yes" to the question, "Have you ever used _____ ?") Note that the survey was changed in 1984–85 to include the use of several additional drugs so it is difficult to discern trends for these drugs. The index of "lifetime prevalence" is very general in that it measures any level of use of a particular drug—even one-time use several years ago. It is a useful measure, however, when looking at the distribution or changing use patterns in a population or when comparing one population to another. To use an extreme example, a lifetime prevalence of 20% for marijuana in a population means something very different from a lifetime prevalence of 60%—the rates for marijuana use in 1989 for Anglo and for Indian 7th–12th graders. When the rate is 60%, it can be assumed that marijuana is highly available and that its use is the norm for that group; everyone probably has access to it, and the pressure to use is very high. A rate of 20% suggests that although the drug is not hard to get, access and pressure to use exist at much lower levels.

Table 12.1   Percent of Reservation Indian 7th–12th Graders Reporting Lifetime Use of Drugs: 1975–1990

|  | 1975 % | 1977–78 % | 1980–81 % | 1982–83 % | 1984–85 % | 1986–87 % | 1988–90 % |
|---|---|---|---|---|---|---|---|
| Alcohol | 76 | 79 | 85 | 81 | 79 | 81 | 74 |
| Get drunk[a] |  |  |  |  | 46 | 49 | 51 |
| Marijuana | 41 | 53 | 74 | 70 | 57 | 61 | 54 |
| Inhalants | 16 | 26 | 30 | 31 | 21 | 24 | 23 |
| Cocaine | 6 | 7 | 11 | 6 | 7 | 8 | 9 |
| Stimulants[b] | 10 | 15 | 24 | 22 | 21 | 25 | 16 |
| Legal stimulants[b] |  |  |  |  | 14 | 15 | 14 |
| Sedatives[b] | 6 | 10 | 9 | 7 | 10 | 11 | 7 |
| Heroin | 3 | 4 | 5 | 2 | 5 | 5 | 4 |
| Psychedelics | 7 | 9 | 9 | 6 | 9 | 10 | 12 |
| Tranquilizers[a,b] |  | 9 | 6 | 3 | 7 | 7 | 3 |
| PCP[a] |  |  |  |  | 10 | 10 | 7 |
| Cigarettes[a] |  |  |  |  | 79 | 78 | 67 |
| Smokeless tobacco[a] |  |  |  |  |  | 58 | 51 |
| N | 1235 | 3105 | 2159 | 1411 | 1510 | 2683 | 5768 |

[a]Data not available for earlier years.

[b]Only illicit, or non-prescribed, use is included.

The results presented in Table 12.1 are somewhat mixed, but one overall trend is evident: for several of the more commonly used drugs there was a dramatic increase in use by Indian youth between 1975 and 1981, and there has been a gradual decline since then. This pattern is clear for marijuana, inhalants and stimulants. Additional data providing support for a general decline in drug use since 1981 among adolescents is provided in this chapter. There is no way to know with certainty the reasons for the upsurge and then the decline; however, it is important to recognize that this same pattern holds true for youth in general in the United States.

The National Household Survey (National Household, 1990) is given every two to three years and includes a representative sample of 12- to 17-year-old youth. The lifetime prevalence data from this survey are plotted for four drugs in Figure 12.1 and are contrasted with the data we have collected from Indian 7th–12th graders. As the methodology for collecting the data in the two surveys was different, the relative rates of use for Indian and non-Indian youth in Figure 12.1 need to be interpreted with some caution. In a number of studies, however, we have compared age and gender distributions and have found that the groups are reasonably comparable.

Indian youth have consistently higher rates of drug use. The differences in use rates are so large that they could not have occurred merely from the method used. The similarity in trends over time for the two major drugs—alcohol and marijuana—are remarkable; the levels of use may differ, but the trends are the same.

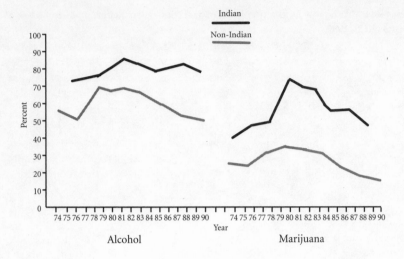

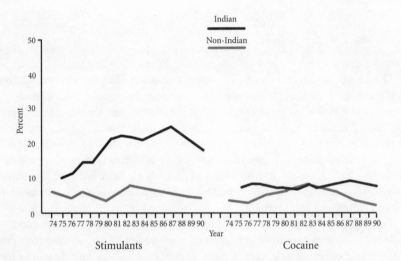

FIGURE 12.1   Lifetime Prevalence Rates for Alcohol, Marijuana, Stimulants, and
Cocaine for Indian and Non-Indian Adolescents

Use increased to a peak about 1981 and dropped after that. Stimulants show a decline as well, but use by Indian youth peaked somewhat later.

The other major source of data on trends in drug use in the United States population, the National Senior Survey (Johnston, O'Malley, and Bachman, 1989),
also very clearly shows the decrease in drug use since the early 1980s. It appears
that broad forces acting in the milieu of adolescents are having similar effects on
both Indian and non-Indian youth, at least for some drugs.

The history of drug use and anti-drug use efforts in the United States may provide a clue as to why there was an increase in drug use followed by a consistent decrease. In the 1970s, as drug use became very common among younger adolescents, there were very few efforts in place to counter this use. Adults were naive about the effects of drugs and were both factually and attitudinally unprepared to confront the growing problem. Without adequate guidance from the adult community and in the absence of firm sanctions, young people were left in a value vacuum and increasingly pursued the short-term exhilaration and social pleasures provided by drugs. Gradually the adult community, bolstered by increasing medical evidence of the harm caused by drugs, mounted an ever-stronger anti-drug response. The early 1980s witnessed the rapid growth of anti-drug parent groups and many other community responses. Anti-drug laws were passed, and the penalties for possession and sale of drugs were radically increased. Federal money and other resources were rapidly mobilized to develop prevention programs. The result has been a general drop in the use of drugs. To date there is still scant evidence that any of these programs had an immediate effect in and of themselves. That is, we cannot conclude that a particular set of prevention activities—whether it is increased recreational opportunities, values clarification exercises, the building of refusal skills, legal penalties, or any of a myriad of prevention activities—has led to the declines we have seen in drug use. What is clear, however, is that through all of these efforts a national consensus was forming, and young people were getting a strong message that drug use was not a tolerable nor a valued behavior in this society.

However it was communicated, the same message seems to have gotten through to the young people in Indian country. Nearly every tribe now has some type of prevention program, and there is a growing movement of sobriety marches and calls for sober leadership on many reservations. The important point is that adolescent drug use is not immutable and that much of what works for society in general has at least some effect on Indian youth. Although there are certainly cultural differences to be recognized in addressing drug problems among Indian youth, there are also similarities with non-Indian populations that must not be overlooked.

Not all of the drugs listed in Table 12.1 are declining in use by Indian youth. Notably, cocaine and psychedelics show small but consistent increases whereas they are decreasing in use by non-Indian youth. We have no explanation for this trend other than the observation in our early work that changes in the use of some drugs by Indian youth lag a year or two behind the national trend. This can be seen in Figure 12.1 where the peak for marijuana use among Anglo youth was about 1979 but among Indian youth was 1981. Another possible explanation for the continuing popularity of these two drugs is related to the supply pipeline. In subsequent papers we will see that marijuana use is extremely common on reservations, and it is possible that the sources of marijuana are also the sources of cocaine and hallucinogens. At least one more data point will be required in order to see whether the trends for cocaine and hallucinogen use are reversing and following the course of trends for non-Indian youth. Furthermore, although there has been a reduction in alcohol lifetime prevalence since 1985, the pattern is uneven. The more important number in Table 12.1 is the lifetime prevalence of "getting drunk." Although many youth report having tried alcohol at some point in their lives, a better indicator of alcohol involvement is getting drunk. Unfortunately, we do not have long-term data on intoxication, but the last three data points indicate a possible increasing level of alcohol involvement. This pattern would match the anecdotal evidence from treatment workers on reservations, where there is an in-dication that alcohol use is increasing among adolescents.

## TRENDS IN RISK LEVEL

As mentioned earlier, the index of lifetime prevalence does not give a complete picture of drug use patterns. Of most concern are youth who are using drugs heavily and on a regular basis as opposed to one-time use or occasional experi-mentation that has not continued. We have developed a classification of drug use that ranks youth on a continuum from essentially no use to continued heavy use (Oetting and Beauvais, 1983). This drug use hierarchy allows us to classify young people into three groups: (1) low-risk non-users—young people who, at the most, have tried a drug but are not currently using any drug; (2) moderate-risk users— youth who are getting drunk once a month or more often and who may be using some marijuana; and (3) high-risk users—youth who are using marijuana more than once or twice a week or who are using other drugs at least once a month. It should be noted that when we refer to moderate- or high-risk users, we mean those youth who are currently using drugs and alcohol in such a way that they may incur some physical or emotional harm from that use.

The reductions that were seen in the lifetime prevalence data are due mainly to a drop in the number of youth in the moderate-risk category and their movement to the low-risk group.

Since about 1977 the high-risk users group has not changed substantially: be-tween 17% and 20% of youth have used drugs enough to place them at high risk. If our hypothesis is accurate that general societal influences have reduced drug use among Indian youth, it appears that there are nevertheless a substantial number of youth—the high-risk users—who do not respond to these societal messages. At the same time, however, it appears that the majority of youth (i.e., the moderate-risk users) can be reached by prevention efforts and will change their drug use behavior.

The existence of a persistent and unchanging high-risk user group has a num-ber of implications. The treatment professionals and people working in hospital admissions, who have been at odds with the epidemiologists for several years, see no reduction in problems even though surveys show less drug use. Both sides may be right. There has been a reduction in use, but it has been among casual users and experimenters. There has been no decrease in the number of high-risk drug users—those who end up in treatment or in the hospital.

Table 12.2  Percent of 4th–6th Grade Indian Students Reporting Lifetime Use of Drugs

|  | *1980–81*<br>% | *1987–88*<br>% | *1989–90*<br>% |
|---|---|---|---|
| Alcohol | 33 | 22 | 21 |
| Marijuana | 23 | 16 | 10 |
| Inhalants | 14 | 14 | 15 |
| Cigarettes | 34 | 33 | 32 |

The fact that there is no reduction in the high-risk group suggests that members of this group probably cannot be reached by the usual prevention efforts. These youth are likely to have multiple problems that need rectifying, and the usual attempts to change attitudes through advertising, by increasing penalties or by building social skills will not work. Many of these youth have probably developed antisocial tendencies and will not listen to messages about social appropriateness.

Prevention, then, must be two-pronged. We should continue what we have been doing in the hope of reaching even more of the moderate-risk youth, but we must also have much more intensive intervention aimed at the high-risk groups. Simply intensifying the usual prevention approaches will not work. Effective efforts to reduce the number of high-risk users will more likely resemble treatment approaches where the multiple and ingrained problems of these youth can be resolved.

## TRENDS FOR YOUNGER CHILDREN

The data for younger Indian children are not as complete as they are for adolescents; they are, however, revealing. Table 12.2 shows the lifetime prevalence for four drugs since 1980. These data show a consistent decrease for alcohol and marijuana but a stable pattern for inhalants and cigarettes. There is no obvious explanation for these differential rates, although it could be that drug prevention activities have not adequately targeted cigarettes and inhalants. Actually, other data suggest that there is a strong need for increased prevention efforts aimed at Indian children for all drugs.

# 13

# HAZHO'S SOKEE'—
# STAY TOGETHER NICELY

## Domestic Violence Under Navajo Common Law

JAMES ZION AND ELSIE B. ZION

## INTRODUCTION: INSTITUTIONALIZED VIOLENCE IN THE NAVAJO NATION

As it is in other parts of the United States, domestic violence is a severe problem in the Navajo Nation. Statistics compiled in a report by the Navajo Nation Department of Law Enforcement show that 0.6 to 1% of Navajos over age 18 are victims of domestic violence.[1] The same report projects that, by 1995, 1.5 to 1.8% of the Navajo Nation population will have been involved in an altercation with parents, children, or siblings, and that in a projected population of 198,000, there will be 3,564 cases of domestic violence among adults over age 18.[2]

In October, 1991, subcommittees of the Navajo Nation Council, in cooperation with the Navajo Nation Judicial Branch, held a hearing on the scope and impact of domestic violence. The hearing, which was held in the aftermath of the deaths of Navajo women at the hands of their husbands, prompted official action. Since then, Navajo Nation Council committees have continually discussed legislative alternatives, and the Courts of the Navajo Nation have issued rules for criminal and civil proceedings to provide remedies.

---

Edited version of J. Zion and E. B. Zion, "Hazho's Sokee'—Stay Together Nicely: Domestic Violence Under Navajo Common Law." Originally appeared in *Arizona State Law Journal* 25:(2) (1993). Reprinted by permission of the *Arizona State Law Journal* and the authors.

This study seeks to reach some preliminary conclusions about the causes of domestic violence and appropriate legal rules and remedies to address the problem. This study accepts an approach to law that consists of norms and values that are identified, applied, and enforced by legal institutions, including traditional bodies.[3] The problem is to identify Navajo norms and values that deal with the subject, and how they can be entrenched in law by Navajo institutions.

It is important to identify the causes of domestic violence. We will argue that Navajo values and morals reject domestic violence because it conflicts with Navajo sexual equality and concepts of harmony. To explain how domestic violence came to the Navajo Nation, we must recognize that it exists in a climate of institutionalized violence, where traditional values of equality and harmony have been broken down, and new forces have caused people to lose hope and replace it with dependence and disharmony.

Following the 1868 treaty between the Navajo Nation and the United States,[4] the government of the United States imposed alien laws, authoritarian governmental forms, and paternalistic institutions upon Navajos. Following World War II, Navajos entered the wage economy, worked outside the Navajo Nation, and learned the values of another culture through population movement, education, and communications media (radio, television, and movies, in particular). Navajos learned about power and authority, as well as its abuses. They also learned about alienation, as it is reflected in family disruption, alcohol abuse, and other forms of escapist activity. In sum, Navajos learned of a new culture that institutionalized violence against people by making them unequal.

A story from Navajo history shows the source of the breakdown well; it is the story of "The Navaho Revolt of 1913."[5] America learned about it in nationwide screamer headlines, including "The Navahos Never Were Subdued by the Whites!"[6] and "The Only Uncivilized Tribe of Indians in the United States Goes on the Warpath!" (Newcomb, 1966:28).

*Hatot'cli-yazzi* lived at Beautiful Mountain, near today's Sanostee, Navajo Nation (New Mexico), which is close to the Arizona border (29). His wife died, so his father, *Bi-joshii,* opened negotiations for a new marriage (29). The intended bride did not want to leave her two sisters to move to Beautiful Mountain, so the talks between parents ended in a marriage between *Hatot'cli-yazzi* and the three sisters (29). In September of 1913, William T. Shelton, the Shiprock Agency Superintendent of the Bureau of Indian Affairs, learned of the arrangement and ordered an investigation (29). When an interpreter advised *Bi-joshii* that the Superintendent expected two of the wives to go away, the elder replied: "Shall we turn them out to wander in the mountains until they die?" . . . "No! That is not the way Navahos do things! These three girls are all members of my family, and their children are my grandchildren. I shall keep them here where they will have good care" (30).

Superintendent Shelton was not amused (30). It was bad enough that Navajos disobeyed his ruling that men could have only one wife, but this was a situation where a noted medicine man and his son openly defied official orders (30).

Shelton sent his police to arrest *Bi-joshii, Hatot'cli-yazzi,* and the three wives (30). The police found only the three women and confined them in a wing of the Shiprock girls' school dormitory (30). On September 17, 1913, *Hatot'cli-yazzi,* a brother, *Bi-joshii,* and nine clansmen rode to Shiprock to take up the matter with Shelton (30). When the men arrived, they found that Shelton was away at the Durango county fair, so the group overtook the policemen, tied them to trees, and released the sisters (30). They then fled to sanctuary on the top of Beautiful Mountain (30–31).

As word of the affair spread across New Mexico, the story grew until a newspaper reported that the Navajos were in full revolt, and that they likely would attack and destroy nearby towns and farming communities. Shelton warned local trading posts to take arms in case the rebellion spread to their areas. Shelton also summoned the cavalry by telegram. Brigadier General Hugh L. Scott, and the Twelfth Cavalry of Fort Bliss, Texas, mounted. Soon, four troops of cavalry (240 men), 5 cooks, 16 mule drivers, 256 horses, 40 mules, and 8 commissary wagons arrived in Gallup. The cavalry subsequently marched north and set up camp at Sanostee on November 26, 1913 (Newcomb, 1966:31–32).

Father Weber of St. Michaels Mission (Arizona) knew the whole affair was overblown, and travelled to Beautiful Mountain to keep things from getting out of hand. *Bi-joshii* agreed to surrender, and went down the mountain to meet with General Scott. The old man held his hand high for all to see and said to Scott, "I see blood on this hand." *Bi-joshii* meant the blood of an enemy he had killed on the way to the U.S. concentration camp Bosque Redondo (Newcomb, 1966:33–34).[7] Waving his fist in Scott's face, the old man said, "I'm afraid there may be blood on this hand again, so I come from my safe place. But I no afraid of you or your men" (Newcomb, 1966:34). The Navajos who defied the Army served a twenty-day unlawful assembly sentence in the Gallup jail, where tourists took pictures of them (34).

That was the end of the "Navaho Rebellion of 1913." We do not know what became of the wives. They likely stayed with their husband secretly, and their lives likely went on as usual.[8]

What was the rebellion about? What does it have to do with domestic violence? Franc Johnson Newcomb, who retold the story, said that *Hatot'cli-yazzi's* first wife died, "and he was looking for another, but the girl he wanted would not leave her mother and her two sisters. *Bi-joshii* started bargaining with the mother and presented her several sheep, so the outcome was that all three girls married *Hatot'cli-yazzi* and came to live in his hogan" (Newcomb, 1966:34). The father and son had a good herd and grazing area, which they would not leave. It was against normal practice for a woman to leave her family to go to the husband's place of residence. Navajo custom provided that the husband and wife would maintain a marital home with the wife's mother and family. This custom was designed to prevent domestic violence. Thus, the negotiated marriage with the three sisters was a means to foster family harmony and protect against mistreatment.

Therefore, we turn from a story of ignorance of Navajo ways to the values that make up the Navajo common law of domestic violence, the causes of institution- alized violence, and an examination of possible ways to institutionalize Navajo values in its place.

## II  THE STATUS OF NAVAJO WOMEN

Problems of domestic violence, rape, sexual harassment, and other forms of vio- lence against women arise from inequality and abuses of power. Sex discrimina- tion comes from those same sources. Rape, one kind of domestic violence, in- volves a hostile, aggressive man who inflicts violence upon a woman; it is not an act of sexuality (Benderly, 1974). Rape-prone societies have a "social use of rape to threaten or punish women," including their own or other women (177). In con- trast, rape-free societies are marked by women's high status: women are respected and influential members of the community; the religion includes a female deity; and the society values essential equality as a goal.[9]

Subordination of women and inequality nurture violence against women in the forms of rape, domestic violence, sexual harassment, and child sexual abuse. Thus, women's status in a given society is essential in identifying these roots of violence.

In traditional Navajo society, women share equal rights with men, and some- times enjoy superior authority and importance (Newcomb, 1966:9). Women have a high social status and contribute equally to the family's economic welfare (Spencer, 1947). Navajo common law reflected these values through women's property ownership and control, the mother's determinative role in tracing an- cestry, and married couples' practice of residing with the wife's family (Kluckhohn and Leighton, 1974). Some cultures treat women as property, or their culture's law retains vestiges of the notion that women are property (e.g., some general princi- ples of American law) (Kanowitz, 1969). In contrast, Navajo common law used property and ownership concepts in a different way: "In marriage, . . . a man be- comes property of a woman, a woman property of a man" (Haile, 1968:14). Thus, Navajo common law conceived the reciprocal relations of a man and woman as an interdependent bond.

Ceremonies and traditions are two primary sources of Navajo norms and val- ues. Ceremonial accounts include incidents of men mutilating women or beating them with a fire poker as punishment for adultery (Spencer, 1947:36–37). However, that sort of physical mistreatment is now only historical lore and is not generally practiced (Spencer, 1947:36; Van Valkenburg, 1938). Rather, women's equal status and dignity are reinforced by Navajo literature, which details Navajo women's important work and essential role in society (e.g., Roessel, 1981). Moreover, the *kinaalda'* puberty ceremony is a visible and continuing means of re- minding Navajos of women's dignity (Begay, 1983; Frisbie, 1967). Navajo origin accounts tell of their greatest deity—Changing Woman—who is also Mother Earth. Changing Woman is the symbol of the female's essential role in life.

Women's importance and high regard are implicit in Changing Woman's part in creating the present world (Spencer, 1947). Navajo ceremonies generally teach and support women's dignity and social importance, which make them central to Navajo society (Kluckhohn and Leighton, 1974). In particular, the *kinaalda'* puberty ceremony is an occasion where young women learn the duties and dignity of women, and through the ceremony, the initiate becomes Changing Woman (Begay, 1983; Frisbie, 1967).

These values are embodied in modern practice and Navajo law. The Navajo Nation Council has taken measures to protect the status of women, including statutory recognition of customary marriage, family planning programs, and placing an Equal Rights Amendment in the Navajo Nation Bill of Rights in 1980 (Shepardson, 1982:161–162).

Navajo norms and values, foundations of the Navajo common law, make it clear that women are equal with men, have a religiously sanctioned status through identity with Changing Woman, and have rights that arise from individual dignity. The essential Navajo value is that while men and women are distinct, they relate as complementary equals (Witherspoon, 1975). That kind of relationship creates, or should create, an environment that views violence toward women as deviant behavior. Under Navajo common law, violence toward women, or mistreatment of them in any way, is illegal.

## III   RULES OF THE NAVAJO COMMON LAW

Navajo norms and values of women's equality and dignity are embodied in rules developed in Navajo legal institutions. In traditional Navajo law, these institutions include the family and clan.

Aside from the *kinaalda'* ceremony, where women are identified with Changing Woman, Navajo marriage ceremonies use the clan as an institution to teach the law of marriage. During the course of the ceremony, elders and clan relations teach the rights and duties of spouses. They include admonishments such as, "Don't get mad at each other"; "Don't talk back to each other"; "Don't divorce each other"; and, "Stay together nicely" (Lamphere, 1977:71). The ceremony specifically addresses spousal abuse, and grooms learn the rule that a man "should never take his hand to his wife (i.e., beat her)" (Lamphere, 1977).

A common American Indian social practice which irritated non-Indians and "proved" the "barbaric" nature of Indians was polygamy.[10] In Navajo society, one of polygamy's purposes was to "obviate dissension and to insure conjugal fidelity" through marriage to a wife's sisters (Franciscan Fathers, 1910:449). A man's potential spouses also included a widow, or divorced woman, and her daughters by the prior union (1949:44). This was a woman-controlled family arrangement, where a man would have difficulty abusing a tight-knit women's group. As is seen by the story of the Navajo Rebellion of 1913, where a woman left her protective family, polygamy was sometimes a marital condition (Newcomb, 1966:33).

The family is a legal institution which enforces these rules. One of the first things an outsider learns about Navajos is that they trace ancestry through their mothers, and that they are members of their mother's clan. They are "born for" their father's clan (Kluckhohn and Leighton, 1974:112).

Traditionally, Navajos practiced matrilocal residence after marriage; the husband went to live with the wife's mother's group (1974:103–104).[11] A woman's family had a corresponding duty to protect her if her husband became abusive (Franciscan Fathers, 1910:54; Leighton and Kluckhohn, 1948:80; Hamamsy, 1957; Spencer, 1947:38–39). Navajo men's life histories show that they understood both the prohibition against domestic violence and the role of the family as an institution to prevent it (Frisbie, 1982). While not all couples lived with the wife's family, there was a protective custom whereby couples did not live alone during their first year of marriage (Leighton and Kluckhohn, 1948:82).

Another rule of Navajo common law, which is reinforced in the family and clan as an institution, is that it is best for couples to reconcile their differences. Navajos use a family meeting to identify sources of conflict, and to make arrangements for an effective reconciliation or an agreed divorce. Another Navajo practice, although fading, is the arranged marriage, entered into for economic benefit and relationships between clans. It shamed clan elders for their children to disrupt family and inter-clan survival by domestic violence. Accordingly, there was strong familial interest in preserving peace among married couples (Leighton and Kluckhohn, 1948:85–86).

The Navajo Nation Courts are a modern Navajo legal institution, and they too have had to deal with the problem of family violence. In the case of *Kuwanhyoima v. Kuwanhyoima,* the district judge of the Tuba City Judicial District dealt with a damage action by a wife whose husband had sexually assaulted and beaten her, causing permanent scarring and disfigurement. The husband assaulted her on two occasions following separation and the commencement of a divorce action. The court ruled in favor of the wife and granted $51,867.20 in damages ($36,667.20 in compensatory damages and $15,200 in punitive damages) on the basis of Navajo common law (Navajo Supreme Court, 1990). The court stated:

> The basic principle applicable to the relationship of a man and a woman is that of *hozho,* or that state of affairs where everything is in its proper place and functioning in harmonious relationship to everything else. Inherent in that concept is proportionality, reasonableness, and individual dignity. In Navajo common law a man does not have the privilege of using unreasonable force against his wife. (2–3, opinion by the Honorable Homer Bluehouse)

On November 1, 1991, following public hearings on domestic violence in the Navajo Nation, the Navajo Nation Judicial Conference resolved to use the legal tools of conditions of release and act-specific sentences in criminal cases, and civil restraining orders, upon an opinion of the Solicitor of the Judicial Branch.[12] The solicitor's opinion outlined the legal foundations for imposing release conditions, sentences for crimes involving domestic violence, and issuing civil restraining orders.[13] The Navajo Nation Supreme Court then adopted domestic violence court rules, based upon Navajo common law,[14] the Equal Rights provision of the Navajo Nation Bill of Rights,[15] principles of the law of equity, and English-American common law (Taub, 1980:241–243).

Navajo Nation judges, as members of the Navajo culture, understand the values of the Navajo People, as reflected in Navajo traditions, ceremonies, and legal maxims. Judges institutionalize these values in rules of law and modern procedures for future recognition.

## IV  THE CAUSES OF INSTITUTIONALIZED VIOLENCE

Unlike any other ethnic group in the United States, American Indians suffer gross extremes of deprivations and violence. Statistical measures of social conditions show that Indians fall at the very bottom of every indicator of well-being.[16] Aside from vehicle deaths, alcohol and drug dependence, suicides, and other forms of self-destruction, Indians are crime victims at rates highly-disproportionate to those of general American society.[17] A 1991 National Congress of American Indians survey of tribal court criminal dockets shows that the most frequent offenses are (1) disorderly conduct, (2) assault and battery, (3) intoxication, and (4) driving while intoxicated.[18] Tribal judges have completed the picture the statistics paint with anecdotal evidence, gained from personal experience, that these offenses largely involve alcohol abuse and personal violence among families, relations, and members of the community.[19] Crime on Indian reservations often makes victims of people who are in continuing relationships with the perpetrators of given offenses.

Crime on Indian reservations is the product of an environment created by the disruption of traditional lifestyles and economies. The crime of domestic violence is caused by economic dislocation, the destruction of traditional institutions, and the introduction of individualism and the individualistic norms of paternalism and patriarchal rule.[20]

Two outside influences have created a climate which promotes domestic violence: one is racist stereotyping of Indians, and the other is male dominance in societal arrangements. The sources of stereotyping and racism in European and American literature are obvious. Accounts of Indian life, both old and new, portray Indian men as brutes and Indian women as long-suffering victims. Indian women were (and are) often depicted as "cruel brutes as a result of their husbands' mistreatment," and as " 'savage women' who were 'as insolent as the men were cruel' " (Riley, 1984:237, 258). Rather than observing the actual state of relations between Indian men and women, non-Indians looked in their cultural mirror to write accounts of Indian life: "Because most Europeans regarded the roles and positions of white women as inferior, it was difficult for them to understand the view of many native groups that men and women were separate but equal" (Riley, 1984:257; Kidwell, 1978:115). This sort of racist stereotyping continues today in popular media, which depict Indian men "as blood-thirsty savages devoted to treating women cruelly" (Allen, 1986). "While traditional Indian men seldom did any such thing—and in fact among most tribes abuse of women was simply unthinkable, as was abuse of children or the aged—the lie about 'usual' male Indian behavior seems to have taken root and now bears its brutal and bitter fruit" (Allen, 1986).

The modern life histories of Navajo women evidence their troubles and worries, including abuse, exploitation, and rape (Frisbie, 1982:20–21). In 1979, a news report stated that rape was the number one crime in the Navajo Nation (Allen, 1986:191). Additionally, a survey of women seen in a five-state Indian Health Service psychiatric service center showed that 80% experienced some sort of sexual assault (Cross, 1982:18). Participants in the October, 1991 Navajo Nation public hearing on domestic violence agreed that the frequency of domestic violence and crimes against women and girls was grossly understated.[21] While it is difficult to compare today's bitter fruit with prerecorded Navajo history, widespread rape, domestic violence, and child abuse likely are recent phenomena among Navajos.[22] We must then ask when and how these forms of institutionalized violence came to the Navajo Nation.

Law is the product of incorporating values into institutions. Whose values nourish a climate of violence? Whose institutions promote it? In 1868, the Treaty between the United States and the Navajo Nation provided for an "agent for the Navajos," who would live among them and enforce non-Indian policies.[23] The treaty also provided for the allotment of agricultural lands among heads of households.[24] In 1883, the Commissioner of Indian Affairs introduced the Court of Indian Offenses for Indian reservations, and the crimes stated in its regulations included polygamy, traditional marriage practices, traditional divorce, and traditional inheritance (Indian Bureau, 1884:300–305). The Navajo Nation received its first Navajo Court of Indian Offenses in 1892 (Department of the Interior, 1892). The agents for the Navajos wore the blinders of their own culture, and insisted that their Protestant-capitalist ethics were superior to those of the Navajos. The agents took strong action to prohibit both polygamy and the many marital traditions designed to protect women. The prohibition of the traditional brideprice denigrated the Navajo practice of cementing relationships between clans through the negotiation of arrangements to share productive wealth (i.e., horses and sheep). In fact, the brideprice was a kind of insurance to prevent abuse of a wife (Kluckhohn and Leighton, 1974:80). Traditional divorce, where a woman was free to get away from an abusive relationship quickly and easily, was prohibited by modern laws that made it difficult for a woman to dissolve her unsuccessful marriage.[25]

The Agent for the Navajos, as it was at other reservations, insisted that the best means to "civilize" Indians was to turn them into farmers with exclusive rights to a fixed area of land.[26] Again reflecting non-Navajo mores, the land allotments under the treaty went to male heads of household.[27]

Another destructive innovation was the adoption of the strong, male leader— "the head man." During the course of negotiating the Treaty of 1868, General Sherman insisted that the Navajos select male leaders; a strong chief and a council of male head men (Underhill, 1956:132–133). Although Navajo women enjoyed a strong role in the public decisions of Navajo clan groups' public decisions (and some were *naat'aanii* or "peace chiefs"[28]) they lost their ability to participate in decisions made by male leaders given absolute power. Thus, alien law and government destroyed traditional relationships and concentrated power in the hands of male leaders. Without the institutionalized protection of Navajo common law, Navajo women suffered. Thus, non-Indian paternalism and patriarchy were introduced to Navajos, and Navajo men learned several Anglo "traditions" including robbing women of economic and political power and wife-beating.[29]

During their period of contact with Spanish (and later Mexican) immigrants, the Navajos adopted a grazing economy (Underhill, 1956:59). That economy was a mainstay of Navajo life for many years, until the period following World War II. That war introduced Navajos to the wage economy; as a result, many Navajos left to work in industries, build and maintain the Santa Fe Railroad, harvest crops, or work in border towns (Iverson, 1981:47, 49). The wage economy required mobility, a fact that created new problems given the shortage of jobs within the Navajo Nation. The availability of jobs in an economy that assumed that the man was the wage-earner required Navajos to move away from their traditional residence areas. Women were taken from their maternal living areas and moved to their husbands' work areas. These arrangements caused women to live with their husbands' parents or with families composed only of parents and children. Navajo women married and lived with non-Indian or non-member Indian men. Those arrangements separated women from their families, and today Navajos will not necessarily honor the tradition of family protection for women. Reliance on wage income causes family conflicts over how wages will be spent, a situation that promotes drunkenness, wife-beating, infidelity, and jealousy (Hamamsy, 1957:107).

In general, social changes, including forced livestock reduction (which destroyed the grazing culture), non-Indian education programs, and the loss of traditional religious orientation, have created stress for Navajos and their children (Hauswald 1988:43–46). One of the most destructive forces was non-Indian education, where children lost their language, received new (and different) cultural values, and were removed from the traditional classroom of their homes (44–46). Rather than becoming assimilated into the dominant society to exercise its learned values, discrimination forced alienated children to return to a society that was then foreign to them. Estranged from their own family and culture, a lost generation of people were caught in the middle (i.e., in the middle of American and Navajo values) and turned to alcohol and learned violence. The cycle of institutionalized violence, created by destructive education policies, continues in new generations of children who do not know their tribe's language, culture, and religion because their parents have lost it. Although many former Navajo boarding school students are now quite successful, they also recognize the validity of traditional values and want to learn about them in order to have a better life.

Increasing population, economic changes, and disruptions of traditional living arrangements have had adverse and destructive impacts on both Navajo women (Hauswald, 1988; Shepardson, 1982; Griffin, 1982; Lamphere, 1989) and on conditions of life within the Navajo Nation in general (Levy, 1989:373–375).

When asked to account for the hardships modern Navajo women must tolerate, some women identify outside influence as a factor. As one Navajo woman put it: "A lot of women are having trouble with their husbands. The only model the men have is the *macho* white man. They try to copy him and Navajo women object" (Shepardson, 1982:163). One approach to the problem of domestic violence is to restore traditional Navajo norms and values in Navajo institutions.

Not all of the factors that contribute to domestic violence are the result of outside influence. One of the major sources of problems between Navajo men and women is adultery. In creation times, adultery caused conflict between the sexes,[30] and prototypical Navajo figures urged the strongest sanctions against it.[31] However, adultery is not an excuse for physical abuse. As medicine man Frank Mitchell instructed, repeating an age-old rule: "If your wife does this, do not abuse her or get jealous of her. She has this privilege; she is a human being. You have the choice of leaving her or staying with her regardless of what she does" (Frisbie 1982:21). There is an accompanying Navajo legal maxim: "One should not sex-jealously quarrel, because one's (pollen) bag becomes blood."[32] In other words, Navajos evolved their own version of the rule of law that provocation is not a defense to assault. This principle, like many Navajo legal principles, is pragmatic; if you cannot work out adultery, then divorce is available.

## V   Navajo Legal Institutions

Professionals who are involved in the process of developing domestic violence laws and policies within the Navajo Nation must not wear the blinders of non-Navajo culture. Consider the following: why is it that while English and American common law goes back to at least the 11th Century (i.e., the Norman invasion of 1066), said common law has not adequately addressed a social problem that is as old as the Christian Adam and Eve? The English common law gave us the "rule of thumb," where it was permissible for a man to beat his wife with a stick no thicker than his thumb,[33] and it gave us the rule of law that it is permissible for a husband to rape his wife.[34] Such laws developed in legal institutions that rely upon hierarchies of power and authority; such is the institutionalization of paternalism and patriarchy. Rape, domestic violence, and sexual harassment are abuses of authority and power, and it is difficult to ask women to respect legal institutions that subject them to such "damnable" injustices.

The Courts of the Navajo Nation are a visible legal institution, as is the Navajo Nation Council. Although the courts and the council may look to recent legislation that deals with domestic violence, most of this legislation is inadequate, does not sufficiently protect victims, and is not enforced in an appropriate manner (Lengyel, 1990; Voris, 1991; Parnas, 1991). While it is true that the Navajo Nation Council and the Courts of the Navajo Nation must strive to create remedies for the victims of violence, they should not simply replicate outside "models." Instead, Navajo legal institutions should search for Navajo values and incorporate them into rules that reflect traditional Navajo expectations.

One of these institutions is the modern Navajo Peacemaker Court. The Peacemaker Court is a court-annexed traditional mediation and arbitration system that uses the traditional Navajo institutions of the family, clan, and *naat'aanii* (Zion, 1985). A *naat'aanii* is a Navajo leader who is selected on the basis of wisdom, ability, and persuasiveness to solve problems by working with people.[35]

Non-Navajo literature and non-Indian professionals who work in the field of domestic violence warn that mediation must never be used to address that problem. The theory is that since mediation works only in situations where there is comparatively-equal bargaining power between disputants, and since women cannot have equal bargaining power (given psychological brutalization and fear), mediation will only further victimize the victim (e.g., Lerman, 1984; Geffner and Pagelow, 1990). That may be true in non-Indian mediation, which attempts to use a completely neutral, independent, and non-related facilitator, whose role is to urge the parties to resolve their own differences. "Mediation" in the Navajo setting is quite different.

First, the Navajo *naat'aanii* is not neutral. He or she can be related to the parties,[36] and most often that person will have a definite conviction about domestic violence as an evil. Navajo mediators are interventionist: they use prayer, an assessment of the positions and values of the parties, and a lecture on Navajo values to address the problem. A *naat'aanii* (or peacemaker) has the responsibility of applying Navajo moral values to find practical solutions to obvious problems.[37]

Second, the process involves not only the parties, but also their families and clan. The traditional procedure was to utilize the family and clan to deal with marital difficulties. Although many Navajos presume that families must preserve a marriage relationship, this concept is not an unbending principle. Navajo law is quite pragmatic and is based on close examination of, and practical solutions to, problems.

Third, the process helps balance the bargaining position of participants. Navajo civil procedure is based upon "talking things out" for a practical resolution of the problem (Tso, 1992). If a woman is psychologically incapable of speaking, family and clan members are available to speak for her.[38] If a session becomes weighted down in anger and recrimination, the *naat'aanii*-peacemaker will either defuse the situation or continue the meeting for another day.[39]

Fourth, the range of options available to the *naat'aanii*-peacemaker for concluding the dispute is completely open. Rather than applying hard and fast legal rules to a problem, as in adjudication, the situation of the parties dictates the recommended outcome. Assuming that modern Navajo *naat'aanii*-peacemakers will abandon a woman to a brutal fate is too simplistic. If we cannot rely upon families to recognize the dynamics of an abusive relationship in order to support victims, then the foundation for Navajo common law has eroded entirely.

Modern law, as imposed by the Government of the United States, impaired the effectiveness of traditional Navajo institutions. However, modern law did not destroy these institutions. The tradition of the family as a legal institution remains intact. Family and clan gatherings are incorporated into the chapter system.[40] The traditional *naat'aanii* never disappeared, and he or she has a revived role in the Navajo Peacemaker Court.

## VI   CONCLUSION

The non-Indian world has taken up the issue of domestic violence as a confrontation between men and women. Domestic violence statutes are debated on legislative floors, with outraged women confronting male authority figures over proper remedies. Too often, male legislators, urged on by (male) police, judges, and lawyers, water down remedies. Even when domestic violence legislation exists, (male) prosecutors, judges, and police deny effective remedies. Throughout, the American system of power and authority in a hierarchical system (i.e., litigation) uses force to address problems of continuing relationships. As a result, people are revictimized in the process.

This study suggests that the proper approach for Navajos is to identify and rethink their traditional values, then use them in both traditional and modern legal institutions. It is true that some of the procedural protections of Navajo common law are either not available or are no longer accepted. Further, reinstitutionalizing matrilocal residence may be impossible, given a wage economy and the shortage of land for a grazing economy. Although many women no longer keep their marital home with their mothers, mothers and other clan relatives are natural battered women's shelters. (Navajos still take in family members during emergencies, while non-Indian families often shun their offspring and relatives.) Although polygamy still exists, it has lost its social foundations and is likely to become an unacceptable social institution.

However, the extended family and clan still have an obligation to victims of domestic violence. Why is it not possible for an abuser to have his own family as a probation officer? Can there be ways for Navajo courts to use a woman's family as a shelter? Another byproduct of imposed Anglo-American law is that only the individual is responsible for his or her own conduct, and there is no liability or role for the criminal's family and clan to deal with violent crime. For Navajos, the options are to build jails for individual offenders, or to reinstitute the family responsible for the actions of members. If courts begin to jail Navajo offenders, or obtain the power to exclude them from the Navajo Nation, protesting family members will soon come forward and assume their traditional responsibilities.

Is it unrealistic to use the Navajo Peacemaker Court to deal with domestic violence? The answer lies in the will of Navajo communities. If domestic violence is, indeed, a problem that disrupts community life, the answer rests in the community. The solution lies with family members who still love and care for their battered clan daughter or their misguided clan son. If the Navajo Nation cannot return justice to the chapters and let them deal with one of the biggest contemporary problems (along with the associated problem of alcohol abuse), then the United States will have achieved its goals of assimilation and authoritarian central control as the means to destroy Indian culture.

Finally, the Navajo Nation cannot deal with the problem of domestic violence using non-Indian methods. The United States has the highest incarceration rate in the world (Mauer, 1992: Table 1), and its legal system uses force in place of problem-solving and restoring people to harmony in continuing relationships. The Navajo Nation is still rural, and people who commit crimes in small communities are either related to each other or live in continuing relationships. Perhaps answers reside in identifying those relationships and how their strengths may be used to restore people to harmony with each other.

Domestic violence is a test of the Navajo culture. Either that culture, with its egalitarian values and rules, is alive or dead. It may have been irrevocably changed by imposed values and the modern climate of institutionalized violence. However, it is more likely that Navajos can successfully address the problem of domestic violence, and associated problems of lost hope (e.g., alcohol and drug abuse, and other kinds of escapism, such as gang activity) by a return to base values.

## Notes

1. Navajo Nation Department of Law Enforcement, Navajo Division of Public Safety, Narrative Report on Domestic Violence [18] (1991) (unpublished statistical data). Participants in an October 1991 hearing on domestic violence generally agreed that these figures are a gross undercount. They are based upon arrest records for only the offenses of assault or battery; they do not reflect either reports of violence without arrest or incidents where victims were discouraged from reporting to the police.

2. Navajo Nation Department of Law Enforcement, 1991:12. This estimate states that the group at risk is aged 25 through 44. Again, the projected number of victims is most likely seriously underestimated.

3. This is Paul Bohannan's theory of "double institutionalization," which has been accepted as an effective approach to the theoretical problem of the nature of "law." Paul Bohannan, The Differing Realms of the Law, Am. Anthropologist, Part 2, Vol. 67, No. 6, Dec. 1965, at 33, 34–37. Bohannan uses the concept of norms as the first prong of his definition, but others insist that law is also a field of values. See generally Watson Smith & John M. Roberts, Zuni Law: A Field of Values (1954).

4. Treaty Between the United States of America and the Navajo Tribe of Indians, June 1, 1868, U.S.-Navajo Indians, 15 Stat. 667.

5. FRANC JOHNSON NEWCOMB, NAVAHO NEIGHBORS 27–34 (1966) (The text that follows is a shortened version of Newcomb's relation of the story).

6. Newcomb (1966:27–28) does not cite the source of this "front-page article."

7. Newcomb, 1966. *See generally* LYNN K. BAILEY, THE LONG WALK (1978). In 1864, most of the Navajo Nation was captured and death-marched to a "reservation" in eastern New Mexico. This period of history was the beginning of the horrors of modern warfare, including the confinement of peoples because of their race, ethnic identity, or religion. The term "concentration camp" is precise, with all its authoritarian connotations.

8. Throughout Indian Country, tribal leaders attempted to warn Indian agents that polygamy was an institution that protected women. Wooden Leg of the Northern Cheyennes, who sat as an early judge of the Court of Indian Offenses, told an offender: "The agent tells me that I as the judge must order all Cheyennes to have only one wife. You must send away one of yours." When a defendant said that both Wooden Leg and the agent were crazy, the judge replied: "No. If anybody is crazy, it is somebody in Washington. All of the Indians in the United States have this order. If we resist it, our policemen will put us into jail. If much trouble is made about it, soldiers may come to fight us. Whatever man does not put aside his extra wife may be the cause of the whole tribe being killed." Wooden Leg, *Judge Wooden Leg Keeps One Wife, in* NATIVE AMERICAN TESTIMONY: A CHRONICLE OF INDIAN-WHITE RELATIONS FROM PROPHECY TO THE PRESENT, 1492–1992, 229–31 (P. Nabokov ed., 1991).

9. Benderly, 1974:178; *see also* Cross, *Sexual Abuse, a New Threat to the Native American Woman: An Overview,* 6 (1 & 2) LISTENING POST: A PERIODICAL OF THE MENTAL HEALTH PROGRAMS OF INDIAN HEALTH SERVICES 22 (1982).

10. In 1882, Henry M. Teller, a Secretary of the Interior from Colorado, was "closing the loopholes" of traditional Indian law. He wrote a directive to require the creation of an Indian court to punish traditional Indian legal practices. Number two on his list of "barbaric" practices was polygamy. FRANCIS P. PRUCHA, AMERICANIZING THE AMERICAN INDIANS 295, 297 (1973). Commissioner of Indian Affairs Thomas J. Morgan complied by issuing the first regulations in 1883 for "Punishment of Crimes and Misdemeanors Committed by Indians." The rule that prohibited "plural or polygamous marriages" stated:

> Any Indian under the supervision of a United States Indian agent who shall hereafter contract or enter into any plural or polygamous marriage shall be deemed guilty of an offense, and upon conviction thereof shall pay a fine of not less than twenty nor more than fifty dollars, or work at hard labor for not less than twenty nor more than sixty days, or both, at the discretion of the court; and so long as the person shall continue in such unlawful relation he shall forfeit all right to receive rations from the Government (300–302).

11. There is some dispute about this custom in the literature, based upon surveys of actual residence patterns. Most agree it is generally true.

12. James W. Zion was present at the meeting in his capacity as Solicitor.

13. Opinion of the Solicitor, Judicial Branch of the Navajo Nation, No. 91-09, *Conditions of Release and Sentencing in Domestic Violence Situations* (December 10, 1991).

14. In the Matter of the Adoption of Rules of Pleading, Practice and Procedure for Domestic Violence Proceedings in the Courts of the Navajo Nation, No. SCJU-02-92 (Supreme Court of the Navajo Nation, June 25, 1992); approved by the Judiciary Committee of the Navajo Nation Council, Resolution No. JCO-13-92 (October 2, 1992).

15. 1 NAVAJO TRIBAL CONST. s 3 (1986).

16. James W. Zion, *North American Indian Perspectives on Human Rights,* HUMAN RIGHTS IN CROSS-CULTURAL PERSPECTIVES: A QUEST FOR CONSENSUS 191, 196–197 (An-Na'im, ed., 1992) (based upon United States and Canadian census data in WALDMAN, ATLAS OF THE NORTH AMERICAN INDIAN 200–201 (1985)).

17. Michael H. Guilfoyle, Indians and Criminal Justice Administration: The Failure of the Criminal Justice System for the American Indian (1988) (unpublished M.A. thesis, University of Arizona); NATIONAL MINORITY ADVISORY COUNCIL ON CRIMINAL JUSTICE, THE INEQUALITY OF JUSTICE: A REPORT ON CRIME AND THE ADMINISTRATION OF JUSTICE IN THE MINORITY COMMUNITY 123–64 (1982).

18. S. REP. No. 168, 102 Cong., 1st Sess. 58–59 (1991).

19. Co-author James W. Zion has worked with tribal courts as a practitioner or staffer for 17 years. This statement is based upon numerous discussions with tribal court judges throughout the United States.

20. Feminists argue that male domination, which includes paternalism, is a product of patriarchal institutions. For an Indian feminist's views, see generally P. ALLEN, THE SACRED HOOP: RECOVERING THE FEMININE IN AMERICAN INDIAN TRADITIONS (1986); MARILYN FRENCH, BEYOND POWER: ON WOMEN, MEN AND MORALS (1985).

21. The co-author, James W. Zion, was present at the meeting and found this consensus.

22. A study of rape and Navajo tradition was unable to locate sources which clearly defined early Navajo rape customs and concluded that rape was relatively absent from early Navajo society. JAMES W. ZION & MARY WHITE, THE USE OF NAVAJO CUSTOM IN DEALING WITH RAPE (1986). Similarly, the available literature seems to indicate that domestic violence and child abuse were known but were an aberration.

23. Treaty with the Navajo Indians, June 1, 1868, U.S.-Navajo, art. IV, 15 Stat. 667, 668.

24. *Id.,* art. V.

25. NAVAJO TRIB. CODE tit. 7, ss 401–97 (1944). The codified marriage procedure prohibited traditional divorce and caused hardship to surviving spouses. *See* Matter of Slim, 3 NAVAJO RPTR. 218 (D. Crownpoint, 1982). The availability of a swift, simple, and inexpensive divorce for domestic violence victims is a domestic violence issue. Such issue may be addressed through the Rules of the Navajo Peacemaker Court, which permit a peacemaker to recommend entry of a divorce decree to the Family Court.

26. DELOS S. OTIS, THE DAWES ACT AND THE ALLOTMENT OF INDIAN LANDS 6–7 (Francis P. Prucha ed., 1973).

27. The allotment of lands to male heads of household, along with antiquated American rules of intestate succession, is an Indian women's issue. KLUCKHOHN & LEIGHTON, *supra* note 39 at 106. When the agent to the Navajos allotted lands, Navajo women sent their men to the agency office to claim the allotments—under the women's war names! *See generally* ROBERT W. YOUNG & WILLIAM MORGAN, THE NAVAHO LANGUAGE 811 (1980) (discussing the significance of feminine war names). One of the theories behind the Dawes General Allotment Act was that individual land ownership would "restore" manhood to Indian men. Sarah Deutsch, *Coming Together, Coming Apart—Women's History and the West,* 41(2) MONT: MAG. W. HIST. 58, 60 (1991). Sitting Bull pleaded with an administrator of the Act to "take pity on my women. . . . The young men can be like the white men, can till the soil, supply the food and clothing. They will take the work out of the hands of women. And the women . . . will be stripped of all which gave them power." *Id.* at 59–60. The administrator, a white woman, ignored the warning. *Id.* The allotment system "was intended to transform Indians who lived under varied kin systems into male-headed, monogamous nuclear fam-

ilies," either ignoring or attacking Indian concepts of family. Scharff, *Gender and Western History: Is Anybody Home on the Range?* 41(3) MONT: MAG. W. HIST. 62, 62–65 (1991).

28. MARY SHEPARDSON, NAVAJO WAYS IN GOVERNMENT: A STUDY IN POLITICAL PROCESS 47–48 (Am. Anthropological Ass'n, 1963). Navajo women also took part in the selection of their leaders, long before American women had the right to vote (see Shepardson, 1963:47).

29. Although the United States had the first woman elected to a national parliamentary body (Jeannette Rankin of Montana), the fact is that today women serve in Congress in lower proportions than the parliamentary bodies of most European nations. *Acceptance and Dedication of the Statute of Jeannette Rankin: Proceedings in the Rotunda Under States Capitol,* S. Doc. No. 32, 99th Cong., 2d Sess. 17 (1985). Further, income disparities among American men and women are notorious, and domestic violence is a longstanding tradition.

30. When the question of gender relations among Navajos arises, the "River of Separation" scripture is often cited. *See,* BERARD HAILE, WOMEN VERSUS MEN: A CONFLICT OF NAVAJO EMERGENCE (1981). Navajo men often cite the separation of men and women over adultery in a prior world as evidence of the superiority of men. However, in this world, Changing Woman demanded equal treatment because of her equality and the need for solidarity and harmony in the universe. *See* Zion, 1985, at 217 n.57.

31. SPENCER, 1977. Jealousy continues to be a major source of violence between the sexes. A 1969 study of Navajo homicide shows that married male Navajos between the ages of thirty-five and thirty-nine years are the largest group of killers, their spouses are the most likely victims, and the most prevalent motive is family quarrels and jealousy (thus making Navajo homicide a "family affair"). Jerrold E. Levy, et al., *Navajo Criminal Homicide,* 25 Sw. L. J. ANTHROPOLOGY 124, 124, 135, 138 (1969).

32. Clyde Kluckhohn, *Navaho Morals, in* CULTURE AND BEHAVIOR 168, 172 (Richard Kluckhohn ed., 1962). A "pollen bag" is a small bag used to carry corn pollen, which is used for prayer.

33. Bernadette D. Sewell, Note, *History of Abuse: Societal, Judicial, and Legislative Responses to the Problem of Wife Beating,* 23 SUFFOLK U. L. REV. 983, 986 n.31, 988 n.39 (1989) (punishment of a wife should be with a rod no thicker than the husband's thumb).

34. Sandra L. Ryder & Sheryl A. Kuzmenka, *Legal Rape: The Marital Rape Exemption,* 24 J. MARSHALL L. REV. 393, 394–95 (1991). It appears that the marital rape exception in the Navajo Nation criminal code came from the Illinois Penal Code. England, where the rule originated, did not abolish it until the Fall of 1991. *Regina v. R.,* 3 W.L.R. 767 (H.L. 1991). Australia has rejected the rule as well. Lea Armstrong, *Farewell to the Fiction of Implied Consent,* 17 ALTERNATIVE L. J. 91, 91 (1992) (discussing *R. v. L.,* 103 A.L.R. 577 (Austl. 1992)).

35. The role of the peacemaker was incorporated into the Navajo Nation Code of Judicial Conduct. *See* Tso, *Moral Principles, Traditions, and Fairness In The Navajo Nation Code of Judicial Conduct,* 76(1) JUDICATURE (1992).

36. The Navajo Nation Code of Judicial Conduct allows peacemakers who are related to parties to preside, without objection by a party. CODE OF JUDICIAL CONDUCT OF THE JUDICIAL BRANCH OF THE NAVAJO NATION (1991).

37. The Courts of the Navajo Nation have a Peacemaker Court project that uses the name for traditional Navajo peacemaking—*Hozhooji Naat'aanii.* The project is exploring traditional Navajo legal procedures, including the roles of the traditional *naat'aanii* and modern peacemaker. A videotape developed by the project (also called "*Hozhooji Naat'aanii*") shows the "interventionalist" and guiding roles of both.

38. The Navajo Nation Supreme Court discussed the Navajo common-law value of traditional representation by family and clan members in Boos v. Yazzie, No. A-CV–35–90, slip op. at 7 (Sept. 24, 1990) and Navajo Nation v. MacDonald, Sr., No. A-CR–09–90, slip op. at 9 (Dec. 30, 1991).

39. The videotape developed by the Peacemaker Court project outlines the traditional role of the Navajo *naat'aanii*-peacemaker. *See* Underhill (1956). The Peacemaker Project of the Navajo courts (*Hozhooji Naat'aanii*) is in the process of developing written explanations of the traditional process.

40. A chapter is a unit of local Navajo Nation government which is much like the New England town meeting form. D. WILKINS, DINE BIBBEEHAZ'AANII: A HANDBOOK OF NAVAJO GOVERNMENT 66 (1987). There are now 110 chapters in the Navajo Nation, and the devolution of power and authority to them is a hot contemporary issue.

PART FOUR

*Police*

# 14

*Law and Order*

# THE ONEIDA TRIBAL POLICE

## Politics and Law Enforcement

BY EDWARD C. BYRNE

*In the middle of the 19th Century, over half of the members of one of the six tribes of the Iroquois Confederation, the Oneida Nation, left their ancestral homelands in upstate New York on a journey that would take them to woodlands west of Fort Howard, a military outpost in what is now the city of Green Bay, WI.*

*Led by an Episcopal priest, the Oneida settled on land that had belonged to the Menominee Tribe. Their rectangular reservation, set at a 30-degree angle from true north, now includes the western edge of the city of Green Bay and two civil townships which straddle a county line. Oneida is in Outagamie County, and adjoining it to the east is Hobart in Brown County.*

*Five miles to the west, in Oneida, is a one-story building, surrounded by trees, that is the headquarters of the Oneida Tribal Police.*

Law and Order, "The Oneida Tribal Police: Politics and Law Enforcement," Edward C. Byrne, February, 1993:59–63. Used by permission.

"When we first started, in 1985, we didn't have any radios, and no cars," Jim Danforth recalled. Danforth, an Oneida tribal member and an officer of the Outagamie County Sheriff's Department, was hired to be the director of what was initially called the Oneida Public Safety Department.

The creation and growth of the Oneida Tribal Police, which now has 20 sworn officers, corresponded to the economic development of the tribe. Under long-time tribal chairman Purcell Powless and his successor Rick Hill, the tribe turned its reservation from a sleepy rural area with overwhelming unemployment to a vital business community.

Profits from tribal bingo, a casino authorized under the federal Indian Gaming Act, and a gaming compact with the State of Wisconsin have been pumped back into the tribal community and into education and jobs for tribal members.

There's the Oneida Radisson Inn, a hotel and convention center, tribal gas stations and convenience stores, a tribal grade school, library and community center, a tribal environmental technology corporation, a flourishing printing business, the tribal museum, a health care center and nursing home. On the horizon are plans for a tribal high school and a new $30-million casino.

Thousands of young Oneida men and women are working and drawing paychecks instead of receiving welfare checks. The tribe is even hiring non-Indians for some positions now. It is a success story with new chapters being written regularly.

In the 1970s, tribal membership voted down a proposal to create a tribal police force and tribal court system, but the success of the tribe's bingo hall saw the creation of a security force. "The tribe needed more services from law enforcement and the counties were not able to provide the level of response that we were asking for," Danforth said. "At that point the tribe decided to go ahead with our own law enforcement agency."

Danforth had been a deputy on the Outagamie County Sheriff's Department for 11 years and the decision to leave it and head up the tribal public safety department was a tough call. But it was an opportunity he decided not to pass up.

"When Jimmy was a patrol officer on the road for Outagamie he had a good reputation and good credibility, as well as good character," Brown County Sheriff Leon Pieschek said. Danforth

was also an excellent athlete, well liked by Indians and non-Indians alike.

"It was a super choice," Pieschek said of the tribe's decision to put Danforth in charge of developing their police agency.

What Danforth accepted was a job as chief of a non-existent law enforcement agency. "There were no vehicles and no communications," he said. Security officers at the bingo hall became the first tribal officers.

"We started out by buying a couple of used police vehicles. We bought also portable radios that enabled us to communicate within the department, but not with other agencies," Danforth recalled.

The tribal police force got no encouragement from either Brown or Outagamie counties. Both counties refused to allow tribal officers on their radio frequencies and refused to have any radio communication with tribal officers. The counties did not recognize that the Oneida officers had any police powers, and there were even threats to arrest tribal officers if they used their red-and-blue emergency lights or sirens.

"Ashwaubenon was our savior at the beginning of our department," Danforth said. "Chief John Konopacki said they were willing to provide us a service of 24-hour radio communication." Ashwaubenon had only recently established its own department.

The dispatch agreement gave tribal officers access to motor vehicle registrations, drivers' records, NCIC and Wisconsin CID files. The relationship with Ashwaubenon continued to grow. When the village had a major homicide, tribal officers secured the scene and assisted in the investigation.

The cool relationship between the two sheriff's departments and the tribal police was part of a larger picture. The tribal government, empowered by strong leadership and successful economic development, made it clear that they intended to exercise their sovereignty over the reservation, despite the fact that the majority of the land had been sold off over the years and was now owned by non-Indians.

The two counties, the town governments of Oneida and Hobart, and Green Bay formed a commission to challenge the jurisdiction of the Oneida Tribe over the lands included within the boundaries of the reservation as it had been established in the 19th century. Recognition of tribal police authority was seen by the counties as admission of the tribal jurisdiction they were challenging in a federal court.

"They (county officials) didn't want their sheriffs to enter into agreements with tribal police with the suit sitting in court," Danforth explained.

Town officials were equally worried. "They were wondering what the jurisdictional boundaries of tribal police authority were going to be," Outagamie County Sheriff Brad Gehring said. (Elected sheriff in 1990, he was the department's juvenile officer at the time of the lawsuit.)

The issue was settled when the court ruled that the Oneida did, in fact, have jurisdiction over the lands within the original reservation boundaries, saying that "jurisdiction" is not dependent upon ownership of the land itself. In essence, the court ruled that the tribe, like the counties and local municipalities, enjoyed concurrent jurisdiction within the reservation boundaries.

With that ruling, Brown County Sheriff Leon Pieschek agreed to have his communications center dispatch Oneida tribal officers. Recognizing the concept of concurrent jurisdiction, Pieschek and the tribe worked out a system of "dual dispatch", where both tribal police and county officers would respond to calls for service in Hobart. Pieschek's department also dispatched tribal officers to calls within the Oneida in Outagamie County.

"Sheriff Pieschek felt he'd had enough political interference in law enforcement," Danforth said. "He felt he needed to know what our officers, as well as his, were doing out there."

Later, the Outagamie County Sheriff's Department agreed to dispatch tribal police as well. Unlike Brown County, Outagamie sends tribal officers to calls within Oneida without also dispatching a county officer.

"Depending on the seriousness of the call, we dispatch the Oneida police and they handle it completely," Sheriff Gehring said. "If they need assistance, our deputy assigned to patrol that area of the county will respond as a backup."

A key step in the growing professional relationship between the tribal police and other law enforcement agencies came about when Brown County formed a multijurisdictional group. This undercover drug unit was overseen by a board of directors that included Danforth and the other chief officers of every law enforcement agency in the county.

"The MJG Unit was on shaky ground at first, and the Oneida Tribe offered an officer to work with the unit at no cost to the taxpayers of Brown County," Pieschek said. Pieschek not only accepted the officer, he also deputized him, an act that angered a number of politicians.

"Having a tribal officer on the MJG Unit, I felt, would be beneficial. I knew he'd get in where non-Indian personnel were not able to," Danforth explained. The tribal officer was assigned directly to the MJG Unit and made a number of key arrests of drug dealers in the tribe's housing project in West Green Bay.

Tribal police officers were also trained as emergency medical service first responders, ready to stabilize trauma patients until rescue squad personnel reached them. That turned out to be a blessing for Sheriff Pieschek, who owns a farm on the Oneida Reservation. "I was cutting wood with a chain saw when the chain came off and cut through my chest, face and chin," Pieschek said. His wife called 911 and within two minutes a tribal officer was giving him first aid. "I'll never forget that. I owe some people out there a lot."

Pieschek's injuries were serious, but he recovered. The incident affected him in another way. "Maybe at one time I was a little prejudiced," Pieschek admitted. "When I moved out there, I became very impressed with the leadership of the tribe, and with the Indian neighbors I had—they are very good people."

After Sheriff Gehring took office in 1991, he moved quickly to deputize Oneida tribal officers living in Outagamie County. Because state law requires a deputy to live in the county

of deputization, Gehring was able to deputize only the Oneida officers living in Outagamie County.

Earlier this year, Pieschek deputized the tribal officers living in Brown County. Pieschek said, "It took a while. It did take a lot of guts to do that, and I'm glad I did it. It's been a great thing for citizens in that part of the county."

The Oneida Tribal Police force has grown to 20 officers: Chief Danforth, Assistant Chief Mark Ninham, a sergeant and 17 patrolmen. All are members of the Oneida Tribe, but Danforth looks forward to the day when that will change, too.

"Hopefully, before I retire, I'll see people besides our own on the department," Danforth said. "It will show the community in the townships of Oneida and Hobart that we're not only utilizing tribal members, but also other people who can work within this department."

Whatever the future holds, there's a consensus among local law enforcement officials that the Oneida police are making a positive impact in the jurisdictions they share with the two sheriff's departments. Gehring is sad that it took so long to overcome political roadblocks and get to this point.

"Law enforcement has to be driven by law enforcement officials," he said. "It cannot be a politically-motivated process.

"Had the Oneida Tribal Police department been allowed to grow, with their officers deputized," Gehring continued, "that area would have seen a drop in the number of calls for service, like they're now experiencing, some time ago."

# 15
## TAKING CONTROL

### Native Self-Government and Native Policing

DOUGLAS M. SKOOG

The overrepresentation of North American[1] Natives in the criminal justice system is well documented. In both the United States and Canada, regions with relatively large numbers of Native American residents send a surprisingly large number of those residents to jail. In Canada Native peoples are the largest single minority group being processed through the criminal justice system. In fact, their incarceration rate is about twelve times that of non-Natives. In the western and northern areas of the country, they frequently constitute well over half of the inmate population (Silverman and Nielsen, 1992; Brantingham, Mu, and Verma, 1995).

In the United States the problem is similar. The work of Marenin (1992:341) suggests that crime rates in largely Native villages in Alaska are about double those of urban rates. Silverman (Chapter 10 in this volume) reports that Native arrest rates are higher than those of Whites—especially in the case of alcohol-related crimes. In general, states with relatively large Native populations have disproportionate numbers of Natives incarcerated (Jayewardene, 1979/1980).

Given this demonstrable relationship between being Native and being in contact with the criminal justice system, attention has been focused on the extent to which certain elements of the justice system contribute to Native overrepresentation. The role of the police is of particular significance. Native leaders feel much the same way as do many African Americans with respect to policing: They see it as discriminatory and lacking in cultural awareness.

Aboriginal people view the police as representatives of a culture which is vastly different from their own. Their encounters with the police are framed by a history of

Written for this volume and used by permission of the author.

cultural oppression and economic domination, during which the use of Aboriginal languages, governments, laws and customs was punished by laws developed by the same legal structures police now represent. (Hamilton and Sinclair, 1991:596)

With that background, North American Native leaders have frequently called for greater control over the policing of their people both on and off Native lands. In both the United States and Canada, some measure of self-determination has been granted, but control of many of the most important elements of the policing process has remained tightly held by non-Native hands.


## NATIVE SELF-GOVERNMENT

At the very center of the issue is the determination of Native peoples to achieve self-governance. Many politically aware Native leaders have argued that their people should be seen as legally autonomous. While many non-Natives may have difficulty with this concept, there is a strong legal-historical argument that can be made for "nation" status for Native groups. In fact, in the period following the American Revolutionary War, the political establishment did regard tribes "as sovereign nations in charge of their own internal tribal affairs" (Peak, 1989:396). This policy was changed by the middle of the nineteenth century for a variety of reasons, not the least of which was a desire to take lands occupied by various tribes. A relationship mixing occasional paternalism and frequent neglect was substituted.

In Canada the situation was fundamentally different. Governments did not historically regard Native groups as sovereign states. From the outset of colonization, a policy of interdependence was developed between Natives and Europeans. This was based almost entirely on the fur trade. The European traders needed furs, and Native people were, of course, experienced trappers. With the collapse of the fur trade beginning in the late 1850s, this was to change. In 1876 the Indian Act was passed and "responsibility" for Natives was given over to the federal government. For the most part, the government provided only minimal services to Native groups until the rise of the welfare state. By the 1950s the government of Canada had adopted a policy of social welfare–oriented paternalism with respect to Natives. Only in recent years has the notion of "nationhood" entered the debate in Canada. It is a theme that has a longer history in the United States than in Canada.

A constituent element of "nationhood" would be the creation of a Native-controlled criminal justice system. In such a system, all segments of the criminal justice system would fall under local control. This, ideally, would include making laws, enforcing laws, dispensing justice, and dealing with wrongdoers. Some U.S. tribes have already experienced considerable autonomy in governance, including the delivery of criminal justice, but none have, as yet, achieved total control. Canadian Native groups have not yet achieved such autonomy, but there is considerable pressure to move in this direction. Thus on both sides of the border,

Native groups can be said to be placing a considerable amount of faith in the continued development of autonomous policing as a means of confirming their belief in nationhood and, perhaps more important, as a means of addressing what they perceive to be an unjust system of justice.

In order to understand the pressure that Natives are exerting to acquire self-direction in policing, one must examine the larger political question. Any community will typically gain a variety of advantages (economic, social, and psychological) if they are able to control their own affairs. In both the United States and Canada, there exists a desire to pursue "self-government." In the case of Canada, the stage has been set by efforts by the government of Canada to rewrite the Canadian Constitution. Native leaders have tried to influence this process and gain some measure of independence. As Sanders (1985:iii) observes, "The constitutional reform process, as it relates to Aboriginal peoples, has come to focus on one major agenda item—Aboriginal self government." At the same time, U.S. congressional proposals that promise to "return government to the people" have provided the opportunity for local constituencies to seek greater control of the law enforcement process. North American Natives are well aware that the 1990s may provide the best shot they will ever have at gaining a larger measure of control over their own affairs.

## CONTROL OF CRIMINAL JUSTICE

Central to any demand for self-government is a demand that communities exercise considerable control over the administration of justice. To some extent, the administration and delivery of justice are seen as representative of the whole idea of "government":

> In many respects the relationship between the police and the Aboriginal community both reflects and shapes Aboriginal concerns about their relationship with government more generally. The police are the first and most frequent contact that Aboriginal people have with the justice system and as such often are seen to represent that system. (Canada, Department of Justice, 1991:33)

The powerful and direct result of this is that issues related to the delivery of justice appear to the Native community as being synonymous with the question of self-government. Thus while the intention is not to denigrate the role of land claims, taxation, and other issues, Natives can rightly be expected to see autonomous policing as central to the entire self-governance issue.

Skolnick (1966:230) points out that "police tend to polarize people into two groups—'respectable' people and 'criminals' who, in their eyes, may include otherwise respectable citizens not conforming to policemen's portrait of respectability." Stereotypes are assigned not only on the basis of legal designations but on the basis of social designations as well. In the officer's effort to carry out what is perceived to be his or her occupational role, Natives may be subjected to greater scrutiny. If a set of beliefs that support the polarization of citizens becomes routinized, it becomes a self-fulfilling prophesy. Evidence of this is found in Jayewardene's (1971) study of violence among the Inuit. Police (correctly) noted that alcohol was frequently a precursor to violence. Because of a conceptual framework that linked Inuit violence to alcohol use, the police frequently intervened when Inuit drank. This swelled the crime statistics with Inuit cases and criminalized the indigenous population. In fact, virtually every violent crime case that came before the courts involved alcohol, whether the accused was Native or White. It was, however, only Inuit drinking that was seen as not respectable.

While some may argue that Native persons do commit more offenses than others, this has no effect on Native people's *perception* that they are singled out for the coercive attention of the police. Studies by Skoog, Roberts, and Boldt (1980) and Skoog and Barker (1989) show that Natives have decidedly uncharitable attitudes toward the police and fault the police for at least some proportion of their overrepresentation in the criminal justice system. This leads, quite naturally, to a belief that autonomous police forces would be more sensitive and hence would serve the needs of Native people more adequately. This must be seen as a key issue in the drive toward autonomous policing.

A somewhat related motivating force in the push for local control involves traditional Native American culture. In recent years, arguments have been forcefully made that the entire body of European-based law and law enforcement is antithetical to Native cultural traditions. Traditional Native culture stresses a variety of factors that are not central to the European adversarial model. Native American justice, unlike the oppositional model that is found in American courts, is based on conciliation and conflict resolution. This discrepancy often leads to inappropriate and insensitive treatment by police officers.

Both the Native emphasis on conflict resolution and on social control are seen as relevant to policing. First, "peacekeeping" is viewed as the appropriate means of conflict resolution, as opposed to the European "adversarial stance" (Depew, 1986). Peacekeeping stresses conflict resolution through informal means and reliance on community resources, such as the Council of Elders and communal reasoning. The solutions that are sought give primacy to community needs and do not stress the "winner-loser" model found in the larger society. Dumont (1990:32) has argued that the purpose of a justice system in traditional society is to restore harmony within the community and to reconcile the accused with their own conscience and the wronged party. As the Report of the Aboriginal Justice Inquiry of Manitoba states, "Peace and harmony, the principal goals to which traditional Aboriginal concepts of justice were geared, have not been accommodated easily by an adversarial and adjudicative system" (Hamilton and Sinclair, 1991:252). Writers who have examined Native culture argue that "policing" as the larger society uses the term may be counterproductive in producing truly just solutions to problems.

Second, traditional culture is seen as a social system that relies on reciprocal constraints that devolve from social relationships to produce social control. The role of the police officer is diminished in such a setting, as individuals are controlled by forces that reflect wider community interests. The notion here (Depew, 1986:94; Griffiths and Yerbury, 1984:155) is that the community's response to crime will reflect sources of action that are "rooted in cultural tradition and custom [and] take precedence over those of a formal, centralized police agency" (Depew, 1986:94). This is a system of social control that relies on the individual's sense of community standards and the ability to control oneself out of conscience rather than on external control by force. The police, as rule enforcers, are seen as having only limited value as agents of social control.

The Manitoba Aboriginal Justice Inquiry sums the cultural theme up this way:

> For Aboriginal people the essential problem is that the Canadian system of justice is an imposed and foreign system. In order for a society to accept a justice system as part of its life and its community, it must see the system and experience it as being a positive influence working for that society. Aboriginal people do not. (Hamilton and Sinclair, 1991:252)

As the Task force on Indian Policing (1990:2) points out, there is reason to believe that "access to culturally sensitive policing on reserves may help to ameliorate the current situation of disproportionate Indian representation in the criminal justice system."

We can then see the juxtaposition of three central themes that provide the motivating force for Native demands for autonomous policing: (1) Changes in government policy in the United States and Canada would bring about new arrangements between citizens and the highest level of government. (2) Concerns about inequality of treatment provide the emotional impetus. (3) An abiding belief in the uniqueness of Native culture provides the framework within which proposals are generated. To have a complete understanding of the issues, these three factors must be kept in mind.

## Contemporary Native Self-Policing

Even though this chapter is most concerned with the *future* of policing, the present situation is important. The future of Native self-policing will quite naturally be influenced by past and present arrangements and to some extent may be an extension of those arrangements.

Moves toward limited Native involvement in policing can be traced to the 1850s, when colonial administrators found that they needed local expertise in order to carry out their tasks. Little recognition was accorded these early Native civil servants, and as Whites gradually learned the "lay of the land," they became expendable. Boldt and Long (1985) argue that federal governments have only recently demonstrated any abiding interest in factoring Native participation into the policing equation. The governments' interest may have been sparked by a number of factors, but certainly much of the motivation was purely practical. It was thought that Native police officers would have the capacity to defuse conflicts between the police and Natives. The Native officer would be seen by his community as less threatening and more sensitive to their concerns. The anticipated result was that the government's task of policing would be made easier and some benefits would accrue to the Native population as well (Depew, 1986:27–28). This model is one that sees Native involvement in policing as being a part of a larger non-Native-controlled police force.

This model has found its fullest expression in the creation of "Indian Constables" in both the United States and Canada. Examples can be found in the 1958 creation of the Navajo Police Department in the U.S. Southwest and the 1973 initiative entitled "Option 3(b)" in Canada. In both instances residents are provided training and act as peace officers. In neither instance were they given full police powers, however. As a general rule, the enabling legislation limited the scope of their responsibilities. In Canada, for example, the directive (Circular 55) allowed constables "to supplement locally the senior police forces but not to supplant them." In the United States the agreement with the Navajo Nation gave jurisdiction over the most serious offenses to the Federal Bureau of Investigation (FBI). These programs, and a host of similar ones, evolved over the years, and in some cases Natives were eventually given full peace officer status. To some extent these programs are not functionally distinguishable from attempts by police departments everywhere to recruit minority group officers. All have as their motive increased minority presence, although none include minority control. For example, many departments in urban Canada have very recently recruited Native members. Such methods of increasing Native representation in policing have received only conditional support from Native leaders (Hamilton and Sinclair, 1991:608–627). The issue is one of control over crucial aspects of the decision-making process. There is little doubt that the ideal situation from the perspective of the Native community is one in which they are part of the most senior levels of decisionmaking. As Havemann et al. (1984:37) note: "Most studies done by or for Indigenous organizations approve of autonomous policing while those done by or for government agencies appear to prefer policing by special constables." Based on recent research utilizing key informants and a review of current public statements by Native leaders, it must be argued that the direction the policing community must anticipate is one that will stress autonomy and local control (Skoog and Barker, 1989).

The approach to Native policing that comes closest to the one advocated by Native leaders is found in the handful of more or less autonomous police programs that have been established in relatively recent times. In general these programs involve local control exercised either by the Band or Tribal Council or a Police Commission composed of Native members and some law enforcement professionals from various levels of government. There are a few of these programs in existence in Canada. Prominent among these are the Dakota Ojibway

Tribal Council Police, the Kahnawake Peace-Keeping Force, the Amerindian Police Program, the Blood Tribal Police, and the Louis Bull Police Program (Pete, 1982; Depew, 1986). In some instances these forces are reduced to the enforcement of laws dealing with less serious crimes. This reduction in the scope of their authority comes about in two ways: First, some are limited by statute from enjoying full peace officer status. For example, the Dakota Ojibway Tribal Council Police have a "written protocol under which Native constables handle less serious offenses, while major Criminal Code violations are reported to the Royal Canadian Mounted Police" (Hamilton and Sinclair, 1991:615). Second, some tribe-managed forces may have full peace officer status but may in actual practice defer to senior forces in the event of a serious crime.

In the United States Native police agencies are more common; however, for the most part, these programs are not autonomous in the truest sense of the word. For example, Native criminal justice agencies in the United States have been historically allowed to deal with relatively minor crimes but have not had authority over sixteen more-serious offenses delineated in the Major Crimes Act (Pommersheim, 1995). This restriction may have been introduced because of a lack of facilities or because of inadequate training or might even have been imposed by pressures from the outside. Peak (1989:405) has argued that "Indian police grapple with jurisdictional confusion, high rates of criminality and problems involving interagency cooperation."

While governments might argue that they are committed to Native control of policing, there are many aspects of the arrangements yet to be worked out. Increased funding alone may not satisfy the demand for self-policing if the funds are tied to models of policing that will not give complete autonomy to communities. Any external control over policing may be seen to give the *appearance* of second-class status in the eyes of some Native leaders. What the community wants is "full control of regional police forces and regional police commissions" (Sinclair and Hamilton, 1991:616). It must be stated categorically that the long-range goal is complete local control of what can be termed "culturally relevant police forces."

Established governments can be expected to resist autonomous police forces. Indeed, the province of Manitoba's justice minister has come under heavy fire from Native leaders for not moving toward local control of policing (*Winnipeg Free Press,* 1992:16). While there may be political *motives* for not creating Native forces, much of the *actual* debate may revolve around the effectiveness of autonomous forces now or in the future. A review of the literature on existing autonomous forces reveals several regularities. First, concern is frequently voiced that the forces need greater levels of professional development which are typically seen to be held back because of inadequate training and substandard resources (Amerindian Police Council, 1979; Depew, 1986; Duncan, 1983; Hamilton and Sinclair, 1991). Tribal police have been described by Harring (1982:102) as having "a singularly bad reputation as being among the worst police forces in America, plagued by nepotism, poor training, high job turnover and low pay." There is little doubt that small regional forces may suffer from relatively low levels of professionalization, but this is not a problem that is unique to tribal forces: Small-town police departments across Canada and the United States face the same problem.

A second criticism is frequently leveled at existing forces of potential political interference. It is argued that "Native politics" may affect the equitable administration of justice. There is no doubt that political favoritism based on family and friendships plays a role in the administration of justice, but to argue that this is an "Indian problem" seems naive. This is a problem faced by all ethnic groups in jurisdictions large and small. It seems unlikely that anyone would ever argue that White people should not have self-governance because they favor their relatives. Favoritism is more obvious in rural areas and thus seems more acute, but it is not unique to Native communities. The National Evaluation of the Social Policy Research Associates/The Evaluation Group (1983) sees external checks as a favorable means of dealing with local political interference. Native leaders can be expected to resist non-Native controls over local policing, as local control of law enforcement is seen as a bulwark against the encroachment of centralized state power.

## ISSUES OF NATIVE POLICING IN THE FUTURE

At this point, we can address the important question of what form Native-controlled policing might take in the last decade of the century. Three models can be identified: (1) the crime control model, (2) the community policing model, and (3) the political sovereignty model. These are conceptually distinct, but in reality there may be some overlap between certain of their features. They are nonetheless based on different motives and priorities, and each model will have a dramatically different impact on the community in which it operates. The models will also affect how Native communities are related to the larger non-Native society.

### The Crime Control Model

Under this model, the style of policing and the goals of policing are not different from those present in the larger society. Maintenance of public order is accorded primacy, and the absolute power of law is used as a means to ensure the safety of the general public. In such a system police departments are hierarchically structured. This is a familiar model, as most contemporary North American police departments adhere to this style. For the most part there is minimal input from citizens with respect to police priorities, policies, and procedures (Trojanowicz and Carter, 1988:4).

Should such a model of policing be adopted by a Native community, it would appear to be essentially indistinguishable from any small-town police department. Administrative control would be in the hands of local political leaders, who may or may not reflect the grassroots concerns of the citizenry. Crime detection, prosecution, and maintenance of order would be stressed. Hiring into a crime control department would be under the direction of local political leaders (tribal governments or chiefs) and, interestingly, employees would not necessarily be of Native descent or even local residents; instead, emphasis would be placed on hiring well-trained officers capable of carrying out the social control function of policing in a professional manner.

It would be an error to assume that the crime control model of policing has no relevance to autonomous programs. There are, in fact, certain pressures at work that will serve to promote this model. The first is citizen fear of crime. Native people have very high rates of victimization. In Canada they are more frequently the victims of serious crimes than are members of any other single group. In the United States high rates of victimization have been similarly reported (Jaye-wardene, 1979/1980). Their high rates of victimization make them especially sensitive to crime control issues. They, like victims everywhere, want the police to make life as safe as possible. Victims of crimes are among those most likely to demand that the absolute power of law be invoked to control criminals. The second source of pressure for Natives to adopt this "White model" may well come from various levels of government, which see alternative models as cumbersome and difficult to administer. Most of our current laws are written in a fashion that reflects crime control concerns. Courts, jails, and aftercare services also reflect these concerns. To allow Natives a justice delivery system that is dramatically different from the one used in the larger society is likely to be seen as problematic. Inasmuch as senior levels of government control funding, they will most certainly try to impose their will. As Griffiths and Yerbury point out,

> While the traditional forms of social control that existed in Native communities are an important consideration, it should not necessarily be assumed that policing schemes should be premised on traditional structures. The report of the Native Counselling Services of Alberta cautions that . . . "purely traditional methods of policing may not be appropriate for Indians living in a changed cultural environment and political system . . . autonomy in policing may not imply traditional Indian policing." (1984:156)

## The Community Policing Model

"Community policing" has been discussed at length in several recent works, including Trojanowicz and Bucqueroux, 1990, and Goldstein, 1987, for the United States and Mitzak, 1991, and Loree, 1985, for Canada. The concept is currently enjoying popularity in mainstream policing literature. With respect to Native thought on the matter, it is significant that the Manitoba Aboriginal Justice Inquiry calls for the adoption of "a community policing approach, particularly in Native communities" (Hamilton and Sinclair, 1991:600). Community policing is generally seen to involve decentralized control and community involvement. "At the core of community policing is the concept of police/community partnership" (Ontario, Ministry of the Solicitor-General, 1991:5). The role of the police in this model moves away from law enforcement and crime control and toward *proactive* crime reduction through techniques of community intervention. This stands in opposition to the typical model in which officers are *reactive* to calls for service. Under a community-based model, the police are asked to develop problem-solving strategies that address the underlying causes of crime (Normandeau and Leighton, 1990).

The community-based model seems to be applicable to Aboriginal communities for a variety of reasons: It has the capacity to be far more culturally sensitive than the crime control model because of its focus on local control and the emphasis on conflict resolution. Both of these factors have been specifically listed by Native leaders as goals for policing. The community policing model might well have some measure of popularity among government leaders in that many non-Native police forces have already initiated trial community policing projects (Mitzak, 1991).

To many parties, the community policing model seems like the ideal goal. Canada's Law Reform Commission (1991:45) comments that "although community based policing is not a complete solution for Aboriginal communities, it is a step in the right direction." The combination of Native and governmental support gives the community policing model a genuine advantage.

Does this mean that the community policing model is clearly the wave of the future? Not necessarily, for there is a significant stumbling block that should be addressed. It involves what can be termed an inherent tension between enacted legal codes and *true* self-control in the delivery of police services. Legal codes, as they are presently constructed, are based on an adversarial system that many Native leaders argue are foreign to them. "The concepts of adversarialism, accusation, confrontation, guilt, argument, criticism, and retribution are alien to the Aboriginal value system" (Hamilton and Sinclair, 1991:37). If community policing were to be established in a Native community, it could be accused of merely enforcing the same old (White) laws in a new way. Although there may be some disagreement in the Native community about this issue, the argument cannot be swept under the carpet. Some will see community policing as a system tied too closely to the establishment and hence reject it. It is, after all, a model that suggests that police forces must work within the framework of existing laws, which are adversarial. Some leaders feel that the entire body of criminal law is antithetical to their traditional way of life and hence should be changed in order to meet their needs. This leads us to the third and final model of autonomous policing.

## The Political Sovereignty Model

This model may be regarded as the most radical of the three. In this model it is assumed that North American Natives would be accorded a considerable degree of control over their own affairs. They would be granted some kind of sovereign nation status and might well control matters ranging from economic development to education. Once Native Americans have won this far-reaching autonomy, it is anticipated that an entirely unique justice system could be created. It would be a system based on a radical reconceptualization of the law as an instrument of social control.

Recognition of this is found in the Law Reform Commission's report on Aboriginal Peoples and Criminal Justice. They state that "the most appropriate response to social problems on a reserve, and the response most in keeping with traditional Aboriginal justice systems, may not be a body operating as what we think of as a police force, but something that performs a much broader social service function—counselling, advising, conciliation and resolving disputes" (1991: 47).

Under this model, Native communities would have their own courts and might well control jails and probation and parole services. The police would form one part of an integrated criminal justice system based on Native values. In this idealized system, the European adversarial approach would be replaced with one based on the principles of peacekeeping, community control, and the autonomy of individuals. In all likelihood, the formal charging of individuals would frequently be replaced by mediation between parties. The courts might be radically different than those seen in White communities. They would be less adversarial and would stress conflict resolution and peacemaking. A wide variety of "sentencing" options would be available, and offenders would only be jailed if they were seen to pose a danger to the community. If incarceration was deemed a necessity, the "jail" might well be a community-based facility or wilderness camp where the milieu would be consistent with traditional Native values.

Some readers might regard this seemingly utopian model as impractical in light of the obvious difficulty of having two different systems of criminal justice operating side by side. There is, however, some evidence that such a criticism is unfounded. In the United States a relatively peaceful coexistence has existed between Native and non-Native systems. As Sanders (1985:vii) notes, "United States Indian law recognizes an inherent Indian right to self government, deriving from the original sovereignty of the tribes before colonization." The result has been the transformation of tribal organizations from "little more than social clubs" into governments (Sanders, 1985:2). There are currently some four hundred tribal courts and widespread development of tribal codes including, in some cases, criminal laws. These courts deal with the bulk of criminal matters. Serious crimes are, however, typically excluded, and defendants are processed by the non-Native system. Two points are relevant here: First, these courts are most often based on the European adversarial model and hence mimic the establishment system. As such, they are not truly Native in their perspective. Second, the establishment of a tribal court system represents only one link in the criminal justice chain. The other links include the elements of policing, punishment, conflict resolution, and aftercare. A fully articulated Native model would have all these elements. It can be said with some certainty that Native peoples have not been accorded control over all these elements of criminal justice. Policing, in particular, remains problematic because of a "crazy quilt" of jurisdictions that hampers effective law enforcement. For example, tribal police frequently cannot arrest non-Natives committing crimes on reservations (O'Brien, 1989:279–281).

Despite the obstacles, many Native leaders remain steadfast in their belief that a truly autonomous justice system could be developed. Such a system would be based on Native historical values and cultural traditions. As such, it would be much more than simply a White adversarial system run by Natives.

In assessing the chances that any of the three models will be successful in reducing Native overrepresentation in the criminal justice system, we should keep one point very much in mind: The latter two models are based, to a greater or lesser degree, on, the singular idea that society can address the issue of Native crime by making police forces culturally sensitive. Both the community policing model and the political sovereignty model can be seen as accepting what may be termed the "cultural solution." Central to this solution is the idea that Native cultures are unique and may be distinguished in a meaningful way from European-based U.S. and Canadian cultures. This is the model that Manitoba's Aboriginal Justice Inquiry clearly chose when making its far-reaching recommendations. Indeed, it places great emphasis on the words of Rupert Ross: "Until we realize that [Aboriginal people] are not simply 'primitive versions of us' but a people with a highly developed, formal, complex and wholly foreign set of cultural imperatives, we will continue to misinterpret their acts, misperceive their problems and then impose mistaken and potentially harmful 'remedies'" (quoted in Hamilton and Sinclair, 1991:36).

Although it is perhaps an unpopular argument to make, it should be pointed out that the cultural solution may be fatally flawed. There is no doubt whatsoever that a truly unique culture existed at the time of first European contact, but it may be that the process of cultural genocide has, to all intents and purposes, destroyed it. As Native people increasingly came into contact with Europeans, their cultural heritage was subjected to vigorous attacks from Christian missionaries and a White-dominated school system that overtly taught that traditional language and culture were worthless. Stripped of their cultural values and denied access to Elders by the residential school system that took children away from their communities, Native youngsters were left in a cultural vacuum. We also know that large numbers of Native people have left the economic poverty of the reserves and sought new lives in urban centers. This has further alienated them from their cultural heritage.

The argument can thus be made that the culture is endangered, if not dead, for many Native peoples. Frideres (1988:373) has suggested that this process has been so devastating that traditional culture, for many, may have been supplanted by a "culture of poverty": "As individuals are prevented from entering the modern economy, a cultural ethos emerges which is quite different from that expressed in the modern economy. Anthropologists have referred to this distinctive ethos as the 'culture of poverty.'" Frideres argues that many Native peoples, separated from their traditional values and not allowed full access to education and jobs in the dominant culture, are left with little to call their own. The day-to-day struggle for survival becomes the focal point of existence.

If traditional culture is no longer relevant for many Native people, then it follows that policing programs based largely on the notion that cultural sensitivity will reduce incarceration rates may be ineffective. The only solution to the "cul-

ture of poverty" is to find a way to erase the tremendous social and economic inequalities that exist between Natives and Whites. It is very doubtful that any
changes in policing would do this. It should be pointed out, however, that most
Native leaders do not believe that the culture is dead or dying, and that as a group
they remain steadfast in their commitment to the development of culturally sensitive policing. Although they acknowledge that their culture has come under fire,
many feel that there is a resurgence of interest in traditional identity. This identity
may not be "traditional" in the strictest sense of the word and can be seen as an
emerging cultural ethos. It may differ from region to region, just as traditional
culture did, but it is nonetheless "Native" in nature and distinguishable from the
dominant White culture.

A second point should be made regarding the presumption that culturally sensitive policing will reduce rates of Native involvement in the criminal justice system: There is a distinct possibility that community-controlled policing will cause
an *increase* in the number of crimes detected and the number of arrests made.
Official crime rates are powerfully influenced by the willingness of the public to
report offenses to the authorities. As community residents gain more control over
their police forces and come to have more faith in them, they will report more
crimes. For example, when Natives gained control over child-care agencies in the
province of Manitoba, the number of children in care did not go down. In fact, it
increased because of better case detection. Native caseworkers had greater access
to information through informal networks than did White caseworkers. A similar
effect will be felt as Natives gain control over policing. Native leaders argue that
the measuring stick should be the appropriateness of policing and argue that local
control would meet that standard.

The chances that one of the three models presented here will be accepted depend on a variety of factors, most of which are outside the control of the criminal
justice establishment. In the United States the current distrust of big government
and "federal cops" may bring about a move to greater local control of policing
generally. At the same time, a reluctance to fund ethnic or racial minority programs will not help the Native cause. In Canada the situation is somewhat different. Above all, the fate of Native issues is tied to the eventual form of the country's
evolving constitutional arrangement. If the "Native Assembly of First Nations"
achieves the extensive political powers it desires, one can anticipate that the political sovereignty model will naturally be promoted by Native leaders. Should the
Assembly not receive those powers, one may assume that one of the two other
models will become preeminent.

It is unlikely that the status quo will remain, however. Native desires to exercise
greater control over the institutions that affect them are simply too strong to ignore. At the same time, governments are frustrated with their inability to deal
with Native crime under current arrangements. The pressures to change are very
much at work. The task of the policing community will be to aid in the selection
of solutions that best serve the needs of the Native community.

# NOTES

1. There is some lack of consensus in North America about what terminology should be employed to describe those residents who were incorrectly labeled "Indios" by the explorer Christopher Columbus in 1492. He reportedly thought he had sailed to the Indian subcontinent and hence thought the indigenous population to be "Indian." In both the United States and Canada many leaders in that community reject the term "Indian," as it devolves from a historical mistake made by a European. Several more appropriate terms have been adopted. In the United States there is a widespread use of the terms "Native American" or "Native." The term "Native" is also widely used in Canada; however, many current Canadian leaders prefer the term "Aboriginal." In this paper I have used "Native peoples" or "Native" most frequently, although some quotes and citations require the use of the term "Aboriginal."

# 16

## POLICING THE LAST FRONTIER

OTWIN MARENIN

The development of policing is a specific historical process. The origins of policing the Native areas of Alaska can be described with some precision, in terms of
specific policies and events by which a foreign culture and system of politics and
law came to be imposed on existing Native norms, routines and lifestyles. What
are the implications of unique processes and events for theorizing about policing?

This chapter focusses on the village Public Safety Officer (VPSO) program, the
latest in a long line of programs designed to bring law and order to the Native
communities of Alaska. How well does it fit the two dominant theoretical models
(contact/social dislocation and underdevelopment/dependency) for explaining
the state of affairs in Native Alaska?

I will argue that the development of policy and the imposition of Western law
and its enforcement in villages was the result of ad-hoc and pragmatic initiatives
taken, in the absence or even in violation of formal regulations, by middle-level
bureaucrats rather than a planned result arising from some larger, long-range design and purpose (Angell, 1978). This piece-meal and adaptive policy making
process has characterized the development of policing in Alaska since 1867. The
VPSO program is the result of the actions taken by many people. A modified theory which can explain form and function—an interested action model—is
sketched. The experience of the VPSO program provides the empirical ammuni-
tion.

Edited version of Otwin Marenin, "Policing the Last Frontier: Visions of Social Order and the
Development of the Village Officer Public Safety Program in Alaska," *Policing and Society* 2:273–291.
1992. Reprinted by permission of *Policing and Society* and the author.

Research for this paper was supported by a faculty development grant from the University of Alaska
Fairbanks, and by a grant from the Fund for Research on Dispute Resolution. The author wishes to acknowledge their support. They are not, of course, responsible for the interpretation of ideas and events
argued here.

First, this chapter describes the organization and functioning of the VPSO program and its place in the long history of policing in Alaska. Then the chapter evaluates how this example of innovation fits into existing explanations of change.

## The Village Public Safety Officer (VPSO) Program

The VPSO program was established in 1980 and as of 1991 fills about 125 positions. VPSOs serve in rural, isolated ('off-road') villages, by themselves, and provide general public safety services. Cost for the program have averaged about six to seven million dollars annually. The money is allocated by the State legislature and passed through the Alaska State Trooper budget to regional Native non-profit corporations using a standard contract. The non-profits, in turn, contract with villages which receive a VPSO position. The contracts spell out mutual expectations and responsibilities. Program money also funds a few oversight Trooper positions and a VPSO coordinator's position in each non-profit. (General descriptions of the program can be found in Alaska Police Standards Council, 1982; Alaska, Department of Public Safety, 1987; Hippler, 1982; Marenin and Copus, 1991; Sellin, 1981.)

Three characteristics of the program stand out, as innovations and responses to demands expressed by Native groups and to the perceived social control needs of Native villages. One, the job of the VPSO extends beyond a narrow crime control or order maintenance role. The VPSO is expected to respond to all disruptions of social life, whether criminal incidents, dogs running loose, villagers overdue on trips, or boating accidents. S/he is also expected to provide support to other state agencies, e.g., adult probation or Family and Youth Services and do proactive work, e.g., help set up fire fighting and search and rescue teams, talk to juveniles on the road to trouble, or advise villagers on safety precautions. Their formal job description and their training emphasize a generalist orientation to work, including order maintenance, crime control, search and rescue support, and fire and water safety. VPSOs are the all-purpose, frontline representations of the state in rural areas, on call and responsible to local councils, the Alaska State Troopers and regional Native non-profit corporations.

Two, they are expected to be responsive to local needs and demands even as they, in their formal authority, represent and enforce Alaska State, that is Western law. Being accountable to local councils and aware of traditional, informal norms and lawways, VPSO also are expected to function as a bridge between the formal Western law which comes to the village, when things really go wrong, in the person of the State Trooper or the Family and Youth Services agent (who removes children from abusive situations) and the informal means and expectations for dispute and conflict resolution practised by villagers. Their discretionary power is guided and circumscribed by both Western/formalized and traditional/informal rules, norms and goals. It is not an easy job.

Three, the VPSO has three 'heads' or bosses. This is the program's most unusual aspect. Day to day supervision is supposed to be by the local village council; administrative control and support and pay are administered by the regional non-profit; and advice and control in serious crime and order matters rests with the Alaska State Troopers. Hiring, training and firing decisions are made jointly by the three heads. There are obvious possibilities for disagreement about what should be done, who should control the VPSO's activities, and how accountability ought to be exercised. The VPSO sits at the bottom of this organizational setup which incorporates public (the Troopers), traditional/local (the council) and private (the non-profit) agencies into oversight and control responsibilities.[1]

All in all, the program looks like a strong version of community policing (but adapted to the multi-cultural environment of rural Alaska), with its emphasis on local control and accountability, the generalist definition of role and with private participation in oversight, administration and policy development.[2]

## The History of Policing Alaska

The VPSO program continues a long history of policing efforts. After the US acquired Alaska in 1867, first the Army and later the Navy, along with the customs branch of the Treasury Department, constituted the government's presence in much of Alaska. (For general overviews see Hunt, 1987; Kynell, 1981; Murton, 1965.) One naval commander instituted the first known example of Native policing, the establishment of an "Indian police system for the maintenance of peace and good order in the native settlements. These policemen were selected from the most influential native men in villages" (Spicer, 1927:48; also Conn and Moras, 1986:14–15; Otto, 1988:17).

Beginning in the middle 1960s, the AST (Alaska State Trooper agency) embarked on a program to train Natives to be village police officers (VPOs). Short training programs were held in Fairbanks and Juneau. The Bureau of Indian Affairs (BIA)[3] provided some money for additional training, beginning in 1966; and the U.S. Department of Labor, in 1968, agreed to chip in money for police training, under its 'new careers' program. The AST applied for Law Enforcement Assistance Administration (LEAA) funds beginning in 1971 and received a total of $542,090 between 1971 and 1977 (Angell, 1978:9). Initially, the AST asked for the money to train officers in how to enforce state laws and to "get the villages to accept our system of law enforcement and justice," as most "village councils [had] no idea of how a Police Department functions in relation to the modern day concepts of law enforcement" (cited in Angell, 1978:12, 11). By 1974, the appropriate role for AST assistance had been defined thusly: to help village councils write rules and regulations "in accordance with State Statutes rather than village custom" and to "train Alaska Natives in the villages as policemen so that they can provide law enforcement in their remote areas, handling minor problems until an Alaska State

Trooper arrives" (cited in Angell, 1978:18). In effect, VPOs had been defined as police auxiliaries.

Later proposals to the LEAA, largely by the participation in their writing by smaller cities having a large Native population, shifted to a different conception of the VPOs role. Earlier submissions had been based on the "assumption that village police training would be primarily an indoctrinary exercise to prepare villages for Anglo-American style law enforcement." Later proposals, "for the first time focus specifically and exclusively on the training of village police for the effective performance of the police role in rural, predominantly native villages" (Angell, 1978:14).

A manual to assist in training was written and the training provided at the academy in Sitka was modified to suit the new definition of the role. The VPO program continues today, but on a reduced scale, and exists only in villages which somehow find the money to pay for their VPOs.

When the VPO program was first established, money to train villagers was not easy to come by. Travel is expensive in Alaska, and getting potential recruits to the academy proved difficult. Some Troopers simply taught as they worked. The one Trooper assigned to the North Slope area began "to hold a 'mini-academy' at his home" in Barrow. "He filled the officers [and VPOs] in on Alaskan rules, regulations and enforcement policies in a bush community" (Davis, 1989:20). Another Trooper resorted to using tickets issued to the AST to transport prisoners from villages to cities to fly VPO recruits to the academy. Members of the AST in charge of training VPOs also found that VPOs, once they returned to their villages, lacked support from their village councils and often had no local law to enforce as no local ordinances had been written. Using LEAA police training money, some Troopers, on their own discretion, began to fly village council members to the police academy in Sitka to teach them how to write local ordinances congruent with state and federal law. This practise lasted for about five years until the LEAA found out and told the Troopers to stop it. In effect, Troopers helped write the law by teaching council members how to write ordinances, and then helped create the capacity to enforce those laws.

The VPO system was criticized extensively. Turnover rates were "astronomical" (AK, Police Standards Council, 1977: 15). Salaries were insufficient to keep officers tied to a job which could be difficult and personally distressing. Funding was always soft, dependent on Federal and State grants.

Policing is a tough job to start with. In conditions where Native VPOs enforced the law in their own villages they worked against existing norms which emphasized reconciliation rather than enforcement, collective consensus rather than individual punishment. Additionally, they were often faced with enforcing State law and village regulations against members of their own families, a situation laden with personal conflicts. Having done their job, VPOs could not escape to the privacy of their homes. Villages are too small and everyone knows everyone and knows what has happened and who has done what to whom. One solution to this personal dilemma was to do nothing (and many VPOs seem to have done that); the other was to resign.[4]

The training provided, between 6 to 12 weeks, was not long enough to train individuals, who often had little formal education, in a complex and demanding job. All that could be taught were a few rudimentary facts about techniques of police work. More importantly, the content, what was being taught, was inappropriate. Lectures stressed norms and procedures relevant to an urban and formal (White) legal environment and failed to sensitize trainees and trainers to the distinctive cultural and traditional patterns of behavior and expectations found in Native villages. The Third Bush Justice Conference (a gathering of Native leaders and non-Native supporters) argued a similar position. Resolution 76–3 asked that "the State of Alaska incorporate cultural training, especially about rural Alaska, on a continuing basis into its training programs for all law enforcement officers." The Conference also asked that "village level recruitment of Natives for positions of law enforcement officers be a matter of highest priority" (McKenzie, 1976:19).

Much of the criminal justice system in rural areas was not really rural. Rather, it revolved around the largest cities and was staffed by non-Natives who "frequently have never visited, not to mention lived in, a rural Native community." Criminal justice agencies claim they serve rural people, but "in reality, the people of rural communities are taken and must travel to the urban centers for services and justice" (Angell, 1981:59). He concluded that, "from the standpoint of justice operations, Native communities are invisible entities" (p. 18).

Generally, then, the VPO program did not work well or effectively. The Alaska Police Standards Council observed that "village police officers generally [are] unable to meet basic APSC requirements and most existing officers simply lack the training and resources to properly do the job" (Alaska Police Standards Council, 1977:15).

## THE THEORETICAL CONTEXTS OF
## POLICING NATIVE ALASKA

Descriptions of the conditions of rural and Native Alaska echo similar themes. The state is vast and settlements are small, isolated and hard to reach. The economies of Native communities are a mix of subsistence activities, transfer payments, limited wage opportunities, cash crops (fish, fur) and the production and sale of artifacts. By standard indicators (e.g., Jorgensen, McCleary and McNabb, 1985; Kruse, Kleinfeld and Davis, 1982; Morehouse, 1989; Robbins and McNabb, 1987), rural areas suffer extensive economic dislocation and low standards of living. Many Natives prefer to live in villages nonetheless, as the alternatives are less attractive. Native cultures are under stress; political and legal conflicts over Native rights and authority abound; a significant public safety and order problem, "a plague of alcohol abuse, violence and self-destruction" (Alaska Federation of

Natives, 1988:650) pervade much of social life and challenge the ingenuity and organizing capacities of public safety agencies and agents which seek to deliver effective and legitimate policing services to rural areas. (For general overviews see *Anchorage Daily News*, 1988; Berger, 1985; Case, 1984; Cornwall and McBeath, 1982; McBeath and Morehouse, 1987; Morehouse, 1989; Morehouse, McBeath and Leask, 1984; Naske, 1985; Otto, 1986; U.S. Senate, 1989.)

Existing explanations of the general state of Native affairs in rural Alaska can be classified into two general frameworks: culture contact/social dislocation and underdevelopment/dependency theories.

The dominant explanation is social dislocation. Culture contact is a catalyst for change. Modern technology, economies and life-styles have reached the bush and have created havoc. Subsistence activities, the material foundation of Native culture, when done with modern technology (guns, snowmobiles, metal boats) are more effective, undermine social and cultural norms and authority based on success in hunting, alter other economic activities and draw Natives into the larger economy (gasoline and bullets cost money). Law both protects and constrains subsistence, converting a traditional way of life into a legally protected right, in turn requiring the assistance of an educated intercessor class (politicians, lawyers, writers) to protect those new rights by new legal and political skills and techniques (Conn and Garber, 1989).

From this perspective, Natives are in the process of an imperfect and so far unrealized transition from traditional lifestyles toward an irresistible and attractive alternative. "Poverty, high mortality rates, levels of victimization are assumed to be due to the inability of natives to adapt to the culture of the superordinate group" (Griffiths, Yerbury and Weafer, 1987:278). Once assimilation and acculturation occurs, such problems will lessen. The social and economic and public order problems which beset villages and villagers are, in a sense, the price of progress and unavoidable. They will have to be suffered through before emerging into a brighter and more stable future. Natives are, as have been other indigenous groups, "victims of progress" (Bodley, 1982). An eight part series in the Anchorage Daily News (1988) vividly dramatized the problems of Native villages as communities "in the throes of self-destruction," (Conn, 1988:10) as on the critical list, awash in booze and almost sedated, individually if not collectively, to their condition.

This analysis is both empirical and normative; it reflects and incorporates as goal the "values of modern liberal democracy and market capitalism: individualism, equality of opportunity, liberty, private property, and limited government. [The aim] is to bring economically and socially marginal groups into the mainstream economy and society, reinforcing the change from traditional to modern values, interests and behavior" (Morehouse, 1989:13).

Interpretations of the origins of and requirements for proper and effective policing or the provision of public safety services reflect their larger theoretical contexts. Policing, in the 'throes of change' perspective, can be little more than a palliative which eases the tensions and the pain of the transition period. Policing responds to the unavoidable harms of learning to be modern. Its motive is benign, an assistance granted to people in need, and its impact progressive.

The second explanation derives from general dependency theory. Social problems are the inevitable end result of incorporating Native groups into an imposed and dominant economy and culture. Natives are, as are other colonized groups, the necessary sacrifices made to a more efficient and rapacious society, but obstacles and resources on the road to improved qualities of life for dominant groups. Natives have become victims "of structural arrangements in society and of a majority/minority relationship" (Griffith, Yerbury, Weafer 1987:278). From the majority perspective, Natives can, at best, be taken care of but they have no rights, no property, no values which can stand legitimately against larger claims.

Incorporation into the capitalist world system has left village people dependent, subsisting on "the leavings—health aides, state magistrates, school janitors and teacher aides, jobs distributed as scarce commodities among families in need of steady wages"—of the larger economy (Conn, 1988:4, 7). As access to subsistence declines as legal constraints tighten, economic underdevelopment is the likely outcome (Jorgensen, et al., 1985:4).

Dependency, in turn, has generated

> attitudes of helplessness and dependence, stimulates individual pathologies, and breeds resentment directed with particular force toward outsiders. The result in many villages is a demoralized and alienated population, thoroughly dependent on the national government but increasingly resentful of its plight. . . . Consequently, villages and communities tend to be severely deficient in effective political institutions (Dryzek and Young, 1985:132, 133).

From the dependency position, all policing is a way of drawing rural Alaska more firmly into the orbit of the dominant culture, law and politics, just another and powerful means of entrenching dependence even further. In Havemann's (1988:72–73) words, even 'progressive' police reforms such as indigenization— "the recruitment of indigenous people to enforce the laws of the colonial power"—merely continue what earlier, imposed policing sought as well, a "disciplined, orderly hinterland suitable for the most efficient mercantile exploitation" yet ultimately "marginal to the mode of production dictated by modern, patriarchal capitalism." Policing is the terror necessary to keep an exploited population in check. If that policing is done by locals themselves, so much the better. It is cheaper and hides the power and interests of the exploiting classes behind the facade of service and accommodation.

The perspectives mingle. Janie Leask (1989), the President of the Alaska Federation of Natives, captures the mix well.

> Social scientists have identified the fundamental issues confronting Alaska Natives as being 'the struggle of previously self-sufficient individuals and family units to adjust to rapid social change largely imposed from the outside'.

Policies and programs themselves which were intended to assist Native families and communities and individuals have, instead, fostered and created dependency rather than self-sufficiency and we can't continue with operating in the same vein and expect to achieve results and solve the problem.

## Theorizing the VPSO Experience

How do the origins of the VPSO program fit both theories? Not very well. Both are partially correct—culture change is going on and incorporation is a fact of life. Yet both fail to connect the acts and motives of actors to the larger processes described, relying instead on functionalist assumptions about causes of change, whether these be cultural or economic in priority.

The origins of the VPSO program fit both the social dislocation and the dependency framework, hence undermine both. The reality of change is both simpler and more complex than either framework can admit or accommodate. The program started from the self-interested motives of entrepreneurs who tried to make things better, as they understood the nature of Native communities and the causes of public safety problems and the likely prospects of policy. Their vision of social order was pragmatic, tinged with the "tacit ideologies" of their profession and culture, yet empathetic of Native ways. It is hard to see a larger purpose at work, though one can characterize the outcome.

The program's origins are also more complicated than either framework predicts. Entrepreneurs, state bureaucrats and Native leaders and Native villagers argued what system of policing would be effective and legitimate and desirable, and all participated, through political and ideological labor, in the creation of the program and its subsequent (though as yet unstudied) impacts on Native communities. The vision of change and order embodied in the program is the social production of many actors.

The origins of the VPSO program and its innovative aspects—the public-private mix in the organizational structure of the program; the multiple functions of VPSOs; the economic as well as public order and safety justifications for creating a position to be filled by Natives; the insistence that policing encourage and serve the political and cultural survival of Native communities; the idea that VPSOs could function as creative resolvers of existing ambiguities and conflicts in law and political authority; the notion that bureaucrats have enough discretion to 'take risks' in implementing and interpreting state regulations—could not have been inferred from a larger theoretical understanding of the conditions of rural Alaska or of the processes which affect and now continue to change rural Alaska. The program was advocated and started by the ideas and efforts of a few entrepreneurs who were lucky enough to be in a position where they could affect the inception and development of the program and, possibly, alter the nature of policing rural and Native Alaska. It was continued by many others, including Native leaders and communities. The program as it exists now is the result of efforts by numerous Troopers, coordinators in Native non-profit corporations, village councils, community members and VPSOs themselves.

This process is on-going. Interviews conducted with all non-profit VPSO coordinators during the summer of 1990 indicate an increasing sense of ownership of the program by the coordinators. They all talk of the VPSOs as their people, whom they have to stand up for against unjustifiable demands for services and time made by state and local agencies. Coordinators have also begun to meet informally as a group, to discuss issues and develop a common position in their negotiations and interactions with state officials and legislators. The program is a valued resource and necessary for the tranquility of the villagers served by each non-profit, and as such has to be defended. Coordinators are not the only ones who see the program in this way. The Alaska Federation of Natives passes a number of resolutions at each year's convention. In the past few years, there have always been resolutions dealing with the need for public safety services to be delivered in culturally appropriate ways.

The dominant models suffer three basic failings. In both frameworks, the motives and acts of individuals count little toward explaining the systems of policing found in rural Alaska. Such acts are but the natural reflections and by-products of larger social processes, little affected by chance, individual ambition or creativity. Specifically, Natives are seen as the passive, almost comatose recipients of change imposed upon them without their consent or much resistance. Natives just suffer and respond, nobly or in dysfunctional ways, to being reoriented or incorporated. There is little sense that Natives actually do anything. They are different, they just take it.[5] In the dislocation framework, Natives seem overwhelmed, flattened by contact, the roadkill of progress on the march. The dependency stance praises resistance when it can be found and condemns the *comprador* instincts of all others' acts (e.g., Anders, 1980).

In short, much mythology, both negative and eulogizing, informs both perspectives. As Dorris remarks (1987:104–105),

> if we stipulate only a few givens—that Indian societies were composed of people of the normal range of intelligence; that human beings *qua* human beings, where and whenever they live, share some traits; that Indians were and are human beings—then we have at least a start. We can dare to leap . . . into the void and attempt to see the world through the eyes of our historical subjects.

Natives are neither savages nor noble savages, they merely differ in their ideas and cultures and practices, in their "usable, pragmatic views of the world" (p. 102). They do not live the elaborations interpreters of their experiences (including themselves) have fashioned for them. They are just people seeking to make sense and find sustenance in a threatened cultural and material environment.

A second common and inaccurate theme is that Native lifestyles are being destroyed, that this process is inevitable and that this destruction is only slowed by remoteness and the absence of desireable resources. Again, this view misses a vast number of actions done by Natives which seek to arrest and reverse what are seen as unacceptable changes, and to actively accept what are seen as useful means and ideas. The underlying assumption, that tradition and modernity exist as dichotomous choices and possibilities, is suspect. Natives live in the here and now, with both tradition and modernity. Change, a voyage from the traditions of the past to the promise of modernity, is a part of Native culture.

A third theme mistakenly reifies 'Nativeness', sees Natives as basically alike and certainly more alike among themselves than they are with other groups. Yet Natives in Alaska, as are aboriginal people elsewhere, are divided within and among themselves (e.g., Cornell, 1987), including identity and issues. Natives and non-Natives have numerous terms to describe such divisions, e.g., village Native, corporation Native, tribal Native, urban Native, and other divisions (generational, regional versus village, pre and post-ANCSA) exist as well. Such labels reflect differences in individual life experiences and are associated with disagreements over issues important to all Natives, e.g., how best to protect subsistence rights, retain ownership of land, or maintain social order in Native communities.

The objection that historical description is of form and explanation is of the underlying structures and their function is unconvincing. Form and function are interactive and neither suffices by itself to explain what happened. Form affects, not merely reflects function. Theory needs to accommodate this reciprocity and can do so only if primary assumptions (function dominates form; functions are historical actors) are modified. Existing dominant theories describe the contexts for but cannot explain the form policing takes, for they lack the theoretical arsenal.

## An Interested Action Perspective

A more accurate explanation argues that change is the result of groups and individuals reacting to circumstances to create new conditions for their lifes. They adapt; they resist; they reproduce material and ideological conditions as constrained by their historically specific economic and cultural conditions.[6] Change arises from the interaction of imposed and created circumstances as ideologized (explained and prescribed) and acted upon by all historical subjects.

The social dislocation and the dependency framework have the same descriptive flaw—they fail to acknowledge the active participation of Natives in the reproduction of new social orders, even if Natives do not succeed in protecting what is of interest to them and even if those orders are harmful to them. This is not an argument that Natives are to blame for their conditions, only that Natives are historical subjects. True enough, their capacity to shape reproduction has been severely limited; but they are not devoid of the status of actors.

As Conn (1985:305–306) remarks, it is incorrect to conceive of change in Alaska as a replacement process—Western ways destroying Native ways. In the public safety field, "the record shows persistent attempts by villagers to construct their own system as a component of the state process." For villagers, "the engagement of the [two] systems is an historical fact. They have sought collaboration on terms reflective of the stronger aspects of the village process and those of the state."[7]

What now exists and what existed earlier as changes from even earlier practises is a process in which multiple actors seek to construct, using whatever ideological tools make sense and seem efficient, new social orders which incorporate selected aspects of the past and of what has been imposed or imported. Natives participate—differentially and unequally in terms of power, successfully sometimes and less so at others, using political and legal means mainly—in the reproduction of new orders, including those which replace or recreate 'traditional' patterns of life. In this process both tradition and change are invented, resynthesized, reproduced within the larger contexts over which small groups have little influence. Change is both continuity and innovation. "Tradition is a living, evolving and still developing reality. [It is] the aggregate of beliefs, customs, habits and practice which develop in a particular culture and, by being continued, give it continuity" (Chief Justice de Weerdt, cited in Bayly, 1988:231). The determining phrase is 'being continued'[8] and everything, including the seemingly firm notion of society and individual, are objects of ideological reproduction (Wolf, 1988).

The interested action framework focusses on power and interests. Within the given yet changing contexts of White contact, economic impact and federal and state power, people, including Natives, compete as interested groups, now as in the past, to protect what is seen as valuable and to create a process which will sustain the continued reproduction of valued interests.

In practice this is an argument for participation. As the "wholesale deterioration of local authority and responsibility in the hands of Native people is one of the fundamental causes of the current epidemic of personal, family and community dysfunctions" (statement by Janie Leask, AFN, cited in US, Senate, 1989:147) a reversal of power is essential. Villages will need to develop "the capacities to participate effectively in the economic, political and social institutions of larger society," yet without, by so doing, losing their cultural identities and rights (Morehouse, 1989:21–22). Natives must compete politically for scarce resources in an environment in which their claims to special status are granted little legitimacy (except in federal law). Natives cannot expect to receive the resources which they now depend on unless they organize politically and use their control of economic resources (land and minerals and investments) and legal and moral claims to create an "indigenist" ideology to argue their case; at that they have been partially successful (Dryzek, 1989:107–109). They are part of the politics of the state and nation and the world, whether they want to be or not, and need to play the game. There is a need for leadership which can "negotiate between the local native community and the larger non-native world" (Fienup-Riordan, 1990:284).[9]

The solution, then is not further movement along the path to progress but the "reconstruction under self-direction of local cultures possessing genuine integrity" and small scale economies (Dryzek and Young, 1985:140), within, some would argue, protected cultural or anthropological sanctuaries (Bodley, 1982:209–216). The process of transforming villagers into "clients and petitioners to neotribal (corporate), state, Federal and even international organizations" must be reversed, by the action of villagers themselves. "There is no substitute for building ambitious programs on small tribal governance." Morehouse (1989:19) summarizes the "tribal model": "the life and death of villages should not be determined by market forces, nor should such forces dictate where Natives live or what economic activities they pursue. Instead, tribal advocates believe that village economies should continue to be based on a combination of subsistence, federal and state transfers, wage employment, commercial fishing and trapping, and other activities common in rural Alaska."

Policing is one way by which the dominant culture can replace Native norms and institutions, can alter the preferred reproduction of social order. In the interested action model, policing is one government policy to be contested in its structure and implementation by interested groups. Policing is something worth fighting for and the struggle shapes both the forms and functions of policing—how it is done and for what purposes and with what impacts.

## Notes

1. No recent evaluation or description of the program as a whole exists. We know little of how well it works, how VPSOs perform their job and how their communities react to and interact with them, or whether the aspirations and goals set by the originators of the program are being achieved. A preliminary evaluation of some aspects of the program can be found in Marenin, 1990.

2. For overviews of community policing see Greene and Mastrofski, 1989; Loree and Murphy, 1986; Skolnick and Bayley 1986; Trojanowicz and Bucqueroux, 1990.

3. The BIA never had a law enforcement presence in Alaska as it did and does in the lower 48 (e.g., Blackburn, 1980; Etheridge, 1977; Hagan, 1966; Wachtel, 1980).

4. This problem persists. At the 1989 Tanana Chiefs Conference (the regional Native organization for the central areas of the state) meeting held in March in Fairbanks, the youths of the region introduced a resolution requesting that the TCC evaluate the performance of village police officers and VPSOs. The first introductory 'whereas' and justification for the request stated that police officers do not enforce the law equally but favor family and relatives (Personal notes taken at the meeting). Angell concluded, somewhat ruefully, that if high turnover rates continue, "entire village populations may eventually be trained as village police officers in the continuing effort to keep officers in each village" (1978:67).

5. As examples, one can point to the 'sovereignty movement' in some areas of the state; legal cases brought by villages to contest state and federal encroachment on their traditional authority over Indian country; and a burgeoning 'Youth and Elders' movement which brings together Elders and youths in annual meetings to resurrect, to reaffirm and pass on 'vision statements' and traditional values and practises.

The dislocation argument overstates its case. Native communities are not as dysfunctional or disappearing as the rhetoric proclaims. Problems exist, but anthropologists find much stability and continuity in their studies of Native villages (e.g., Ellanna, 1991).

6. LaPrairie (1988:379–380) argues that "to leave the discussion at the macro level of colonization and underdevelopment is to ignore the nature and form of these adaptations to change." Adaptations refers to the "contemporary Native social structures" developed differently by different Indian bands. They are not all alike.

7. Similarly, Angell (1978:55) argues that the VPO "program facilitated, and likely stimulated, the adoption of many Anglo-American criminal justice methods in Native communities. Whether these methods actually replaced traditional Native ways, and if so, whether they are more effective than old ways" needs to be asked and investigated. It cannot be assumed.

8. Fienup-Riordan (1990:264–313) argues this thesis convincingly in her description of the 'Yupit Nation', the best known sovereignty movement among Alaska Natives. The Yupit Nation is a traditionalist movement in its emphasis on the importance of oral discourse, yet also a "radical innovation" in that it seeks a regional movement.

9. I sat in on a class on Native leadership given at the university last year. Natives who had succeeded in traditional and Western activities addressed class meetings. Without fail, they all stressed to the students in the class (almost all of whom were Natives) the need to continue with their education. They would be needed back home in their communities to act as go-betweens between Native and Western societies; they would have to be able to 'walk in two worlds' for walking in one had become impossible or was undesirable.

# PART FIVE

# *Courts*

# 17

*The (Toronto) Globe and Mail*

## ABORIGINAL JUSTICE CITED AS WAY TO COMBAT CRIME

### Incarceration Expensive System That Is Not Working, Judge Says

BY PETER MOON

WINNIPEG—The criminal-justice system should take a look at what is being done by some Aboriginal communities to successfully combat crime, says a senior judge of Manitoba's Provincial Court.

Nine out of every 10 dollars spent in Canada on crime prevention ends up being spent on the costs of locking people up—an expensive system that does not work, Associate Chief Judge Murray Sinclair told the Canadian Congress on Criminal Justice in a speech on Saturday.

*The Globe and Mail,* "Aboriginal Justice Cited as Way to Combat Crime," Peter Moon. Monday Oct. 2, 1995: A3. Reprinted by permission.

An Ojibway, Judge Sinclair was co-chairman of the Manitoba Aboriginal Justice Inquiry that recommended in 1991 that a separate justice system should be established for First Nations peoples.

The Canadian justice system is becoming more remote from the communities it serves, he said. It is run increasingly by professionals, such as police officers, lawyers and judges and the general public no longer feels it has any meaningful part in the process.

The result, he said, is an ever-increasing reliance on imprisonment, with "more and more demands to build jails with higher walls, more fences, stronger gates, more guards."

Justice means nothing if the process does not belong to the community, he said, and communities must be allowed to play a bigger role in the administration of justice.

Judge Sinclair said Hollow Water First Nation, a Manitoba Ojibway community at the centre of a population of about 1,500 people of Aboriginal descent, is an outstanding example of local people becoming involved in dealing with sexual offenders after it decided the criminal-justice system was not working.

"We would catch them, sometimes," he said. "We would prosecute them, not always successfully, but we would always lock them up if we convicted them.

"And those people who were being locked up and were coming back out into the community were repeating their offences . . .

"They [the community] took it upon themselves to establish a program that brings together the victim, the offender, the community and the justice system in a way that causes us in the justice system to do things differently than we have always done with those kinds of offenders in those kinds of circumstances."

In the Hollow Water program, sexual offenders who plead guilty are no longer routinely jailed but are placed on three years probation. Specially trained community members employ an intensive, holistic approach to heal the victimizer, the victim and their families. The result has been a dramatic reduction in rates of recidivism.

Judge Sinclair cited similar successful approaches to local crime problems by four other Aboriginal communities in Manitoba. The results, he said, have been so successful the courts rarely have to visit the communities any more.

"The emphasis in our [non-Aboriginal] system is on the punishment of the deviant, of the offender, as a means of making that person conform or as a means of protecting society or members of society," he said.

"But in an Aboriginal society, the purpose of justice is to restore peace and equilibrium or balance within the community, primarily by reconciling the accused with his or her own conscience and with the victim or their families."

# 18

*Lewiston (Idaho) Morning Tribune*

# WHO'S THE LAW OF THE LAND?

## BY JOAN ABRAMS

Nez Perce Tribal Prosecutor Kimron R. Torgerson said a University of Idaho law student recently told him the tribal court wasn't what he expected.

"He had this vision of a system where people were railroaded," said Torgerson. The surprise came when the student saw the court was firmly grounded in constitutional rights.

That prejudice about tribal law and order isn't unusual, he added. The Idaho Department of Motor Vehicles, for instance, has yet to recognize the provisions of tribal courts.

The misapprehension is more simple than a cultural bias, according to Torgerson. "There's always a concern for due process, for a fair hearing, that you're dealing with people not schooled in the law."

That's far from the truth in Lapwai. Torgerson, Chief Judge Eishe Kayar-MacGregor and the court's judge pro-tem are all experienced attorneys. The tribe made an effort to fill the offices with people well-schooled in traditional law, he said. Judge Kayar-MacGregor was not available to be interviewed for this article.

Fred W. Gabourie Sr., chief judge for the Kootenai Tribe and prosecutor of the Coeur d'Alene Tribe, says state and local authorities sometimes have a hard time understanding tribal ways of solving problems. Often, modern-day tribal methods take a cue from traditional peacemaking.

For instance, Gabourie said a tribal member convicted for drunk driving in tribal court may not receive the state's standard $500 fine. Instead, the fine will be smaller, but the offender will be ordered to cut firewood for an elderly community member.

Hunting violators may be ordered to provide meat for other tribal members

Edited version of *Lewiston Morning Tribune,* excerpt from "Who's the Law of the Land?" Joan Abrams, November 26, 1994: F6. Reprinted by permission.

to serve at wakes or celebrations. A juvenile offender will be counseled by a panel of Elders, not placed in detention.

"Sometimes the penalty may not satisfy the judges in the state court, but they are tailored to get better results on the reservation."

Gabourie said the recently established State Court–Tribal Court Forum is going a long way toward establishing mutual respect between the two systems. In fact, "Idaho is probably one of the more advanced states trying to resolve issues between the state, counties and Indian people."

He said in some instances, state officers are now less reluctant to send Indians to tribal court instead of state court on traffic infractions, because "they know (we're) not going to give the courthouse away."

The issue of respect for tribal jurisdiction came to a head earlier this year when attorneys for Nez Perce tribal member Marcus W. Mathews successfully argued before the Idaho Supreme Court that police had no right to gather evidence that was used to obtain a guilty plea to first-degree murder.

The evidence was seized on the reservation with a state search warrant that had not been reviewed by a tribal judge and therefore violated tribal sovereignty, the high court ruled. Mathews was given back his guilty plea and the evidence disallowed.

The Supreme Court has agreed to rehear arguments in the case.

The initial decision drew a loud outcry from politicians and the public, but tribal representatives say the episode is a tragic example of how state and local authorities ignore Indian jurisdiction.

"These Lewiston police officers would not have even thought of going over to Clarkston and serving an Idaho judge's search warrant," Kane said. "If they will respect state jurisdiction, why ignore the tribe's sovereignty?"

She says Indians will not be happy if Mathews is guilty and he is set free. "But don't blame sovereignty. Look at the facts and how it came about. . . . It's an issue of respect."

The push toward more self-governance, including a tribal police force and an experienced court, has a lot to do with gaining that respect, Kane believes.

"We want to be recognized as a sovereign government. Part of that is having the responsibility for our own process and part of that is having a court system that has respect."

# 19

*(Tucson) Arizona Daily Star*

# Navajo Project Links Culture to Legal Realm

BY ALISA WABNIK

"How do you plead?" is a tough question to answer if you don't understand the word "guilty."

For many Navajos who end up in U.S. courts, the answer is anything but clear. Their native language contains no equivalent for the term.

So it becomes even more essential that they have court interpreters whose credentials are backed by the federal government.

The Federal Court Interpreter Certification Project, directed by University of Arizona professor Roseann Dueñas González, provides those credentials to qualified individuals—so far, to only nine Navajos nationwide.

But that number is likely to rise now that González has formed the first interpreter training institute in the Navajo language.

The weeklong intensive program met for the first time last month at the UA. Thirty Navajos from New Mexico and Arizona attended the seminar's 10-hour daily sessions, learning how to translate the legal intricacies of subjects ranging from drunken driving to sexual abuse.

González started a similar program in 1983 for Spanish-speaking interpreters.

The New Mexico state government provided $100,000 for the Navajo program, dubbed the New Mexico Court Interpreters Training Institute. Tucson philanthropist Agnese Haury donated an additional $20,000 to help pay for students' transportation, lodging and food, González said.

*Arizona Daily Star,* "Navajo Project Links Culture to Legal Realm," Alisa Wabnik, January 2, 1994: B8. Reprinted by permission.

New Mexico sponsored the course because it wants to supplement federal certification with its own local test, González said.

Robert Yazzie, chief justice for the Navajo Nation and a certified court interpreter, said there are more than 200,000 Navajos nationwide who could be affected by the program.

If they end up in court, having access to qualified interpreters will improve Navajos' ability to participate in the proceedings, said Yazzie, who attended the seminar with his wife, Esther, also a certified Navajo interpreter and seminar faculty member.

"If they do not (participate), then their rights are at stake," he said.

Roselyn Johnson, a Navajo from the University of New Mexico's court advocate program who attended the seminar, said she needed the program, even though she speaks fluent Navajo, because it provides some legal training.

"I'm here to learn the Navajo legal language, which is a whole different ballgame," Johnson said. "It's so formalized and it has to be so accurate, so information gets across to your client."

But she said learning the terminology is worth the extra work.

"There are a lot of decisions that are made through the judicial process that are unfair to my people," Johnson said. "They are accused of crimes they don't commit. They need an eye and an ear that can help them get through the process."

# 20

# LEAVING OUR WHITE EYES BEHIND

## The Sentencing of Native Accused

RUPERT ROSS

## AUTHOR'S NOTE

This chapter was written to convey my growing conviction that we in the mainstream culture remain largely ignorant of the fact that Native people—and Native communities—operate under a scheme of ethical commandments which vary significantly from our own. When, at sentencing, our focus shifts from a particular act to assessments of the attitudes and resources of the accused and of his community context, failure to make *accurate* assessments of their realities will necessarily imperil successful attainment of the goals of sentencing.

If, as I suspect, we fail to properly interpret what we see and hear, we will in all likelihood reach for sentencing alternatives destined if not for failure then for showing markedly less success than we had hoped for. In short, it is my sense that we must learn, as best we can, to leave our white eyes behind to a very significant degree.

## INTRODUCTION:
## SEEING THROUGH THE RULES

In the 1970s, a group of Mohawk from southern Ontario hosted a sporting tournament to which they invited a group of James Bay Cree. On the Saturday night they prepared a feast. The Mohawk, an agricultural people long before contact

Edited version of Rupert Ross, "Leaving Our White Eyes Behind: The Sentencing of Native Accused," [1989] 3 *Canadian Native Law Reporter* 1–15. Reprinted by permission of *Canadian Native Law Reporter* and the author.

with Europeans, had developed a custom of always setting out considerably more food than could ever be eaten. In this way they demonstrated both their wealth and their generosity. The Cree, however, had a different custom. A hunter-gatherer people for whom scarcity was a daily fact of life, their custom involved always eating everything that was set before them. In this way they demonstrated their respect for the successful hunter and for his generosity.

Needless to say, there was a problem when these two sets of rules came into collision. The Cree, anxious to show respect, ate and ate and ate until a number became seriously ill. They thought the Mohawk gastrointestinal sadists were determined to poison them. The Mohawk thought the Cree ill-mannered boors who were determined to insult the Mohawk generosity. Each group went away believing that the other had intentionally shown insult and disrespect. Each group had, of course, been going to great pains to try to show exactly the opposite. The problem lay in the fact that each group had developed its own unique rules governing not just actions, but, more importantly, the sending of signals meant to convey attitudes. When acts are seen but their signal-content misinterpreted, we cannot help but form inaccurate impressions of motivations and attitudes and states of mind which may be well off the mark.

Most Europeans, for example, have an expectation that someone who will not look you straight in the eye is demonstrating an evasiveness. We suspect that we are being either brushed off or lied to. When we wish to demonstrate our own sincerity and respect, we make a point of squarely facing the other and establishing the strongest eye contact we can sustain. I have learned, to my chagrin, that in some northern reserve communities looking another straight in the eye is taken as a deliberate sign of disrespect, for their rule is that you only look inferiors straight in the eye. Fortunately, I have not insulted too many people, though only because they knew I was just an ignorant White man who did not even know *how* to behave civilly. More unfortunate was the fact that for many years I have been misinterpreting them, especially on the witness stand. I have been reading evasiveness and insincerity and possible lies when I should have been reading only respect and sincerity.

These two illustrations serve to underline the wisdom of R. D. Laing's cryptic but critical observation that "until you can see through the rules, you can only see through the rules." We interpret what we see and hear through our own cultural eyes and ears. When we deal with people from another culture, our *interpretations* of their acts and words will very frequently be wrong. It follows that when we *respond* to their acts and words, relying upon our interpretations of them, we will respond by doing and saying things which we would never consider appropriate had we known the truth.

Sentencing is nothing more than an institutional response to an act or a word. Sentencing Native people—or people from any other culture—poses a very substantial challenge. Sentencing is not, after all, an end but a means to other ends. It is a tool employed in an effort to accomplish rehabilitation of the individual, deterrence to him and to others in the community, and protection of that community. It requires that we learn as much as we can about that individual and about the context in which he lives. The greater our misinterpretation, the less likely it is that our sentence will produce the results we intend.

I do not propose to explain Native people and Native communities, because I can't. After twenty years in northern Ontario, I am only just beginning to realize how much I don't know. I propose instead to point out areas in which we should exercise great caution in interpreting the acts and words of Native people. My experience is only with the hunter-gatherer peoples of northwestern Ontario, and I have no way of knowing how applicable that experience is in dealing with Native people in other parts of Canada. If nothing else, I hope to underline one conviction only: we have not understood the degree to which the rules of their culture (or cultures, as the Cree-Mohawk feast story illustrates) differ from ours. We must learn to *expect* such difference, to be ever wary of using our own cultural assumptions in interpreting their acts and words, and to do our best to discover their realities and their truths. Until we do, we will be serving neither our goals nor their interests.

I wish to emphasize that the communities with which I deal are remote, isolated and self-contained. The majority are accessible only by aircraft. They did not have sustained contact with the majority culture until some thirty years ago, and even now it is sporadic. In fact, they did not *exist* as year-round, multi-family communities until schools were built, in some cases only twenty years ago. Traditional ways and rules remain strong, as does the conviction that each individual's interest is secondary to the community interest. Their isolation, both geographically and culturally, from the rest of Canada gives rise to a very pronounced conviction that the community has both a right and a responsibility to be an active player in all aspects of community life, including the criminal law process. Sentencing is, most emphatically, an enterprise in which each community feels a very pronounced interest and may be able to play a very important role. Understanding the attitudes and approaches of each community becomes critical if sentences are to show promise of attaining the goals we intend.

## ASSESSING THE INDIVIDUAL

Central to sentencing deliberations is an assessment of the individual accused. Whether the material reviewed consists of pre-sentence reports, psychiatric assessments, reports from detention facilities or simple observations of his demeanour, we are obliged to do what we can to become familiar with him. Only then can we come to conclusions about his prospects for rehabilitation and about what sanctions may be necessary to accomplish our goal of specific deterrence. It is my experience, however, that we very frequently misinterpret the information gathered and draw unfair negative conclusions.

## Assessing the Prospects for Rehabilitation

If I have any picture of a Native accused, it is of a silent person, someone who says little or nothing to me, to psychiatrists, to custodians, to the court or to anyone. I regularly receive reports from numerous sources who all use, to varying degrees, the same descriptive words and phrases: uncommunicative, unresponsive, unable to offer insights into his actions, unwilling to confront his past, unwilling to explore his feelings towards himself or his victim or his surroundings. On occasion I have received reports indicating that an accused withdrew completely into himself and absolutely refused to enter into any form of dialogue or respond to any efforts at communication. They are, without question, what we would call negative reports. In turn, they lead us to very negative conclusions about the prospects for rehabilitation. If he won't even explore why he did what he did, if he won't confront his personal demons or open up his feelings or acknowledge the sources of his anger, we assume that he is not *interested* in rehabilitation, not *motivated* towards helping himself. We then assume we are left with sentencing options that concentrate instead upon deterrence.

What if we are wrong in our interpretation of what he is and is not apparently willing to do? What if his refusal to cooperate stems from the fact that he objects to our *processes* of rehabilitation rather than the *goal* of rehabilitation? Further, what if that refusal was based on *ethical* objections? Would we not then have a very different picture of that individual, seeing not someone apparently devoid of concern for himself and others but someone who was able to resist all our imprecations by virtue of his *allegiance* to ethical precepts? Would that not alter our conclusions about the prospects for rehabilitation?

I was first alerted to the existence of such ethical precepts by the work of Dr. Clare Brant, a full-blooded Mohawk from the Tyendinaga Reserve in southern Ontario and a practicing psychiatrist. Everything I have seen in the three years since being exposed to his insights confirms them: there are very pronounced ethical commandments which have traditionally forbidden Native people from doing many things which we expect all people would "naturally" do. We have seen them only through our own rules.

One such rule requires that grief, anger and sorrow be quickly buried. They should not be expressed, for that only serves to burden the person who hears. They should not be explored or indulged privately, for doing so results in a lessened capacity to contribute the fullest energy, attention and skills which the hunter-gatherer society needed to maintain survival. Expressions of anger or criticism would serve only to create friction, a dangerous luxury to a people who required the maximum cooperation of all. Even the *thinking* of critical thoughts about others was to be avoided. Quite simply, the past was the past, and its negative parts were to be buried and forgotten as quickly as possible.

This set of rules results in a variety of responses. Amongst the Ojibway, for instance, it is improper to use the name of a family member who has died for six months after death, or to openly recount their lives for a year. It is not uncommon still for relatives to go into the home, remove and destroy clothes, keepsakes, pictures and mementos, and to alter the configuration of interior walls so that there is virtually no trace of his physical existence. On one large reserve, band members took chain saws and thoroughly destroyed a relatively new community coffee shop after a fight (which started inside) resulted in a killing; while outsiders could use the building materials for any purpose, the only purpose permitted band members was as firewood.

While such overt observances of these rules are declining, it remains a central tenet of life in many communities that it is wrong to speak of your hurts and angers and criticisms, wrong to indulge your private emotions. Instead, you bury and you carry on, resisting the backwards glance. I recall one teenage rape victim who refused to testify when her assailant finally came to trial more than a year after the event; her reason was simply that he should have paid his penalty by now and be getting on with his life. For her, it was simply too late to put him through it. The past was the past.

Asking a Native accused to explain what it was that aggravated him to such a degree that he attacked his victim is the subject of a special constraint, already referred to, which forbids the criticism of others. It extends to things both large and small, from how your spouse cooks potatoes to whether or not they are destroying the family through alcohol. It precludes the giving of advice or what we call constructive criticism. Each person is to be left entirely free to make his own choices. Even when those choices are obviously leading to harm it is rude and improper to interfere. If, as I have personally seen, your friend or brother is about to drive his boat onto a reef, it is your duty *not* to jump up and warn him away. Similarly, in circumstances where we would spend hours telling our friend what car he should buy or diet he should try, such "friendly advice" would be looked upon as a rude and arrogant interference in another's choices. I should add that this rule, which Dr. Brant terms the Ethic of Non-Interference, extends even to children, forbidding parents from telling their children when to go to school, what to eat, when to come home, that they must see the dentist, etc. Children too are to be left free to make their own choices, to learn from their own mistakes. It goes without saying that we interpret the absence of parental direction and control as signs of a lack of concern. I suspect that in fact most Native parents who see their youngsters getting into dangerous circumstances now *wish* they could interfere, but struggle with the force of their traditional prohibition. I recall one Native father who was asked by the judge what he did when he learned that his son had done a great deal of damage to the teachers' lounge at 4 a.m.; his response was that he had hidden the boy's shoes at night. That, to us, was as feeble a demonstration of care and concern as we could imagine, while to him it was probably further than he *should* have gone in interfering with his son's life. In many instances parents seem to welcome the intervention of the court, for it will do what they believe is necessary but what allegiance to traditional ethics forbids them from doing.

When their actions are seen in this light, we can see that we may be regularly misinterpreting *why* they do what they do and why they *refuse* to do what we expect. They are not us. Their rules are not our rules. When they refuse to jump into group therapy, to delve into their pasts, to recreate their emotional states and their trains of thought, that refusal stems not from an unwillingness to change things for the future but from a cultural prohibition against both reliving the traumas of the past and burdening others, even professional helpers, with their private woes. As one young Native boy told the court only recently when asked why he had not taken advantage of all the therapeutic resources offered to him in earlier placements: "It's not that I'm afraid or embarrassed. It's just that it isn't right."

The degree to which such things were not considered "right" is revealed by two dispute-resolving mechanisms from traditional times which have been described to me. The practice in one Inuit village was to call the entire village together, and to put the actual event forward as a *hypothetical* event which might happen some time in the future. All people, including the miscreant and his victim, were required to put forward their views as to how things might be handled peacefully and properly were the situation ever to arise. There was no blaming, no pointing of fingers, no requirement of explanation, nor was there ever any discussion, much less imposition, of either punitive or restitutionary response. At an Ojibway reserve in my district similar dynamics governed. While the miscreant and his victim were summoned before an Elders panel, there was never any discussion of what had happened and why, of how each party felt about the other or of what might be done by way of compensation. Nor was there any imposition of punishment. Each party was instead provided with a counselling Elder who worked privately to "cleanse his spirit." When both counselling Elders so signified by touching the peace pipe, it would be lit and passed to all. It was a signal that both had been "restored to themselves and to the community." If they privately arranged recompense of some sort, that was their affair. As far as the community was concerned, the matter was over. While I have not learned what the private counselling did consist of, I have been told that it did not involve retrieval and re-examination of the past in either its factual or emotional facets. It concentrated upon the future, and its spiritual component was central.

As a footnote, such ethics also cast the behaviour of Native victims in a very different light. Refusal or reluctance to testify or, when testifying, to give anything but the barest and most emotionless recital of events, may of course have been prompted by fear of the accused, by fear of the court, by love for and forgiveness of the accused or by any other such "sensible" reason (including the possibility, of extreme rarity in my experience, that they are uncomfortable because they are lying). Another reason, culturally foreign to us, could be that giving testimony face to face with the accused is simply considered wrong. It was not part of the traditional processes described above, where in fact every effort seems to have been made to *avoid* such direct confrontation. I recall one Indian woman who repeated her entire story of abuse to me in vivid detail before going into court and then asked me to do whatever I could to have the court send her very dangerous assailant to jail for as long as possible. Ten minutes later she took the witness stand and absolutely refused to say anything of an accusatory nature. When such witnesses regularly ask why they have to repeat their stories in court when they have already told "us" (meaning the police and the Crown), I have come to suspect that it is more than fear or embarrassment at work. I suspect instead that it is perceived as ethically wrong to say hostile, critical, implicitly angry things about someone *in their presence,* precisely what our adversarial trial rules have required since Sir Walter Raleigh's defiant dare. In fact, we have taken his legal challenge into our daily lives, exhorting each person to open up with the other, to be honest and up front, to get things off our chests, etc., all of which are, to traditional Native eyes, offensive in the extreme. When they refuse to follow the exhortations of our rules, we judge them as deficient in rule-obedience or, worse still, as rule-less. In our ignorance we have failed to admit the possibility that there might be rules other than ours to which they regularly display allegiance, an allegiance all the more striking because it is exercised in defiance of our insistent pressures to the contrary.

I therefore urge great caution whenever we are faced with descriptions of Native accused filled with words starting with "un-." We may well be faced with someone *un*willing, *un*responsive, *un*communicative, etc., because he truly does not care what happens to him or to anyone else; it is at least just as likely, however, that he is acting as he is out of long-established notions of propriety which forbid his acquiescence to our recommendations or requirements and that he truly does want to change his ways and avoid repeating his past misconduct.

I earlier mentioned that on rare occasions I have received reports that an accused had withdrawn completely into himself and absolutely refused to enter into any form of dialogue. Dr. Brant terms this phenomenon the Conservation-Withdrawal Tactic, and its rule stipulates that when faced with unfamiliar situations the wisest response is to step back into yourself to conserve both physical and psychic energy and to study all surroundings with great care until they are familiar enough that you can participate in confidence. It was a bush survival strategy where *not* acting was necessary until the choice of action was carefully made. It is a learned response which varies significantly from our own. Just as a great many lost white hunters react with a frenzy of unproductive, energy-consuming and potentially dangerous activity, so too we frequently respond to the stress of a cocktail party full of strangers by a frenzy of blabber. The Native, by contrast, will retreat to a wall and observe until the stress of unfamiliarity subsides and he can join the proceedings with confidence.

It is not hard to imagine the stress felt by a Native youngster who is arrested and flown to a detention facility in some faraway, non-Native community. On rare occasions the withdrawal is so complete that psychiatric examinations are quickly arranged. According to Dr. Brant, there have been significant mis-diagnoses made wherein people experiencing intense conservation-withdrawal have been diagnosed as psychotic or schizophrenic, simply because we fail to recognize learned responses other than those *we* learned. Their apparently catatonic state is not a symptom of schizophrenia nor is it a psychotic episode; it is a learned response which will pass in time without massive pharmaceutical intervention.

The point I wish to make is that refusals of Native people to do what we assume all truly repentant people would do if they were genuinely motivated towards rehabilitation, should not automatically lead us to the conclusion that they are remorseless individuals with *no* desire for rehabilitation. Native refusals can just as easily be strong indicators that they maintain a determined allegiance to ethical considerations, amongst which may well be a heartfelt desire to see to it that they never repeat their anti-social act.

It should be noted in passing that a number of Native communities are now taking revolutionary steps to break with some of those traditional ethics. The Alkali Lake Reserve in British Columbia is perhaps the most famous illustration. Their first enemy was alcohol, but in the process of receiving alcohol treatment they began to encourage each other (and other bands across Canada and the United States) to open up to each other, to share their hurts and their sorrows, to express their discontentments as well as their dreams. The second enemy was sexual abuse and its legacy of pain, suffering and repeated abuse. The two-segment "Man Alive" series on CBC Television showed them gathering *as a community* to speak of such hidden things, to comfort each other and to forgive and heal each other. While most of Canada may have been shocked at the extent and origins of the abuse, the even more startling aspect was, for me, the degree to which such efforts contravened the traditional rules requiring suffering in silence and putting it all behind you. A reserve in the Kenora District played a variation on the same theme several months ago when they held a three-day community session which both encouraged and instructed parents on the proper kinds of interference in the lives of their children which year-round life in multi-family communities now requires.

What strikes me regularly is the possibility that these tiny communities may not only change from the old ways in an historically very short period of time, but that they will move well beyond the lip service which, by and large, is the extent of our observance of rules requiring full and honest disclosure of our emotional burdens. Because they are real communities, and because the community still holds immense power over individual decisions, there is every chance that these "new" ethics may become powerful ethics in fact practiced by the majority. If so, they may well get at the issues of domestic and sexual violence in their communities faster and more thoroughly than we will in ours. It might serve us well to watch them closely in an effort to study the most efficacious response to such phenomena, for I suspect that left to their own devices, they will choose a more strongly rehabilitative, less punitive approach. And, like it or not, it is my sense that in most isolated reserves very little comes to the attention of the court in this context.

## Assessing Specific Deterrence

This too is a complex area, not only for those of us in the court party but for the communities themselves.

In traditional times, such deterrence was accomplished without much man-directed intervention. In the first place, the social group was the extended family, with the result that any harm done was harm to family members. Secondly, Mother Nature was the great enforcer, for anti-social conduct almost by definition diminished the capacity of the group to maintain bare survival in the woods. If man failed, Mother Nature punished. The overriding threat was banishment from the group, banishment into the wilds where, without the help of others, there was every likelihood of death. It was critical to each person that he maintain the welcome of the group, for without it he was lost.

What has caused great turmoil in many northern reserves is the fact that the old deterrence no longer seems adequate. People no longer need the group in the same essential way they once did, for their physical survival. Nor is the social context restricted to a small group of blood relatives, for today's northern reserves have populations up to 1,500 and are made up of many families, some of whom are mutually antagonistic. For a great many reasons too numerous and too complex to go into here, the incidences of anti-social behaviour have escalated dramatically, sometimes to crisis proportions (one court docket had 222 *Criminal Code* charges against 129 people, just over 10 per cent of the entire community's population). Some reserves have adopted a deterrence regime whose harshness I am uncomfortable with, while others emphasize rehabilitation and counselling almost exclusively. They retain their threat of banishment, and use it when all else fails.

This is not to suggest, however, that specific deterrence can only be accomplished through the threat of fines or jail. I suspect that most such tiny, isolated communities promise deterrence mechanisms largely unavailable in our larger towns and cities.

A number of Elders have told me that before the courts came they kept order through gossip. I am coming to understand that being talked about negatively hurts them, in their context, far more than it does me in mine. Even though people no longer count on each other for physical survival, there is still a remarkable sense of each person being important to the group, with its corollary sense of shame whenever an individual lets the group down. In such tiny communities no indiscretion goes unnoticed, no anti-social act undiscovered (in fact, regardless of what the CRTC stipulates, community radio stations routinely broadcast the most personal gossip imaginable, far more interesting to the listening audience than soap operas!). They have been taught to care deeply about what others think, while we are regularly instructed to ignore what others say. We do not fear rejection by the group in the same way, because we can always move to a new city, make new friends, start all over again. We know that we may be punished by the court, but we also know we will never be banished. Further, our indiscretions and criminal acts, while potentially the subject of wide media coverage, are in all likelihood going to be known only to a few, and a few strangers at that.

I think we forget, or fail to recognize, that a Native person who offends his own tiny community and is taken to court (or before council, which may be more intimidating still) very frequently feels degrees of personal shame and of fear about

losing his community's welcome which in themselves stand as significant deter-
rents to repeated misbehaviour. They know that their acts will be remembered by
all and be the subject of comment by all (not to his face, of course) for long into
the future.

I suspect we also forget the degree to which the misbehaviour of one person
brings shame upon his whole family. The very fact that they must *bear* his shame
adds to the regret and discomfort of the individual who caused it all. He knows
that wherever his family members go, they too will be gossiped about.

One illustration brings this dynamic into clear focus. On one reserve a drunken
young man passed out while slowly driving his parents' car down a gravel road.
The car went into a steep ditch and rolled. A friend in the back seat was thrown
forward out an open window and then crushed by the rolling car and killed. The
driver was charged with impaired driving causing death, an offence which in
southern centres routinely attracts sentences ranging from eighteen months to
three years, almost regardless of the situation of the individual accused.

That particular reserve has a justice committee which regularly speaks to me and
to the court on the issue of sentence. Their primary focus is on rehabilitation, but
they agreed that there had to be a jail term here to highlight the danger of drinking
and driving. They advised me that they thought our southern sentences much too
severe, and that they were prepared to support a sentence of six months. They also
advised that the accused was agreeable as well, and would enter a guilty plea. As I
soon discovered from the defence counsel, however, the accused was *not* agreeable.
He had no memory of driving and suspected that the third boy in the car was trying to blame him. He wanted, quite properly, to require the Crown to prove its case.

What is of interest here is that it made little difference to the justice committee
whether we had charged the right boy or not. What was important to them was that
we had charged the son of the family who had provided the car to three intoxicated
youngsters in the first place. Their son should go to jail, driver or not, because that
would punish *them*, the parties they considered primarily responsible. Just as that
family already bore the shame, so too should it bear the punishment.

At trial it was clearly proven that the accused boy had in fact been the driver,
and he was convicted. His sense of shame, and his family's, was palpable. He
would carry that shame, as would they, for the rest of his days. The accident scene
now boasted a huge sign in English and syllabics saying "Don't Drink and Drive,"
a sign which that boy would have to pass every time he went out to the airport or
over to another part of the community. He would, quite literally, be forever re-
minded, as would all other people travelling that route. His name was not on it,
but everyone would know. There are white crosses at accident sites now in other
communities. Jail seemed an almost inconsequential burden compared to having
to live out his life with that sign, especially when he knew he had visited his family with that same burden.

Even when no signs are erected, there are ways in which community reaction
can contribute significantly to specific deterrence. Probation terms requiring
community service work appear to be effective not only because of the punish-

ment aspect of working for free but because being seen performing it prolongs each individual's public exposure as someone who has injured his community. I have been told that they are very conscious of being seen, of the talk continuing. Coincidentally, community service work may well assist in individual rehabilitation, in that it permits an individual to be seen paying back his debt, at the end of which both he and the community can close the books and mark them "debt paid." This too is important to Native people. They feel obliged to acknowledge their misbehaviour and they are anxious to be given an opportunity to atone for it so that it can be put behind them and their welcome can be restored. In this respect it is of more than passing interest to note that they *want* to plead guilty when they are. Amongst the Mohawk, one of the most serious of crimes is lying, which would include not acknowledging those acts of which you were properly accused. Three convictions for lying results in automatic banishment, and convictions follow you for life. Pleading "not guilty" is, to them, a lie because it means denial of the truth of the allegation. For us, of course, a not guilty plea does not mean "I didn't do it"; it means instead that we require the Crown to prove it, as is our right. It is little wonder that there are so many guilty pleas from Native accused, for it is likely that the offence with which they are charged is less serious *to them* than lying about their involvement in it, precisely what a "not guilty" plea would represent for them. They *welcome* the opportunity to come to court, to confess their transgressions and to do their penance, for in this way they can earn the continuing welcome of their community. To deny their involvement and to successfully escape penance would bring upon them nothing but disdain, likely a more severe disdain than the original crime would have produced. They do not understand the thinking behind our right to enter a plea of "not guilty," do not understand how it can co-exist with our Christian rule that requires confession and acknowledgement before there is the possibility of forgiveness and redemption. Put in that context, quite frankly, neither can I!

This is not to say that all Native people approach things in the way I have described them. A great many have been off to university or have lived for considerable periods of time off the reserve. Many understand our system perfectly. The fact remains, however, that a great many are still puzzled by it, see our rules as perplexing and sometimes contradictory. When they do not act in automatic conformity with them we should not interpret that inability or outright refusal as a sign of an anarchist existence. They have their own notions of propriety which are several thousands years old, and they differ markedly from ours in some very fundamental respects. There is even a chance, much as we might resist admitting it, that some of their rules show a humanity and a respect for the integrity and rehabilitative potential of each person which we would be well to emulate.

I hope I may be forgiven that editorial comment, but I am growing a little weary of our assumption that we have little to learn from what we call a "primitive" society. I no longer hold the view that their survival as a people requires that they "catch up" to us, adopt all of our ways, and become indistinguishable from us. There is no doubt that they are searching for *new* ways in recognition of the fact that rules appropriate to the survival context may be wholly inappropriate now. When they refuse, however, to adopt some of our ways, perhaps we should take heed. What they ultimately *do* create will be new, and it may well be superior in many respects to what we are doing now. There is no reason that we cannot learn from each other.

We should also be alert to the fact that for many Native people incarceration carries consequences more burdensome than those experienced by non-Natives. This fact was recognized by the Ontario Court of Appeal in *R. v. Fireman* (1971), 4. C.C.C. (2d) 82, [1971] 30 O.R. 380 originating from the District of Kenora and argued by a Kenora lawyer. There is often a language problem which results in the accused being held in a state of *de facto* isolation. Being held indoors amounts to a special deprivation for many Native people, as does the fact that virtually all recreational and rehabilitative programs may be completely foreign and incomprehensible. Even the food is likely to be strange and unsatisfying. We must also remember that for many Native people the practical impossibility of family contact, either in person or by telephone, adds an extra sense of deprivation and loss, especially when, as is the case with a great many Native people, close involvement with every member of the extended family is the most important enterprise of life. Even the degree to which they worry about the worry which their *families* feel adds an extra burden. Their absence means that others will have to stack the wood and haul the water, check the traps, etc. They feel great shame that they have added to the burdens of others. For these and other reasons, it is my conclusion that for a great many Native people, each day in jail poses hardships and occasions feelings of grief and sorrow which would not be experienced to the same degree by their non-Native cellmates. Specific deterrence through the use of jail terms may not, in other words, require the same length of sentence for many Native accused. There are others of course who are largely institutionalized from past jail terms, and others who, disturbingly, commit crimes in the *hope* of escaping intolerable community dynamics and going to a place where they are at least well-fed and safe. I merely wish to indicate that when we look at jail as an instrument of specific deterrence that we also look carefully at the individual we propose sending there, for very frequently even a short stay will have a very substantial deterrent effect simply because of certain specific factors in the Native background.

## ASSESSING THE OFFENDER'S COMMUNITY AND FAMILY CONTEXT

It is also our duty to examine the context in which the offence took place and to which the offender is likely to return. An accurate reading of that context is required before we can hope to assess the opportunities for rehabilitation. Acknowledging that it may be a contentious proposal in some quarters, I also suggest that the family and community context peculiar to the accused may be an important element in considering the issue of general deterrence. I will canvass this latter contention first.

Conventional wisdom has it that general deterrence focuses on the Canadian community as a whole. It speaks to national concerns, expresses national revulsions requiring national denunciations and sets national standards. I have a problem with this in an Ojibway-speaking community three hundred air miles north of Thunder Bay. It is my sense that its inhabitants are not in the least touched by a *Globe and Mail* report of a deterrent sentence announced by the Court of Appeal in Toronto. They are, however, immediately and deeply affected by any sentence handed down in their own community. In fact, it is precisely the isolated and self-contained nature of those communities which guarantees that measures aimed at effecting general deterrence will have that intended effect.

The case involving impaired driving causing death which I mentioned earlier provides a very good illustration. Every person in that community knew what had happened. They witnessed the results of drunk driving first-hand for, as is their custom, they all went to the funeral. They did not need explosive headlines, for they saw the body. They did not need court-inspired depictions of the tragedy, for they watched the dead boy's family weep, and joined in the weeping themselves. In short, there was no court denunciation which could come close to telling them what they already knew, what they already felt, what they had already learned first-hand. In the year it took to get that case to sentencing, impaired driving charges in that community had dropped from sixteen to one and that involved a Ski-Doo. These communities, because of their size and their isolation and their sense of community, are capable of learning lessons from events themselves, and so have less need of the court's drafting of responses aimed at making such lessons clear. In the result there is, in my view, much less need to do something I find very difficult to do, sacrificing an individual and his family for the sake of communicating a message. I acknowledge that it has the *appearance* of sending different signals to Native and non-Native communities. I have even heard accusations that it means that the court takes the loss of an Indian life less seriously than the loss of a non-Indian life. I proposed to the court in that particular case a sentence of three months jail, plus lengthy probation with various counselling and abstention terms, a proposal which the court accepted. Even then there was immense regret in the community as the young lad was taken into custody. They felt that he had learned his lesson, that in the year since the tragedy he had demonstrated his commitment to abstention and to becoming an involved and contributing member of the community, and that imprisonment would serve no purpose whatsoever. It appeared that even members of the victim's family shared those sentiments.

In that particular community I was also heavily influenced by the fact that the community leadership feels a very distinct responsibility for each person. When they get into difficulty, the band assists. When they *cause* difficulty, the band intervenes. Every arrested person is taken before the chief and council. I don't know what happens there, but it seems to work, for the court dockets in that community are dramatically lower than on other reserves of equal population size, economic opportunity, etc. When they tell me that their activities with a certain accused or family seem to be working, I believe them, for they are not reluctant to come forward and state to the court that other parties refuse their help, cannot be controlled and must be removed to jail as a regretted last result. The simple truth is that an active and interventionist chief and council can accomplish a great deal more than all the social agencies in our towns and they know the trials and tribulations he has faced and must overcome. Secondly, they have a personal commitment to his rehabilitation for they too must live with the results if they fail. Thirdly, the accused himself has a number of special reasons to listen to them, not the least of which is that they control virtually all allocation of jobs, housing and welfare benefits. When they tell the court they believe they can work with him, and when the accused indicates his willingness to abide by their direction, it is likely that both can be counted upon to follow up. In short, there are many Native communities where the chances of successful rehabilitation are much enhanced by dynamics which do not exist in ours. There are others, of course, where such intervention does not yet exist, where they prefer to have the court intervene or where, unfortunately, the social chaos (or political infighting) guarantees that virtually nothing of any substance gets accomplished. Each community requires individual and careful scrutiny. If forced to generalize, however, I would have to guess that the *opportunities* present for successful rehabilitation in such communities exceed those available in ours. In making that guess, I also rely heavily on the central role of family earlier referred to, on their determination not only to avoid further loss of face but also to see their good name restored.

The unique nature of northern reserves also promises that general deterrence which *requires* jail terms can frequently be accomplished with somewhat lighter terms. The very fact of removal is itself significant, and the departure of the police airplane with the accused waving from a window often takes on the character of a community spectacle. Everybody knows he has gone. Everybody senses the shame on his family. Everybody knows that now others will have to perform whatever chores he usually contributed to family well-being. Just as importantly, his extended family will miss him sorely, and those who are left behind will see that grief and determine not to be the cause of such grief themselves. While the length of the sentence of course matters to the accused and his family, I am less certain that it adds significantly to *general* deterrence. It is the simple fact of removal which seems to have the greatest impact. Lengthy sentences, save where required for community protection from uncontrollable accused, seem to be viewed as exercises in gratuitous punishment serving little useful long-term purpose.

As a final matter, I think that we should be alert to the fact that many Native communities seem to be prepared to take substantial risks for the sake of making efforts to assist each accused with his rehabilitation. While our cities regularly show vociferous protest at proposals to establish group homes or half-way houses in residential neighbourhoods, Native communities frequently show themselves more than ready to welcome back even those who have done the most monstrous harm. Many genuinely feel that an individual's violent act is a sign that they, as a community, have failed to provide him with the guidance and nourishment he required. In that sense they seem more than ready to pay a price for what they perceive on some level to have been a community failure. At the very least, they are often prepared to take significant risks with dangerous people, premised on the hope that they can turn them around, help them find themselves and, in the phrase earlier quoted, restore them to themselves and to the community. If they are willing to take such risks, I have some difficulty convincing myself that I have a duty to interfere. It is an attitude of community responsibility which I find admirable in the extreme.

## Sentencing and the Calls for Aboriginal Justice Systems

A growing chorus of voices across Canada is now calling for the establishment of alternate systems of criminal justice for Native people. Some of those calls are based on more fundamental assertions of absolute sovereignty. I suspect that the majority, however, do not necessarily have that assertion as their cause, and that the source of the complaint can be predominantly traced to dissatisfaction with the sentencing and post-sentencing process.

We must recall that for the most part "our" crimes are crimes to them as well. Even if our procedures of allegation, plea and proof are foreign, they too believe that harmful activity requires a response. It is my sense that it is at this response stage, at sentencing, that many individuals and communities feel to a large degree either invisible or excluded, perceiving themselves as being without power at precisely the instant when their fates as individuals and as communities are most directly and dramatically affected. They see their futures being decided by people who, in their view, frequently don't known them and, worse still, do not appear to expend much time or effort in *trying* to get to know them. It is my growing suspicion that it is this perception of being powerless at time of sentence which is the greatest contributor to their dissatisfaction with the justice system as a whole.

My own experience, limited as it is to remote northern bands, strongly suggests that the very careful, often very protracted, sentencing hearings which we are attempting to foster in the Kenora District go a long way towards empowering individuals and, where efforts are made to involve community leaders, the communities themselves. Their sense of being processed, of being left out in the cold, seems to diminish rapidly if sentencing deliberations both invite and respond to detailed presentations of their perspectives and suggestions. Even when the sentencing judge does not accede to community views, his or her careful review and discussion of those views still leads to a markedly higher level of community satisfaction with the justice system as a whole. In this respect, they share with us a conviction that justice involves guaranteeing that each individual will not only be given an opportunity to be heard, but be understood. With Native people on reserves, the community itself has that same expectation.

If we can show ourselves at sentencing to be sensitive to their realities and supportive of their best efforts to effect the changes which *all* parties desire, it is my sense that we can add significantly to their acceptance of and faith in the justice system.

We should also be alert to the fact that there may be as many methods of involving Native communities in sentencing—and in carrying out the particulars of any sentence imposed—as there are Native communities. I doubt that any blanket strategy will be either appropriate or productive, for individual communities have wildly varying capacities, power structures, aspirations and emphases. It will fall to each court party to investigate, encourage and support local initiatives. We will be greeted by varying degrees of skepticism about the genuineness of our efforts and the strength of our commitment to expanding their role. Some communities will choose not to respond, for participation in their eyes may be akin to collaboration with a force for disharmony, so long have we been doing, in their view, counter-productive things out of ignorance of their reality. Some will wish only to make *private* representation to the Crown and defence counsel. Others will make presentations to the court, but only to argue in favor of reliance on rehabilitative measures. Still others will have no hesitation in indicating that community measures have proven unproductive with particular individuals and that the only recourse is jail. Some will come to court urging the use of extensive, local rehabilitative services as sentencing alternatives, while others may take years to even establish them. The variety of response will be, without a doubt, wide. It remains my conviction, however, that involvement must be both encouraged and utilized.

I reiterate my earlier proposition that many of these communities possess unique capacities for effecting both deterrence and rehabilitation, our central and common goals. We may never come to a full understanding of them but we have, in my view, an obligation to investigate and try them, even when their precise dynamics remain mysteries. If they are unsuccessful, it will be those communities themselves which will be the poorer and, ultimately, the wiser. There will not be overnight success, for many communities are still grappling with relatively new varieties and degrees of disorder which may well require substantial modification of their traditional methods of dispute resolution. I suggest, however, that many of *their* experiments promise greater chances for success than ours, because they at least know where they come from, as individuals and as communities. If they can be acknowledged as contributing architects of those measures we employ to attain deterrence and restitution, and if they can be granted significant roles in the carrying out of the terms of dispositions, we may well achieve two critical results: *effective* rehabilitation and deterrence and, in the process, an acknowledgement that our justice system can indeed accommodate, to a very significant degree, the aspirations of Native people in the justice field.

The above is not to suggest, however, that there can always be harmony. There will continue to be certain spheres in which substantial disagreement will arise. The conversion of band funds to the personal use of fund managers is an issue to which we attach much more significance than do many members of individual bands. Spousal assault, recently the subject of increasing attention (and rising sentences) in the mainstream culture, has not yet attained that status in many remote communities; in fact, I've seen instances where it was the complaining spouse who was effectively banished from her community. In the same fashion I have seen adolescent victims of sexual assaults virtually excommunicated, even by family members, while their assailants retain their good standing. Such matters—misuse of government funds and intra-family violence—will continue to show differences in attitudes which may give rise to disagreements at sentencing. If, however, our courts take the time to listen carefully and to respond with a detailed explanation of the reasons behind the sentence imposed, a great deal can be accomplished.

There will also be occasions upon which the court will have to come to grips with customary ways. In one community, for example, a man beat his wife black and blue over a period of three days. It was discovered that it had been a marriage arranged by the two families, against the wishes of the two young people. When the husband discovered his new wife was significantly retarded and had been sexually abused prior to marriage, an anger and frustration set in, ultimately leading to the violence against her. Remarkably, both families remained insistent that when he completed his jail term he return to her. The court chose to face that issue directly, advising the couple to exercise their individual rights against family and community pressures if the situation was as intolerable as past events seemed to indicate. Protection of the wife from the husband and protection of him from community coercion were put, in that instance, at a higher level than protection of the traditional custom of arranged marriages.

Despite the inevitable value conflicts, however, it remains my view that a great deal can be accomplished if we make conscious and sustained efforts to invite Native involvement in the course of sentencing deliberations. That involvement should, in my view, consist of fulsome representation of the background factors which gave rise to the offence as well as detailed presentations of community and individual views on sentencing alternatives. Finally, bands should be encouraged to establish and administer community rehabilitation and deterrence programs which *they* anticipate can be productive for their own people. While we share the same goals in most respects, it is my sense that achieving those goals in Native communities frequently requires such band involvement, and that it is the lack of such involvement which has given rise to a significant portion of the dissatisfaction now being voiced from so many quarters.

## CONCLUSION

Sentencing is, at all times, a complex process which requires close scrutiny of each individual accused and of the context from which he came and to which he will return. For the foreseeable future it is not an exercise involving the rote recitation of certain formulae and the selection of a standardized response showing systematic conformity. It instead borders on an art wherein the ultimate sentence imposed reflects the court's selection of the particular instrument best suited, in all the circumstances, to the attainment of essential and lofty goals.

Where those circumstances involve Native accused and Native communities, very different instruments may well show themselves as being better suited to the attainment of those goals than the instruments we are accustomed to reaching for. Our selection process demands that we pay close attention to the goals of sentencing, and to the reality of each individual and his community. Accurate pictures of that reality will require that we do our best to discard our own cultural filters and to see things through theirs. We should as a matter of routine expect them to hear different commands and, equally, not to hear many of ours. When they appear to refuse to follow ours, we must learn to ask where that refusal stems from. The handy explanations we are used to in dealing with our own accused may form no part whatever of their decisions. In the same fashion we should be alert to the possibility that their unique family and community contexts may provide opportunities for attaining the goals of sentencing which are not present in either kind or degree in our communities.

Finally, it is my suggestion that we not be in the least professionally discomfited if, in the end, the final quantum of sentence varies dramatically from that generally imposed in the rest of Canada. Our task as professionals is not uniformity of quantum but uniformity of goal-attainment. Natives and non-Natives alike deserve nothing more and nothing less.

# 21

# THE PROCESS OF DECISION MAKING IN TRIBAL COURTS

CHIEF JUSTICE TOM TSO

In this essay, I would like to discuss the process of decision making in tribal courts. I will speak about the Navajo Tribal Courts because that is what I know. It is difficult to discuss the process without first discussing the history and the background from which the Navajo courts developed.

## HISTORICAL PERSPECTIVE

The history of the Navajo Nation and of the Navajo Tribal Courts is one of challenges. Today, we still face challenges to our sovereignty, our jurisdiction, and our right to exist as a people different from the dominant society. The ultimate challenge to the Navajo has always been survival. Those familiar with the history of the Navajo will recall that the Spanish and the United States Cavalry both attempted to exterminate us. In 1864, the United States Cavalry under Kit Carson succeeded in rounding up and driving thousands of Navajo several hundred miles from their traditional homes in Northern Arizona to Fort Sumner. The true objective of this mass removal, known as "The Long Walk," is unclear. What is known is that the Cavalry engaged in the intentional, systematic destruction of Navajo villages and the herds and crops that supported the people. The starving Navajo were then forced to walk four hundred miles in inclement weather with inadequate food and clothing to their new "home"—a reservation surrounding Fort Sumner which was to be shared with the Mescalero Apache. Once located on the

Edited version of Chief Justice Tom Tso, "The Process of Decision Making in Tribal Courts," *Arizona Law Review* 31(2):225–235. 1989. Reprinted by permission of *Arizona Law Review* and the author.

reservation, the Navajo, numbering between eight and ten thousand, were forced onto farming land poorly suited to agriculture. Failure of crops and the unwillingness of the government to provide the tools, clothing, and food necessary to permit the people to survive resulted in the government's abandonment of the Fort Sumner reservation. In effect, four years after the disastrous Long Walk, the government threw up its hands, telling us to take our sheep and go home. The return of the Navajo to their ancestral home marked the beginning of the end of federal governmental efforts to terminate our physical existence.

Since that time, the challenges have been to our cultural identity and existence. These challenges reflect the false assumption on which relations between Indians and the Anglo world have always been conducted. The false assumption is that the dominant society operates from the vantage point of intellectual, moral and spiritual superiority. The truth is that the dominant society became dominant because of military strength and power.

Examine this from the Navajo perspective. When people live in groups or communities they develop rules or guidelines by which the affairs of the group may proceed in an orderly fashion and the peace and harmony of the group may be maintained. This is true for the Navajos. As far back as our history can be verified and further back into the oral traditions of our origins, there is a record of some degree of formal organization and leadership among the Navajos. In the earliest world, the Black World, which was the first phase of our existence, it is said that the beings knew the value of making plans and operating with the consent of all. In a later world, Changing Woman appointed four chiefs and assigned one to each of the four directions. These chiefs convened a council, established clans, and organized the world. The chiefs and councils of Navajo oral history made decisions for the larger group and regulated the clans. The oral traditions indicate that there was a separation of functions between war leaders and peace leaders. One of the major responsibilities of the Navajo headmen was offering advice and guidance.

The people chose the headmen from among those who possessed the necessary qualities. The headmen needed to be eloquent and persuasive, since they exerted power by persuasion rather than coercion. Teaching ethics and encouraging the people to live in peace and harmony were emphasized.

One of the important functions of a headman was dispute resolution. When a dispute or conflict arose in the community, the people would go to the headman for advice. If the matter involved what we today would call a criminal offense, the headman would meet with the wrongdoer, his family, the victim, and the victim's family to discuss how to handle the matter. The discussion usually involved two issues: how to compensate the victim or his family for the wrong and how to deal with the wrongdoer. The discussion continued until everyone was in agreement as to what should be done.[1]

Prior to Kit Carson's arrival, we lived in communities. You might say we had a decentralized, grass roots government. We had our own mechanisms for resolving disputes. We had a profound respect for the separation of functions. Not only did we have various leaders for war and peace, we had our medicinemen, who occupied a very important role in the operation of our society. The training and the teachings of the medicinemen were respected, and no one interfered with their function. We had our own concepts of fairness in the way we handled disputes, seeking both to compensate the victim and to rehabilitate the wrongdoer.

After we returned to our land in 1868, the federal government began to tell us all the things we had to have. We had to have an organized government and a tribal council. We had to have courts. We had to have jails. We had to have separation of powers.[2] These things and many more have been instituted. They work very well in the Navajo Nation. I believe the main reason the Navajos have, by Anglo standards, the most sophisticated and the most complex tribal court system is because we were able to build upon concepts which were already present in our culture. Navajos are also flexible and adaptable people. We find there are many things which we can incorporate into our lives that do not change our concept of ourselves as Navajo.

## THE NAVAJO COURT SYSTEM

I regret that the outside world has never recognized that Navajos were functioning with sophisticated and workable legal and political concepts before the American Revolution. I regret even more that the ways in which we are different are neither known nor valued by the dominant society. Because we are viewed as having nothing to contribute, much time has been wasted. Let me be more specific. Anglo judicial systems now pay a great deal of attention to alternative forms of dispute resolution. Before 1868 the Navajos settled disputes by mediation. Today our Peacemaker Courts are studied by many people and governments.[3] Anglo justice systems are now interested in compensating victims of crime and searching for ways to deal with criminal offenders other than imprisonment. Before 1868 the Navajos did this. Now Anglo courts recognize the concept of joint custody of children and the role of the extended family in the rearing of children. Navajos have always understood these concepts. We could have taught the Anglos these things one hundred and fifty years ago.

Today the Navajo courts are structured very much like those in the state and federal courts. We have seven judicial districts. The district courts are courts of general civil jurisdiction and of limited criminal jurisdiction. Civil jurisdiction extends to all persons residing within the Navajo Nation or who cause an act to occur within the Nation.[4] The limitations on criminal jurisdiction are determined by the nature of the offense, the penalty to be imposed, where the crime occurred, and the status and residency of the individual charged with an offense.[5] Each district also has a children's court, which hears all matters concerning children except for custody, child support and visitation disputes arising from divorce proceedings, and probate matters.

The second tier of the Navajo court system is the Navajo Nation Supreme Court, composed of three justices. The Supreme Court hears appeals from final lower court decisions and from certain final administrative orders. The Supreme Court abolished trial de novo at the appellate level and now only hears issues of law raised in the lower court record. In addition, the Peacemaker Courts, established in each judicial district, use traditional mediation processes and are supported by the district courts' supervision and enforcement of the agreements reached through mediation.

The tribal government is rapidly developing an extensive network of administrative bodies with quasi-judicial functions. The final decisions of bodies such as the Tax Commission and Board of Election Supervisors are appealable directly to the Navajo Supreme Court. Recourse from the decisions of other administrative bodies is sought through an original action in the trial court.[6] All opinions of the Navajo Supreme Court, and some of the opinions of the district courts, are published in the *Navajo Reporter*. Additionally, the Navajo courts have established rules of procedure for criminal, civil, probate and appellate matters.

## THE SELECTION OF JUDGES

Navajo judges and justices are chosen through a process designed to insulate them from politics. When a judge is to be selected, interested persons submit applications to the Judiciary Committee of the Navajo Tribal Council. The Judiciary Committee screens the applicants and draws up a list of the most highly qualified people according to the qualifications set forth in the Navajo Tribal Code.[7] This list is then sent to the Tribal Chairman who appoints a judge from the list for a two year probationary period. Each appointment must be confirmed by the Tribal Council. During the probationary period, the judge receives training from carefully selected judicial education establishments which offer a quality legal-judicial education. There are currently two such establishments: the National Judicial College in Reno, Nevada and the National Indian Justice Center in Petaluma, California. The Navajo Nation Bar Association, the Judiciary Committee and the Chief Justice all evaluate the probationary judge.

If the probationary judge receives an adequate performance evaluation and satisfactorily completes his or her course of training, the Chief Justice and the Judiciary Committee recommend the judge for permanent appointment. This permanent appointment must be confirmed by the Tribal Council. Thereafter, the judge remains in office until retirement or removal under procedures established in the Tribal Code.[8] Permanent judges continue to be evaluated each year and receive training in areas where the evaluations show that knowledge and skills are lacking. Through its careful selection process, its vigorous educational programs and its thorough evaluation procedures, the Navajo Nation maintains a high standard for its judiciary.

## SUBSTANTIVE AND PROCEDURAL LAW
## IN THE NAVAJO TRIBAL COURT SYSTEM

### Representation in Court

All parties may represent themselves in the courts. If a party chooses to be represented by counsel, a member of the Navajo Nation Bar Association must be chosen. Membership in the Navajo Nation Bar Association requires passing the
Navajo bar examination, which is given twice a year. Both law school graduates
and those who have not been to law school may practice in tribal courts. The practitioners who have not been to law school are called advocates and must complete
either a certified Navajo Bar Training Course or serve an apprenticeship.

The contribution of the advocates to the Navajo court system is beyond measure. Both our language and our traditions make Anglo court systems strange to
us. In traditional Navajo culture the concept of a disinterested, unbiased deci-
sionmaker was unknown. Concepts of fairness and social harmony are basic to us;
however, we achieve fairness and harmony in a manner different from the Anglo
world. For the Navajo people, dispute settlement required the participation of the
community Elders and all those who either knew the parties or were familiar with
the history of the problem. Everyone was permitted to speak. Private discussions
with an Elder who could resolve a problem was also acceptable. It was difficult for
Navajos to participate in a system where fairness required the judge to have no
prior knowledge of the case, and where who can speak and what they can say are
closely regulated. The advocates helped the Navajos through this process, and the
advocates continue to be an important link between the two cultures.

### The Applicable Law

The law the Navajo courts must use consists of any applicable federal laws, tribal
laws and customs. The structure of our courts is based upon the Anglo court system, but generally the law we apply is our own.[9] When the Navajo Tribal Courts
were established in 1959, the Navajo Nation did not have extensive laws of its own,
and there were no reported opinions to guide the judges in the decision-making
process. In 1959, the Navajo Tribal Code required the courts to apply the applicable laws of the United States, authorized regulations of the Interior Department,
and any ordinances or customs of the Tribe not prohibited by such federal laws.
Any matters not covered by tribal or federal law had to be decided by the law of
the state in which the case arose. As the Navajo Nation encompasses land in three
states, this sometimes led to confusion and the application of different laws in different parts of the reservation.

In 1985, the Tribal Code sections regarding applicable law were amended. Now,
the courts are required to apply the appropriate law of the United States and laws

or customs of the Navajo Nation that are not prohibited by federal law.[10] If the matter is not covered by tribal or federal law, the courts may look to any state laws and decisions for guidance,[11] *or* Navajo courts may fashion their own remedies.[12] The Navajo Nation Supreme Court makes the ultimate decisions on these issues, thereby developing an internal body of law. As a result, many of the briefs filed in that court and many of the opinions issued by it cite only Navajo cases.

It is easy to understand that the Navajo Tribal Code contains the written law of the Navajo Nation, and that this law is available to anyone. When we speak of Navajo *customary* law, however, many people become uneasy and think it must be something strange. Customary law will sound less strange if I tell you it is also called "common law." Our common law is comprised of customs and long-used ways of doing things. It also includes court decisions recognizing and enforcing the customs or filling in the gaps in the written law. The common law of the Navajo Nation, then, consists of both customary law and court decisions. In a case decided in 1987, the Navajo Nation Supreme Court observed that:

> Because established Navajo customs and traditions have the force of law, this court agrees with the Window Rock District Court in announcing its preference for the term "Navajo Common Law" rather than "custom," as that term properly emphasizes the fact that Navajo custom and tradition *is* law, and more accurately reflects the similarity in the treatment of custom between Navajo and English common law.[13]

The Navajo Nation Supreme Court through case decisions is developing rules for pleading and proving Navajo common law.

## The Integrity and Independence of the Decisionmakers

Once a court makes a decision, that decision is subject to change only through judicial processes. No other part of the tribal government has the authority to overrule that decision. The basis of the concept of a separate and independent judiciary is found in both Navajo common law and in the Tribal Code. The Tribal Code establishes the Judicial Branch as a separate branch of government.[14] The integrity of court decisions, however, has its basis in the respect given to the peacemakers as leaders who helped settle community disputes. In a case decided in 1978, the Navajo Supreme Court ruled that the respect given the peacemakers extends to the courts because Navajos have

> a traditional abiding respect for the impartial adjudicatory process. When all have been heard and the decision is made, it is respected. This has been the Navajo way since before the time of the present judicial system. The Navajo People did not learn this principle from the white man. They have carried it . . . through history. . . . Those appointed by the People to resolve their disputes were and are unquestioned in their power to do so. Whereas once the clan was the primary forum (and still is a powerful and respected instrument of justice), now the People through their Council have delegated the ultimate responsibility for this to their courts.[15]

## The Old and the New Way

A close look at the Navajo Tribal Government would reveal many characteristics that appear to be Anglo in nature. Actually, many concepts have their roots in our ancient heritage. Others are foreign to our culture but have been accommodated in such a way that they have become acceptable and useful to us. Ironically, the Navajo, whose governmental structure and operation are perhaps most like those of the Anglo world amongst United States Indian tribes, is the tribe that has no constitution. The Anglo world places much value on the written word and there is a tendency to believe that if things are not written down, they do not exist.

Navajos have survived since before the time of Columbus as a separate and distinct people. What holds us together is a strong set of values and customs, not words on paper. I am speaking of a sense of community so strong that, before the federal government imposed its system on us, we had no need to lock up wrongdoers. If a person injured another or disrupted the peace of the community, he was talked to, and often ceremonies were performed to restore him to harmony with his world. There were usually no repeat offenders. Only those who have been subjected to a Navajo "talking" session can understand why this worked.[16]

Today we have police, prosecutors, jails, and written laws and procedures. I am convinced that our Anglo-based system of law enforcement is no more effective than the ways we traditionally handled law enforcement problems. Our present system certainly requires more money, more facilities, more resources and more manpower. But we have this system now, and it works as well as those of our brother and sister jurisdictions. My point is that the Anglo world has said to tribes, "Be like us. Have the same laws and institutions we have. When you have these things perhaps we will leave you alone." Yet what the Anglo world has offered, at least as far as Navajos are concerned, is either something we already had or something that works no better than what we had.

The popular concept of tolerance in America is based upon its image as a melting pot, where everyone blends together to form an indistinguishable mixture. This is fine for people who come to this country and *want* to jump into the pot. The melting pot can, however, become a good place to hide people. When differences cause discomfort or problems, it can make everyone the same. The real measure of tolerance and respect for tribes may well be how successfully the outside world can coexist with tribes. We are part of the total environment of America and at least as important as the snail darter or the California condor. What a tragedy if fifty years from now a news commentator should report on how the government has set aside a preserve in the desert where nine Indians are being saved from extinction and how it is hoped they will reproduce in captivity.

As economic development plans progress, the Navajo Nation Courts are likely to face a wide range of issues. The jurisdiction statutes of the Navajo Nation provide that the tribal courts have jurisdiction over all civil causes of action where the defendant resides within the Navajo Indian Country or, regardless of residence, has caused an action to occur within the territorial jurisdiction of the Navajo Nation.[17] Future litigation involving the land and resources of the Navajo Nation will no doubt challenge tribal court jurisdiction. In light of recent federal court decisions, however, these questions will be decided in the Navajo Nation Courts.

Beyond the jurisdictional issues, questions of what law will be applied in civil disputes are likely to arise. Whether federal law will attach in a specific case will depend on the facts. In cases where federal law does not apply, tribal common law and statutes will be used. The Navajo Uniform Commercial Code, Navajo Nation Corporation Code, Water Code, and Mining Code are examples of statutory provisions enacted to regulate on-reservation business ventures and the use of natural resources.

Non-Indians may have concerns about the impact of tradition and custom on case decisions. Navajo custom and tradition are unlikely to call for law entirely different from that expected in Anglo courts. They are more likely to supply additional factors to consider in an already familiar context. For example, the Anglo system is familiar with the concept of valuation and payment for the taking of land.[18] Compensation for the loss of use to the surface user of land is an accepted concept in both Anglo and Navajo law. The difference will be in the valuation. Land that may appear to have little value to a non-Indian may be very valuable to a Navajo. It may have spiritual or historical value that has little to do with the income it can produce. The difficulty will be in assigning a dollar figure to values that have no measure in the market. This is not an impossible task. It is done every day in tort cases where damages are assessed for intangible harms like pain and suffering, intentional infliction of emotional distress, and loss of companionship.

Navajo courts will differ in the emphasis we place on the traditional relationship between Navajos and nature. We refer to the earth and sky as Mother Earth and Father Sky. These are not catchy titles; they represent our understanding of our place. The earth and sky are our relatives. Nature communicates with us through the wind and the water and the whispering pines. Our traditional prayers include prayers for the plants, the animals, the water and the trees. A Navajo prayer is like a plant. The stem or the backbone of the prayer is always beauty. By this beauty we mean harmony. Beauty brings peace and understanding. It brings youngsters who are mentally and physically healthy and it brings long life. Beauty is people living peacefully with each other and with nature.

Just like our natural mother, our Mother Earth provides for us. It is not wrong to accept the things we need from the earth. It is wrong to treat the earth with disrespect. It is wrong if we fail to protect and defend the earth. It would be wrong for us to rob our natural mother of her valuable jewelry and to go away and leave her to take care of herself. It is just as wrong for us to rob Mother Earth of what is valuable and leave her unprotected and defenseless. If people can understand that the Navajo regard nature and the things in nature as relatives, then they will easily see that nature and the Navajos depend upon each other. Understanding this relationship is essential to understanding traditional Navajo concepts which may be applied in cases concerning natural resources and the environment.

We Navajos find it difficult to separate our lives into fragments or parts. Our ceremonies are religious, medical, social, and psychological. The seasons tell us how to live and what ceremonies to have. The earth gives us our food, the dyes for our rugs and the necessities for our ceremonies. These may be seen as *everyday* things. Today, the earth gives us income and jobs from mining, from oil, and from the forests. Water and earth combine to give Navajo Agricultural Products, Inc. the ability to produce large amounts of food for the Navajo people. Snow and rain and proper runoff from the mountains give us lakes for fishing. These may be seen as *commercial* things.

We cannot separate our needs and our relationships in the same fashion. This is why our laws and judicial interpretations must accommodate *both* of these things. For example, our tribal law requires that persons who want to harvest or remove anything from the forests have a permit. An exception is made, however, for persons who need to gather plants and forest products for ceremonial purposes. In a recent Navajo Supreme Court probate case,[19] the court held that any further division of the land would defeat the agricultural purposes of the land. Under Navajo common law, the parcel went to the heir who was best able to use the land for agricultural purposes. The other heirs were given set-offs in other items of the decedent's property. This case illustrates the Navajo Tribal Court system's ability to accommodate traditional values.

## CONCLUSION

I have tried to give you a brief overview of the judicial decision-making process in the Navajo tribal courts, and to indicate some of the ways we attempt to accommodate the best from two cultures so that the Navajo Nation may proceed to develop within a framework that is familiar to us. We, the people, are a natural resource. Our culture and our history are natural resources. We are so related to the earth and the sky that we cannot be separated without harm. The protection and defense of both must be preserved. On the other hand, the dominant society views things in terms of separateness, of compartmentalization. For this reason, the Navajo Nation is best able to make the laws and decisions regarding our own preservation and development.

I have spoken of the Navajo experience, but I believe that much of what I have said applies to all Indian tribes. Understanding the challenges facing tribes is the first step toward meeting them. The process of making judicial decisions in the Navajo Nation reflects our response to these challenges.

## NOTES

1. This historical information previously appeared in Tso, *The Tribal Court Survives in America*, 25 JUDGES' J. 23 (1986).

2. Government regulation of Indian tribes has been anything but consistent. In the century since the Navajo return to the homeland, political philosophy and opinion have undergone dramatic changes, changes that resemble a pendulum swinging from one extreme to another. The overriding philosophy has been to assimilate Indians into the Anglo society and can be seen in most of the policy enactments. After assimilation as a stated policy failed, the new policy became allotment. After allotment, we saw the Indian Reorganization Act, which was followed by termination, which in turn was followed by self-determination.

It was, however, the Indian Reorganization Act that dictated the structural changes in Tribal organization referred to here. In so doing, the Act imposed the Anglo model of government on Indian Tribes and granted additional benefits and latitude in internal matters in return for compliance. *See generally* V. DELORIA & C. LYTLE, THE NATIONS WITHIN (1984); V. DELORIA & C. LYTLE, AMERICAN INDIANS, AMERICAN JUSTICE (1983); E. SPICER, CYCLES OF CONQUEST (1962).

3. See Bluehorse and Zion in Chapter 22 and Zion, *The Navajo Peacemaker Court: Deference to the Old and Accommodation of the New,* 11 AM. INDIAN L. REV. 89–109 (1983).

4. NAVAJO TRIB. CODE tit. 7, § 253 (Cum. Supp. 1984–1985).

5. The most important criminal law statutes are the Indian Country Crimes Act (18 U.S.C. § 1152), extending federal enclave jurisdiction to interracial crimes which take place in Indian country; the Major Crimes Act (18 U.S.C. §§ 1153, 3242), punishing Indian offenders for commission of 17 articulated felonies in Indian country; and the Assimilative Crimes Act (18 U.S.C. § 13), permitting federal prosecutions for state law offenses.

For a discussion of criminal jurisdiction in Indian country, see Clinton, *Criminal Jurisdiction Over Indian Lands: A Journey Through a Jurisdictional Maze,* 18 ARIZ. L. REV. 503 (1976).

6. In a decision upholding the power of the Navajo Nation to tax mineral lessees on tribal lands, the United States Supreme Court said: "The Navajo Government has been called 'probably the most elaborate' among tribes. The legitimacy of the Navajo Tribal Council, the freely elected governing body of the Navajos, is beyond question." Kerr-McGee Corp. v. Navajo Tribe, 471 U.S. 195, 201 (1985) (citations omitted). Clearly, the thrust of this decision is to uphold the exercise of substantial autonomy in governing the internal affairs of the Navajo Nation.

7. NAVAJO TRIB. CODE tit. 7, § 354 (Cum. Supp. 1984–1985).

8. *Id.* at §§ 352–353.

9. *See* Williams v. Lee, 358 U.S. 217 (1959).

On June 1, 1868, a treaty was signed between General William T. Sherman, for the United States and numerous chiefs and headmen of the "Navajo nation or tribe of Indians." Implicit in . . . [the] treaty terms . . . was the understanding that the internal affairs of the Indians remained exclusively within the jurisdiction of whatever tribal government existed. . . . Today the Navajo Courts of Indian Offenses exercise broad criminal and civil jurisdiction which covers suits by outsiders against Indian defendants.

*Id.* at 221–22 (footnotes omitted).

10. NAVAJO TRIB. CODE tit. 7, § 204(a) (Cum. Supp. 1984–1985).

11. *Id.* at § 204(c).

12. *Id.* at § 204(b).

13. *In re* Estate of Belone, 5 Navajo Rptr. 161, 165 (1987).

14. NAVAJO TRIB. CODE tit. 7, § 201 (Cum. Supp. 1984–1985).

15. Halona v. MacDonald, 1 Navajo Rptr. 189, 205–06 (1978).

16. See M. SHEPARDSON & B. HAMMOND, THE NAVAJO MOUNTAIN COMMUNITY 128–56 (1970) for a discussion of social control methods among the Navajo. For a description of traditional legal practices among other tribes, see K. LLEWELLEN & E. HOEBEL, THE CHEYENNE WAY (1941).

17. NAVAJO TRIB. CODE tit. 7, § 253 (Cum. Supp. 1984–1985). The definition of Navajo Indian Country is consistent with the federal definition:

> The Territorial jurisdiction of the Navajo Nation shall extend to Navajo Indian Country, defined as all land within the exterior boundaries of the Navajo Indian Reservation or of the Eastern Navajo Agency, all land within the limits of dependent Navajo Indian communities, all Navajo Indian allotments, and all other land held in trust for, owned in fee by, or leased by the United States to the Navajo Tribe or any Band of Navajo Indians.

*Id.* at § 254.

> Except as otherwise provided . . . the term "Indian country". . . means (a) all land within the limits of any Indian reservation under the jurisdiction of the United States Government, notwithstanding the issuance of any patent, and, including rights-of-way running through the reservation, (b) all dependent Indian communities within the borders of the United States whether within the original or subsequently acquired territory thereof, and whether within or without the limits of a state, and (c) all Indian allotments, the Indian titles to which have not been extinguished, including rights-of-way running through the same.

18. U.S.C. § 1151 (1982). The fifth amendment of the United States Constitution provides that "no person shall be . . . deprived of life, liberty or property, without due process of law; nor shall private property be taken for public use, without just compensation." U.S. CONST. amend. V.

19. *In re* Estate of Wauneka, 13 Indian L. Rep. 6049 (1986).

# 22

# HOZHOOJI NAAT'AANII

## The Navajo Justice and Harmony Ceremony

### PHILMER BLUEHOUSE AND JAMES ZION

The Navajos in today's Arizona, New Mexico, and Utah had their own justice methods for centuries. Despite that, the government of the United States imposed adjudication methods on Navajos in 1892. After almost a century of adjudication, in 1981, the Courts of the Navajo Nation began a process of consciously returning to traditional ways. While Navajo judges used principles of traditional law prior to that time, it was only recently that the Navajo Nation judiciary began an open and intentional program of reviving it.

As it is with other American justice planners, the judges and lawyers of the Navajo Nation are attempting to bring individuals into the dispute resolution process so they can resolve their own problems. That was one reason the Navajo courts returned to traditional mediation and arbitration. However, there is a difference: traditional Navajo "mediation" is not mediation as others understand it, and Navajo "arbitration" is different as well.

Navajos are very aware of their justice traditions and, as Associate Justice Raymond D. Austin of the Navajo Nation Supreme Court puts it, Navajos are "going back to the future" by reviving traditional justice methods (Austin, 1993). To go forward into the next millennium (and the next half-millennium of contact with non-Navajos), there is a return to old justice ways. That includes initiatives to use Navajo common law in opinions and policy documents, the return of justice responsibilities to communities through the Navajo Peacemaker Court, and research on Navajo values to use as principles of law.

Edited version of P. Bluehouse and James Zion, "Hozhooji Naat'aanii: The Navajo Justice and Harmony Ceremony," *Mediation Quarterly* 1993. Reprinted by permission of *Mediation Quarterly* and the authors.

The Navajo courts are a leader among the 170 or more American Tribal Courts: they preserve Navajo cultural values to an unusual extent, and Navajos are actively using their contemporary traditional law (that is, ancient law in modern settings). That persistence, which is the product of the Navajo language, religion, and traditions, motivates conscious judicial initiatives. The Courts of the Navajo Nation apply Navajo common law as the law of preference. This approach reflects the customs, usages, and traditions of the Navajo People, formed by Navajo values in action.

In 1982, the Navajo Nation Judicial Conference created the Navajo Peacemaker Court (Zion, 1983). This unique method of court-annexed "mediation" and "arbitration" uses Navajo values and institutions in local communities. Today, it struggles to overcome the effects of adjudication and laws imposed by the U.S. government. The alien Navajo Court of Indian Offenses (1892–1959) and the Bureau of Indian Affairs (BIA) Law and Order Code (written in 1934; adopted by the Navajo Nation in 1959) made Navajos judge others, using power and force for control. That arrangement is repugnant to Navajo morals. The BIA court and code illustrate the failure of legal structures and methods imposed on Indians by non-Indian outsiders. Given the contemporary enthusiasm for alternative dispute resolution, Navajo judges must also guard against new imposed methods. Navajo justice has different goals and methods, which are more successful than imposed or imported models. This article describes the foundations of traditional Navajo justice and traditional dispute resolution methods and makes comparisons with non-Indian mediation and arbitration.

## K'EI: A HORIZONTAL SYSTEM OF JUSTICE

Alternative dispute resolution allows an escape from adjudication in judicial systems. The dynamics of adjudication and mediation are different. Adjudication uses power and authority in a hierarchical system. A powerful figure (the judge) makes decisions for others on the basis of "facts," which are developed through disputed evidence, and by means of rules of "law," which are also contested by the parties. Decisions based on those competing versions of "truth" and "law" are enforced using coercion (the power of the police). (In a 1992 presentation to the Royal Commission on Aboriginal Peoples of Canada, Professor Leroy Little Bear of the University of Lethbridge wondered how it is that a [non-Indian] "law shaman" can declare "the truth," based on "lies" presented by lawyers.) In sum, adjudication is a vertical system of justice, which is based on hierarchies of power, and it uses force to implement decisions (Barkun, 1968:16).

In contrast, mediation is based on an essential equality of the disputants. If parties are not exactly equal or do not have equal bargaining positions, mediation attempts to promote equality and balance as a part of its process. It is a horizontal system, which relies on equality, the preservation of continuing relationships, or the adjustment of disparate bargaining positions between parties.

Most modern-world systems of municipal law are vertical and positivist and use sanctions. That makes law authoritarian. Authoritarianism is an abuse of authority, and abuses are easiest in systems which rely on hierarchical or class authority as the source of decisions and that utilize force as their instrument.

The primary examples of horizontal legal systems are international law and the laws of many Native peoples (Barkun, 1968:14–55). The core of the common law of most Native peoples is the "segmentary lineage system," which is a method of tracing relationships and adjusting disputes among people who are related to each other in various ways (Barkun, 1968:17–24). With Navajos, the method of tracing relationships is the clan system.

The traditional Navajo legal system—a horizontal one—is based on clan relationships. All Navajos identify clan membership through their mother. They are members of their mother's clan and are "born for" their father's. Thus, each Navajo has relationships and relatives in extended families. Differences or disputes can be adjusted between individuals using learned values and with the help of family or clan members on the basis of the strength of relationships.

The two dynamic forces of traditional Navajo law are *k'e* and *k'ei*. *K'e* translates into English as compassion, cooperation, friendliness, unselfishness, peacefulness, and all the other positive values which create an intense, diffuse, and enduring solidarity (Witherspoon, 1975:37). Navajo ceremonies, stories, and traditions, and for that matter the language itself, teach and reinforce those values and the utility of solidarity. *K'e* is an essential part of the clan system and is the dynamic which makes it work as a horizontal system of law and dispute resolution. *K'ei* is a special kind of *k'e:* it refers to the clan system of descent relationships and groups of relatives a person is connected to, tied by the virtues of *k'e* (p. 37). Thus, Navajos know their clan relatives and interact with them, prompted by strong values which create Navajo solidarity. Those values are virtues which become an engrained emotional cement to bond the individual to the clan and the clan to the individual. Navajo children learn the importance of their clan relationships, and they express them in daily life by introducing themselves by clan, parentage, and grandparentage. The *k'e* values are expressed in traditional lore, stories, and ceremonies which are a common part of Navajo life, and Navajos cite them in ordinary conversations as a kind of case law. In Navajo culture, words often have more powerful connotative force than in English. It is difficult to describe the powerful impact of the terms discussed here.

The Navajo language has great connotative force. Words are strong, taken literally, and they often have a great deal of meaning by connotation. The way a Navajo speaks tells the listener a great deal about his or her state of Navajo knowledge or ability to relate to traditional values. If the individual appears to be aloof, that may mean that he or she does not know the values being related to the listener. If the individual is abruptly direct, given the great weight of words, that most likely means that the person knows the values. This cues the peacemaker and allows him or her to set the stage for the person's response to peacemaking. In addition, the way a person speaks will let the peacemaker know the nature of the problem and the individual's response. The peacemaker wonders, "Is it *hashkeeji* (moving toward disharmony) or *hozhooji* (moving toward harmony)?" Language is a powerful tool and an essential component of peacemaking.

Most Americans have heard of the Indian concept of "Elders." An "Elder" is not simply a person who is old and thus wise. An Elder is a distinguished person who earns that status. As is true of most Indian groups, Navajos identify their Elders by recognizing their spirituality, good works, and personal achievements. For Navajos, that person is the *naat'aanii*.

The word *naat'aanii* has been inaccurately translated as "headman" or "principal leader." This unfortunate translation is the product of American Indian policy. Non-Indians need to have some powerful leader to deal or treat with to conclude peace or take land. Most tribes did not have strong leaders with absolute or hierarchical power, as was typical of European vertical systems of authority. Most tribal leaders were persuasive and not coercive. The Navajo "peace chiefs" were civil leaders, and the word *naat'aanii* refers to a person who speaks strongly, wisely, and well. They are leaders who are known for their ability to guide others and plan for community solidarity and survival. Their authority comes from the force of *k'e* in *k'ei* relationships. Beyond relationships in the family and clan, Navajos acknowledge their *naat'aanii* as community leaders because of demonstrated leadership abilities.

In Navajo society, there are war leaders or war planners (*hashkeeji naat'aah*) and peacemakers or peace planners (*hozhooji naat'aah*). Both have demonstrated leadership abilities, depending on whether war or peace is necessary. In the way of warfare, leadership is a tool of last resort. Peace planning has been a predominant force in Navajo life, as is reflected in the Emergence narrative, where peace planning was done with the intent of promoting peace. War is avoided at all costs. This dictates always seeking peace and harmony. Peacemaking guidelines were established in the Emergence narrative. As one elder peacemaker said, "I have waited for the day I would hear again of the peacemakers as was provided for in the Emergence *No Sleep* Ceremony. I'm glad we are getting away from war ways, which our children have learned much of—they are so used to war ways, they have become our own enemy. We must speak of peace and harmony to be back in *hozho*." The modern term for a peacemaker is *hozhooji naat'aanii*—Peace and Harmony Way Leader, the key person in the Navajo Peacemaker Court and its operation.

The Navajo horizontal (peace planning) system of justice uses Navajo norms, values, moral principles, and emotions as law. *K'e* and *k'ei* are only two of these precepts. There are many others, which are expressed in Navajo creation and journey scripture, songs, ceremonies, and prayers. Navajos also have sayings which are in fact legal maxims. The denial of *k'e* and *k'ei* is expressed in the maxim, "He acts as if he had no relatives." A person who acts that way betrays solidarity and kinship; he or she is not behaving as a Navajo and may behave in a "crazy" way (see Kaplan and Johnson, 1964:216–217).

# Hozhooji Naat'aanii

The Navajo term *hozhooji naat'aanii* denotes the process of peacemaking. Navajo common law is a process which uses principles that are internalized by songs, prayers, origin scripture, and journey narratives. It builds on *k'e* solidarity in a procedure to summon assistance from the Holy People and humans to diagnose how people are distant from *k'e* or their *k'ei* relations (to identify the disharmony which creates disputes), teach how Navajo values apply to the problem, and restore the continuing relationships of the parties in their community. It is in fact a justice ceremony.

In the Navajo worldview, disharmony exists when things are not as they should be. This condition is called *anahoti*, the opposite of harmony. *Hozho* is a fundamental Navajo legal term, and it is related to the forces of solidarity (*k'e*) and clan membership (*k'ei*). It is difficult to translate *hozho* into English, because of differences in perceptions. According to Philmer Bluehouse, *hozho* measures the state of being in complete harmony and peace. It provides the framework of Navajo thought and justice. It takes into account both the *hashkeeji naat'aah* (war planning or war philosophy) and *hozhooji naat'aah* (peace planning or peace philosophy). *Hozho* is the balance obtained from the two plans. Peacemaking applications are simple, because *hozho* measures the root cause of one's conduct and prompts the participants to seek solutions to regain that *hozho*. It means that reality and the universe are unified, and there is a unity in existence itself. Reality is not segmented or compartmentalized in the Navajo worldview. There is no separation of religious and secular life. Everything has its place in reality and in a relationship to the whole which is something like the clan relationship. All animate and inanimate beings, and all supernatural beings (or forces), have their proper places and relations with each other. Thus, *hozho* is a state of affairs or being where everything is in its proper place, functioning in a harmonious relationship with everything else (Witherspoon, 1975:8). It is also a state which sometimes translates as "beauty," as in the phrase non-Navajos often hear, "walk in beauty." The term *hozhooji* refers to the Beautyway, one of the fundamental Navajo ceremonies. As with the Beautyway, the goal of *hozhooji naat'aanii* is to restore disputants to harmony.

*Hozhooji naat'aanii* is itself a ceremony. Navajo prayers are based on the concept that the processes of prayer and ceremony create *hozho* or harmony. Many Navajo prayers (including those said by Christians) end with a repetition of the phrase *hozho nahasdlii* four times. This repetition expresses a feeling of the restoration of *hozho,* meaning something like "the world is *hozho* again" (Farella, 1984:165, 167). At the conclusion of the prayer, which ends a ceremony, individuals are again in their proper place, functioning harmoniously and in beauty with everything else. *Hozho nahasdlii* is the end goal of *hozhooji naat'aanii,* which, as a peacemaking ceremony, uses a similar orientation as the Beautyway ceremony.

The process is closely related to Navajo concepts of illness and healing. When people are ill, they are out of harmony and must be restored to harmony to be well. Some describe Navajo healing as holistic, where supernatural power can be directed to remove or overcome evil and to restore order (Kaplan and Johnson, 1964:221). Navajo healing ceremonies are effective and use two major processes: suggestive words and symbols to purify the patient, and a reaffirmation of solidarity with the community and deities by making the patient the center of goodwill and reintegration with the group (Kaplan and Johnson, 1964:228). The process of helping a patient return to harmony involves invoking supernatural powers for assistance, driving out evil forces, and utilizing the force of solidarity (k'e) to help the patient achieve a return to continuing relationships with the group.

The peacemaker's role in the justice ceremony is to guide the parties to *hozho*. The peacemaker's authority is persuasive, not coercive. Coercion (forcing someone else to do one's will) is alien to Navajo thought about human relationships. It is contrary to Navajo morals and can be an evil in itself. (This overstates some very subtle Navajo thought; one can use *coercion* in the sense that one can "force" the assistance of the supernatural through prayer. Just as authoritarianism is an abuse of authority, an abuse of supernatural coercive power is witchcraft, one of the most feared evils.) A *naat'aanii* uses authoritative (not authoritarian) persuasion to lead and guide others. Navajos have a great deal of respect for tradition, so relevant information from Navajo narratives helps provide authority.

For example, if there is a land dispute, this story may be told by the peacemaker to guide the parties:

> Before humans assumed their present form, the Holy People had their own problems to address. During that time, Lightning and Horned Toad had a dispute. Horned Toad was walking on some land, when suddenly Lightning confronted Horned Toad and asserted that he, Lightning, owned the land and Horned Toad must leave immediately. Horned Toad replied, "My brother, I don't understand why you should have possession of this land, and I certainly don't lay claim to it." He continued along. Again, Lightning asserted his claim, and he threw a bolt of lightning as a warning. Horned Toad said, "I am very humble, and I can't hurt you as you can hurt others with your bolt of lightning. Could we talk about this tomorrow? I'll be waiting to talk with you on top of the refuse left there by Brother Water." Lightning agreed.
>
> The following day, Horned Toad arrived, wearing his armor. Lightning announced his arrival and asserted his power by throwing more lightning bolts at Horned Toad.
>
> Horned Toad sat atop a pile of driftwood, which was left behind after a storm. From atop that pile, he discussed the matter with Lightning. Horned Toad said, "You are very powerful; you can certainly strike me down with a bolt of lightning." "I certainly can," said Lightning. "That's not what we are here about," said Horned Toad. "We are here to discuss the land ownership issue, and we must talk." "There is nothing to discuss; the land is mine!" Lightning got angry and threw another bolt of lightning, which hit Horned Toad. "Brother, you did not hurt me," he said. The bolt bounced off Horned Toad's armor. "Brother," he said, "this armor was given to me by the same source as your bolts of lightning. Why is it we are arguing over the land, which was also loaned to us?"

This story takes land complaints back to the true "owner," and it is a forceful traditional precedent to take the parties to common ground.

In the process, a *naat'aanii* will teach Navajo values to guide people in the right way. Many values use the strong moral and emotional connotations of *k'e*, particularly in the context of *k'ei* obligations.

The peacemaking ceremony has stages and devices to instruct and guide disputants in their quest for *hozho*. It begins with an opening prayer to summon the aid of the supernatural. The prayer also helps frame the attitudes and relationships of the parties to prepare them for the process. There is a stage where the peacemaker explores the positions of the parties in the universe, verifying that they are in a state of disharmony, deciding how or why they are out of harmony, and determining whether they are ready to attain *hozho*. It is similar to diagnosing an illness to find causes. There are lectures on how or why the parties have violated Navajo values, have breached solidarity, or are out of harmony. Lectures are not recitations or exhortations of abstract moral principles, but practical and pragmatic examinations of the particular problem in light of Navajo values. The peacemaker then discusses the precise dispute with the parties to help them know how to plan to end it. The word *hozhoojigo* describes a process of planning—another Navajo justice concept. It means to "do things in the good way" or "go in the right way" by identifying practical means to conform future conduct with values. The entire process is called "talking things out," and it guides parties to a noncoercive and consensual conclusion to restore them to harmony in an ongoing relationship within a community. The relationship aspect is central, because the community is entitled to justice and the return of its members to a state of harmony within it. As with the process of ceremonial healing, the method is effective because it focuses on the parties with goodwill to reintegrate them into their community, in solidarity with it.

## COMPARISONS WITH OTHER FORMS
## OF MEDIATION AND ARBITRATION

General American mediation uses the model of a neutral third person who empowers disputants and guides them to a resolution of their problems. In Navajo mediation, the *naat'aanii* is not quite neutral, and his or her guidance is more value-laden than that of the mediator in the American model. As a clan and kinship relative of the parties or as an Elder, a *naat'aanii* has a point of view. The traditional Navajo mediator was related to the parties and had persuasive authority precisely due to that relationship in a *k'ei* way. The Navajo Nation Code of Judicial Conduct (1991) addresses ethical standards for peacemakers and states that they may be related to the parties by blood or clan, barring objection.

Peacemakers have strong personal values, which are the product of their language and rearing in the Navajo way. Those values are also the teachings of Navajo common law. A peacemaker, as a *naat'aanii*, is selected because of personal knowledge of Navajo values and morals and the demonstrated practice of them. Peacemakers teach values through prayer and a "lecture" to tell disputants what is right and wrong. Navajo peacemakers, unlike their American mediator counterparts, have an affirmative and interventionist role to teach parties how they have fallen out of harmony by distance from Navajo values.

A peacemaker is a guide and a planner. As a guide, a peacemaker helps the parties identify how they have come to the state of disharmony. Non-Indian dispute resolution tends to focus more on the act which caused the dispute. Navajo peacemaking is more concerned with the causes of the trouble. A peacemaker tries to find the sources of disharmony and conflict. Persuasion and guidance help the parties make practical plans to resolve problems. Lectures—which are not simply speeches that urge people to do good and avoid evil—help them explore concrete means of repairing disharmony.

A peacemaker intervenes but is not coercive. Navajos have definite opinions about good and evil and about how parties can be at variance with *hozho* and the good way. The intervention has the end of making the parties come to feelings of being at one with all, of being beautiful in the resolution of the dispute at hand, and of having restored a good relationship with others. The peacemaker summons supernatural help through prayer and uses ceremonial knowledge as a guide to promote goodwill, self-examination, and reintegration in continuing relationships. Navajo peacemaking, like Navajo healing, actively involves the disputants in the process. This is not a doctor treating a passive patient; the patient is actively involved in the cure.

Peacemaking is not quite "mediation," in the sense of a completely neutral intermediary who leaves the process wholly in the hands of the parties. It is almost, but not quite, "arbitration." Peacemakers generally do not make decisions for others, because coercion is wrong. (But under the rules of the Peacemaker Court, a peacemaker can make decisions for others, where the parties agree to use that method.) The peacemaker's authority is persuasive, but it has an element of arbitration. An individual selected for personal qualities and respect can use guidance, instruction, and persuasion to help others, and if they respect what the peacemaker does, they will most likely follow the guidance they receive. It is much like the process of complying with the healing instructions of a medicine man or woman. Perhaps we can best say that a *naat'aanii*'s word is law.

These attempts to translate Navajo legal terms into English show that it is dangerous to use English terms to describe what Navajos actually do. For that reason, non-Navajos should take great care when applying an English term to describe Navajo processes. The English words *mediation* and *arbitration* do not accurately reflect how Navajos feel about their justice ceremony. Navajo legal terminology shows that Navajo culture approaches justice processes with different values and procedures from mainstream American society. Just as the non-Native society is now having problems with adjudication in courts, Navajos also suffer because of this approach. Navajos are still coping with a century of coerced law—law that makes individual acts criminal and subject to punishment, rather than emphasizing restoration to harmony with others and the community. Given the differences between Navajo and general American alternative dispute resolution processes, no outsider should come in to impose any other way of handling social problems.


## CONCLUSION

Navajos have a valuable system of law that is different from the American adjudication system. It is a horizontal system of justice which relies on the essential equality of Navajos and on their solidarity in kinship relations. It differs from modern alternative dispute resolution, which attempts to avoid state coercion or authoritarianism (when coercion is excessive) by perhaps going too far in the direction of neutrality. Navajo peacemaking is an example of restorative justice.

The Navajo Peacemaker Court and its *hozhooji naat'aanii* are a model for non-Navajo initiatives. The dynamics of community solidarity, reinforcement of relationships, and wise guidance by community leaders who have the people's respect can be developed in other systems. Following the creation of the Navajo Peacemaker Court in 1982, officials and leaders from Australia, New Zealand, Canada, and South Africa studied it as a possible model. In 1991, the Manitoba Public Inquiry into the Administration of Justice and Aboriginal People recommended the use of Native peacemakers in that Canadian province (Public Inquiry into the Administration of Justice. . . , 1991:654). A group of South African visitors which came to the Navajo Nation recognized the similarity of peacemaking to their native processes, and some of them said that Navajo peacemaking would work there. In 1992, the Canadian Royal Commission on Aboriginal Peoples examined the operations of the Peacemaker Court for possible use in Canada.

As Navajos go back to the future, others can join them.

PART SIX

---

*Sentencing*

# 23

*Associated Press*

# BANISHED TEENS SENT TO PRISON

EVERETT, Wash. (AP)—A judge sentenced two Indian teen-agers to prison for an attack on a pizza delivery driver, cutting short an experiment in justice in which the youths were banished to remote Alaskan islands.

Snohomish County Judge John Allendoerfer said Tuesday he was ending the yearlong judicial rehabilitation experiment because of "flaws which unfortunately threaten its credibility and integrity."

The judge said he saw dramatic changes for the good in Simon Roberts and Adrian Guthrie, but there were too many problems with banishment—including reports of unauthorized travel and infighting among Alaska tribal judges.

"It is time to end this experiment while it can still be ended on a positive note," Allendoerfer said.

The experiment was to have run for another six months, but the judge had reserved the right to recall the 18-year-olds at any time.

Allendoerfer sentenced Roberts to four years and seven months in prison, and Guthrie to two years and seven months. Both were credited with about a year they spent in jail before being banished to separate islands in southeast Alaska to undergo traditional Tlingit rehabilitation.

The judge also ordered them to jointly pay about $36,000 restitution to Tim Whittlesey, the driver they robbed and severely beat in August 1993. Whittlesey has said he suffers dizziness, headaches, hearing loss and balance problems from the beating.

Roberts and Guthrie were 16 at the time of the robbery. Roberts got the longer term because he wielded the bat.

"I think the judge made a good decision," a somber Roberts said after the hearing, adding that he had always expected to serve prison time.

*Associated Press,* "Banished Teens Sent to Prison," Wednesday October 4, 1995. Clarinet.News. Reprinted by permission of the Associated Press.

Guthrie declined comment.

Prior to Allendoerfer's decision, both teens said they had benefited from their banishment.

Roberts told the judge that at first he thought the banishment would be "like a camping trip." But as time went on and he learned to fend for himself in the wilderness, he said he grew up "mentally, emotionally, spiritually and physically."

Guthrie likewise thanked Allendoerfer. He said the experiment gave him a chance "to become that which I need to be—a man."

Whittlesey, the victim, told the judge he supported continuing the experiment. He said later he hoped to visit the youths in prison.

While addressing the judge, Roberts turned to Whittlesey and said, "I'm very, very sorry, Timothy, for what I did."

In giving them sentences at the low end of the state's standard range, the judge said he took into consideration the teens' improvement in attitude. Prosecutors had recommended prison terms of about 5 ½ years for Roberts and about 3½ years for Guthrie.

"I find that each of you has matured significantly," Allendoerfer told the teens.

Deputy prosecutor Seth Fine, who opposed the banishment, once calling the teens "two dangerous, unremorseful offenders that presented a serious danger," said the prison sentence should have been imposed a year ago.

"I don't believe in experimenting with public safety," Fine said.

# 24

*Minneapolis (Minnesota) Star Tribune*

## PELTIER'S 3RD TRY FOR
## NEW TRIAL REJECTED

### Court Rules Prosecution Was Legitimate

BY DUCHESNE PAUL DREW

American Indian activist Leonard Peltier lost his third bid for a new murder trial Wednesday when the Eighth U.S. Circuit Court of Appeals rejected the request.

Peltier, who has been in prison for 17 years, is serving two consecutive life terms for the murder of two FBI agents on the Pine Ridge Indian Reservation in South Dakota in 1975.

Peltier, 48, has become a national figure over the years. His case has been the subject of books, movies, and a "60 Minutes" TV report. In fact, many regard him as a martyr of the American Indian Movement. Among his supporters are Amnesty International, actor Robert Redford and the Canadian government, which submitted a letter on his behalf to the court.

Federal authorities maintain that Peltier and the other men wounded agents Jack Coler and Ronald Williams in an ambush and then shot them in the head at close range. But Peltier argued that he and his codefendants didn't know Coler and Williams were federal agents and that they fired on them in self-defense.

Peltier's attorneys maintain that federal prosecutors switched their theory of what happened between his 1977 trial and later arguments. In the appeal, defense lawyers asserted that prosecutors initially pinned Peltier as the triggerman, but later backed off, viewing him as an accomplice.

*Minneapolis Star Tribune,* "Peltier's 3rd Try for New Trial Rejected," Duchesne Paul Drew, July 8, 1993. Reprinted with permission of the *Star Tribune,* Minneapolis–St. Paul.

The court, however, rejected that assertion and ruled that the government tried the case on alternative theories that proposed that "Peltier personally killed the agents at point-blank range, but that if he had not done so, then he was equally guilty of their murder as an aider or abettor."

Defense attorneys also argued that Peltier was denied a fair trial because of government misconduct. But the court held that those issues had either been argued in previous appeals or should have been.

Lynn Crooks, the assistant U.S. attorney who prosecuted the original case in 1977 and who represented the government on this appeal, said Peltier's legal options are exhausted and that the matter should be put to rest.

"This case is essentially a case where Mr. Peltier has gotten a fair trial and a fair review and hopefully this will be the legal end of it," he said.

Reflecting on the amount of attention Peltier's case has received, Crooks said Hollywood's interest may be motivated by guilt from years of producing B-movies that cast Indians in a negative light. It was "a relatively straightforward murder case, and it's turned into a cause," he said.

Although FBI officials would not comment on the specifics of the decision because they had not had a chance to read it, Bill Carter, an FBI spokesman, said the agency was "gratified" by the ruling.

Peltier's lawyers found the court's decision difficult to accept. "To say that we are disappointed is to really minimize what we feel about this," said Bruce Ellison, one of Peltier's attorneys.

William Kunstler, another member of the defense team, said Peltier has become a pariah. "For some people there is absolutely no chance of justice in this system," he said.

Noting that none of the other three men indicted for the gunfight was convicted, Kunstler said, "He's the only one, and they had to get him by fabrication."

Crooks said, however, that the critical difference between Peltier's case and that of the two co-defendants, who were acquitted in a prior trial in Cedar Rapids, Iowa, was the government's witnesses.

"The simple fact of the matter is they were different cases and different evidence," he said.

Nonetheless, Peltier's attorneys maintain that the government's case against their client was part of an orchestrated effort to quash the civil rights movement within the Indian community.

Ellison said that the defense would not give up on the case and that they will try "anything that we can think of that will bring the light of day on this case."

"It will go away when justice is done," he said. "It will go away when the government is not allowed to do ever again what they did to the people of Pine Ridge."

Ellison said he would either petition the Eighth Circuit for another hearing or petition the U.S. Supreme Court, which refused to rehear Peltier's case in 1978 and again in 1986.

Peltier received fleeting support from members of the Minneapolis City Council in December. Thirteenth Ward

Council Member Carol Johnson submitted a resolution calling for a new trial, but withdrew it when more than 60 FBI agents, Hennepin County sheriffs and other law enforcement officers made a show of force at the council meeting. At the time, Johnson said she did not have the votes to pass the resolution.

# 25

# DISCRIMINATORY IMPOSITION

## OF THE LAW

### Does It Affect Sentencing Outcomes
### for American Indians?

RONET BACHMAN
ALEXANDER ALVAREZ
CRAIG PERKINS

American Indians have long been neglected in research examining the differential or discriminatory application of the law in the United States. Typically, for example, most studies investigating adjudication outcomes such as convictions and sentences have focused their attentions almost exclusively on the legal treatment of African Americans by the agencies of justice (for reviews see Kleck, 1981; Mann, 1993; Petersilia, 1983). Leiber (1994) points out that in research of this kind, minority groups other than African Americans are usually excluded or are grouped together under some all-inclusive heading. Research specifically investigating discrimination in the application of the law toward American Indians remains sparse (Bynum, 1981; Bynum and Paternoster, 1984; Feimer, Pommersheim, and Wise, 1990; Hall and Simkus, 1975; Leiber, 1994; Pommersheim and Wise, 1989; Williams, 1979). This lack of research attention exists despite evidence indicating that other minority groups, such as Latinos, are also likely to be discriminated against in the legal process (LaFree, 1985; Zatz, 1984, 1985). Additionally, American Indians, like African Americans, have been found to be overrepresented in arrest and prison data relative to their numbers in

Source: R. Bachman, A. Alvarez, C. Perkins, "Discriminatory imposition of the law: Does it affect sentencing outcomes of American Indians?" (written for this volume).

the general population[1] (Bachman 1992; Feimer, Pommersheim, and Wise, 1990; Flowers, 1990; French, 1982; Stewart, 1964), and they are subject to racist and dehumanizing stereotypes that encourage discrimination (Hanson and Rouse, 1987, 1990; Levy, Kunitz, and Everett, 1969; Stratton, 1973; Zatz, Lujan, and Snyder-Joy, 1991). Economically, American Indians are among the poorest and most deprived in our society and are therefore least able to resist the discriminatory application of law (Reddy, 1993). These factors suggest that American Indians are also likely to be subject to differential or discriminatory treatment in the application and administration of law. Clearly, there exists a need to address this deficiency in the literature and to examine the legal treatment of American Indians.

In this chapter, we explore the extent to which differences exist in sentencing outcomes for American Indians and Whites within five states: Arizona, California, Minnesota, North Carolina, and North Dakota. After reviewing the available literature on the differential legal treatment of American Indians, we examine differences between Indians and Whites for two adjudication outcomes within separate felony crime categories: (1) sentence received for new state prison admissions and (2) percent of sentence served for new state prison releases. We then discuss the results of this exploratory analysis in light of relevant theoretical considerations, and we also consider implications for future research.

## Previous Research

Among the first to conduct research on American Indians and the discriminatory application of the law, Swift and Bickel (1974) found that American Indians received longer sentences than did Whites in federal courts. Hall and Simkus (1975) found similar results in their analysis of sentencing in a western state, asserting that the sentencing differences that they uncovered can in part be attributed to negative and stereotyped labels affixed to American Indian defendants, as well as to their absolute lack of political, economic, and social power. As they nicely summarize:

> The native American's relative lack of power and influence, his subjection to the remaining influence of old negative stereotypes as a "drunken, brawling, (horse) stealing Indian," his increased "visibility" outside of the reservation boundaries, and his position in social and economic conflict with the white community may constitute a handicap in his ability to avoid being labeled and incarcerated. His inability to hire effective lawyers, to meet bail demands, and to engage effectively in plea negotiations may further reduce his chances to avoid the more severe types of sentences. (1975:215–216)

Focusing on arrest and disposition rather than sentencing, Williams (1979) found in his analysis that American Indians were treated more severely than were Whites. Flowers (1990) has also found evidence of discrimination in terms of how Indians are treated within the justice system. He argues, however, that discrimination alone cannot fully explain the extreme overrepresentation of Native peoples in arrest and incarceration statistics; rather, one must also examine issues such as substance abuse and economic determinism.

While Bynum and Paternoster (1984) found that American Indians served significantly more of their sentences before being released on parole than did Whites, they also found that Whites received longer sentences. In fact, Bynum (1981), Feimer, Pommersheim, and Wise (1990), Leiber (1994), and Pommersheim and Wise (1989) all found that American Indians in some cases received more lenient sentences than did non-Indians. Based on these few studies investigating disparities in adjudication outcomes between American Indians and Whites, the only unequivocal finding appears to be that if discrimination is operating against American Indians, it is not uniform in its application.

## DATA SOURCES AND METHODS

Data utilized for this study were obtained from two different sources. Data for Arizona were obtained directly from the Arizona Department of Corrections.[2] Data for California, Minnesota, North Carolina, and North Dakota were obtained from the National Corrections Reporting Program (NCRP) sponsored by the Bureau of Justice Statistics. The NCRP was begun in 1983 and continues today on a yearly basis.[3] Both sources rely on data obtained from correctional facility populations. Two types of sentencing outcomes will be examined for American Indians and Whites from NCRP data in 1990: (1) sentence received for new admissions and (2) percent of sentence served for new releases. Because data for Arizona were derived from present inmate populations, only information on sentences received were available for Arizona.

### Sentence Length

Data on mean sentence length refer to the average sentence received in months (except for the Arizona data, which necessitated measurement in years) within each category of felony. Sentence lengths used for this mean calculation were based on the convicted offense with the longest sentence. Whenever a sentence had both a minimum and a maximum term, the maximum was used to define the sentence length.

### Time Served

The percent of prison sentence actually served before release refers to the average amount of time spent in prison for American Indians and Whites between the date of admission and the date of release. It should be noted here that this proportion may actually underestimate the actual time served because data on time spent in jail that was credited to the prison sentence were not available for most inmates.

## RESULTS

Data on sentence length and time served for California, Minnesota, North Carolina, North Dakota, and Arizona are presented in Tables 25.1 through 25.5 respectively. A glance across these tables quickly reveals that sentence differentials

between American Indians and Whites vary considerably depending upon the
crime committed and the state in which it was committed.

Data from California, presented in Table 25.1 reveals that, except for the crimes
of homicide and drug trafficking, American Indians received longer sentences
than did Whites. On the other hand, Whites served larger proportions of their
sentences for all crimes except sexual assault, although in some cases the differences were minimal.

Sentence length and sentence served data for Minnesota are presented in Table
25.2. Variation in patterns of treatment are again evident. American Indians received longer sentences for all crimes except sexual assault and larceny, and they
also served a longer proportion of their sentences for all crimes. In short,
American Indians in Minnesota are usually sentenced to longer terms of imprisonment (except for sexual assault and larceny) and always serve more of their sentences than do Whites.

North Carolina data presented in Table 25.3 reveal a somewhat different pattern. Here, American Indians received longer sentences than did Whites for all
crimes examined except robbery. In terms of the percent of sentence served,
American Indians served a much larger proportion of their sentence for every

Table 25.1    Sentence Lengths in Months for Whites and American Indians by Most
Serious Charged Offense for California, NCRP 1989

|  | White | American Indian |
|---|---|---|
| Homicide |  |  |
| Mean sentence (months) | 73 | 72 |
| % of sentence served | 24% | 10% |
| Sexual assault |  |  |
| Mean sentence (months) | 64 | 75 |
| % of sentence served | 24% | 28% |
| Robbery |  |  |
| Mean sentence (months) | 34 | 39 |
| % of sentence served | 30% | 25% |
| Assault |  |  |
| Mean sentence (months) | 37 | 42 |
| % of sentence served | 29% | 17% |
| Burglary |  |  |
| Mean sentence (months) | 31 | 36 |
| % of sentence served | 24% | 11% |
| Larceny |  |  |
| Mean sentence (months) | 22 | 27 |
| % of sentence served | 21% | 17% |
| Drug trafficking |  |  |
| Mean sentence (months) | 34 | 33 |
| % of sentence served | 51% | 24% |
| Public order |  |  |
| Mean sentence (months) | 21 | 25 |
| % of sentence served | 25% | 16% |

Mean sentence lengths were calculated from admission data; proportions of sentences served were calculated from release data from state correctional facilities during 1990.

Table 25.2   Sentence Lengths in Months for Whites and American Indians by Most
Serious Charged Offense for Minnesota, NCRP 1989

|  | White | American Indian |
|---|---|---|
| Homicide | | |
| Mean sentence (months) | 137 | 184 |
| % of sentence served | 2% | 8% |
| Sexual assault | | |
| Mean sentence (months) | 62 | 52 |
| % of sentence served | 3% | 11% |
| Robbery | | |
| Mean sentence (months) | 49 | 82 |
| % of sentence served | 1% | 5% |
| Assault | | |
| Mean sentence (months) | 38 | 44 |
| % of sentence served | 2% | 17% |
| Burglary | | |
| Mean sentence (months) | 31 | 35 |
| % of sentence served | 1% | 11% |
| Larceny | | |
| Mean sentence (months) | 24 | 20 |
| % of sentence served | 1% | 9% |
| Drug trafficking | | |
| Mean sentence (months) | 33 | —[a] |
| % of sentence served | 1% | 23% |
| Public order | | |
| Mean sentence (months) | 27 | 28 |
| % of sentence served | 1% | 5% |

[a]Indicates there were no American Indian cases.

Mean sentence lengths were calculated from admission data; proportions of sentences served were calculated from release data from state correctional facilities during 1990.

crime. This state has consistently applied the law more severely toward American Indians than toward Whites.

The North Dakota data, presented in Table 25.4, again, reveal a different picture. Only for cases of robbery and drug trafficking did American Indians receive longer sentences than did Whites. Whites received longer sentences for assault, burglary, larceny, and public order offenses. For the crimes of homicide and sexual assault, Whites and American Indians received comparable sentences. When the proportion of sentence served is examined, we see that American Indians served much larger proportions than did Whites for virtually every type of crime. Interestingly enough, however, the total percentages of time served for both American Indians and Whites, for all crimes, are remarkably small. The highest percentage of sentence served was for American Indians convicted of larceny, and this was only 8 percent.

Mean sentences in years received by the inmate population in Arizona by type of crime are presented in Table 25.5. As noted earlier, because data for Arizona was derived from present inmate populations, we were not able to calculate the percent of sentence served. Except for the theft-related crimes of robbery, burglary, and larceny,

Table 25.3    Sentence Lengths in Months for Whites and American Indians by Most
Serious Charged Offense for North Carolina, NCRP 1989

|  | White | American Indian |
|---|---|---|
| Homicide | | |
| Mean sentence (months) | 151 | 158 |
| % of sentence served | 7% | 20% |
| Sexual assault | | |
| Mean sentence (months) | 139 | 185 |
| % of sentence served | 4% | 8% |
| Robbery | | |
| Mean sentence (months) | 147 | 120 |
| % of sentence served | 4% | 13% |
| Assault | | |
| Mean sentence (months) | 41 | 55 |
| % of sentence served | 10% | 27% |
| Burglary | | |
| Mean sentence (months) | 71 | 77 |
| % of sentence served | 8% | 25% |
| Larceny | | |
| Mean sentence (months) | 42 | 48 |
| % of sentence served | 9% | 34% |
| Drug trafficking | | |
| Mean sentence (months) | 68 | 96 |
| % of sentence served | 9% | 54% |
| Public order | | |
| Mean sentence (months) | 26 | 38 |
| % of sentence served | 20% | 44% |

Mean sentence lengths were calculated from admission data; proportions of sentences served were calculated from release data from state correctional facilities during 1990.

Arizona data reveal that White inmates received longer sentences than did American Indian inmates. American Indians received longer sentences for robbery and burglary, and Whites and American Indians received equivalent sentences for larceny.

Although these descriptive statistics provide important information about variability in sentencing outcomes for American Indians and Whites, the limited nature of the data necessitates qualifying the interpretations and conclusions drawn from this analysis. There are many factors other than discriminatory practices by the criminal justice system that may be responsible for the disparities found. Since these data allow for only a limited univariate analysis, we are unable to control for other relevant factors that may contribute to the disparate treatment of American Indians relative to Whites. For example, previous research has found that a defendant's prior felony record is one of the most important influences on the length of sentence received (Adams and Cutshall, 1987; Chiricos and Waldo, 1975; D'Allessio and Stolzenberg, 1993; Spohn and Weich, 1987; Welch, Gruhl, and Spohn, 1984; Welch and Spohn, 1986). In addition, factors such as prison overcrowding or prison infractions committed by an inmate may influence the proportion of sentence served. The results, however, do suggest the possibility that at least a portion of the differential treatment found in this analysis

Table 25.4    Sentence Lengths in Months for Whites and American Indians by Most
Serious Charged Offense for North Dakota, NCRP 1989

|  | White | American Indian |
|---|---|---|
| Homicide |  |  |
| Mean sentence (months) | 56 | 55 |
| % of sentence served | 1% | 2% |
| Sexual assault |  |  |
| Mean sentence (months) | 60 | 60 |
| % of sentence served | 1% | 6% |
| Robbery |  |  |
| Mean sentence (months) | 77 | 120 |
| % of sentence served | 1% | 3% |
| Assault |  |  |
| Mean sentence (months) | 64 | 55 |
| % of sentence served | 1% | 4% |
| Burglary |  |  |
| Mean sentence (months) | 47 | 40 |
| % of sentence served | 1% | 6% |
| Larceny |  |  |
| Mean sentence (months) | 50 | 31 |
| % of sentence served | 1% | 8% |
| Drug trafficking |  |  |
| Mean sentence (months) | 46 | 60 |
| % of sentence served | 1% | 6% |
| Public order |  |  |
| Mean sentence (months) | 23 | 13 |
| % of sentence served | 1% | 1% |

Mean sentence lengths were calculated from admission data; proportions of sentences served were calculated from release data from state correctional facilities during 1990.

is the result of discrimination, especially in light of the body of evidence showing discrimination against African Americans and Latinos. If this is indeed the case and American Indians experience discrimination in the application of law, how can we theoretically and empirically explain this discrimination and these results?

## THEORETICAL EXPLANATIONS

The recognition that the law in the United States operates to the disadvantage of some groups has long been acknowledged in a large body of theoretical writing. This differential treatment has been explained most often in terms of power differences between different groups in society (Chambliss and Seidman, 1971; Hills, 1971; Quinney, 1970; Turk, 1969). These conflict-based arguments contend that those with the least social, economic, and political power will be sanctioned the most harshly because they lack power and are therefore unable to resist legal sanctioning (Turk, 1969) and also because they are also often defined as representing a threat to existing power relationships (Gordon, 1973; Hawkins, 1987; Quinney,

Table 25.5  Mean Sentence Length in Years Received by White and American Indian Inmates Within All State Correctional Facilities in Arizona by Type of Crime, 1990.

|  | White | American Indian |
|---|---|---|
| Homicide[a] | | |
| Mean sentence (years) | 175 | 74 |
| Number of cases | 1,238 | 94 |
| Sexual assault | | |
| Mean sentence (years) | 26 | 19 |
| Number of cases | 2,094 | 110 |
| Robbery | | |
| Mean sentence (years) | 27 | 37 |
| Number of cases | 1,971 | 589 |
| Assault | | |
| Mean sentence (years) | 14 | 8 |
| Number of cases | 2,062 | 330 |
| Burglary | | |
| Mean sentence (years) | 6 | 8 |
| Number of cases | 2,480 | 893 |
| Larceny | | |
| Mean sentence (years) | 4 | 4 |
| Number of cases | 4,752 | 236 |

[a]Means for homicide rates also included those who were sentenced to death or life. Life sentences were recoded to equal 505, fifteen years above the maximum for the remainder of the distribution, and death sentences were recoded to equal 510. There were 502 Whites and 20 American Indians sentenced to life, and 53 Whites and 2 American Indians sentenced to death. These differences will have undoubtedly produced a positively skewed mean distribution for homicide sentence lengths.

Data were obtained for 1990 from the Arizona Department of Corrections, Phoenix.

1970; Spitzer, 1975). In short, these conflict theorists have argued that the inequalities extant in our legal system result both from direct discrimination against poor and minority groups and from their lack of access to the resources required for successful defense.

Utilizing a non-conflict-based model, Black (1976, 1989) has more specifically outlined a model for the differential application of the law. Black's model is based on the idea of stratification, which he defines as the vertical dimension under which social life operates, or more simply, as the unequal distribution of and access to wealth. According to Black (1976), each person is higher or lower than others based on his or her access to resources and his or her resulting status in the stratification system; the application of law varies depending on the relative rank or status of the actors (e.g., victim and offender) involved in the crime drama. Specifically, he asserts:

> An upward crime [one committed by a lower-ranked person against a higher-ranked person] is more likely to receive a serious charge. . . . The wealthier a thief is, for instance, the less serious is his theft. It is possible to order the seriousness of deviant behavior according to its vertical location and direction, at once. All else being constant, upward deviance is the most serious, followed by deviant behavior between people of

high rank, then between people of low rank and finally downward deviance. The quantity of law decreases accordingly, and this applies to law of every kind. In cases of homicide, for example, the most severe punishment befalls a poor man who kills a wealthy man, followed by a wealthy man who kills another equally wealthy, then a poor man whose victim is equally poor, while the least severe punishment is given to a wealthy man who kills a poor man. (1989:25)

Essentially he argues that the law is applied differently depending on the social relationship between the involved parties. It is important to note that according to this argument, in some cases minority group members will in fact receive more lenient treatment in the application of law because their offenses are committed against other minority group members. Conversely, at other times, minority group members will receive harsher treatment because their offense is directed against a person of higher rank. This is very similar to a conflict-based argument made by Hawkins (1986, 1987), who asserts that because of the devalued status of African American life, when African Americans kill each other it is defined as a less serious offense, whereas if an African American kills a White, whose lives are valued more highly, that act will be defined more seriously. Theoretically, this would have the effect of greater leniency of treatment for some offenses and harsher treatment for others depending on the racial identities of the victim and offender vis-à-vis each other.

Utilizing a labeling-based perspective, others have argued that stereotypes are the operant force in the discriminatory application of the law. Swigert and Farrell (1977) suggest that cultural stereotypes of criminals and minority groups influence the determinations of legal authorities. In their study, they described a diagnostic category, a personality type that they termed a "normal primitive." It is a stereotyped depiction of what is essentially a neo-Lombrosian atavistic personality. According to this stereotype, certain individuals and groups lead "primitive" lifestyles characterized by deviance, criminality, and violence. Specifically, this "normal primitive" was characterized by Swigert and Farrell as being

comfortable and without mental illness. He has little, if any, education and is of dull intelligence. His goals are sensual and immediate—satisfying his physical and sexual needs without inhibition, postponement or planning. There is little regard for the future—extending hardly beyond the filling of his stomach and the next pay or relief check. His loyalties and identification are with a group that has little purpose in life, except surviving with a minimum of sweat and a maximum of pleasure. (1977:19)

Swigert and Farrell found that this stereotyped belief in the innate and social predisposition to violence and criminality was invariably applied to African American and lower-class defendants, who were subsequently less likely to obtain bail or receive a jury trial and who consequently received more severe sentences. This image of the "normal primitive" is comparable to many of the stereotypes of American Indians (for example, drunken, savage, etc.) that are so prevalent in the United States. Research has shown that these negative and racist portrayals are not only

widespread but also serve to foster negative, dehumanizing, and degrading definitions of American Indians (Berkhofer, 1978; Hanson and Rouse, 1987, 1990; Levy,
Kunitz, and Everett, 1969), and these portrayals have also been shown to contribute
to the discriminatory application of the law (Miethe, 1987; Miethe and Moore,
1986; Swigert and Farrell, 1977). Additionally, there is ample evidence that these
stereotypes specifically affect the treatment of American Indians within the legal
system (Hall and Simkus, 1975; Stratton, 1973; Zatz, Lujan, and Snyder-Joy, 1991).

## DISCUSSION

In this analysis disparities between American Indians and Whites were examined
for the length of sentence received and the amount of sentence served; the analysis was based on state prison admission and release data from California,
Minnesota, North Carolina, North Dakota, and Arizona.

In the aggregate, our data indicate that American Indians received longer sentences more often for offenses such as robbery and burglary, as well as for drug
trafficking and public order offenses, while Whites more often received longer
sentences for larceny. The results for homicide, sexual assault, and assault were
more closely matched. These patterns, however, showed much variation by crime
and state. Our results indicated that for some categories of crimes in some states,
American Indians received more lenient sentences than did Whites. This does not
necessarily mean that there is no discrimination in those states. The greater leniency in some cases may, in fact, be consistent with certain theoretical propositions discussed earlier. For example, if we specifically examine the data from
Arizona, we see a pattern in which Whites generally received longer sentences for
crimes of violence, whereas American Indians generally received longer sentences
for property offenses. If we interpret this from the standpoint of the context of the
crime, the pattern we observe from these data is not inconsistent with the theory
espoused by Black (1976, 1989) and with that of Hawkins (1986, 1987). It has long
been recognized that the crime of homicide is predominately intraracial (Federal
Bureau of Investigation, 1990). We can assume, then, that a larger proportion of
those allegedly killed by American Indian homicide defendants from these samples were American Indians themselves. Extrapolating from Black's (1976, 1989)
work, as well as Hawkins's (1986, 1987), we can also assume that the killing of an
American Indian by another American Indian would be very low in the perceived
seriousness hierarchy and that the perpetrator would be sentenced accordingly.
Interpreted from this perspective, mean sentences received by American Indians
convicted of homicide would naturally be lower than mean sentences received by
White defendants.

Because robbery has been found to be one of the most interracial crimes
(Bureau of Justice Statistics, 1993), the fact that robbery and burglary in Arizona
were the only crime categories in which American Indians received harsher sen-

tences than did Whites is also consistent with this interpretation. As the victims of these crimes committed by American Indians were more likely to have been White than were the victims of homicide committed by American Indians, the severity of the sentence handed down to American Indian robbers relative to White robbers should also have risen accordingly. In other words, because a crime characterized by a minority group member victimizing a member of the majority is thought to be more serious, it follows that we should see harsher sentences handed down to American Indian defendants for committing crimes that are more often interracial (that is, involving White victims), such as larceny, than for crimes that are more likely to be intraracial (that is, involving Indian victims), such as homicide. Application of this theory to Arizona, although provocative and suggestive, remains speculative at best, and although this perspective may aid in the interpretation of the patterns found in Arizona, it remains much more problematic in its application to other states that evidenced different patterns. For example, although American Indians in Arizona, California, and North Dakota received more lenient sentences for homicide, they received longer sentences in Minnesota and North Carolina.

The extent to which differences were found in proportion of sentence served between American Indian and White inmates showed a clear pattern of American Indians serving higher proportions of their sentences in every state except California, for every crime. Since this descriptive data was the only information available to us on the issue of time served, attributing these differences to discriminatory practices is, again, speculative at best. As noted earlier, a number of factors may be responsible for these differences, including such things as the number of prison infractions committed by inmates. The findings, however, are consistent with previous research, which found that American Indians served significantly higher proportions of their sentences before release from prison than did non-Indians and which does lend qualified support to the discrimination argument (Bynum and Paternoster, 1984).

Are discriminatory practices by the criminal justice system responsible for the disparities in sentence length and in the percentage of sentences served that we found in this analyis? The results of this analysis certainly do suggest the possibility that at least some degree of discriminatory behavior on the part of the criminal justice system does exist against American Indians in the United States. The extent and nature of this discrimination is still unclear and cannot be definitively explored with the present data. Clearly, much more research needs to be devoted to this area. In recent years, some have pointed out that discrimination exists intermittently and may therefore be evident in one jurisdiction or state but not in another and at one stage of the legal process but not at another (Crutchfield, Bridges, and Pitchford, 1994; Frazier, Bishop, and Henretta, 1992). In our present study, we were only able to examine two later stages in the application of law for certain specific states, and we can therefore not speak to any possible discrimination that may or may not be present at earlier stages or in other states. Future research should therefore attempt to utilize multistage analyses in order to control for the sporadic application of discriminatory practices. Analysis could include earlier decision-making stages, such as arrest, prosecution, and trial, as well as sentencing and time served in order to trace the differential handling and disposition of American Indians throughout their contact with the apparatus of justice. One related issue that clearly needs further study is that of the victims' characteristics. Data on the demographics of victims of American Indian crime would substantially aid theoretical discourse and explication in terms of establishing the validity of the theoretical arguments reviewed in this study. In the absence of data on the race of victims relative to the race of offenders, the validity and relevance of neither Black's (1976, 1989) argument nor Hawkins's (1986, 1987) argument can be established. Crime-specific data, such as that presented in this study, may approximate the effect of victim-specific data; however, victim identity is clearly preferable. Ethnographic work could also be conducted in order to establish the extent to which stereotypes influence the application of law to American Indians. As reviewed earlier, the literature certainly suggests this as one factor affecting the legal treatment of American Indians. Although beyond the scope of this project and these data, it could certainly be further explored. It is hoped that this work will be a catalyst for other researchers to pursue the inquiry further.

## Notes

1. This overrepresentation has also been found among Native populations in other countries, such as Canada (LaPrairie, 1984; Griffiths and Yerbury, 1984; Bonta, 1989).

2. For a detailed accounting of the state correctional facility population in Arizona for 1990, see Arizona Department of Corrections, 1990.

3. For a more detailed discussion of this data reporting program, see Perkins, 1993.

# 26

## "I Fought the Law and the Law Won"

C. HUTTON
F. POMMERSHEIM
S. FEIMER

### INTRODUCTION

One of the inveterate marks of sexism is the general invisibility of women as subjects of research in important institutional settings. This is particularly true in the criminal justice setting, exponentially vivified from the prairie perspective of the upper plains. Compounding the problem is the possible overlay of racism on sentencing decisions applied to both men and women.

In an effort to address the question of what role race and sex play in the sentencing in South Dakota, the researchers examined the files of women incarcerated in the South Dakota Penitentiary between 1980 and 1988 to determine whether there was substantially significant disparity in the sentences imposed on white and Native American women. As a supplement to the statistical analysis, the researchers also asked the current inmates to describe their perceptions of the equity of the sentencing process. Finally, the study included a statistical comparison of the sentences received by female and male inmates for selected offenses.

### BACKGROUND

#### A. Race as a Factor in Sentencing

As two researchers have noted, "the quality of justice available to NativeAmericans [sic] and the quality of treatment they receive under the law has been a major con-

Edited version of C. Hutton, F. Pommersheim, and S. Feimer, "I Fought the Law and the Law Won," *New England Journal of Criminal and Civil Confinement* 15:2. 1989. Reprinted by permission of *New England Journal of Criminal and Civil Confinement* and the authors.

cern in South Dakota" (Pommersheim and Wise, 1987). As Pommersheim and Wise have observed, although these concerns have been discussed for many years (1987:19), little research has been done in the state to either confirm or deny that unequal treatment exists (1987:19).

According to the Bureau of Census, Native Americans constitute the largest minority in the state of South Dakota, representing approximately 6.5% of the state's population of 609,768.[1] Consistently, however, they constitute a much higher percentage of the prison population (1987:1). As of December 1987, Native Americans made up twenty-three percent of the male prison population.[2] Of the women offenders incarcerated as of December 1987, nineteen of fifty-three, or thirty-six percent were Native Americans.

> These figures highlight a serious disparity between the representation of Native Americans in the general population and their representation in the state prison population. This disparity is even more disturbing when viewed in light of the fact that the state only has jurisdictional authority over Indians for offenses committed off the reservation and outside of Indian country. (Pommersheim and Wise, 1987:20)[3]

The reasons for this over representation of Native Americans are difficult to pinpoint. Whether it might be due, at least in part, to discrimination in sentencing is the focus of this study.

## RESEARCH AND METHODOLOGY

The primary focus of this study was to determine from the data whether there is a relationship between punishment severity and race during sentencing. In other words, do Native American women, as a group, receive more severe punishment than their white counterparts? Related to this issue is the question of which factors (*e.g.,* age, criminal history, number and ages of children) are most important in determining punishment? And, are these factors different or similar among Whites and Native Americans? The results of this part of the study appear in Part A below.

A second focus of the study was disparity in sentencing between males and females. Because the information was collected in South Dakota, the researchers thought it appropriate to compare available data on males and females within the state in an effort to provide as complete a picture as possible of the state's sentencing patterns. To this end, the data from the 1985 Pommersheim-Wise study (1987) were compared with the data on women collected for this study. Those results appear in Part B below.

### A. Race as a Factor in Sentencing: Native American and White Women

### 1. Statistical Assessment of Disparity

*a. Sample Selection*

Base line data used in this study were collected during the spring and summer of 1988 from records at the Springfield Correctional Facility, which houses all female inmates and some male inmates of the South Dakota State Penitentiary. The study population consisted of all women sentenced to a term of imprisonment and incarcerated from January 1, 1980, to July 1, 1988, a total of 307 inmates.

The primary focus of the study was disparity between sentences for White and Native American inmates; other minorities were omitted from this study. In addition, since the study required a comparison of sentences, offense categories involving only one race were eliminated. These two limiting factors left a total of 272 inmates in the study; 180 were White, 92 were Native American.

Finally, because inmates are often convicted of more than one offense, it was necessary to develop a scheme for defining the primary offense which would be analyzed in the study. Inmates with more than one charge were assigned to an offense category based on the crime for which they received the longest sentence. If sentence lengths were identical, the offense which carried the most severe maximum penalty was used.

### b. Operationalizing Punishment Severity

Reaching definitional agreement on punishment severity has always proved to be troublesome, simply because judges, jurors, victims and convicts all have differing views on the issue. For purposes of this study, punishment was operationalized as *the percentage of maximum penalty sentenced, minus years suspended.* For example, if one is convicted of aggravated assault, a Class 4 felony, which carries a ten year maximum penalty, and is sentenced to eight years with two years suspended, then that prisoner receives sixty percent of the maximum penalty. In this way, punishment is described as the portion of sentence received relative to the maximum penalty.

### c. Prisoner Data

During the intake interview, prison authorities collect a variety of information relating to conviction, offense, age, race, defense type, prior felonies, juvenile record, and employment status. Although much of the information is obtained as "self-reported" statements, prison officials are able to verify most of the factual data (i.e., prior felonies, conviction status, juvenile records). In all, the data base contained information from twenty-six variables.[4]

### d. Felony Classification

In South Dakota, criminal offenses are classified into one of eight felony classes, each with a different maximum penalty. Table 26.1 includes a list of offenses of which women have been convicted by felony class and the maximum penalty, with the number of offenders included for each offense.[5]

### e. Demographic Characteristics

Often differences and similarities between groups can be detected by examining frequency and percentage distributions. In this section, the demographic variables of marital status, number and ages of children, age, education, criminal history, and employment are considered.

Because female inmates were the subject of this study, the researchers chose to examine marital status and the number and ages of the inmates' children, not only to determine whether they play a role in sentencing but also as a descriptive device. As a whole, twenty-seven percent of the inmates were currently married, while seventy-three percent were divorced or never married. The breakdown by race was virtually identical to this percentage. With respect to children, the researchers endeavored to determine whether the inmates had any children, and if so, what their ages were. Thirty-four percent of the inmates had no children. Fifty-six percent of the inmates had between one and five children under age ten. Twenty-six percent of the inmates had children ten years of age or older.[6] Most inmates in the study were relatively young. Sixty-eight percent were thirty or younger, and almost half (49.3%) were twenty-five or younger. Seventeen inmates were forty-five or older, with sixty-three being the age of the oldest inmate. When race was factored in, 70% of White inmates were thirty or younger, as were 65.2% of Native Americans. The Native American inmate population was slightly older than the White inmate population, with a mean of 29.5 years and a median of 28 years, compared to a mean of 27.8 years and a median of 25 years for the White inmates.

The years of education for White and Native Americans differed significantly. The mean for Whites was 11.2 years of formal schooling (or GED) and for Native Americans, 10.2 years. Fifty-seven percent of the Native American women had formal education of ten years or lower, while 27.2% of White women ended their education at that level. As a group, the female inmates averaged 10.9 years of formal schooling.

During the intake interview, inmates were asked to provide information about their juvenile and felony record. In some cases, the information was confirmed by a pre-sentence report. The inmates reported that 83.8% of their number had no juvenile record and 79% had no prior felony convictions as adults.

In examining the intake sheets, it became apparent that most of the inmates had been employed in some capacity, but most had been marginally employed and often for very brief periods. Because many of the jobs were comparable and almost no inmates had professional training, we organized the data to reflect only whether they had ever been employed. Nearly all—90%—had been employed in some capacity, although White inmates reported 95.6% employment and Native Americans, 79%. Furthermore, it was not clear from the intake interview whether the inmate was employed either at the time of committing the offense or at the time of sentencing, so we could not determine what role, if any, employment played in the sentencing decision.

### f. Testing for Differences in Punishment Severity

Many studies of racial discrimination in the criminal justice process use only descriptive statistics for analysis. However, by using inferential statistics not only can we generalize from a sample to a population, but we can test hypotheses. In this case, a student's t-test was used to analyze the difference between White and

Table 26.1   Offense Type by Felony Class with Frequency of White–Native American Convictions

| | | Number of Casts | |
|---|---|---|---|
| | | White | Native American |
| Felony Class | 1 | | |
| Maximum penalty | *Life imprisonment* | | |
| | Manslaughter | 1 | 1 |
| | 1st arson | 2 | 1 |
| Felony class | 2 | | |
| Maximum penalty | *25 yrs* | | |
| | 1st robbery | 2 | 1 |
| | 1st burglary | 1 | 2 |
| Felony class | 3 | | |
| Maximum penalty | *15 yrs* | | |
| | 2nd burglary | 6 | 2 |
| Felony class | 4 | | |
| Maximum penalty | *10 yrs* | | |
| | Aggravated assault | 3 | 10 |
| | Grand theft | 28 | 4 |
| | Possession of stolen property | 1 | 1 |
| | 3rd burglary | 8 | 5 |
| | Vehicular homicide | 1 | 1 |
| | Accessory to manslaughter | 1 | 1 |
| | Child abuse | 5 | 3 |
| | 2nd robbery | 1 | 1 |
| | Dist. of controlled substance | 11 | 2 |
| | Intentional damage to property | 1 | 3 |
| Felony class | 5 | | |
| Maximum penalty | *5 yrs* | | |
| | Forgery | 38 | 20 |
| | No account checks | 22 | 5 |
| | Distribution of marijuana | 5 | 2 |
| Felony class | 6 | | |
| Maximum penalty | *2 yrs* | | |
| | 3rd DWI | 30 | 21 |
| | Possession of forged instrument | 1 | 2 |
| | NSF checks | 12 | 4 |

Native American female inmates on our operationalized punishment variable. Using all felony classes, and after subtracting for years suspended, White inmates, on average, are sentenced to 44.3% of their maximum penalty, whereas Native American inmates are sentenced to an average of 45% of their maximum penalty, a difference of 0.7%.

Our research question was "how likely is it to see a difference of 0.7% in sentences received in the population?" About 86% of the time a difference of 0.7% in sentence received would occur between Whites and Native Americans when the

Table 26.2    Percent of Maximum Penalty with Years Suspended by Offense

| Offense | Number of Cases | | Percent of Maximum Penalty with Years Suspended (Average) | |
|---|---|---|---|---|
| | W | NA | W | NA |
| Aggravated assault | 3 | 10 | 31 | 34.4 |
| Grand theft | 28 | 4 | 33.3 | 25.3 |
| Forgery | 38 | 20 | 39 | 38.2 |
| No account check | 22 | 5 | 40.2 | 44 |
| 3rd DWI | 30 | 21 | 73.6 | 67.2 |

two population means are equal. Given these findings, it appears unlikely that for female inmates a statistically significant relationship exists between punishment severity and race.

In an effort to evaluate the statistical information more critically, we examined the offense categories with the greatest number of inmates to see if disparity in sentencing existed there. Most inmates in the study were convicted of Class 5 felonies (33.8%), followed closely by Class 4 (33.4%) and Class 6 (25.8%). Because of the small total number of inmates in the study (272), we were reluctant to differentiate among classes and attempt to draw universal conclusions. With that caution, separating the offenses into felony classes did not change the overall result: White and Native American women receive equivalent percentages of the maximum penalty.

By further examining the individual offenses of which the largest numbers of inmates were convicted, we hoped to discern any differences in sentences between the two groups. Again, as Table 26.2 indicates, the sentences were comparable, although not identical.

### g. Empirical Model Building

In addition to discovering any relationship between punishment severity and race, we were interested in knowing which independent variables or variable combinations best explained any variance in punishment severity. For example, does having a juvenile record, prior felony conviction or using a weapon affect sentencing decisions? And, do the same factors apply for both Whites and Native Americans? [At this point in the original article, results of the statistical analysis are presented.]

In short, these variables, whether taken individually or in the aggregate do not seem to make a significant impact on punishment severity either for White or Native American female inmates.

## 2. Inmate Perceptions of Disparity

To gain further insight into the existence of disparity in sentencing, the researchers developed a questionnaire which was distributed to all female inmates currently incarcerated at the Springfield Correctional Facility. A group meeting was held between the inmates and researchers to follow up on the initial questionnaire, and individual interviews were also conducted at that time. One life-term inmate incarcerated since 1973 dictated several hours of tapes to provide us with her insight into the existence of disparate treatment in the system, as well as its strengths and weaknesses. We analyzed this data in an effort to determine whether personal experiences and observations support the statistical results suggesting that there is no disparity in sentencing. We anticipated that the personal accounts might fill in some of the details which cannot be gleaned from a statistical analysis—such as whether discrimination occurred in a particular case. We should note that at the time of completing the questionnaire, the inmates did not know the results of the statistical analysis and so had relied on their own, admittedly limited, observations.

The results were an interesting mix of impressions, with both Whites and Native Americans reporting no discrimination against their own or the other race. Almost half of those responding thought Native Americans receive longer sentences because of prejudice or unfortunate stereotypes. Some relied solely on a comparison of their own case with other inmates',[7] while others gave more generalized impressions.[8] Some thought Native Americans were treated more leniently, or that the races were treated equally once they had been found guilty and the decision made to impose a prison sentence.

The women suggested several reasons other than race to explain perceived unfairness in sentencing. One suggested that South Dakota communities are too small to be fair and tend to exaggerate minor crimes. Another claimed the prosecutor in her case was not striving for justice, but only for "another notch on his gun." Another thought women aged twenty-four and younger tend to receive shorter sentences and are released sooner. Finally, one inmate said South Dakota "slams lengthy sentences on everyone," and wondered, "[i]s it Midwestern tradition?"

When asked whether men or women receive harsher sentences for the same crime, many of the inmates responded that judges sentence women more harshly. Some of the reasons cited were: "they assume mothers are born perfect mothers;" "women aren't supposed to get in trouble;" and it is worse when the offense "isn't accepted by the puritanist attitude most men still harbor towards women." Other women disagreed, pointing out that "many women come in with sixty days, ninety days, and the same guy comes in with five years." One woman suggested there should be a difference in treatment, saying "judges are harder on the women here in South Dakota than they are on men. Showing no compassion for the babies and husband they are separated from."

The inmate who gave us her detailed observations had conflicting impressions about discrimination, which resulted in a more complex picture of the sentencing and incarceration process. With respect to racial discrimination she commented:

> I don't feel that a Native American Indian is any worse off than the whites. If they are treated different in the system, I have noticed they come in with a chip on, and they seem to think they have more rights because they're Native American or their attitude is bad. I have some good friends, and I'm a half breed; however, it is not the whites

who are prejudiced in the prison system it is the Indian themself [sic]. They are very, very prejudiced against white inmates, against guards, against the system, and they expect better treatment than anybody else gets.

But upon further reflection, she added:

I do believe that if the American Indian is treated any different, it's because they usually are very, very quiet people. I have found them easier to do time with because they do stay to theirselves [sic], but they usually hang out with their own, but they're very, very intimidated by the white status authority. So rather than speak up to get what they want, or to not get walked all over, or whatever, they will let it slide and then somebody will say, '[w]ell you can't do that, it's against your rights,' and all of a sudden they realize they have rights. But it is not with intent that the staff shows favoritism.

With respect to the effectiveness of prison as a method of rehabilitation she commented:

Actually, something you find very interesting is the fact that once women come in here, they revert back to almost high school days. You know, they talk parties, and men, and dress, and makeup. If they're 40 years old, they begin to flit and flop around, wear their hair in ponytails, and try to be 15 again. I'm not quite sure I understand, unless it's the lack of responsibility in prison. . . . [A]ctually every bit of responsible characteristics that we are taught to respond to are taken from us in a system devised to dominate. I think it subdues us because of the authority.

She emphasized this lack of responsibility and its detrimental effect on those who will be released from prison, pointing out how easily people become institutionalized, how the lack of responsibility causes recidivism, and how the personal growth people experience on the outside is completely lacking in prison.

Based on these comments it is evident that many inmates of both races perceive the existence of racial discrimination. Their personal observations may be limited and not unbiased, but equally likely, they reflect the continued existence of disparate treatment in at least some cases.

## B. Sex as a Factor in Sentencing—Males and Females Incarcerated in South Dakota

Although the primary focus of this study was to detect racial discrimination in the sentences given to Native American and White women in South Dakota, the researchers thought it would be useful to compare the sentences given to women and men in the state. The rationale was that the study of female inmates had a methodology similar, although not identical, to the 1985 study of male inmates of the South Dakota penitentiary. We hoped to gain a more complete picture of sentencing in the state by making the comparison.

At the outset, it is important to note that the data from the two studies are different in significant ways, so any conclusions reached are tentative, at best. First, the period of time for the two studies is different, with that of the male inmates

Table 26.3   Percent of Maximum Penalty by Sex for Selected Offenses with Prior Record Considered

|  | Nbr. Cases | Percent of Max. | Nbr. Cases | Percent of Max. | Nbr. Cases | Percent of Max. |
|---|---|---|---|---|---|---|
|  | No Prior Felonies | | One Prior Felony | | Two or More Prior Felonies | |
| Aggravated assault | | | | | | |
| Men | 19 | 55.2 | 7 | 60.0 | 11 | 61.8 |
| Women | 10 | 33.7 | 3 | 33.3 | 0 | -0- |
| Grand theft | | | | | | |
| Men | 41 | 37.5 | 25 | 42.8 | 40 | 62.7 |
| Women | 26 | 34.3 | 4 | 23.2 | 2 | 24.0 |
| Forgery | | | | | | |
| Men | 19 | 57.8 | 7 | 68.5 | 15 | 73.3 |
| Women | 42 | 38.2 | 9 | 41.1 | 7 | 52.4 |
| Passing no account check | | | | | | |
| Men | 8 | 50.0 | 3 | 40.0 | 17 | 62.3 |
| Women | 21 | 40.5 | 0 | -0- | 3 | 43.3 |
| DWI, 3rd offense | | | | | | |
| Men | 20 | 76.6 | 15 | 88.3 | 15 | 90.0 |
| Women | 43 | 70.9 | 5 | 70.0 | 3 | 73.3 |

measuring sentence lengths of inmates sentenced between 1981–1985 still in the penitentiary during the summer of 1985, and that of female inmates measuring sentence lengths from 1980 through 1988. One reason for the differing time periods is the very small number of female inmates. Their low number, compared to the relatively large number of male inmates, makes a comparison of sentencing data more difficult because of the inability to make reasonable generalizations. Related to the population size is the problem of criminal behavior—most of the women were incarcerated for non-violent, less serious offenses than the men. Finally, the study of male inmates did not include an analysis of the number and ages of their children, so it is not possible to compare the nature of each group's families to see whether that plays an important role. These methodological problems render it impossible to completely explain differences in sentences between the two groups.

With these qualifications in mind, the researchers assessed the sentences imposed on female and male offenders in the state. The methodology was described in the original article with the further modification that the only offenses with a sufficient number of females to compare to the males were aggravated assault, grand theft, passing no account checks, forgery and driving while intoxicated (DWI). Table 26.3 lists the offenses and percentages of maximum penalty minus years suspended for both sexes.

As is apparent from the figures, women receive significantly lower sentences than men convicted of the same offense in the five selected categories. Explaining the differences is problematic. For example, the relatively low sentences for women convicted of aggravated assault could be offense-based, that is, that their conduct was relatively less culpable than their male counterparts. On the other hand, paternalism could be a factor, in that a judge could view a woman's deviation from her expected conduct as an anomaly and less of a threat than a similar act by a male. Also, the relatively small number of cases could explain the judge's perception of women as law abiding citizens, making the need to punish an individual offender less pressing.

Such proffered explanations are less persuasive when a sex neutral offense such as DWI is under consideration. In that type of case, the conduct of an offender is similar, regardless of sex, yet the punishments are disparate. It is interesting to note, however, that the punishments are closer for this offense than for any of the others, and that the penalties for both sexes are relatively high, at eighty-four percent of the maximum penalty for men and seventy percent for women.

In an effort to scrutinize this data, the researchers chose to control for prior felonies to see whether that had an impact on the punishment received. Table 26.3 lists the percentages of the maximum penalty for offenders of both sexes, breaking the groups into those with none, one, and two or more prior felonies.

The effects on the male offenders of a prior conviction are what would be expected: the penalties for all but one category increase with each conviction. For the female inmates, however, the effect of prior felony convictions is negligible, with the exception of one offense category. Why a judge would consider a prior felony an aggravating circumstance for a male and not a female is certainly not apparent from the data. Perhaps other factors in the individual woman's file would justify the different treatment—for example, that the prior felony was non-violent or not particularly egregious, or that the woman had become the sole parent in her family. Such explanations are speculative, however, for the data reveal no concrete rationale for the difference in treatment.

## Conclusion

The statistical analysis of the sentences imposed on Native American and White women during 1980–1988 indicates that the sentences for both groups are comparable for similar offenses. On its face, the study suggests that judges do not discriminate based on race in the imposition of sentences for female offenders. Such a conclusion would be overbroad, however, for it fails to account for discrimination which might have occurred in individual cases but it is not statistically significant. In addition, since this study addresses discrimination in sentencing, it does not attempt to measure the disparity in treatment in other phases of the criminal process, such as arrest and plea bargaining.

Furthermore, whether or not actual disparity exists, the perception of unfair treatment does, as is indicated by the comments of some of the penitentiary inmates of the penitentiary. Their impressions reflect the views of many in the state who allege that discrimination permeates the system.[9] Such conclusions may be erroneous, but may also indicate the existence of discrimination in other phases of the system.

The statistical analysis of sentences imposed on female and male offenders for selected offenses indicates that sex does play an important role in sentencing, and that in South Dakota, a woman will likely receive a significantly lower penalty than a man convicted of the same offense. This conclusion must be qualified because of the flaws in the data compared. However, even with the differences in study populations accounted for, it appears women receive lighter sentences. Why that happens—whether because of paternalism, single parenthood or less violent offense—is not apparent from the data. Likewise, whether that result is appropriate, because of legally relevant factors such as prior convictions, is not explained by the statistics. Further exploration of this information should precede any decision to lengthen women's sentences or shorten men's merely to achieve statistical equality. The factors resulting in disparate results may represent valid differences in the position of the female and male offenders and not represent discrimination because of sex.

As one director of studies of sentencing practices quipped: "[a]fter fifty years of research on whether or not there are racial or ethnic disparities in sentencing, there is only one generalizable finding: Sometimes judges discriminate and sometimes they don't" (Unnever and Hembroff, 1988:53).

The results of this study indicate that as a general proposition, judges in South Dakota might discriminate on the basis of sex, and probably do not discriminate on the basis of race for female offenders. Why they behave in this way remains unanswered, though the data and inmate commentary suggest a rich source for continuing investigation.

## NOTES

1. U.S. Department of Commerce, 1980, South Dakota 43–10 (1982). "These figures reveal significant growth since the 1970 census figures which showed a Native American population of 32,365 comprising 4.9% of the state's total population (665,507)" (Pommersheim and Wise, 1987:20, citing U.S. Department of Commerce 1970, South Dakota Table 17-(1971)). "Bureau of Census population statistics for Native Americans are generally conceded to be low and estimates of the Indian population in South Dakota vary significantly. Nevertheless, the census data indicate a population increase of 39 percent [sic] for Native Americans between 1970 and 1980" (Pommersheim and Wise, 1987:20, citing U.S. Commission on Civil Rights. South Dakota Advisory Committee, 1977:3). Whether this is due to population growth or improved counting procedures is unknown.

2. South Dakota Board of Charities and Corrections, 1987. Two hundred forty-six out of one thousand seventy-five inmates were Native Americans. This compares to the November 1976 figures of 131 out of 500 inmates or approximately 26% of the prison population.

3. See also 18 U.S.C. §§ 1151, 1152, and 1153 (1982 Supp. II 1984) (defining Indian Country and preserving tribal and federal criminal jurisdiction over all Indians who com-

mit criminal offenses on the reservation, on trust land, or in dependent Indian communities off the reservation).

4. County; offense; number of convictions; sentence length; maximum penalty; percent of the maximum received; judge; whether there was a defense attorney; type of plea; race; whether a weapon was used to commit the offense; alcohol, drug or mental problem; age; education; military status; whether the person had ever been employed; juvenile record; number of prior felonies; sentence data; length of sentence minus years suspended; percent of the maximum penalty with suspension; sex; number of children under age ten and age ten and over.

5. Class A and B felonies include murder, with a maximum penalty of death or life imprisonment. None of the inmates in the sample were convicted of either class of offense.

6. Broken down by race, of the 92 Native American inmates, 31 (33%) had children 10 years of age or older and 57 (52%) had children under 10 years of age. Of the 180 inmates, 40 (23%) had children 10 years of age or older and 96 (53%) had children under 10 years of age. Eighty women, including twenty-one Native Americans and fifty-nine whites, had no children.

7. Interview with an unnamed inmate at the Women's Correctional Facility, Springfield, South Dakota (Mar. 1987) (transcript on file with authors). "I came in with white women and they both got lesser time and are already paroled."

8. (As note 7). "I also did time in Oklahoma and Wyoming. It was true in all these places that Indian women received longer sentences."

9. E.g., Giago, "Harsh Penalties for Indians Suggest Dual Justice System," *Sioux Falls Argus Leader,* Sept. 4, 1988:7; Young, "Liberty and Justice for All?" *Sioux Falls Argus Leader,* Aug. 10–13, 1986 (4-part series).

PART SEVEN

# *Corrections*

# 27

*The Durango Herald*

## SWEATING IT OUT

### Religious Ritual Helps Inmates Pass Time

BY JUAN ESPINOSA

FLORENCE—Man goes to prison; man finds religion—it's a familiar tune with a new beat.

Indians at state and federal prisons across the nation are rediscovering their indigenous religion. Their church is the ceremonial sweat lodge and the beat for the prayer ceremonies is pounded out of a small drum.

The federal prison camp near here recently became the latest prison to get a sweat lodge.

Under direction of Lenny Foster, director of the Navajo Nation Corrections Project, a dozen inmates spent three hours building a lodge that

*The Durango Herald*, "Sweating It Out: Religious Ritual Helps Inmates Pass Time," Juan Espinosa for the *Pueblo Chieftain*. Sunday, May 30, 1993. Used by permission.

will be used for weekly religious services.

After Foster discussed the layout of the ceremonial area with the inmates, the inmates eagerly went to work digging a fire pit and setting the first willows for the lodge.

"The sweat lodge is a very important and ancient practice of our indigenous people of North America," Foster said. "It's a central part of the ceremony and provides spiritual foundation for ceremonies and practices."

Through the sweat lodge, Indians believe they receive insight, cleansing and purification.

"It helps give a person insight into their behavior and attitudes and helps them reflect on that. That's why the sweat lodge is the most important function for Native Americans when they're incarcerated," Foster said.

Donovan Long, 21, who is part Hopi, was one of the most enthusiastic of the inmates.

"We've been waiting a long time to get this sweat lodge together," he said. "It's a good day to sweat; it's a good day to be alive."

While Foster and the inmates worked, three prison employees watched—chaplains Rev. John Lamsna and Rev. Anthony Wojcinski and executive assistant Julie Alba. They offered reserved endorsements of the project.

Wojcinski was the most ardent. He said he has had three to four years of experiences with a sweat lodge community inside the Fremont Correctional state prison in Canon City.

"As the Indian community became more and more immersed in Indian traditions and religious beliefs, it truly has had a transformational effect on them," he said. "You would find a dramatic difference from before the time they had sweat lodges and today."

Ms. Alba said allowing inmates to have sweat lodges is required and she hopes it will be beneficial.

"This is helping them find a way to cope with being incarcerated," she said.

"Mother Earth is giving us a lesson today. . . . We are very small compared to everything else," said Buddy Goddard, a Shoshone, as he looked up at the sky.

Goddard said he has found that entering the sweat lodge relieves his anxieties and helps him have a spiritual attitude. He made no attempt to contain his excitement.

"I've tried other religions and this is my church," he said. "I've been looking forward to this day. This is our day. This is it! It's going to help me a lot for the rest of my time here."

Long also said the sweat lodge would make serving time easier.

"It helps me deal with being incarcerated," he said. "It helps me maintain a positive attitude. I feel I can share with my brothers. In the lodge, I pray for everybody. We're all brothers."

After the sweat lodge was built, Foster led the group in a prayer service at which a cornhusk cigar filled with a sweet wild tobacco was smoked.

"You guys did a good job," said Foster. "You put your good efforts into it. It's a continuation of our struggle. It's a beautiful cause. I encourage you to make that vow to carry on these ways. They're not in books. We didn't go by any textbooks. We did it right because it's in our hearts."

A second sweat lodge was supposed to have been built at the medium security prison in the general complex, but Indian inmates were not satisfied with its proper location, Foster said.

# 28

# AMERICAN INDIANS IN PRISON

E. GROBSMITH

Nebraska Indian prisoners have served as a model for Indian inmates nationwide since they began the process of asserting their rights to religious freedom. The dissemination of information concerning Indian prisoners has now become widespread, and two major channels of communication have served to inform both correctional administrators and inmates of what practices are commonly accepted in prisons across the country: Native American travel in and out of the state of Nebraska, and legal decisions handed down by the U.S. District Court in Nebraska, Eighth Circuit, which have guided correctional policy as it pertains to Indian prisoners. Correctional authorities in other states have contacted the Nebraska Department of Correctional Services for information on ways in which they have addressed Indian inmates' concerns, and firms such as the Native American Rights Fund in Boulder, Colorado, have provided information to prisons on issues they have litigated. Native American prisoners also have strong communication links with brothers in other penal institutions, supported by regular publication of newsletters such as the *Iron House Drum* and *Journal of Prisoners on Prisons* and national conferences sponsored by the Native American Prisoners Rehabilitation Research Project. Reprints of scholarly publications on issues of incarceration are requested by Indian inmates in a number of states, resulting in an increase in interprison communication and plans for initiating new litigation. Within a decade, it is likely that prison policy concerning Native American cultural and spiritual practices will be significantly more uniform and culturally tolerant.

Because there is a paucity of published information concerning Native American prisoners nationwide, I designed a survey and sent it to all state and federal correctional facilities in the United States during 1988 and 1989. All six fed-

Edited version of "American Indians in Prison," reprinted from *Indians in Prison: Incarcerated Native Americans in Nebraska*, by Elizabeth S. Grobsmith, by permission of the University of Nebraska Press and the author. © 1994 by the University of Nebraska Press.

Table 28.1   Indian Prison Population by State

| State | Number of Native Americans | % of Prison Population† | Tribes Represented |
|---|---|---|---|
| Alabama | * | 0.0 | |
| Alaska | 800 | 31.9 | Tlingit, Haida, Inuit |
| Arizona | ** | 3.1 | ** |
| Arkansas | * | | * |
| California | 362 | 0.5 | Pomo, Sioux, Pit River |
| Colorado | 47 | 1.3 | * |
| Connecticut | 12 | 0.1 | Cherokee, Maliseet, Passamquoddy, Choctaw, Penobscot, Aleut, Shawnee |
| Delaware | 2 | 0.1 | Nanticoke |
| District of Columbia | * | 0.0 | * |
| Florida | 16 | * | * |
| Georgia | * | 0.0 | * |
| Hawaii | 12 | 0.9 | * |
| Idaho | 42 | 4.3 | Shoshone, Nez Perce |
| Illinois | 27 | 0.2 | * |
| Indiana | 15–20 | 0.2 | * |
| Iowa | 43 | 1.6 | Sioux (and others unknown) |
| Kansas | 50 | 1.4 | Kickapoo, Yakima, Potawatomi, Navajo |
| Kentucky | 1 | 0.4 | * |
| Louisiana | 2 | * | * |
| Maine | 19 | 1.0 | Penobscot |
| Maryland | 7 | <1 | * |
| Massachusetts | 12 | 0.2 | * |
| Michigan | 108 | 0.4 | Ojibway, Chippewa |
| Minnesota | 207 | 8.3 | Sioux, Chippewa |
| Mississippi | 8 | 0.1 | Choctaw |
| Missouri | 18 | 0.2 | * |
| Montana | 234 | 18.3 | Kootenai, Salish, Cree, Chippewa, Crow, Blackfeet, Sioux |
| Nebraska | 100 | 3.9 | Omaha, Winnebago, Sioux, Chippewa, Cherokee, Ponca |
| Nevada | 56 | 1.4 | Washoe, Paiute, Shawnee |
| New Hampshire | * | 0.3 | |
| New Jersey | 4 | * | * |
| New Mexico | ** | 3.0 | |
| New York | 25 | 0.2 | Mohawk, Onondaga, Seneca, Cayuga |
| North Carolina | 360 | 2.2 | Lumbee, Cherokee, Tuscarora, Haliwa |
| North Dakota | 106 | 22.2 | Sioux, Chippewa |
| Ohio | ** | 0.0 | |
| Oklahoma | 360 | 5.7 | Cherokee, Creek, Choctaw, Seminole, Chickasaw, Ponca, Araphao, Kansa, Osage, Caddo, Comanche, Otoe, Cheyenne, Apache, Sioux, Chippewa, Shawnee, Kiowa, Potawatomi |

*(continues)*

Table 28.1   *continued*

| State | Number of Native Americans | % of Prison Population† | Tribes Represented |
|-------|---------------------------|------------------------|---------------------|
| Oregon | 107 | 2.2 | Klamath, Modoc, Siletz, Sioux, Eskimo, Shoshone, Umatilla, Warm Springs, Paiute, Tlingit, Cherokee, Comanche, Blackfoot, Grand Ronde |
| Pennsylvania | 8 | 0.1 | * |
| Rhode Island | 3 | 0.2 | Narragansett |
| South Carolina | 13 | 0.1 | * |
| South Dakota | 262 | 25.4 | Sioux, Winnebago, Omaha |
| Tennessee | ** | 0.0 | ** |
| Texas | 4 | 0.01 | * |
| Utah | 42 | 3.4 | * |
| Vermont | 0 | 0.0 | * |
| Virginia | * | 0.0 | * |
| Washington | 258 | 3.7 | Yakima |
| West Virginia | * | 0.1 | * |
| Wisconsin | 148 | 2.2 | Chippewa, Oneida, Winnebago, Menominee |
| Wyoming | 43 | 5.4 | Skoux, Shoshone, Crow, Arapahoe, Cheyenne |

†Figures from Camp and Camp 1992:4–5, except where no data are available; in these instances, percentages reflect survey data.

*Too few to count or unknown.

**No survey response (data may be available elsewhere).

eral correctional facilities in the United States during 1988 and 1989. All six federal facilities and all but three states responded.

## SURVEY RESPONSE FROM STATE PENAL INSTITUTIONS

Since states were inconsistent in the manner in which they responded to the survey, the numbers of Indian prisoners may be greatly underrepresented. For example, in one state only one correctional facility may have responded to the survey, while another state system duplicated the survey and sent in responses from five or six different facilities. Some states, such as Oklahoma, collated responses from all their institutions and provided a single summary for the entire state. In the interest of consistency, Indian prison population figures from *The Corrections Yearbook 1992* are presented in Table 28.1, Indian Prison Population by State. In most instances, those figures were very close to the survey figures.

The identification of tribal affiliations in prisons was also problematic. During intake, administrators usually ask for an inmate's racial or ethnic identity, but the intake officer may record this information based solely on appearance. The tribes represented in Table 28.1 reflect only those *known* by the prison administration. The race/ethnic affiliation on intake forms in "Native American," not a specific tribe; further, if an inmate is Native American but doesn't necessarily conform to the stereotype of what Indians look like, he or she is likely to be classified by intake officers as black, Hispanic, or "other."

In twenty-one states the Indian inmates make up 1 percent or more of the state prison population. Approximately half the states in this grouping are located in the plains. In South Dakota, Indians comprise 7 percent of the state population but represent approximately 26 percent of all inmates in the State Penitentiary in Sioux Falls (Grobsmith 1989:286). Other states with relatively large Indian populations also have disproportionately large Indian prison populations, notably Idaho, Minnesota, Montana, North Dakota, Oklahoma, Oregon, Washington, Wyoming, and Alaska. Alaska has the highest population of incarcerated Indians and Alaska Natives, but this is not surprising since they represent proportionately such a large percentage of the general population. In Nebraska, the Indian prison population has ranged in the last several years between 3.1 percent and 4.4 percent, approximately triple the percentage of Indians residing in the state.

# 29

# DISCRIMINATION REVISITED

T. BYNUM AND R. PATERNOSTER

*[Editors' note: In the original, the authors performed statistical analyses that have been omitted from this version.]*

## INTRODUCTION

The relationship between "extra-legal" attributes and criminal justice system processing has occupied the attention of legal scholars and sociologists for over twenty years. One such attribute which perhaps has received the most attention is the race of the defendant. This interest in race is rooted in two major theoretical traditions, the conflict perspective and labeling theory.

Conflict theorists have generally emphasized the role of economic, political and cultural power in the creation and maintenance of social order (Coser, 1956; Dahrendorf, 1957; Collins, 1975). In terms of legal system processing this has meant that criminal sanctions are used by the powerful as a mechanism through which those who threaten the interests of the status quo may be controlled (Gordon, 1973; Spitzer, 1975; Quinney, 1977). As power is distributed along class and racial lines in American society, threats to the existing power structure are seen by conflict theorists as identified by class and racial group membership. Members of racial minorities, inasmuch as they are disproportionately members

Edited version of T. Bynum and R. Paternoster, "Discrimination Revisited: An Exploration of Frontstage and Backstage Criminal Justice Decision Making," *Sociology and Social Research* 69(1):90–108. 1984. Reprinted by permission of *Sociology and Social Research* and the authors. Copyright © University of Southern California 1984. All rights reserved.

The authors would like to thank Kurt Siedschlaw for collecting the data used in this article and Katherine McCracken of the Social Science Bureau at Michigan State University for her editorial assistance.

of the lower economic class, can be expected to be subject to more frequent and more severe treatment at all levels in the criminal justice system. In an early statement of the conflict position, Chambliss (1969:86) noted this tendency of class bias in American criminal justice: "A consequence of the unequal ability of members of different social classes to reward the legal system is that at every step of the legal process the lower class person is more likely to feel the sting of the law enforcement process." Although most conflict theorists speak in terms of *class* conflict and *class* bias in the operation of the legal system, conflict theory can also be used to derive propositions about racial disparity. Although there is a strong relationship between race and social class position, this is not to say that race and class effects are coterminous. Racial disparity and class bias, though interrelated, are independent features of differential legal processing.

Within the conflict perspective, there are several reasons to expect racial disparity within official criminal justice activities. One of these emphasizes the powerlessness of racial minorities in American society. Conflict theorists, such as Turk (1969:163) suggest that racial minorities are more likely to receive harsh treatment in the legal system because they lack sufficient resources and power relative to norm enforcers: ". . . there is no doubt that nonwhites in the United States are more powerless than are whites to affect legal decisions or to resist their implementation . . . every indicator continues to point to the relatively disadvantaged position of the nonwhite in this country." According to Turk, the relative powerlessness of non-Whites will ensure a one-way flow of criminalization because their behavior is both more subject to criminal definition and because (p. 169) "nonwhites are less able than whites to resist enforcement." The relative inability to resist enforcement occurs not only at the police "street level" of justice but at bail, access to counsel, sentencing and beyond.

Labeling theorists entertain a similar expectation concerning the discriminatory application of the criminal sanction to racial minorities. One reason for this expectation is identical to that offered by conflict theorists—the relative lack of power of racial minorities and the threat to social order posed by the powerless in the eyes of the powerful. Similar to Turk's (1969:70) contention that "the greater the power difference in favor of norm enforcers over resisters, the greater the probability of criminalization" is the claim of one labeling theorist (Lofland, 1969:14) that: ". . . deviance is the name of the conflict game in which individuals or loosely organized small groups *with little power* are feared by a well-organized, sizable, minority or majority who have a large amount of power" (emphasis added). Furthermore, just as Turk expressed that the greater probability of criminalization for Blacks in America is, in part, a product of their powerlessness, Becker (1963:12–13) noted that: "The degree to which an act will be treated as deviant depends also on who feels he has been harmed by it. Rules tend to be applied more to some persons than others . . . the law is differentially applied to Negroes than whites."

In his discussion of labeling processes, Schur (1971) noted that outcomes of deviant events are not determined solely by the behavior of deviance-processing organizations. Between those labeling and those being labeled there is considerable bargaining and negotiation that significantly influences if a deviant label is applied and if so, of which type. In terms of negotiation and bargaining over the application of criminal labels, racial minorities, because of a lack of resources (competent legal counsel, bail money, etc.) are more likely to find themselves in a disadvantageous position, and so receive more severe treatment.

In addition to the relative power position of non-Whites, conflict and labeling theorists posit other reasons for expecting racial disparity in the outcomes of legal processing. Turk (1969:169–170), for instance, claims that non-Whites are more likely to be criminalized than Whites because they are more likely to disagree over legal norms and because they are less likely to make "realistic" or "sophisticated" (i.e., conflict-reducing) moves vis-à-vis norm enforcers. In a similar vein, labeling theorists would predict a greater severity of treatment for minorities because of the existence and use of racial stereotypes at the organizational-processing level (Lofland, 1969, Simmons, 1969; Schur, 1971; Hawkins and Tiedeman, 1975). The stereotyping of particular racial minorities as "crime prone" and the considerable discretion within which such typifications could operate would be expected to result in minority group members being more severely sanctioned by deviance control organizations.

As can be seen, there are important theoretical convergences between the conflict and labeling perspectives which would lead theorists from both traditions to predict racial disparity in the application of legal sanctions. Theorists from both perspectives would agree that in American society racial minorities have been economically and politically suppressed, putting them in a subordinate position both in organizationally-based negotiation processes and in large-scale power conflicts. In addition, there is a rich tradition of stereotypes around their criminality, stereotypes shared not only by the general public but by "norm enforcers."

Although the expectation that racial minorities will receive harsh treatment by the legal system is derived from at least two well-established theoretical perspectives, the empirical evidence in support of it has been less than conclusive. Research on the relationship between suspect's race and the decision to make an arrest have provided inconsistent support for the racial disparity hypothesis. While most studies have shown that Blacks are more likely to be arrested, some researchers have concluded that this is due to legal considerations, such as the seriousness of the offense (Terry, 1967; Black and Reiss, 1970; Black, 1971), the antagonistic demeanor of Black suspects (Black, 1971), or the dispositional preference of complainants (Black and Reiss, 1970; Lundman, et al., 1978). Other studies, however, have suggested that the race/arrest relationship is not artifactual (Black, 1968; Lundman, 1974; Visher, 1983; Smith, 1984).

Research on the relationship between race and the sentencing decision has been no more conclusive. While some studies have found that the race of the defendant does affect either the type or length of sentence (Chiricos, et al., 1972; Thomas and Cage, 1977; Lizotte, 1977; Liska and Tausig, 1979; Thornberry, 1979; Farnworth and Horan, 1980; Unnever, 1982), others have found either very weak or no such effect (Burke and Turk, 1975; Chiricos and Waldo, 1975; Bernstein, et al., 1977; Cohen and Kluegel, 1978; Hagan, et al., 1979).

It might appear from the literature on racial correlates of arrest and sentencing that the conflict and labeling proposition about racial disparity in legal decision making has been discredited. Consideration of the *context* of the arrest and sentencing decisions within the overall system of social control, however, may bring to light both a possible interpretation of the lack of evidence of racial disparity at these levels and suggestions for alternative research strategies. In examining why so little support for the racial bias hypothesis has been found, it is helpful to remember that some legal decisions are highly visible ceremonies, taking place in the "front region" (Goffman, 1959) of the legal system. Inasmuch as sentencing is a public ceremony, conducted in places easily accessible to public view, as is the decision to arrest in the presence of a complainant, it behooves the personnel in the system to follow the officially espoused ideology of egalitarianism. Operating under an official ideology of equal treatment before the law, and hemmed in by the public and quasi-public nature of its proceedings, police and court workers are at times relatively restricted in the opportunity to use extra-legal information in decision making. This is not to say, of course, that there is no disparity along racial lines in the legal system; rather it is to say with Green (1964:357) that if there is, it is "more apt to occur in the less public phases of the administration of justice."

If there is racial bias in the criminal justice system, then it is more likely to appear in less visible ceremonies. Goffman (1959:113) has referred to these regions of social interaction as "backstages." As "backstage" areas, the events occurring within them are often totally withheld from public view: "the back region will be the place where the performer can reliably expect that no member of the audience will intrude." Shielded from public scrutiny, the performance of actors "backstage" may often violate official or public expectations. Indeed, as Goffman (1959:111–112) makes clear, because they are not open to public view, backstage events may deliberately contradict the impression created in the more visible front region:

> . . . when one's activity occurs in the presence of other persons, some aspects of the activity are expressively accentuated and other aspects, which might discredit the fostered impression, are suppressed. It is clear that accentuated facts make their appearance in what I have called a front region; it should be just as clear that there may be another region—a "back region"—where the suppressed facts make an appearance.
>
> A back region or backstage may be defined as a place, relative of a given performance, where the impression fostered by the performance is knowingly contradicted as a matter of course.

In front region ceremonies, such as police-suspect-complainant interactions and criminal trials, proceedings are deliberately imbued with a spirit of legal equality. Discrimination may yet appear in backstage events, with "suppressed facts making an appearance." A limitation of previous studies on the role of race in legal decision making, then, is that they have often been conducted in frontstage regions.

There are, however, regions in the legal process which are more nearly protected from public inspection and scrutiny, regions where only criminal justice system actors have access. In these areas research showing racial disparity in treatment has been more consistent. Studies on the prosecutor's issuing of arrest warrants (Hepburn, 1978); access to private counsel (Swigert and Farrell, 1977; Unnever, 1982), and release on bail (Lizotte, 1977; Unnever, 1982; Bynum, 1982) show either a direct or indirect effect for the defendant's race. One other backstage, low-visibility decision point in the criminal justice process which has received relatively little research attention is the granting of parole.

Except in those states with rigorous determinate sentencing laws, the decision to release an offender from incarceration has been in the hands of paroling authorities. With but few exceptions parole decisions have been made at hearings conducted within prison walls beyond the purview of all but parole board members and inmates. In addition, paroling authorities have virtually unguided and untrammeled discretion (Stanley, 1976; Coffee, 1978; von Hirsch and Hanrahan, 1979). The few studies that have focused on the impact of race on paroling decisions suggest that at this stage racial minorities may receive more severe treatment than Whites. In their study of parole decision making, Carroll and Mondrick (1976) found that Black inmates served a significantly longer proportion of their sentence than Whites before being released on parole. In a study of early exit from prison on "shock probation," Peterson and Friday (1975) found that race was the strongest factor in predicting this form of release.

In summary, the inconsistent evidence found in previous research for the unequal treatment of racial minorities in legal processing may reflect the *context* within which that treatment takes place. Frontstage regions are exposed to public intervention and intrusion making it difficult for norm enforcers to depart from the espoused ideology of equal legal treatment. Such departures from the official ideology of the legal system can more readily be conducted in hidden or backstage regions, such as parole hearings. Past research has ignored this contextual element, which may explain the inconsistencies in the literature.

A second limitation of this racial disparity literature is that for the most part studies on the effect of race in legal system decision making have restricted their attention to the difference in how Whites and Blacks are treated. Little research has been done on how the legal system treats other minorities, even though in some states Chicanos and Native Americans comprise a significant proportion of the non-White population. Of the published literature, only the studies of Lundman (1974), Hall and Simkus (1975), Lizotte (1977), Hagan (1975), Hagan, et al., (1979), and Unnever (1982) have included non-Black samples. An examination of the legal treatment experienced by Native Americans would provide a clear test of the conflict/labeling hypothesis since they are perhaps the most oppressed minority group in American society (Talbot, 1981).

In summary, although the proposition that racial minorities will be more severely treated by the legal system is predicted by two major theoretical perspectives, research efforts to date have been inconclusive. This may reflect the fact that researchers have ignored an important contextual variable, the location of the event in the front or backstage of legal processing. In addition, the scope of their inquiry has been unnecessarily restricted to an examination of Black-White differentials, with little attention directed toward the treatment of other racial minorities.

This paper reports on an attempt to explore criminal justice decision making in a backstage region. It focuses on how one American minority group, the Native American, fares in the decision to grant parole. In keeping with previous research findings and the theoretical expectations they have given rise to, we hypothesize that although Native Americans may not be treated more severely in the frontstage sentencing decision, they are more likely to receive more harsh treatment in the backstage decision to release on parole. In an earlier study, Swift and Bickel (1974) found that Native Americans in the federal prison system served 15 percent more time in prison than Whites before being released on parole. It is not clear from the Swift and Bickel study, however, whether this was due to racial discrimination since they also reported that Indians received longer sentences than Whites, and they did not consider other relevant parole criteria such as prison infractions and prior criminal history. The present study will incorporate controls for relevant legal factors and social characteristics in an attempt to more precisely address the issue of parole release and Native Americans.

## Data and Method

The data employed in this analysis came from an upper plains state with a relatively large Native American population. At the time of the study an indeterminate sentencing system was in effect, with inmates being eligible for parole after serving one-fourth of their maximum sentence. Furthermore, there were no parole guidelines in operation which would restrict parole board decisions. Thus, in the absence of such formal criteria, parole board members possessed wide discretion in the granting of release from prison.

In order to allow sufficient time for most offenders to either be paroled or released, data were gathered from institutional records for a cohort of offenders admitted to the state prison system during 1970. Excluded from the sample were those offenders who were not eligible for release during this period (i.e., those serving life or extremely long sentences). Thus, all individuals in the sample had completed their sentence either through release on parole or serving their maximum sentence.[1] Excluded, too, were categories of offenses so singular (e.g., child molesting, extortion, [total excluded = 7]) that their inclusion might have distorted the analysis. This procedure resulted in a sample of 137 offenders, of which 54, or 39 percent were Native Americans.

In the following analysis, several approaches are used to determine the severity of sanction imposed as well as the importance of various factors in the parole decisions. Initially the relationships between the independent variables and two indicators of sanction severity, mean length of sentence imposed and proportion of time served prior to parole, are explored. Rather than simply looking at time served before parole this latter measure relates time served to sentence imposed to obtain a single measure of severity of sanction.[2] An offender who serves two years of a four-year sentence has served longer than one who has served eighteen months of a two-year sentence, but the second offender has clearly been punished proportionately more severely. Following such a procedure overcomes a traditional weakness in parole studies and one that is particularly problematic for Swift and Bickel's (1974) earlier study of parole decisions involving Native Americans.

Two variables representing the "legal" factors influencing the parole decision were used: the number of prior felony convictions of the offender and the number of major infractions committed while incarcerated. (Major infractions were defined according to department of corrections policy and included such actions as assaults, refusing to obey orders, and possession of weapons). Sixty-five percent of the sample had at least one prior felony conviction and 50 percent had at least one major prison infraction. Additional information concerning behavior in prison that may influence parole decisions, such as participation in correctional programs, was not available. While having finalized a parole plan including adequate job and living arrangements is an important aspect of the actual date of release, in this study the release date was calculated using the date of parole approval which may have been in advance of the submission of a complete parole plan.

Three variables—Indian status, age at admission to prison, and educational level—were used to represent the impact of social factors upon parole decisions. Further measurements of social status, such as income or occupation were not consistently available. The mean age at admission was 29.3 years, while the mean educational level was 9.5 years.

## Findings

To examine the differences between front and backstage ceremonies, Tables 29.1 and 29.2 present the relevant independent variables, the mean length of sentence imposed and the proportion of time served. The length of sentence imposed is a decision made in a front region (courtroom) where the theme of equality is paramount. The proportion of time served is the outcome of a series of events played out backstage and it is here that we would expect nonlegal criteria (e.g., race) to become important.

Although most individuals in the sample were serving sentences for property crimes, the variation in type of offense may be responsible for a portion of the variation in the dependent variables. While analysis based upon a single offense does not negate the potential importance of the type of offense, it does control for the influence of this factor in decisions regarding those individuals sentenced for this offense. Thus, a secondary analysis was conducted on a reduced sample of offenders sentenced for burglary offenses only (n = 43). Table 29.1 presents the mean length of sentence imposed for both the full (all offenses) and reduced (burglary offenses) samples. In both cases the difference between sentences imposed upon Indians and non-Indians was statistically significant. But it is important to note that sentences imposed upon Indians were shorter than sentences imposed upon non-Indians. In the full sample, non-Indians received an average sentence of 26.5

Table 29.1    Mean Length of Sentence Imposed by Race for Burglary Offenses and for All Offenses Combined

| | *Overall* | *Age* | | *Education* | | *Prior Convictions* | |
|---|---|---|---|---|---|---|---|
| | | *25 and Under* | *Over 25* | *Through 9th* | *10th and Above* | *None* | *1 or More* |
| All cases | | | | | | | |
| Indian (N=51) | 18.6[a] | 20.0 | 17.4[a] | 19.5 | 18.1[a] | 17.3 | 19.7[a] |
| Non-Indian (N=82) | 26.5 | 23.9 | 29.6 | 22.5 | 29.9 | 24.7 | 28.6 |
| Burglary cases | | | | | | | |
| Indian (N=19) | 16.2[a] | 18.6 | 13.6[a] | 17.0 | 14.9 | 16.8 | 16.0[a] |
| Non-Indian (N=24) | 24.8 | 21.5 | 30.4 | 24.3 | 25.3 | 20.0 | 28.9 |

[a]Statistically significant.

months while the sentences given Indians averaged 18.6. More importantly, in the more homogeneous sample of burglary cases, non-Indians received significantly longer sentences than Indians (24.8 and 16.2 months respectively). Table 29.1 also presents a comparison of the mean length of sentence imposed for Indians and non-Indians under first-order controls for age, education, and prior convictions. For both samples, in each of the categories of the control variables non-Indians received longer sentences than Indians. Particularly interesting is the length of sentence imposed among different categories of age at admission. While the difference between sentences imposed on Indians and non-Indians age 25 and under was slight, there was a sizable and significant difference between older inmates. This is particularly the case in the burglary sample: the average sentence imposed on whites (30.4 months) was over twice as long as the sentence imposed on older Indian defendants (13.6 months). A similar situation was observed when controls were introduced for prior felony convictions. In the burglary sample those non-Indians who had one or more prior convictions received sentences that averaged over a year longer than the sentences imposed on Indians with similar records.

Thus, in the frontstage region of sanctioning, Native Americans are apparently not only not subjected to more severe sanctions, they are seemingly sentenced more leniently. Several comments are in order about this apparent anomaly. First, and most important, since these data come from only an incarcerated population, we are limited in our ability to make conclusions about the sentencing process. Furthermore, it is altogether possible that Indians may be less likely than Whites to be sentenced to nonincarcerative sanctions. Such a situation would result in Indians being sentenced to prison for less serious offenses; a fact that may explain the consistently shorter sentences Indians received.

The second dependent variable of interest in this analysis was the proportion of sentence served before release from prison. Table 29.2 presents the mean propor-

Table 29.2   Mean Proportion of Sentence Served by Race for Burglary Cases and for All Offenses Combined

| | Overall | Age | | Education | | Major Infractions | | Prior Convictions | |
|---|---|---|---|---|---|---|---|---|---|
| | | 25 and Under | Over 25 | Through 9th | 10th and Above | None | 1 or More | None | 1 or More |
| **All cases** | | | | | | | | | |
| Indian (N=51) | .86[a] | .77 | .92[a] | .86 | 1.84 | .84 | .91[a] | .71 | .89[a] |
| Non-Indian (N=82) | .75 | .71 | .82 | .82 | .670 | .76 | .75 | .65 | .80 |
| **Burglary cases** | | | | | | | | | |
| Indian (N=19) | .84[a] | .77 | .93[a] | .83 | .88 | .86[a] | .84 | .59 | .94[a] |
| Non-Indian (N=24) | .64 | .60 | .70 | .67 | .61 | .58 | .69 | .47 | .66 |

[a]Statistically significant.

tion of sentence served for Indians and non-Indians and the first-order controls for age, education, major prison infractions, and prior convictions. In the all-cases-combined sample, non-Indians served an average of 75 percent of their sentence before release from prison, while Indians served an average of 86 percent of the sentence imposed. This difference is even more striking in the burglary sample, where non-Indians served an average of 64 percent and Indians served an average of 84 percent of their sentence. (This difference is statistically significant in both samples.) Furthermore, in each category of the control variables, Indians served a larger proportion of their sentence than non-Indians. These relationships are particularly strong in the burglary sample. Indians with at least one prior conviction served an average of 94 percent of their sentence while non-Indians with similar criminal records served on the average only 66 percent of the sentence imposed. The findings were similar for Indians who were older, had more education, and had committed more prison infractions.

In both samples, Indians were found to be slightly older, to have more prior convictions, to have fewer major prison infractions, to receive shorter sentences, and to serve a higher proportion of the sentence imposed.

These results tend to support the hypothesis that members of racial minorities may receive disparate treatment in the backstage regions of criminal justice decision making. One explanation of the finding that Indians serve a higher proportion of their sentence is that they get shorter sentences, that is, those offenders receiving short sentences are more likely to complete a larger proportion of their time before being released. With a 12-month sentence, the parole authority may simply not bother to grant parole for such a short period of supervision. The data lend evidence to such a tendency, in both samples there was a negative association between sentence length and the proportion of sentence served. Since Indians more often received shorter sentences, it becomes clear that the difference in the proportion of sentence served by Indians and by non-Indians cannot be accounted for solely by the fact that Indians received shorter sentences than non-Indians.

## DISCUSSION

The conflict and labeling perspectives hypothesize that legal sanctions will be more severely imposed on members of racial minorities. While little support for these expectations can be found in the literature, it could be that discriminatory treatment in the legal system is most likely to occur in backstage decisions that are highly discretionary and not very visible. Further, there has been little study of discriminatory treatment of non-Black minority groups. The data presented in this study reveals the existence of differential treatment of Native Americans in a low visibility criminal justice decision—the decision to grant parole. The analysis reported here showed that of several explanatory variables, race was a major determinant of parole release, with American Indians significantly less likely to be released than whites.

The major questions about these findings may now be raised: What is it about being a Native American that may induce the parole board to impose a more severe sanction? Do Indians have a higher recidivism rate and parole boards are simply following a policy of predictive restraint? Are Native Americans more likely to be seen by parole board members as more in need of "prison treatment and education" than Whites? Hawkins's (1971) study of parole in New York demonstrated the importance of the inmate's appearance and demeanor at the parole hearing in determining parole release. In a similar vein, Piliavin and Briar (1964) found that demeanor was of major importance in the police decision to arrest and that demeanor was strongly correlated with race. Thus, Blacks were more likely to be seen as having a "bad attitude" than Whites and consequently were handled more severely. It is possible that a similar process may be occurring in the decision to grant parole, with Indians being perceived as having a poor presence at their parole hearing and consequently treated more harshly. They may also be viewed as having inadequate community support, such as a poor prospect for employment or an unstable living arrangement. This is compatible with Talbot's (1981) description of high rates of unemployment, poverty, idleness, and family disruption in Indian society. Although suggestive, at present there are no data to address these questions—clearly, they warrant further study. An important direction for future research would be direct observational data of parole board members' attitudes and perceptions of American, as well as the behavior of Indian inmates in the parole hearing.

While the present study has found support for the hypothesis that Native Americans are likely to receive more harsh treatment in backstage legal decisions, a major anomaly of these findings remains unexplained. If Native Americans were the object of discriminatory treatment, why did they receive significantly shorter sentences? There are several possible interpretations for this phenomenon. First,

Indians might be given prison sentences for offenses or in circumstances for which Whites would receive probation. If Whites are generally given probation for less serious crimes and only incarcerated for serious offenses or when less serious crimes have serious factual elements associated with them, then their sentence length in the aggregate may actually be as long or longer than those received by Native Americans. Rather than reflecting judicial leniency for Indians, however, this reflects the fact that for similar offenses Indians are less likely to receive non-incarceral dispositions. In this case, it would appear consistent to argue that Indians who receive a relatively shorter term of incarceration were actually being treated more harshly than similarly situated Whites who avoided incarceration. Thus, what is needed to supplement the present length-of-incarceration argument is an analysis of the *type* of sentence given to similar Indian and White offenders. Hall and Simkus (1975) performed such an analysis and reported that for similar offenses, Native Americans were more likely to be incarcerated than Whites.

Secondly, the shorter sentences given to Native Americans might reflect the fact that their crimes are most likely to be directed against other Indians rather than Whites, and these offenses may be perceived as either less severe or less threatening than those that cross racial boundaries. This suggests the idea of a *race-specific* definition of offense severity and may account for the shorter sentences of some Indians.

While the findings from this study differ from a number of other studies dealing with the treatment of other racial minorities in the legal system, they are consistent with other studies about the discriminatory legal treatment of Native Americans. This consistently reported disparity at several decision points may suggest the existence of cumulative discrimination (Liska and Tausig, 1979) that should be addressed through a more comprehensive analysis of the treatment of Native Americans at each stage of the criminal justice process.

## Notes

1. Those offenders who were paroled and returned to prison as a result of parole violation were included in the parole group even though they may have served their complete sentence since they at one point did receive a favorable parole decision.

2. In this state, "good time" was awarded at a rate of two months for every ten months of good behavior. Thus, for a one-year sentence, an inmate would have to serve ten months unless he committed prison infractions that would result in the loss of this good time. Proportion of time served was computed by calculating the actual sentence (sentence imposed minus goodtime) and viewing the time served as a percentage of this amount. Thus, those inmates who were released at the expiration of sentence would have a proportion of time served equal to 1.0. However, if an inmate lost good time and was released at his sentence expiration, the proportion of time served might be greater than 1.0. All variables were measured continuously except race which was coded "1" for Indians and "0" for non-Indians.

# 30

## ABORIGINAL SPIRITUALITY
## IN CORRECTIONS

J. B. WALDRAM

Canada appears to be on the verge of substantial changes in the relationship between Aboriginal peoples and the justice system. Recent research in Manitoba,
Saskatchewan and Alberta has demonstrated the extent to which Aboriginal peoples are disproportionately represented in the courts and the correctional system.
As the movement for Aboriginal self-determination sweeps the nation, talk is
emerging of the implementation of Aboriginal justice systems, including policing,
courts, and traditional laws and punishments.

The area of corrections has received considerably less attention than other aspects
of the justice system with respect to the integration of traditional approaches.[1] One
area of corrections which has seen some attempt to accommodate Aboriginal offenders as culturally different from other offenders, and therefore requiring other
programs and services, is the provision of religious services. Known euphemistically
as "Native Awareness" programs, these involve the provision of spiritual services by
Aboriginal Elders to Aboriginal prisoners. However, it appears that these services
have been categorized as "religious" in nature, analogous to services provided by

Edited version of J. B. Waldram, "Aboriginal Spirituality in Corrections: A Canadian Case Study in
Religion and Therapy." Reprinted from the *American Indian Quarterly*, volume 18, number 1 (spring
1994) by permission of the University of Nebraska Press. Copyright © 1994 by the University of
Nebraska Press. Used also by permission of the author.

The research upon which this paper is based was funded, in part, under contract to the Correctional
Service of Canada. However, the views expressed herein are those of the author, and do not necessarily represent the views of the service. The author acknowledges the support of the Correctional Service
of Canada, and in particular Drs. Arthur Gordon and Steve Wong, and the psychology and treatment
staff at the Regional Psychiatric Center in Saskatoon. The author also wishes to gratefully acknowledge the assistance of those Aboriginal Elders and offenders who agreed to be interviewed.

prison chaplains. This paper will argue that the therapeutic aspect of Aboriginal spirituality is not being fully recognized in correctional programs.

## RESEARCH SETTING

The site of my research is the Regional Psychiatric Centre in Saskatoon, Saskatchewan. The RPC is one of three such institutions in the country operated by the Correctional Service of Canada. Its mandate is to provide treatment primarily to federal offenders with sentences of two years or more. The Saskatoon facility primarily serves offenders from western and northern institutions.

Opened in 1978, the RPC has the capacity to house 106 offenders or "patients" in five units. The two main units, from which the research participants were drawn, concentrate on the treatment of sexual offenders and those diagnosed as having "personality disorders." Treatment includes a combination of group therapy, instructional groups, and individual counseling. Psychiatric and registered nurses work with psychiatrists, psychologists, and social workers to identify psychological and behavioral problems and to treat the patients.

Over a thirteen-month period in the early 1990s, I interviewed thirty Aboriginal offenders at the RPC, and observed a variety of psychological and traditional Aboriginal treatments. I used an ethnographic interview approach, using open-ended questions and discussion to detail the respondents' cultural and prison experiences. Aboriginal Elders who worked with the Aboriginal offenders also have been interviewed. All interviews were tape-recorded. Participant observation was used to gain a better understanding of the offenders' experiences with various spiritual and traditional healing components.[2]

## CORRECTIONAL VIEWS OF
## SPIRITUAL PROGRAMMING

Aboriginal spirituality programs generally depend on the services of Aboriginal Elders retained on a contract basis, often through agencies independent of the Correctional Service. Providing such services is relatively recent, used in western Canada only since the early 1980s at the insistence of Aboriginal inmates.

The Elders offer spiritual guidance and cultural education, and are clearly the hub around which the programs revolve. Many Aboriginal offenders (perhaps one-third) lack any knowledge of their Aboriginal cultures or languages as a result of residential school or foster home/adoption experiences. For many, the Elders are able to begin the process of cultural education. More importantly, the Elders provide spiritual and, it is argued here, "healing" services. These would include guiding fasts and undertaking sweat lodges (or "sweats") in the prisons. The Elders also provide counseling for Aboriginal inmates in a manner which, on the surface, appears similar to that undertaken by Eurocanadian therapists.[3]

The other component of prison Aboriginal spirituality programming that deserves mention is the Native Brotherhoods, volunteer organizations of Aboriginal (and sometimes non-Aboriginal) inmates who meet on a regular basis to undertake spiritual services (with or without an Elder), and to discuss political, recreational, and social concerns. The Brotherhoods are often vehicles for bringing into the institutions resource people from the outside.

In general, the correctional system in Canada appears to view Aboriginal spirituality programs primarily as "religious." In other words, the services are made available because of constitutional guarantees regarding the right of the inmates to practice their religion. Recent studies done for the correctional service would bear this out, as they emphasize the struggle of Aboriginal peoples to have their spirituality services, and Elders, recognized in a fashion analogous to the chaplains.

A 1988 report for the Solicitor General's office noted that "there seems to be an increase in Native culture and spiritual awareness among Native inmates" (Canada Solicitor General, 1988a:5). Further, the report noted:

> Many Native offenders have special social, cultural and spiritual needs. These include the observation of such traditional group ceremonies and rituals as pipe ceremonies and the sweat lodge. For Native offenders who have not had much prior contact with traditional culture and spirituality, the opportunity for instruction and participation in these areas can become an important part of their incarceration experience (Canada, Solicitor General, Ministry Secretariat, 1988a:5).

The report then suggests that, "beyond spiritual and related cultural needs, however, the unique program needs of natives are not well understood or documented by correctional systems." I would suggest that the extent to which these "spiritual and related cultural needs" are truly understood is questionable, primarily because of the report's view of these as religious in nature. Indeed, the report indicates that there have been complaints about Aboriginal spirituality not being recognized as a "religion" (1988a:33), and recommends that "Aboriginal spirituality shall be accorded the same status, protection and privileges as other religions," and Elders "recognized as having the same status, protection and privileges as religious officials of other religions" (Canada Solicitor General, 1988a:34). Although suggesting that these programs appear to be having positive effects on inmates, the report fails to broach the issue of such programs as inherently therapeutic.

On the heels of this report, the Task Force on Aboriginal Peoples in Federal Corrections (Canada Solicitor General, 1988b) recognized the "traditional Indian view" of health (Canada Solicitor General, 1988b:13) and that services for Aboriginal offenders "must take their spiritual and cultural background into account" (Canada Solicitor General, 1988b:14). But the report stops short of recognizing the explicit therapeutic value of the spirituality programs, recommending only that Elders and their spiritual programs be recognized with the same status as chaplains and other religions. Only when the report suggests that "exposure to Aboriginal spirituality and culture can make a major contribution to rehabilitation" (Canada Solicitor General, 1988b:69) of alcohol and substance abusers is the issue of therapy raised. Unfortunately, the discussion goes no further.

Recently, the three prairie provinces have experienced inquiries into the process of justice and Aboriginal peoples (Hamilton and Sinclair, 1991; Cawsey, 1992; Linn, 1992). The report of the Aboriginal Justice Inquiry of Manitoba (Hamilton and Sinclair, 1991) is typical of all three on Aboriginal spirituality programs and the employment of Elders. It calls for the recognition of Aboriginal Elders on par with chaplains, and for a policy guaranteeing Aboriginal offenders the right to spiritual services "appropriate to their culture" (Hamilton and Sinclair, 1991:447).

At the RPC itself, Aboriginal offenders lamented that spiritual services were less available than in their parent institutions.[4] In fact, Aboriginal spirituality has continued to have problems being recognized as equivalent to other religions. Although the Correctional Service of Canada has established councils of advisory Elders, and is attempting to change the manner in which spirituality is treated, many Elders still feel that they are subject to discriminatory treatment at the hands of guards. The searching of medicine bundles and sacred pipes continues to be an issue in many prisons. This is in contrast to the accepted practice of allowing priests, for instance, to enter prisons without being subjected to searches or having certain items, such as sacrificial wine, inspected.

## THE THERAPEUTIC NATURE OF ABORIGINAL SPIRITUALITY PROGRAMS

Little research (e.g., Waldram, 1993) has been done on the effects of Aboriginal spirituality on Aboriginal offenders in Canada. My research suggests the spirituality programs had a significant effect on the mental health and well-being of offenders.

The offenders report that the benefits of spirituality programs tend to fall into four categories. First, spirituality programs provide a mechanism for coping with the stresses of prison life, reducing conflict with other inmates and staff, and opening up the individual to other prison programs. The sweat lodge experience in particular seems to be important. As one offender stated "It brings up my spirit, especially when I come out of a sweat, eh. When you come out of that sweat, there's nothing that can disturb you."

The second category of benefits relates to the role of Elders as therapists, a role which reflects to some extent that of other correctional staff but in a more culturally appropriate manner. Many offenders noted that they could talk more openly with Elders, indeed that it was sacreligious to lie to an Elder, and that they had a great deal more confidence in Elders than in other correctional staff. Individual counseling involved dialogue on specific Aboriginal cultures (i.e., an educational component) as well as the individual offender's life. Offenders found that the Elders were better able to understand the reserve context, the problems of alcohol and substance abuse in Aboriginal communities, and physical abuse. The

Elders were highly valued because of their ability to be empathetic, a quality that was not characteristically ascribed to Eurocanadian treatment staff. According to one offender:

> I was talking to both of them [treatment staff and Elder] about the same problems. The reason I went to an Elder was because he was Native, you know. He understood what went on in my community, what happened to me.

The third category of benefits relates to what could be termed "culturally specific" mental health problems. Some Aboriginal offenders retain strong beliefs in the power of traditional healing and in what is known as "bad medicine." Bad medicine refers to the ability of one individual to cause harm, misfortune, or illness to befall another through supernatural means (e.g., Young et al., 1989). A few offenders in this study expressed a belief in the existence of bad medicine, and a concomitant belief that they had been the targets of someone's malicious intent. Bad medicine can only be treated in a culturally appropriate manner. Likewise, only Elders can make the appropriate "protection" medicine available to individuals who fear bad medicine.

Some Aboriginal offenders also expressed a strong belief in dreams, that messages encoded in dreams are purposefully sent to them. These messages can be disturbing and require interpretation. Elders are particularly valuable in offering the culturally appropriate interpretations.

The fourth category of benefits pertains to questions of identity. Some Aboriginal offenders express profound conflicts in this area; this is particularly true of those who have been raised primarily in a Eurocanadian cultural milieu. These individuals are Aboriginal in heritage and have been victimized as Aboriginals through racism, yet know nothing of that heritage. Indeed, frequently they have found themselves ostracized by both groups: by the Aboriginal population because they appear to follow the "White way," and by Eurocanadians because they are visibly Aboriginal. The Elders, in conjunction with workshops on Aboriginal culture and history, are often able to lessen the consequences of, and sometimes resolve, this identity conflict and instill pride in Aboriginal offenders.

## Spirituality as Healing: A Case Study

It would be useful to demonstrate the great potential for the "healing" of Aboriginal offenders through Aboriginal awareness and spirituality programs by presenting a case study. I have found numerous cases similar to this one, though the apparent change in this individual is perhaps the most striking.

"Jack"[5] was an individual of mixed ancestry. His father was Aboriginal, his mother Eurocanadian, and he grew up mostly in the city. I first met him at a meeting of the Native Brotherhood. My first impression of Jack was that he was an intensely angry man, who seemed suspicious of everyone and who spewed venom with every comment. He shouted angrily, denouncing the police, the judges, the

RPC staff, and finally me. He was particularly upset that I proposed to examine the case management files for those offenders I interviewed. In his view, the files contained nothing but lies concerning his background, and that once something was written in the file it was seen as "truth." A man's reputation, as documented in his file, followed him everywhere, and conditioned prison officials' responses to him.

Jack's case management files generally supported my initial impression of him as an intensely angry individual. At the time he was interviewed by me, he was in his early thirties, and was doing a long sentence for a violent offense. At the time of that offense, he had been on the street just one day since completing an earlier sentence. His criminal convictions began at age 16, and he had at least seven convictions between the ages of 16 and 21. His most serious offenses included armed robbery, hostage takings and gun battles with police. He had been in institutional care since the age of twelve.

His prison record showed many incidents of violence, escape, and other problems. He had also been involved in prison hostage taking incidents, and had spent more than two years "in the hole" (segregation) and in the special handling unit, available only in some prisons and designed to handle the most dangerous offenders.[6] According to his file, "up to approximately one year ago, his behaviour in prison was disruptive, rebellious, and often a threat to institutional security." As a result, he had served time in most Canadian prisons capable of handling him. He let it be known that he hated anyone in authority, especially prison guards and believed that both the guards and some other inmates were constantly out to get him. One report stated that "he showed no signs of major mental illness, although he is very sensitive to imagined slights." A report at another institution documented that

> The patient had deteriorated into a paranoid agitated state and had developed some delusions concerning a couple of other inmates. . . . There was also considerable mood disturbance and he had in fact made a significant suicidal gesture by cutting quite deeply into his arm.

An earlier attempt at obtaining treatment at one RPC had ended in failure after only three weeks, when he requested transfer back to his parent institution "because the open discussion of personal problems and the atmosphere of the unit were making him very anxious." While waiting for the transfer, Jack asked to be secluded in the most secure unit in the institution: "He has stated that he cannot handle being around other patients and staff in an open environment." An RPC psychiatric report contained the following passage:

> He stated that he hated people and the system had made him avoid them, especially women and now he was forced by the same system to be in this atmosphere wherein he had to deal with a lot of women. His hatred for people is very apparent. . . . He has poor control of his temper, his frustration tolerance is low and often has the urge to take it out on other inmates, however he did say he would never harm a female, for that goes against his self-respect.

He was diagnosed as having a "personality disorder," including a substance abuse problem, "difficulty coping with stress resulting in aggressive behaviour, and difficulty interacting with authority." Indeed, many prison staff were fearful of him.

Although Jack had originally rejected my request for an interview, eight months later he was more than willing to sit and, in his own words, "do the best I can." This remarkable turnaround will be discussed shortly. First I would like to elaborate on his past from information obtained in that interview.

Jack's father had grown up on a reserve, but Jack had spent relatively little time there as a child. His formative years were spent in the city, and he never learned his Aboriginal language. He had very little cultural knowledge of his people.

It is evident that his childhood was quite disturbing, filled with alcohol abuse and violence:

> My dad was an alcoholic and my mom, she used to take lots of beatings, lots of screams, stuff like that. And I saw my father rape one of my sisters. And then I said, "fuck that shit," and I ran away from home.

His description of his prison experiences was considerably more graphic than what his record described:

> I find the time I spend in the jail wasn't easy, either. I watched a few hostage takings, took part in a riot . . . had both guards tied. I spent six years in the SHU out of fourteen years . . . The rest I spent in normal population, but I was bad ass up there. They kicked me out of [one province] . . . they booted me out after a few years there . . . they transferred me back [to another prison] . . . got in a riot there. They made me spend two and a half years in the SHU over that. I come out of the SHU and [my home province] didn't want me. So they sent me to [another province]. [There] I did the same thing. I escaped . . . did lots of pipings, stabbings . . . So spent lots of time in seg[regation] and they just booted me out . . . When I arrived at [one prison], there, they [guards] tried to torture me, tried to hang me, smashed three of my ribs. I got nineteen stitches in the back of my head. They really did put a number on me. And all those friends that I had when I first came in when I was sixteen, most of them today are dead. The pigs killed them. So I don't know, I got a hatred, a hatred. I just can't handle them around me.

Despite his relatively weak links to his Aboriginal heritage and his pale complexion, he was subjected to racism and taunting as a child. His response was to fight, and he was cajoled by his father if he appeared to have lost any such encounter. After witnessing his father rape his sister, on two occasions he attempted to kill his father but was charged only once, with assault.

The most pleasant memories of his childhood were the brief times he spent on the reserve, ironically often the result of trouble he had encountered while in the city. He stayed primarily with his aunt and uncle, and received a cursory introduction into Aboriginal culture and spirituality. On the reserve he found a refuge from the racism of the city.

Despite this early exposure to an Aboriginal culture, by the time he entered prison as a young adult he knew very little, and he would ultimately experience a personal and spiritual awakening. He explained his reasons for becoming involved in the prison's Aboriginal awareness and spirituality programs:

> I see some of my friends, they were there before me—they were in the SHU and when I hit [the prison] I don't know, I saw a change in those guys. They were fucking nuts like me before . . . I couldn't understand how come they were changing like that. And they used to tell me, "You try this, you listen, you see. You try this and you see." So I put myself into it, and I believe it today.

It was in prison that Jack experienced his first sweat, and began to learn more about Aboriginal culture. But his real awakening came when he entered the RPC and began to work with the Elder:

> When I started to talk to that guy it was easy to relate to him. He knew a few of my friends. That was our first conversation there, of a couple of people we know and we talked about that. And then we talked about myself. And I was sitting in my cell one day and I said, "Fuck, that's not my dad. That's what I would like to have fucking gone to my dad [for]." So to me he is a friend, he is a dad. He's everything, that guy. And that was the first person to come along and be willing to put everything on the line for me, so that means lots to me. That was the first person that came along, crossed my road and asked me if I wanted help, and was willing to give me a hand. . . . And you know for me that means a lot, because I never had anybody come along and ask me those things before. I wish somebody did, but it never happened.

Then Jack added reflectively:

> Now it's funny. I never feel that I want to beat anybody up. I never feel I want to escape. I never feel like taking hostages no more. I just want to be out with [the Elder] and learn about my people, and learn about me. Learn about me more.

This remarkable change was noticed by RPC staff. Reports in Jack's case management file stated:

> Since being at RPC, [he] has developed a relationship with the Native Elder. The Elder has offered him ongoing support in the community. . . . On the unit, [his] participation in groups has been consistent. He has always been attentive, but his active participation is limited.
>
> A great deal of [his] efforts at identification of self have been through the Native Brotherhood. He has worked closely with the Native Elder . . . In fact, they have bonded to the extent that [Jack's] plans for MS [mandatory supervision] release are to reside with the Native Elder.

RPC staff members were quite surprised by the change in behavior. By the time I interviewed Jack, he had been at the RPC almost fourteen months, and the intense, angry man had given way to one who readily smiled and joked with the staff. It is simply not possible to say to what extent the work of the RPC staff, and prison therapists at other institutions, contributed to this remarkable change, relative to the work of the Elder. A report in Jack's file stated that, beginning in 1986, he had started therapy with a prison psychologist, which signaled "the start of a change in his behaviour which continued throughout the eighteen months he was [there]." But there is no denying that the man who presented at the RPC appeared to be as angry and tense as any person could be.

Jack's view of his change places the responsibility more firmly with the Elders he has worked with, and particularly the one at RPC. But other aspects of the RPC program have contributed as well. Jack states:

> A year ago, I wouldn't talk to anybody. I wouldn't talk about myself. I would fight all the time. At least once a day I would fight. I don't say that to try to look bad or nothing, but that's exactly the way I was. I was really hurt and I learned how to talk about that hurt. Talk about it. Spend lots of time with the Elder. Spend lots of time with those psychologists down in the psychologists' office here. Spend lots of time by myself, reading those handouts they gave to me.

According to Jack, the Elder has been instrumental in helping him remain calm and deal with the stresses of prison life, stresses which contributed to his poor incarceration record:

> Usually lots of time [the Elder] used to come and fuck I wasn't ready to go, you know? And . . . I fought four times and I used to ask [the Elder], forget the sweat because I was so angry inside. [But] I would go in that sweat and I would pray hard and I would ask him for understanding and that did help me. No matter what anybody says, that did help me.

One particular incident seems to have been the turning point for Jack. Despite having been abused by his father, Jack was particularly troubled when news of his father's death reached him, followed by news that he would not be allowed to attend the funeral. Indeed, he was so upset that the security staff became nervous that he might become violent. The Elder was there to assist:

> I asked [the Elder] for a special sweat, there he made a special sweat. He made two rounds instead of three. And it was for me and my father. And I was sitting down and I asked him for more, more understanding. I went through what basically I went through when I was a kid. I talked basically about all my life . . . the pain and the hurt. And he showed me how to pray, how to get a better understanding of myself. And since I did that, I do feel better, because when you grow up like that, you just keep those things inside you. That's why you become so bitter.

Jack's story was corroborated in a separate interview with the Elder. The Elder explained that Jack broke down and cried in the sweat as he related his story and particularly his difficult relationship with his father. Because of his image in prison as a tough "con," this was something he simply could not let himself do; but in the security of the sweat lodge, alone with the Elder, his true pain came out. The Elder saw this as a turning point.

Jack's relationship with the Elder was quite different from that he had established with the nurses and other staff at RPC. He suggested that there was a great deal he would not bring up in his counseling sessions with the nurses, and chastized them for always looking at their watches to gauge session time. As Jack said, "[it's] hard to trust when you see a person act this way." In his estimation, he had obtained some benefits from the group therapy sessions, but his lack of trust of the staff clearly inhibited his participation. In contrast, his work with the Elder was built upon a foundation of trust. His respect for the Elder stemmed, in part, from his respect for the knowledge the Elder had gained over the course of his life, and he contrasted this with the knowledge of the nurses:

> How come somebody twenty-four years old, twenty-five years old, can sit down in front of you and talk to you about life when you're a lot older? I don't know. To me it's hard to understand. If somebody is able to talk to me about life, somebody is going to be older than me, somebody that has seen more than me . . . I can learn from that person. Somebody younger than me didn't even go through half what I've gone through. How can I learn from that person?

Jack was subsequently transferred to another prison to await his release on mandatory supervision.[7] His release plans at the time centered on continuing his work with the RPC Elder. In fact, the Elder had invited Jack to work with him as his helper, an opportunity which Jack initially could not resist. He had been in prison since the age of sixteen, and now he stated emphatically, "I don't want to fuck up the next thirty years." However, he also recognized how seriously institutionalized he had become, and that he still required treatment in order to adjust on the outside:

> Actually, I seriously believe I've hurt a lot of people and I have to try to make up for it. More sweats to go through. More suffering I have to give for the people that I made suffer all my life. I wish to help some other people like [the Elder] . . . I want to be working with some kids, try to give them understanding, talk with them. Because I remember when I was a kid, that was one of my dreams. To see somebody come along, sit down, kind of talk with me and tell me what's wrong. I never had that happen when I was a kid, and I know when I was a kid I was needing that. So maybe that is the way I will pay back . . . But I am not going to go [home] until I am strong. Until I can walk on my two legs without no worry. That is the time I am going to go there.

In the end, Jack's release plans were changed, and he went to reside with a sibling (but not in his home community). Two years after his release, the Elder was able to report that he was still out of prison, and had been in contact several times over that period. The Elder's invitation to come stay at his place remains open, but it is difficult for newly released offenders to obtain permission to travel outside their parole jurisdictions. It is not known the extent to which Jack has remained involved in Aboriginal spirituality.[8]

## DISCUSSION

Sam Gill (1983:107), in summarizing the elements of Aboriginal "religion" noted that:

> Quite clearly, matters of health and healing are not restricted to conditions of a simple physiological and biological order, but rather these matters are laden with meanings and concerns that reach the highest cultural, and even cosmological, levels. The

state of health speaks to Native Americans of the conditions of the world in which they live. Consequently, matters of health and healing are commonly central to the religious concerns of many Native American tribes.

Anthropologists, and others who have studied religious and healing systems in various cultures, reinforce Gill's assertions. For instance, Foster and Anderson write that:

> In many non-Western societies . . . the dividing lines between medicine on the one hand and religion, law and society on the other hand are much less distinct. In these societies religion and medicine, or etiological beliefs and social control, may be inextricably intertwined in the same institutional context. The efficacy of medical systems in these societies must therefore be measured by their ability to successfully play roles that lie far beyond the cure of illness and the maintenance of health. (1978:125)

But can spirituality, broadly conceived, be considered therapeutic? Foster and Anderson (1978:125) have suggested that the efficacy of any treatment must be seen in its proper cultural context, and the ability to "satisfy the expectations of the people served" is crucial. In this sense, what is considered "therapeutic" is largely socially and culturally defined, which is not surprising given that "illness" itself (as opposed to "disease") is also socially and culturally defined.

The pivotal individual in these healing traditions are the shamans, healers, or medicine men and women. Alland (1970:128) has described these individuals as "social adjudicators as well as religious functionaries" who treat "social cause rather than disease." Hence, the inter-relationship between the religious and the medical is clear not only in terms of social institutions and cultural practices, but also in the many functions of the healers themselves.

A considerable amount of research has been undertaken on the parallels between religion and psychotherapy, and especially the therapeutic aspects of religious or spiritual activity (Dozier, 1966; Kiev, 1973; Ness, 1980; Pattison, 1973; Skultans, 1976). In some ways, Eurocanadian religion seems to have drifted away from the therapeutic component of spirituality (although certain denominations, such as the Pentecostals, engage in "miracle healing"). This seems to be the case with Eurocanadian and correctional views of Aboriginal spirituality: recognizing its religious nature is relatively easy but accepting spirituality as complementary to, or as an alternative to scientific, biomedical, or psycho-social treatment is considerably more problematic.

Do traditional healers "heal?" Many anthropologists have written that traditional medicine is particularly useful in the treatment of psychological and psychiatric problems (Kleinman and Sung, 1979; Jilek, 1982). Even the Canadian government has accepted this position, as evidenced in the submission of the Department of National Health and Welfare to the Special Committee on Indian Self-Government (the Penner report):

> We have come to appreciate very much the relevance and the utility of traditional approaches, particularly to mental health problems—approaches which address the suicide rate, approaches which address addiction problems. We believe that in areas such

as those the application of traditional medicine and native culture perhaps can be more successful than anything we could offer in terms of contemporary psychiatric approaches to those kinds of problems. (Penner, 1983:34)

This is quite an overwhelming show of support for traditional Aboriginal medicine, all the more significant in that National Health and Welfare has no concrete evidence if, and how, traditional medicine actually works. Indeed, it may simply be an act of faith on the government's part, taking at face value assertions of the efficacy of traditional medicine, perhaps mindful of the political "incorrectness" of questioning such practices precisely because of the wider cultural issues. Yet, among those who study traditional medical systems around the world, there is considerable concern regarding the weak methodological approaches which have been brought to bear on this question (Anderson, 1991; Weibel-Orlando, 1989).

One American study of prison spirituality programs and their effect on Aboriginal recidivism rates and substance abuse was inconclusive, due in part to a lack of a proper measure of treatment "success" (Grobsmith and Dam, 1990). Nevertheless, there exists a strong belief among incarcerated Native Americans that "celebration and revitalization of indigenous religion is a more successful avenue to achieve sobriety and rehabilitation," and that such participation precludes the use of alcohol and drugs (Grobsmith, 1989:144, 145). In another American study, Bachman (1991:479–480) quoted a prison psychologist who noted that involvement in spiritual activities resulted in significant positive behavioral changes for participants. An earlier Canadian study by Jilek and Roy (1976:210) established a link between a lack of exposure to a "traditional Indian lifestyle" and the early onset of criminal activity, and noted that "positive Indian self-identification was associated with experiencing educational and therapeutic benefits from incarceration." Unfortunately, we are left to speculate about the possible relationship between involvement by offenders as part of their quest for an identity and positive therapeutic outcomes. Couture (1992:209–210) has addressed this concern:

> The issue of the rehabilitative value of a Native religious/cultural program has been raised several times. Fairness would require a comparison with short-term and long-term results of other rehab programs, keeping in mind that this program has barely started, and also keeping in hand testimony of several Native service organizations who attest that there are a small but growing number of Native inmate "recoveries" attributable to Native spiritual influences. The primary argument lies in the inherent validity of Native spirituality and religion.

Coming back to our case study, the positive therapeutic effects of the Aboriginal spirituality program were evident in Jack's case, but it is not possible at this level of analysis to separate the spirituality benefits from those of the other RPC programs. Even the Elder who worked with Jack saw his work as only a part of the overall treatment, and this is probably the best way to view it. However, developing a better understanding of the contributions of the spirituality component is important. While some patients at the RPC appear to combine in an eclectic manner the spiritual treatments with those offered by the RPC staff, many patients noted areas in which the two were in conflict. Furthermore, the "how" and "why" of the efficacy of these programs need further investigation. The first reason would be to demonstrate specifically what aspects of the spirituality programs are working, and how, so as to enhance these aspects of the programs. Such an investigation would ease the integration of traditional approaches with current correctional programs to develop a more coherent treatment strategy. At the present time, the correctional system seems not very interested in examining what goes on under the guise of "spirituality" programs, in a manner reflective of biomedicine's disinterested attitude toward traditional medicine in general.

In addition, some aspects of spirituality programs may actually cause some degree of harm (e.g., Ness, 1980:175). Some Aboriginal offenders in the original study demonstrated identity confusion linked to their participation in spirituality programs: their personal views of their "Indianness" were challenged when presented with certain elements of Aboriginal spirituality.

To suggest that the correctional system needs to view Aboriginal spirituality programs as therapeutic leads to other more complex questions. If we are to argue the therapeutic benefits of these programs, are we also suggesting that they be critically and scientifically examined in the same way as are other programs for offenders? Clearly, to suggest this is to invite controversy for, in spite of a few examples (e.g., Young et al., 1987, 1989), traditional Aboriginal healers in Canada have been reluctant to have their healing documented and assessed. Such an approach will require extensive dialogue with the healers themselves. Nonetheless, to fail to address this issue will likely mean that Aboriginal spirituality programs remain fundamentally "religious" in scope and outside the parameters of correctional therapeutic programs. The implications of this have been experienced for many years. Some Elders continue to be searched, resulting in the desecration of sacred bundles, pipes and other spiritual objects. Some Elders have reacted by refusing to bring certain items into prisons, which greatly reduces the kinds of services they can offer. Elders are rarely thought of as being part of an offender's treatment team, are rarely if ever consulted about an offender's progress, and have little input into case management assessments. They experience many scheduling conflicts in their activities; they are told when sweats will be held, and for how long. One Elder reported that he once was told he had fifteen minutes to undertake a pipe ceremony (he declined, of course, because such ceremonies take considerably longer). Many prison officials openly wonder why Aboriginal spirituality cannot be practiced just like the Christian religions, for instance through a one-hour service on Sundays. The idea that a traditional fast requires four days of isolation is foreign to them and seems absurd. There are even some officials who openly question offenders' involvement in spirituality, suggesting they simply use it to get out of other programming, or burn sweetgrass and sage to mask the smell of marijuana.

## CONCLUSION

Jack's transformation was nothing short of extraordinary. He is not exceptional in comparison with others in this study, but his case is particularly noteworthy because of the great distance he has traveled, spiritually, emotionally, and intellectually, in such a short time. The Aboriginal spirituality program which he has experienced has clearly had a profound therapeutic effect, although the dynamics of that effect are not well understood in relation to other RPC programs. His case demonstrates the extent to which Aboriginal people have little trouble combining traditional and biomedical/psychological approaches in seeking treatment (e.g., Waldram, 1990a, 1990b).

Aboriginal spirituality programs have a "healing" component, and are not simply educational and religious programs narrowly defined, as the Correctional Service tends to view them. Offenders are not always able to articulate precisely how that healing works, but the data suggest it is no longer possible to deny its existence. It would not be prudent to suggest that Aboriginal spirituality represents a therapeutic "magic bullet;" it holds great promise, yet there are no magical solutions in the area of forensic treatment. To formally recognize the therapeutic nature of these programs raises many difficult questions, and the answers to these can only be achieved through extensive dialogue between Aboriginal healers and spiritual leaders, on one hand, and correctional service treatment personnel on the other. The current system of disinterested non-communication between the Aboriginal and biomedical healing systems appears to be having some detrimental effect on the spirituality programs, in that restrictive conditions are placed on the spiritual activities, under the assumption that these are, after all, "religious" in nature and therefore analogous to the work of the various Christian denominations in the prisons. It is suggested here that in failing to consider the inherently therapeutic nature of Aboriginal spirituality, the ultimate loser becomes the Aboriginal offender, an individual whom everyone, from government ministers on down, suggests requires special attention.

## NOTES

1. Recently, the Canadian government and the Correctional Service of Canada announced plans to construct two new facilities for Aboriginal offenders, one at Maple Creek, Saskatchewan for females, and the other at Hobbema, Alberta for males. It is not clear at the time of writing the extent to which traditional approaches will be incorporated in the development of treatment programs, though most observers expect this to occur to some extent.

2. The research reported here was but a small component of a larger study of the cultural characteristics of the Aboriginal offenders and the way they interact with the RPC staff and programs as cultural beings.

3. In fact, individual Elders are quite idiosyncratic in their spiritual practices in prison, depending in part on their own cultural traditions and views as to what is appropriate for a prison setting. For instance, not all Elders will bring sacred pipes or bundles into prisons.

4. Since this research was first commenced, the availability of Aboriginal programs and Elders has improved significantly at the RPC.

5. "Jack" is a pseudonym. Certain details of "Jack's" life have been altered to ensure anonymity, without sacrificing the integrity of the case study. For the same reason, his own words are reproduced here with some editing.

6. The Special Handling Unit is not the same thing as "segregation." Most prisons have a segregation unit, used to punish inmates who have committed institutional infractions, or to isolate them from the other inmates because of fears of violence. "Jack" has spent time in both segregation ("the hole") and the SHU.

7. Mandatory supervision release is now known as "statuatory release," and means that the inmate is released automatically at the two-thirds point in his sentence, though there are exceptions. This form of release is not identical to parole, for which the inmate must apply, but both types of release come with conditions such as where they live, curfews, and abstention from alcohol and drugs.

8. It is apparent that many Aboriginal offenders find it difficult to continue to follow the spiritual path once out on the street. Not only are they faced with the many problems associated with their past (such as their criminal record and old friends still following a criminal lifestyle), but they are also ill-equipped to pursue spiritual activities outside the heavily regulated prison environment.

PART EIGHT

*Justice Initiatives*

# 31

*Edmonton Journal*

## COUNSELLING JUDGED TO GIVE NATIVES A FAIRER SHAKE

BY MIKE SADAVA

Chester Cunningham mortgaged his house for a $20,000 bank loan so Natives could get a fair shake from the court system.

His efforts have paid big dividends for thousands of Aboriginals who have managed to stay out of jail, or at least go to jail with a better understanding of what has happened in court.

Before he started Native Counselling Services 25 years ago, Aboriginals charged mainly with alcohol-related offences encountered a revolving door in the justice system, and often went to jail simply because of a failure to communicate.

At the time, nearly 60 per cent of provincial inmates were Native, but within five years of the introduction of Native counselling, that number had fallen to 28 per cent.

"I went down to the courthouse and it was just like going to a supermarket." Cunningham says.

Some Natives would assume they were guilty merely because they had been arrested, while others looked at the clerks, judge, guards and other court workers and felt they would automatically lose because they were outnumbered.

Some would be denied bail because they didn't know their street address but knew where they lived through local landmarks.

And many didn't understand their right to get a lawyer.

"To have fair and equitable treatment sometimes that means you have to do additional things for Native people," Cunningham says.

*Edmonton Journal,* "Counselling Judged to Give Natives a Fairer Shake," Mike Sadava, Monday June 5, 1995: B1. Reprinted with permission of *The Edmonton Journal.*

- Average daily number of adult offenders in provincial jails—2,718

- Percentage Native—35 percent

- Average daily number of young offenders in custody—611

- Percentage Native—29.5 percent

Former provincial court assistant chief judge Carl Rolf, who is now retired, was the judicial spark plug to get counselling for natives.

Rolf's view from the bench was that a lot of Natives were pleading guilty to alcohol-related charges, going to jail for short spells and not getting any help with their problems.

"You had no way of communicating with these people, and that's where counselling came in," he says.

Rolf attributes a lot of Cunningham's success in his ability to see through the song and dance of some people, and steer them into treatment and other constructive programs.

Although a need for Native counselling was recognized by judges, starting the organization wasn't easy.

Cunningham has an original Bank of Montreal chequebook that puts the account of the organization "in trust" to his name. "It's funny that no bank would lend money to a Native organization at that time," he says.

He had been doing court work through the Native Friendship Centre for about seven years, but started a new organization because the centre's boundaries were limited to Edmonton, and the services were needed all over the province.

The Metis Association of Alberta provided some seed money, but Cunningham had to go through long negotiations with the federal and provincial governments to get permanent funding.

The money ran out before long-term funding was obtained, which meant that staff members worked for nothing for four months.

"When I found out there was a commitment, I mortgaged the house and car so I could pay the staff," Cunningham says.

He encountered other roadblocks, such as less than co-operative guards in the cell lockup who felt there were already enough "do-gooders."

But the organization managed to thrive, and today has a $6-million budget, a staff of 150 and provides a wide range of services for Natives.

It still has counsellors in adult, youth and family court, but it also provides services such as family counselling and group homes for young offenders.

The organization runs the Stan Daniels Centre—a half-way house for federal and provincial inmates who are close to being released—as well as bush camps, and it does parole supervision.

Cunningham, 62, has been named to the Order of Canada for his efforts and has received achievement awards from the Queen, Prince Charles and the province, as well as an honorary Doctorate of Law degree from the University of Alberta.

But his single-handed approach to running Native Counselling has irked some Native political organizations, including the Indian Association of Alberta.

The board of Native Counselling Services is self-appointed, and Indian

Association president Mel H. Buffalo says only an elected board would be accountable.

"If they had to be accountable every year, they would have to show to the membership they're doing the job they should be doing," Buffalo says.

Having a voice in this organization is especially important for urban Natives, who are not represented by anybody, he says.

But Cunningham said they are accountable to the thousands of clients they have served over the years without the support of the political organizations.

"We have a hell of a lot of credibility with the grassroots Native people as well as within the criminal justice system . . . I'm prepared to sit and report to them, but I don't want them to tell me who to hire; I don't want them to dictate to me."

# 32

*Edmonton Journal*

# Brothers Hold Court
# for Troubled Natives

## BY MIKE SADAVA

"The brothers" are a fixture around the courthouse and the Remand Centre.

Brian and Gary Shanks regularly keep company with people facing charges, but they aren't habitual criminals.

They're court workers with Native Counselling Services, and they're available to anybody needing help with the often baffling court system.

They help people access lawyers or legal aid, explain some of the options they have, or help them raise bail.

And while they're not lawyers, the court workers also act as agents for people in the courtroom, arranging adjournments and speaking to sentencing.

On a recent day, Brian Shanks was helping two people on a variety of drug

charges arrange to reserve their plea until they can talk to a lawyer.

Later in the morning, Shanks spoke on behalf of the mother of a 13-year-old boy who was being sentenced on charges of cocaine possession and failure to appear in court.

Although in this case the woman has a common-law husband who will look after her son, Shanks and other court workers often find themselves involved in the family problems of their clients, such as arranging guardianship while someone is in jail so the children aren't apprehended by Social Services.

"You really feel sorry for these people, the lives they've led," Brian says. "A lot are trying hard to get out of it, but the system seems to just lead them back."

Their day starts early, with a visit to the Remand Centre to see if anyone just arrested wants help from Native Counselling Services.

Their clients come from a number of other sources as well, including lawyers and families. They even get the odd call at home.

They spend much of the morning and afternoon running between docket court, trials and even the Alberta Court of Appeal, where they are occasionally asked to make a statement about the appropriateness of a sentence.

Raising bail can also be time-consuming.

The client might have the money, or relatives who have the money but no phone. Or they might be treaty Indians with oil royalties, but unable to arrange with the Remand Centre for the money to be transferred to Edmonton.

Their clients vary, from the frightened young person from a small northern community facing his first charge, to veterans of the criminal justice system.

"I've had little old ladies in there for the first time," says Gary Shanks. "They're frightened. You have to empathize with them, help them out."

For some clients, Native Counselling Services is a lifeline to the outside.

Brian has a client who was in and out of jail, followed the straight and narrow for a couple of years, and now is in Edmonton Institution for a few years.

He still hears from him a couple of times a week, and wonders if he'll get his life together when he gets out.

"I'm still hopeful," Brian says.

# 33

# FINDING THE WAYS
# OF THE ANCESTORS

E. J. DICKSON-GILMORE

The Mohawk People of the Kahnawake Nation have a history of being at the centre of things, whether in balancing the interests of French and British in the colonial context, or more recently in the rising activism of Native Nations within Canada against the continued imposition of Canadian law. While they have often paid high costs for their activism, and continue to do so, it is arguable that, through it, they have retained an important element of power through which the potential to return to a state of self-determination is enhanced. Much of that power is currently being directed to the realization of a separate legal system in Kahnawake, one which is grounded firmly in Mohawk traditions of dispute resolution and premised upon an historical precedent recognizing the right of the Mohawk Nation to administer Mohawk law to the Mohawk people.

This recognition is embodied in the 1664 Albany Treaty, wherein the British agreed to respect Mohawk political and legal institutions and to give "all due satisfaction" in cases where disputes crossed National borders (O'Callaghan, 1853–57, 3:67–68). The details of this satisfaction were contained within that aspect of the treaty recorded in Mohawk tradition as the doctrine of the Two Row Wampum, and which asserted that those living within a particular culture, having been raised within and shaped by that culture's laws and customs, should be tried for their wrongdoing within it, under laws and systems which they understand and which have relevance for them. Thus any "English, Dutch, or Indian (under the protection of the English)" committing an offence within Mohawk territory would, upon their being discovered, be returned to the English, who would ensure the offender would be punished and "satisfaction" for his or her act would be made. The same arrangement was agreed in regard to Mohawks found to have committed a criminal act within lands claimed by New York: the Mohawk would be returned to the Mohawk Nation, the latter ensuring punishment of the of-fender and the making of satisfactory compensation to the British.

What is significant about this treaty and the Two Row Wampum is their testi-mony that the Mohawks, even at this early date, had a pre-extant legal structure for resolving disputes which was sufficiently developed for the British to recognize it for what it was and respect both its existence and its jurisdiction. Unfortunately, time was ultimately to suggest that this respect was very much situationally de-fined, and when the moment arrived in which the Mohawk were no longer needed as economic or military allies, the legal traditions which the British had previously respected underwent a redefinition, along with most other Native traditions. In this new light, Mohawk legal traditions were not simply different, they were infe-rior, and thus the colonial powers felt justified in imposing their putatively supe-rior western legal tradition.

The practical consequences of the subsequent British and Canadian drives to impose their culture, languages, laws, and legal traditions upon Native nations have been to substantially erode much First Nations' traditional knowledge. As a consequence, many of those nations, who would wish to resurrect their tradi-tional legal structures as alternatives to remaining under Canadian law, are faced with limited sources from which to draw the traditional stuff from which such structures might be constructed. The magnitude of this challenge varies across nations in accordance with the degree of success governments have had in wast-ing away traditional knowledge, for as knowledge is lost, so is the means from which a new system, or an old system for that matter, might be constructed in the modern context.

The Mohawk have been more fortunate than many Native nations in regard to retention of traditional knowledge, for while it cannot be denied that much oral history and records were lost in the colonial assault on the Mohawk language and culture, traces of this knowledge remain and can be augmented by the relative wealth of early written records describing Mohawk culture and traditions. This is not to say that there are not problems with these records, originating as they do from predominantly non-Mohawk writers and thereby carrying all the potential defects accompanying those origins; however, once sifted of their biases and for their common threads, such documents can work together with oral tradition to offer a more substantial picture of traditional cultures and histories.

As the Mohawks, and Native people elsewhere, begin to draw together their tra-ditional knowledge and articulate 'new' traditions of Aboriginal justice and dis-pute resolution, there rise from some quarters the inevitable cries that, insofar as what is proposed deviates from an often shifting baseline of tradition, many of the 'new' traditional systems are in fact something less than traditional. Such charges may emerge as much from the anticipated, outside sources as from within Native nations, as these spawn internal competitions for control of the 'new' institutions and competing claims to traditional truths. Regardless of their origins, however, attempts to undermine the credibility of tradition, whether as a justification for or blueprint of separate legal systems, overlook more compelling concerns about the origins of tradition in general and the fundamental grounds upon which separate Native justice systems may be justified. The discussion which follows attempts to understand competition of traditions through the critique of the theory of invention of tradition, looking specifically at the so-called invented tradition of Longhouse justice at Kahnawake.

## I. The Ultimate Adversarial System: The Feud as a Foundation for Modern Traditional Legal Systems

It is within the realm of the present-day competition of legal traditions that the traditionalist Mohawks of Kahnawake, like many other Aboriginal nations, face one of their most compelling challenges, namely: the re-creation of traditional legal systems subsequent to nearly a century of government efforts to eradicate those traditions. Within the Mohawk context, it must be recognized that there remains little original, purely oral record outlining those traditions. Rather, much of what remains comes from two sources, one being the contemporary written records of non-Mohawks, such as Thwaites' edited collection of the journals and letters of the Jesuit Missionaries (1896–1901, hereafter JR), and O'Callaghan's New York Colonial Documents (1853–87). Additional secondary sources include those of Lewis Henry Morgan (1851), Horatio Hale (1883), Arthur C. Parker (1916), and Henry R. Schoolcraft (1846), which were derived in whole or in part from knowledge taken from 'acculturated' Iroquois well-after the entrenchment of the colonial enterprise. Such materials can be complemented by information extrapolated from modern ethnographic studies which deal with dispute resolution in similar cultural groups, such as the Huron (Trigger, 1976) or Cherokee (Reid, 1970). Insofar as it will never be possible to ascertain just how true to the original traditions these records are, the Mohawks find themselves in a position different primarily by degree to that of other First Nations for whom much tradition has been lost, but no records exist. Thus there is a gap here, albeit a different sort of gap, and one for which there would seem, at least potentially, to be more 'cultural mortar' from which to reconstruct legal traditions.

Accepting the above, it is possible to launch into a brief elucidation of what is known about early Mohawk traditions of responding to disputes, a subject which has been discussed at length elsewhere (Dickson-Gilmore, 1991). Morgan's *League of the Ho-De-No-Sau-Nee*, as perhaps the best-known of the secondary sources on Iroquois culture and society, describes a society remarkably free from criminal in-

teractions, but which nonetheless maintained a limited 'criminal code' outlining
the proper response to four types of crimes: sorcery, female adultery, theft, and
murder (1851, 2:330). Murder was the sole act for which Morgan described in detail the process of resolution, and as reconciliation of murder is also well-docu-
mented in the *Relations,* focusing upon this offence offers an excellent elaboration
of early Iroquois dispute resolution.

An act of wrongful killing could occur either intentionally or unintentionally,
and rights of responding to it fell within the jurisdiction of those clans whose
memberships were involved directly in the event. Upon the killing reaching public notice, all interested members of the clans of the victim and offender would
meet in separate councils, wherein the details of the death would be examined and
consideration would be given to possible modes of response. Within the clan of
the accused, pressure would be applied to the killer to confess and make atonement for the crime; should the accused agree to do so, a messenger would carry to
the clan of the victim a strip of white wampum symbolic of the killer's confession,
regret, and apology for the death (Morgan, 1851, 2:333). Acceptance of the
wampum "forever obliterated and wiped out the memory of the transaction"; its
rejection constituted notice of the intention of the victimized clan to act upon
their right of blood revenge against the killer's clan. To this end, they would appoint one relative who "resolved never to rest until life had answered for life"
(Morgan, 1851, 2:332).

The *Jesuit Relations* inform of a slightly different process of restoring community relations subsequent to an act of murder, although there appears to be agreement on the matter of clan responsibility for the acts of its individual members.
Taking this matter of jurisdiction further, however, the *Relation* of 1636 reports
that responsibility for a murder fell not just upon the clan of the murderer, but
upon the entire village, or nation, depending upon whether the involved parties
crossed familial, community or national boundaries. At the inter-clan level, the
resolution process involved an intricate interplay of rights and responsibilities
whereby the offended family was given two options. First, on the basis that all
members of the offender's clan were equally responsible for the actions of their
kin, anyone of them could be killed in vengeance for the original murder. This action, while possibly satisfying a sense of retaliatory justice, had the effect of transforming the victims into offenders, and transferred their original right of blood
vengeance to the clan responsible for the first murder (JR, 10:221). This could lead
to yet another retaliatory killing and another, and so on, setting in motion the destructive give and take of a full-blown blood feud.

Perhaps in recognition of the costs of such exchanges, a means of avoiding feud
evolved whereby a highly structured process of gift-giving could compensate for
the taking of a life. This was the second option open to the victim's clan in the
event of the killing of one of their membership: they could approach the clan of
the murderer and demand restitution by a specific number and type of presents,
the quantity and value of which were pro-rated with the importance of the deceased person. Among the Huron Iroquois, the basic rate for death of a man was

thirty presents and, for a woman, forty; women being of greater value as populators of earth. These amounts would increase proportionally with the significance of the victim to the clan as a provider, leader, and so on (JR, 10:217). Although the *Relations* do not mention Morgan's "white wampum", they do inform that each gift had a symbolic utility, such as drying the tears of the bereaved or removing "all bitterness and desire for vengeance" (JR, 10:215–225; JR, 19:269). These presents were delivered to the clan of the victim in a meeting of the involved clans; their acceptance of this compensation, which was often the result of extensive and protracted negotiation (JR, 10:221), removed the victimized clan's right to avenge the death and ended the matter. There were, of course, times when a murderer's clan was unwilling or unable to meet the costs of reparations for a killing. In such circumstances, they could abandon the offender to the vengeance of the injured clan with a promise that no blood revenge would be taken for his or her death, or they could effect a similar compensation through appointing one of their own membership to do the killing, thereby guaranteeing an absence of revenge. Either of these courses were common where the person responsible for the dispute was either incorrigible or unvalued, and not considered worth the cost of reparations to the bereaved clan.

The process differed only slightly at the higher level of killings involving members of different villages and nations. According to Reid, wrongful deaths occurring at this level may have been the most necessary to resolve, as the equivalent of the clan blood feud here was, quite simply, war (Reid, 1970:153–155). His assertion is supported by accounts in the *Jesuit Relations* (33:229–249; 38:273–287), and by Hale, who observed that

> The wars among the Indian tribes arise almost always from individual murders. The killing of a tribesman by members of another community concerns his whole people. If satisfaction is not promptly made, war follows, as a matter of course (Hale, 1883:68).

The disadvantages of the feud are relatively clear and are such that no Native nation would be likely to insist upon resurrection of this tradition in its fullest sense. Yet there are clearly core philosophies to the later form of restitution which evolved out of the feud; philosophies which are certainly amenable to articulation within a modern legal structure and in terms of wrongful acts other than murder, namely: clan and societal responsibility, negotiation, and compensation for wrong-doing to the wronged parties. Yet while it is possible to revitalize such philosophies into a tradition-based structure similar to that which once existed, it can be argued that this would be feasible and successful only in relatively isolated, cohesive social contexts, and that few of the present-day Mohawk settlements are characterised by such qualities. If one chooses to focus only upon the Mohawk Nation at Kahnawake, which is surrounded on all sides by Canada and its western legal tradition, there is no isolation, and time in the community reveals that there is only limited internal social cohesion (Dickson-Gilmore, 1991:30–32).

As a result of such pressures, and the reality that the modern social problems faced by present-day legal systems often require more complex responses than pure tradition can provide, the traditional people of the Longhouse at Kahnawake, those who represent themselves through the secretariat of the nation office, have chosen to focus upon the core philosophies of their traditional modes of dispute resolution, but with a twist. The proposed "Longhouse Justice System" maintains the philosophy of restitution and responsibility, but adds these to the traditional political process of deliberations 'over the fire'. This process provides the structure through which the traditional values of dispute resolution will be articulated, and which will constitute the modern, separate traditional legal system of Kahnawake. The result is a system which is new insofar as it blends previously distinct, albeit related, traditional structures into a 'neo-tradition', but one which is made truly Mohawk insofar as it is a creation of the Mohawk people, their traditions and unique world view.

## II. A Blending of Traditions: The Traditionalist Longhouse Justice System at Kahnawake

The "neo-tradition" of Longhouse justice at Kahnawake proposes the blending of dispute resolution and political traditions as a means of responding both to a degree of attrition in traditional knowledge and to the different demands placed upon a modern, separate legal system, but in a way which maintains the integrity of traditional responses to deviance. Reflecting the latter, the Longhouse justice system values the restoration of harmony as much as possible between the parties to a dispute and, unlike the Canadian justice system, rejects the intensively adversarial emphasis upon determination of the guilt of one party over another, and the allocation of punishment. Acknowledging that the Canadian system has met with little success either in regard to satisfying victims or preventing future deviance by offenders, Longhouse justice assumes that by requiring and respecting the maximum involvement of both the disputants and their community in the resolution process and negotiation of restitution, it is more likely that justice will be both done and seen to be done.

Like many other legal systems, the Longhouse justice system is prefaced by a level of informal dispute resolution, wherein parties to a dispute attempt to resolve their differences amongst themselves or with the assistance of an unofficial mediator. In Kahnawake, special emphasis would be placed upon disputants to ensure they have entirely exhausted all possibility of informal resolution before invoking the Longhouse system, as to do otherwise would breach an all-important ethic of social responsibility—an ethic which residence in the community reveals remains remarkably strong.[1] If all attempts at informal resolution prove fruitless, either or both of the disputants would be free to bring their trouble to an Elder, clan mother, or faithkeeper, who would either confirm that genuine efforts have been made at informal resolution or, where it is believed all avenues of compromise have not been explored, send the disputants away to reconsider their options and reach a possible Elder-mediated resolution.

When it is no longer debatable that an informal resolution is impossible, the Elder or leader to whom the dispute was originally brought would approach the Turtle clan leaders to ask them to consider whether the dispute is the appropriate stuff for inclusion in the Longhouse justice system. The Turtle clan, as the Firekeepers of the Mohawk Nation, are those who carry the responsibility for calling government councils and overseeing their content and proceedings, and they would perform the same function with the Longhouse justice system. Thus, upon having a dispute brought to their attention and agreeing that it is deserving of consideration in the Longhouse, the Turtle clan leaders would arrange for a meeting of all the leaders of the Mohawk clans, including with the Turtle leaders those of the Bear and Wolf clans, in a community council to hear the dispute.

Once in council, the process followed would be that outlined within the Constitution of the Five Nations, which is commonly referred to as deliberations "over the fire" (Parker, 1916:30–34). The latter term most probably derives from the physical structure of the council within the Longhouse, whereby leaders and members of the Bear and Wolf clans sit along either side wall, separated by a central fire burning between them; a fire which is tended by the Turtle clan leaders, who sit with their clan members toward one end of the Longhouse. As articulated in the Constitution, the deliberations would be initiated by the Turtle clan sachems, who would introduce the matter to the council by deliberating it first among themselves, and then passing their conclusions "over the fire" to the Wolf clan for their consideration. The Wolves would in turn consider the Turtle clan's recommendations and, if they found fault with them or wished to alter them in any way, they would return their suggestions for change to the Turtles, who would have to reconsider and again refer their conclusions to the Wolf clan. This type of exchange would persist until the Turtle and Wolf clans agreed upon the best possible outcome, which the Turtles would then pass across the fire to the Bear clan, thereby initiating a further set of negotiations. When all clans finally reached an accord, the Turtle clan, having ensured an outcome consistent with the laws and principles of the Kaianerakowa, or "Great Law of Peace", would return the council's decision to the people (Barnes, 1984:34).

As a forum for hearing disputes and negotiating resolutions, the community council would involve not only the clan leaders, but the disputants and their speakers, if they wish to have someone speak for them, as well as any other interested parties. After hearing from the disputants, their witnesses and any other interested persons, the sachems of the three Mohawk clans would deliberate the matter in accordance with the processes defined above, giving special attention to three matters: (1) the facts of the offence; (2) its nature/severity; and (3) possible resolutions. When the clan leaders reached a concordance on the first two matters and what they agree constitutes a good and proper resolution, the disputants would be asked if they accept the leaders' view of the matter and their suggested reconciliation. If the disputants agree and accept the means of reparation, the council process is concluded, with the matter being ended with the satisfaction of all elements of the accepted resolution.

Whether settled privately or within the Longhouse, the pivotal condition of resolution is the satisfaction of all parties regarding its equity and propriety. In this way, the need for a separate appeals process is eliminated as it is implicit within the system: the Longhouse must remain in deliberations until the disputants and the community are satisfied with the resolution. Where a consensus at the community level proves impossible, or where the dispute is too severe or the result of an ongoing pattern of incorrigibility in the offender, it would be elevated to the next tier in the system: The Mohawk Nation Council of Chiefs.

At this level, the earlier procedure of deliberations over the fire is repeated involving sachems from other communities within the Mohawk Nation, but with three important alterations. First, the deliberations would be preceded by what might best be termed a "preliminary investigation", wherein the chiefs would meet in a private audience with the clan leaders from the community council bringing the dispute, to hear the facts and determine whether the business warranted a meeting of the Nation Council, or would best be returned to the community level. If the former were deemed appropriate, arrangements would then be made by the Firekeepers to call the various clan leaders, the disputants and their witnesses to a council of the chiefs. Here, as at the previous level of the Community Clan Council, the facts would again be presented and deliberated over the fire, with a view to reaching a resolution compatible with the needs of the involved parties and the community.

Where it becomes apparent that a satisfactory resolution is impossible even at the level of the national council, two options would become available. If the council feels resolution is impeded by an absence of evidence or information material to a satisfactory outcome, the clan leaders may set the matter aside until additional evidence becomes available. It has been suggested that, where a dispute is set aside, the parties might be directed to some manner of mediation to prevent further alienation and hardship during the "stay of proceedings."[2] Where the inability to resolve could not be attributed to gaps in evidence, application would be made by the Nation Council direct to Onondaga for the matter to be raised before a meeting of the Grand Council of the Haudenosaunee.

As the "court of last resort" among the members of the Mohawk Nation (and all others who ascribe to the Longhouse model), the Grand Council would incorporate all the powers and processes which precede it, as well as extraordinary authority to conclude disputes. Thus while it is empowered to set cases aside, as at the Nation level, or to conclude cases through consensus and resolution, a further option is open to the Grand Council through its right to determine and impose the best possible compromise.[3] This would, one surmises, constitute an extraordinary means of resolution to be used only in those cases where the failure to resolve is in some way due to unreasonableness on behalf of the parties, or where no additional evidence is anticipated as forthcoming, and the desirability of a return to normal group relations necessitates an imposed compromise.

## III. TRADITIONALISM AND THE INVENTION OF TRADITION: WHEN IS A TRADITION NOT A TRADITION?

If one compares the earliest tradition of feud outlined in the first part of this work with the Longhouse justice system, it rapidly becomes clear that these manifest significant differences both in terms of process and, in many cases, outcome. And yet at the same time, both the processes of the initial 'pure feud' and those of the modern Longhouse justice system are similar in that they are clearly the offspring of historically valid traditions, albeit in the case of Longhouse processes traditions that were at least in part directed to mending ruptures of policies or relations between nations, as opposed to individual rifts. In this way, the 'new system' is both new and old—it blends the philosophies inherent in the 'old tradition' of feud with the equally ancient structures and processes of 'deliberations over the fire' into a 'neo-tradition'; one which is neither completely within Mohawk tradition nor a creature entirely apart from it.

The question which this situation raises in some minds, both Mohawk and non-Mohawk, is whether 'neo-traditions' are 'real' traditions, insofar as they depart from a putative 'original' tradition and thus may lack the seal of approval of antiquity. To the degree that the Longhouse system constitutes both a new and a recent tradition of Mohawk justice, its authenticity as a 'true tradition' is thrown into question. That it seems not only to be new, but also something which has been consciously "constructed and formally instituted" (Hobsbawm, 1983:1), in response to immediate pressures favouring its creation, further undermines its legitimacy; for while traditions must be of a seasoned vintage, it would seem they must also have evolved slowly, almost imperceptibly, and never under the conscious manipulation of human beings. To be invented is to be fraudulent, and essentially untraditional, apparently notwithstanding the value or necessity of the invented tradition.

What is curious, however, is that many traditions which are considered legitimate in non-Native societies can be shown to have been, at one time or another, the product of invention, usually by the state, but not uncommonly by others within a given society (Hobsbawm, 1983:15–42). And while it is mostly the passage of time and their continued, regular practice which accords them legitimacy, there may be aspects to these 'invented traditions' which set them apart from other types of tradition, and which render them vulnerable to varying assessments of their authenticity.

*Editors' note: At this point in the original article, the author offers an extensive analysis of traditionalism and the invention of tradition. The idea is that "traditions" can be invented and be different from "old" traditions. Much of the discussion derives from the work of Hobsbawm. The reader is encouraged to see the original for the full discussion.*

Clearly many Native nations are committed to the resurrection of their traditions within the realm of separate justice, so that their people will no longer have to bear the costs of the imposed Canadian criminal legal system. Taken in this light, whether what they propose is 'really traditional' is secondary to the importance of alleviating the current position of Native people within Canadian legal traditions. Thus what may be central here is not whether the systems are based on 'rightful' traditions, but whether those systems are the right ones for the Native Nations who will administer them. And that, in itself, is a matter which Native Nations only can determine.

## Notes

1. This observation is based on a period of residence in the community by the researcher in the autumn of 1989.

2. Interview with Kanatase, Justice Committee, Mohawk Nation Office, 20 September, 1989.

3. This right of the Grand Council to impose a decision to which there is not "warrantable dissent" was reported to the researcher by various informants at Kahnawake, but a clear statement of such a right is not present in the Constitution (Parker, 1916). The best possible approximations of such a power are found in article 6 which instructs that it "shall be against the Great Binding Law to pass measures in the Confederate Council after the Mohawk Lords have protested against them"; while article 8 directs that "Every Onondaga Lord (or his deputy) must be present at every Confederate Council and must agree with the majority without unwarrantable dissent, so that a unanimous decision may be rendered". Both these sections appear to offer no more than a simple power of veto, which cannot be viewed as a true extraordinary power given the requirement of unanimity placed upon all Council determinations. Thus, while it is difficult to determine the origins of the Grand Council's right to impose a decision, it may be the case that "warrantable dissent" is defined only as that which bars a proposed outcome and yet also provides an alternative to it. If this is not the case, and there exists no other similar provision for "imposed compromise", the powers of these sachems in a juridical context might have to be modified under article 16 (provision for amendment and law reform) in order to render them an effective supreme council.

# 34

# THE NECHI INSTITUTE ON ALCOHOL
# AND DRUG EDUCATION

MAGGIE HODGSON

*In the mid-1800s there was an Hopi prophecy which said: "Our Indian people
are in midnight and we will come out of our midnight into our day to be world
leaders. This change will start when the eagle lands on the moon."*

No one understood this business of an eagle landing on the moon. In the 1960s
when the first space ship landed on the moon, they sent word back to the world,
"THE EAGLE HAS LANDED." That week the first Indian Alcohol and Drug Program
was set up. The Native Alcohol Programs in North America have been the primary
instruments in dealing with addiction prevention and treatment from the holistic
way. They have been catalysts in the renewal of the Indian Culture. For good social change to happen, it has to have a "spirit" of healing to it, an energy, a vision,
and movement. The Native Alcohol Programs have been the rebirth of our culture. *See the Spark!*

This prophecy has evolved in the Canadian Indian population. I will take you
on our Indian Communities' journey into drug addiction to where we are today.
This journey has been one which has involved our people, our government, and
our partnership in building one of the leading programs to effectively deal with
alcohol and drug abuse within our indigenous population of Canada.

## HISTORY

In the 1800s, the Canadian Government entered into a number of treaties with our
people. These treaties laid the foundation for Government's responsibility in the

Edited version of Maggie Hodgson, "The Nechi Institute on Alcohol and Drug Education: The Eagle
Has Landed," *Canadian Woman Studies* 10(2/3):101–104. 1990. Reprinted by permission of *Canadian
Woman's Studies* and the author.

areas of health and education of our population. Education was offered through the development of an institution called a residential school. Canadian Indian children were forced to leave their homes to attend these schools away from their region from age 5 and often remained in these facilities until age 20. They returned home once a year, if they were lucky. When they entered these schools, they spoke their own dialect of Indian and followed Indian customs and religion.

The intention of the government was to provide them with education and opportunity to learn English and a Caucasian religion to enable them to fit into mainstream society. The results were there was a period of 100 years when our population was removed from our language, our parents and our Elders, which are all the integral elements of our culture and values. Emile Durkheim described the effect on cultures when this phenomena happens: a state of anomie sets in, a valueless society in which there is a loss of the original culture and an inability to adapt to the new culture. The results of the anomie within our Indian population manifested itself in the form of alcohol and drug addiction in pandemic proportions. By 1970, 50% of the Canadian Indian population was 20 years old or younger because we had such a high death rate from drug addiction. One hundred percent of our population was affected by alcoholism directly or indirectly.

The Province of Alberta responded with programs designed to deal with mainstream societal drug abuse in the early 1960s with little success in attracting into treatment Indigenous peoples who were addicted.

In the early 1970s three Alberta Indigenous programs were developed, administrated and staffed by our people. These programs were funded by AADAC. Alberta is one of the first provinces in Canada to be willing to listen to our population's requests to develop or unfold our own vision of dealing with our addiction and the state of anomie within our population.

There were many barriers to this happening. The primary barrier was the lack of academically qualified Indigenous people to staff these programs. Our position to Government was that our people share the same experience and will be able to effectively deal with substance abuse from a cultural perspective. AADAC had the wisdom to listen.

We did not only lack the academics to deliver treatment programs, we also lacked academics to deliver training programs. AADAC trusted us to develop ourselves in this arena, with the benefit of limited funding in 1972.

The treatment programs were set up in old buildings (usually old houses) and operated on a minimal budget with limited staff. These programs were administrated by Indian controlled Community Boards, administrative staff and counsellors. AADAC did assist when requested and largely maintained a "hands off position." Funders operated on faith because all our people involved at that time had no previous experience in this industry and our programs were operated by recovering alcoholics or recovering drug addicts. Newly recovered to boot! Contemporary research says that it is not the way to go if you want success, but when you have nothing, the only place you go is up.

The treatment centre staff required training; a former director of one of the treatment programs developed our organization. He was a very young newly recovering alcoholic. While the Nechi Institute in Edmonton is now the largest in Canada, at that time we were the only training centre which operated from a store-front facility. The first graduating class held their training sessions in a teepee on the grounds of the University. They had all of 10 days of training to equip them to deal with this pandemic in our community. Brave eh?

## Vision

Our culture operates within a symbol called the Medicine Wheel. The Medicine Wheel teaches many cultural beliefs which manifested themselves through the years. One such form is as follows:

The four peoples of the earth are equal. White people bring movement; the Yellow people bring vision; the Brown people bring relationship or feelings; the Black people bring patience. Each race contributes our own gifts to development. The Medicine Wheel symbolizes the four seasons of spring, summer, fall and winter. Morning, noon, dusk and dark and all of these phases continue into infinity.

The beginning to the wheel is Vision. The vision of the originators of Nechi was one of identifying the need to have many Indigenous programs to deal with drug abuse.

The initial training program was set up in an experiential model of training. The average grade level of counsellors employed in the field was grade seven or basic elementary. This model enabled the trainers to transfer skills without worrying too much about reading levels and testing. The focus of the training from 1973 to 1980 was largely directed at community development skills. The content was divided with a 30% focus on alcohol and drugs and 70% on personal and community development. The average counsellor in training had a history of personal deprivation in their cultural, emotional, physical and spiritual lives.

Our model developed differently from the mainstream model in which the counselling relationship is between the client and the agency. The social change and counselling relationship is one which starts with how the counsellor relates to himself, his children, his family, friends, his community and finally how that affects how he will relate in his agency. His clients see him in the first four roles and build their trust level based on what they saw in how that counsellor was able to be within his or her extended family system. Our culture is based on relationships, formal or informal extended family systems. Social change within our community is founded on that principle.

The community development training modules focused on the mobilization of those social structures. We focused on the development of informal leaders to formal leaders and proposals to government for new treatment facilities. The average grade level was grade seven and from 1974 to 1982, there were 13 treatment facilities, detoxification facilities and half-way houses started and 26 urban and rural community based programs opened and funded by both AADAC and the National Native Alcohol and Drug Abuse Program of Health and Welfare Canada.

## FEELING

Community Development utilizing DeBono's model of stretching our ability to analyze a situation was encouraged. One Indian community developed a model of "the community is a treatment centre," as the philosophical base for their program. This community had 100% alcoholism in 1972.

A member of their community was motivated to seek treatment because his daughter wanted to live with her grandmother because of the drug abuse in their home. He sobered up and systematically approached people and referred him or her into treatment until he had a whole council sober. They attended our training and broadened their strategies. They charged all people illegally selling alcohol in the community, including the Chief's mother. They fixed up people's houses when they went for treatment. They commenced training of all who sobered up in a counsellor training program, building on a peer counselling model and social norms of community responsibility.

They set up small businesses which served the communities' basic needs, which employed the people returning from treatment. They cut off social benefits to all drug impaired residents and only gave them the necessities. They rewarded success and supported each other in a nurturing manner. They reintroduced traditional Indian religion and cultural dancing. They commenced sober dances. They actively directed all their energies at the development of sobriety as the new social norm. Within ten years, they moved from 100% alcoholism to 95% sobriety. They moved from a death a week to one death per year, from 75% of the children in the care of the government to 100% of the children returned to their homes; from thirty convictions of impaired driving per year to one conviction in the last three years; from two suicides per year to two in the last five years. They moved from people dying of alcoholism to people dying of old age.

## THINKING

Training has moved from 30% on alcoholism and 70% personal and community development to 30% on personal and community development and 70% on alcohol and drug addiction. We address primary prevention and secondary and tertiary skills development. The academic level of entrance to the program has moved from Grade 7 to Grades 11 and 12; from no exams and ten days of training to two years of training and exams; from no reading to regular curriculum with extensive reading requirements; from no planning to extensive Planning in Level of Prevention. Counsellors stay in the field for an average of 2½ years. Studies of a random sample of 300 participants of the 2000 people we have trained reflect that 36% have gone on to further education, 49% moved into leadership positions and 65% sit on community boards and associations. The key issue is that we only train non-drinkers, whether they be recovering addicted people or co-dependents.

The model which was set out in 1974 is bearing fruit. We are moving from anomie to a societal norm where an Indian leader who is a social drinker said, "You know it is quite trendy to be a sober Indian; I feel like apologizing for having a social drink. I sure know how you smokers feel: you are the minority and I am quickly becoming the minority." The training is effectively developing new norms for every sector of our society. It's like a germ which is spreading into every facet of our society—except this germ carries health.

## DOING

One community has expanded on a mobile treatment model. They chose to refer a minimum of 5 to 10 people to treatment together at a time to ensure there would be a peer support system built in. They had all members of their Council go for treatment within six months of being elected. They then referred all service givers, whether they were addicted or co-dependents. Their purpose was to build on role modelling and the relationship model. They set up a special program for their inhalant abusers. They referred a total of 50 of their community of 400 to a residential centre within a year. They utilized the cluster referral processes. They then brought out a mobile treatment team to work with their counsellors in the delivery of a day treatment program. Community members celebrated the opening day with an attendance of 250 people: imagine 2/3rds of your population out to celebrate sobriety!

The community development model and clustering resulted in community members cooking for the clients. They babysat for them and donated food for those in the treatment program, which was operated in the school gym. The cost per client day of this futuristic treatment model is $30. The costs of residential treatment within the NNADAP funding structure is $50 to $70 per day per treatment bed. The community which followed this model has moved from 100% alcoholism to 85% sobriety within 2½ years. One Elder said, "Our extended family system is our greatest strength. If we ignore addictions and enable the people we love to drink, it becomes our greatest weakness." This model erodes enabling and ensures our greatest strength does not become our greatest weakness.

## SOBRIETY AND BEYOND ISSUES

The two communities I referred to have had to deal with the aftercare issues of maintaining the sobriety for the adult population and developing programs for the children raised in addicted homes. Once sobriety was a reality, the violence which existed in these homes became uncovered. They have identified community safety as their primary concern to address the primary prevention with the youth.

They are facing 50 charges of child sexual abuse in one community because they are changing the "don't talk, don't trust and don't feel rules" to "talk about dysfunction." They are now trusting and allowing the rage out about the massive parental neglect, child abuse and the cultural abuse perpetrated by the residential school supervisors. It will take a minimum of two more generations to develop people who are reared in violence-free and substance abuse-free homes. They are developing and delivering programs which first deal with substance abuse and secondly treat the violence to ensure our children do not have to drink to cover up their pain and sadness.

## EVALUATION

Our program requested and underwent a formative evaluation process in 1984 with a review of the implementation of those recommendations in 1986. We implemented 56% of the recommendations and partially implemented 36% for a total of 92% of the recommendations. We increased our program by 100% with a 21% cut in our budget. Our purpose is program quality improvement and role modelling the importance of evaluation to the 45 programs we serve. We, too, role model change.

We have a research department which has developed a new model of management, from a management by objectives to a management by values of relationships model. We have researched a new employee assistance program to address the increase in Indian self government programs. We are presently researching the relationship between the decrease in family violence and the decrease in addictions in those two communities. We are presently working with the Solicitor General's department in tracking the reduction of impaired drivers in communities which have elected to develop a community as a treatment centre model versus other communities which continue to deal with substance abuse from an individual client model. We have implemented a treatment program for our Board of Directors and our staff in Co-Dependency and Children of Alcoholics because our research identified Adult Children of Alcoholics (A.C.O.A.) and Co-Dependency as major stumbling blocks in problem solving in sobriety and beyond communities. As a result of our leadership, three other communities have implemented an A.C.O.A. treatment program for their leaders and staff. The key here is this A.C.O.A. treatment is 100% organization funded. It has evolved from 100% government funding alcohol treatment to 100% of the A.C.O.A. of sobriety and beyond being funded by Indian organizations. That is the proof in the pudding of how our model works and how the faith of the government was the right strategy for them.

We have moved from 100 people attending a sober Pow Wow (a Native traditional dance), which was 100% government funded, to 3000 people attending, which was 100% government funded, to 5000 sober Indians with prize money of $25,000, which is 100% funded by volunteer hours raising funds for this cultural activity. We have moved from a 100% dependency relationship to one of greater autonomy in social service, education and policing.

We have Nechi graduates who have continued on into and are completing their education in the faculties of psychology, nursing, social work, education and into the Royal Canadian Mounted Police.

Our facility is a 6½ million dollar facility funded by our Provincial Government. Our total training and research budget from foundations and different levels of government is one million dollars per year. We have fifteen computers and a trainee data analysis system which is funded 100% by non-government funds. Our organization is now staffed by Indian academics and paraprofessionals. These are the results of the Alberta Government's faith in Indian people's ability to deal with Drug Addiction. We have trained and hosted Indigenous students from Australia, New Zealand, Thailand, Malaysia and Nicaragua to enable them to see how they might harness the energy of their paraprofessionals in the delivery of treatment, training and prevention programming for their Indigenous people.

We are networking with Indigenous groups to lobby the United Nations to declare one year World Drug Prevention Year of the Community because drugs affect the child, the woman, the homeless. It is possible!

*Can you see that prophecy come true? "Nechi" means "my spirit touches yours." I hope in some small way my spirit and the spirit of our Indian people has touched yours.*

# 35

## THE FUTURE FOR
## NATIVE AMERICAN PRISONERS

E. GROBSMITH

Trying to reorient the direction of Native American incarceration is akin to reversing the course of Indian history and all its consequences. Economic, cultural, and social oppression have contributed not only to a culture of poverty but to the emergence of a particular subculture within that, reflecting both urban and reservation styles. Indian urban ghettos, well known in large metropolitan cities, have been the subject of numerous books and films (*The Exiles* was a particularly poignant film about the San Francisco urban Indian population following the period of government relocation). This subculture has been dominated by disproportionately high rates of alcohol addiction and has accordingly suffered its devastating effects.

Changing this course is a monumental and daunting prospect, given the host of factors that have contributed to the problems—economic poverty, high unemployment, inadequate health care, lack of access to social welfare programs, and so on. Nor can one alter the historic vacillation in federal policy, or modify the principles that underlie funding patterns to tribal peoples. It is unrealistic to expect a total redirection in American Indian health care priorities, community alcoholism education, employment profiles, and juvenile delinquency. One can, however, work at the micro level, to provide analysis, evaluation, perspectives, and observations to inform future policy recommendations. Setting realistic goals is crucial, and the most basic and central one is to provide a path to sobriety. Positive change

Edited version of "The Future for Native American Prisoners," reprinted from *Indians in Prison: Incarcerated Native Americans in Nebraska,* by Elizabeth S. Grobsmith, by permission of the University of Nebraska Press and the author. © 1994 by the University of Nebraska Press. Editors' Note: In this chapter the author draws extensively from her work in Nebraska; hence, Nebraska inmates are used as examples throughout.

*is* occurring, and although it is hampered by national economic recession and the accompanying cuts to social welfare programs, results are beginning to be tangible. The important documentation of the Canadian band of Shuswap at Alkali Lake, which achieved nearly 100 percent sobriety, demonstrates the potential for community action. Representatives of this model group have visited tribes throughout the nation to share their message of hope in reversing the course of reservation alcoholism.

In the area of Native American incarceration, approaches to relief involve a clear set of objectives that must be embraced by all participants before any measurable effects can be achieved. Strategy must be proactive rather than circumstantial and must involve the united efforts of all involved parties: the inmates, who want to reverse the increasing trend toward alcoholism, criminal involvement, and incarceration; the states, represented by correctional authorities, who direct the use of public funds toward societal benefits; parole authorities, who bear responsibility for bringing offenders into rehabilitative opportunities; and the courts, which are ultimately responsible for interpreting how constitutional rights must be interpreted within state penal institutions. Getting all parties to agree on the problem—much less the solution—may seem unlikely, but on a state-by-state basis negotiations can be developed. The issues, as I see them, are: (1) the political relationship between correctional authorities and Indian inmates, (2) federal support for Indian relief through prison litigation, (3) the state's commitment to alcohol treatment and rehabilitation in prison for offenders with serious alcohol and drug dependency problems, and (4) articulation of such programs with parole policies and procedures as inmates prepare to resume their participation in the greater society. Each of these issues will be discussed in turn.

## The Political Relationship Between Correctional Authorities and Indian Inmates

Indian people have become accustomed to having to draw major attention to their concerns before they are able to obtain relief; it will be no different for Indian prisoners. The history of Indian militancy reflects the frustration Native American people have experienced in having their needs addressed, and Indians have periodically had to resort to drastic measures to bring national attention to a crisis situation. Like the leaders of such organizations as the National Congress of American Indians and the American Indian Movement, Indian prisoners (many of whom were active AIM members or "militants") have campaigned first within the penal institutions and ultimately in the courts to make Indian religious freedom an accepted tradition in prison. Long before the passage of the American Indian Religious Freedom Act in 1978, a strong commitment to activism was reflected within the Nebraska penal system.

Inmates in Nebraska have certainly taken the lead nationwide, and now in approximately twenty states, prisons have sweat lodge facilities and permit some form of Indian religious and cultural activity. But there is little long-term under-standing and acceptance of such practices, and the hold on them seems tentative, fragile, and perhaps endangered. Ongoing battles between correctional authorities and Indian prisoners seem to indicate that the authorities comply with Native American requests only when forced to do so by the courts. Conversely, letting up on litigious behavior appears to result in a loss of privileges previously allowed.

"Irreconcilable differences" pose obstacles to peaceful relations between Indians and the prison system. Twenty years have passed since Nebraska Indian inmates first pursued litigation to protect religious freedom, but the Nebraska penal system still provides no in-depth cultural training of guards or correctional officers. Although some generic ethnic sensitivity training is offered, there is not sufficient focus on particular cultural groups' needs, nor is there regular enough incorpora-tion of such elements in training to resolve the problems. As a result, daily conflicts between prisoners and guards continue to occur with regard to religious practices and paraphernalia. For example, sweat lodge services are officially approved at Hastings, yet during one period inmates were not permitted to use their towels at the sweat lodge. The prison authorities know that the men sweat with no clothes on and use towels when they emerge from the ceremony. Provision of blankets for use as tarps over the sweat lodge structure was also prohibited, so the Indians took the blankets off their bunks. The sweat lodge was shut down for lack of "supplies." Eventually the prisoners requested my intervention. In my negotiation with the ad-ministration, I urged them to comply with the Consent Decree's mandate of "ac-cess to the sweat lodge" by permitting the use of the prison's towels and providing the inmates with some tarps or blankets, explaining that cooperation would be much more productive than more litigation—and the prisoners' requests were *not* unreasonable. Correctional intervention—discussion between inmates and prison administrators—yielded a mutually satisfactory outcome. Such conflicts need not occur if administrators remain sufficiently informed about the protections of the decree and *comply with them.*

Another continuing conflict is caused by the relegation of the Native American cultural group to the status of a "self-betterment" club. While the purpose of such clubs is for inmates to expand their connections in the business community, such categorization by definition conflicts with the goals of NASCA, the Indian orga-nization. Inmates see it as a religious, cultural, *and* spiritual group (hence its name: Native American Spiritual and Cultural Awareness group); however, ac-cording to prison regulations, it must be classified as either a club or a religious group (not both), because each category is entitled to different privileges within the institution. This conflict has fostered endless disagreements and has been the source of ongoing conflict for at least seven years. Requests for approval of Indian activities such as powwows, Hand Games, Native American Church services, *yuwípi* meetings, and the like all come back to the issue of whether NASCA is a club or a religious group; requests by inmates are denied on the grounds that NASCA is, according to prisoners, a club, and so cannot sponsor activities that re-quire longer periods of time (as religious events may). The prison's explanation for denials of requests is that approval would mean treating one self-betterment club different from another. Not infrequently, the result is cancellation and rescheduling of an activity because of a lack of agreement on its time or length, the type of food served (and whether Native Americans may have access to the kitchen to prepare traditional foods), the guest lists, or other policy measures. In the absence of a clear guideline for Indian activities, every request on the part of the Native Americans is met with resistance and a long series of "kites" (official memos of correspondence). The resulting grievances and the responses they engender become the exhibits offered into evidence in the many trials arising from inmates' accusations of non-compliance with the Consent Decree. While it might seem that classifying NASCA as a religious group rather than a club would resolve these conflicts, that would result in a loss of privileges for weekly meetings, symposia, and banquets.

One issue that is likely to continue to be a thorn in prisoners' sides for decades to come is the issue of family members no longer being admitted to NASCA activities. Because NASCA is classified as a club and no self-betterment clubs are permitted to have family members participate in their activities, Indian prisoners find themselves not being able to invite family members—or anyone on their visiting lists, for that matter—to their special cultural or religious events. From the Native American perspective, no celebration or ceremony is proper without family members present.

The irreconcilable conflict between prison and prisoner ultimately lies in the fact that the prison believes it must treat all inmates in the same way, and perhaps in the view of the courts they must. But the Indian inmates perceive themselves as a special class, and according to federal law, they are. No group in the United States has an entire branch of the federal government devoted exclusively to it except for Native Americans. No other group in the United States has free health care nationwide simply as a result of treaty negotiations. No group but Native Americans has access to controlled substances such as peyote, or religious articles from endangered species such as eagle feathers. So to make the argument that Native Americans in prison ought to be treated the same as other inmates is one that is inconsistent with federally recognized modes of accommodation. Nevertheless, prisons are state institutions and in their funding, policy, and procedures, they insist that they apply regulations uniformly to all inmates. In obtaining the support from prisoners to write my book, several admonished me to be sure and focus on this very important issue.

Another indicator of irreconcilable differences is the continual disagreement about the use of religious articles in prison and the access to sites of religious worship. The use of plants in Indian ceremonies is something that does distinguish Native Americans from other religious groups in prison, and the burning of plant substances has caused grief and will probably continue to do so. The burning of sage, cedar, or sweet grass in Indian prayer is tolerated at the sweat lodge but prohibited in the cells because of fire hazards and the confusion caused by their aromas. So the inability of an inmate to burn sage or sweet grass in personal prayer continues to be regarded by inmates as a denial of a basic personal freedom and a violation of constitutional guarantees of freedom of religion.

Use of ceremonial foods, while not posing the same risks to security as the use of plants, also raises conflict. Indian culture demands that ceremonies be accompanied by native foods and traditional ways of serving them, from offerings made to the spirits before food is consumed to offering relatives leftovers to feed their families at home. The Nebraska penal system has barred such activities. It is not that the prison cannot accommodate these wishes; they can and historically have. The conflict arises when inmates who have enjoyed these privileges for years are suddenly denied such requests with no explanation except "equal treatment" arguments as they pertain to other self-betterment clubs. The inmates see this sudden inflexibility as arbitrary and capricious.

Conflict appears to be increasing over the desire of other cultural groups to have access to a sweat lodge. Because of the Nebraska prison's requirement to allow equal access to religion for all groups, they cannot prevent the Odinists or other non-Native Americans from worshiping in a manner acceptable to them. But the proximity of these "other" sweat lodges to the Indians' sweat lodges poses perceived threats, not only to the uniqueness of their activities but to the isolation and solemnity of the site set aside for spiritual activity.

All of these issues have one thing in common: rather than taking a proactive role in establishing a policy that regulates all Indian cultural activity, the prison *reacts* to every proposal and grievance and has to negotiate anew each privilege every time. Postponement or cancellation of banquets, celebrations, powwows, ceremonies, and Hand Games due to breakdown in the negotiation process is routine, a fact that builds anger and defensiveness among the inmates. Such breakdown further alienates them from the prison administration, resulting in more litigation. And so the cycle continues in Nebraska.

The lack of guidelines, the lack of proactive policy, the lack of guard training, the disproportionately low number of Indian correctional employees, and the irregularity in the services of a religious coordinator to assist Indian inmates leave the relationship between administrator and inmate ambivalent at best, and hostile and resentful at worst. The result is more and more litigation, more use of attorneys and time in the courts, and endless negotiations that result in recommendations that either fail to be implemented or are not followed until litigation forces the prison administration to comply.

An informed, ongoing consultative relationship between Native American inmates and the prison administrations could result in positive planning and produce negotiations that clarify policy and privileges. Many of the confrontations cited above might have been resolved with some dialogue. But prisoners are not normally entitled to sit down and discuss their views. They correspond with the administration via one-way directives and receive only formal written responses. A positive, interactive negotiation process would yield significant benefits for both parties: it would reduce the barrage of grievances thus reducing paper work for the prison, and simultaneously provide the inmates with a clear framework for their religious and cultural practices.

## Federal Support for Indian Relief Through Prison Litigation

Without the decisions that have been made in federal court, there would be no special provisions for accommodating Indian religious needs in prison. Fortunately, the court has upheld Native Americans' rights of access to their religious practices, and has recognized the uniqueness of their religious requirements. It has at the same time drawn a clear line with regard to the use of normally illegal substances in prison, such as peyote. The issue of prison security has colored every decision, for whether an inmate has the right to sweat alone, to drink peyote tea, burn sage in his cell, or carry wrapped-up articles with the sacred pipe, all depend on what protections the court can provide without jeopardizing state concerns for prison security. Without court protections, the principles of religious freedom cannot be upheld, and whatever privileges are gained could be easily lost.

## The State's Commitment to Alcohol Rehabilitation in Prison

This is a complex and extremely serious issue. The first aspect of the problem is that inmate intake procedures, including assessments of the extent of alcohol and drug addiction, are inadequate and unable to discover the true extent of addiction in this population. In an era of economic recession and state budget reductions, it may be impossible to correct the situation. Such underestimates effectively limit the dimensions of alcohol treatment programs that can be considered for a prison population, both quantitatively and qualitatively. First, the number of inmates requiring intervention and the appropriate degree of intervention are not really known. Perhaps more importantly, the quality or nature of the interventions cannot be anticipated without more accurate assessments of the ways in which alcoholism plagues this population. Without more sensitive instruments and procedures, the endemic nature of substance abuse, addiction, and the deep social pathologies will never be fully discovered, much less addressed.

Even if processing corrections could be made, actually providing improved therapeutic rehabilitation would involve monumental problems, not the least of which is funding. Prisons may not be prepared in the coming decades to meaningfully address inmate psychological problems; realistically they may only provide protection to the public as well as security and isolation for social offenders. But the costs of recidivism must be factored into the decision as to what rehabilitation can be afforded—surely when two out of three offenders return to incarceration, the cost of *not* rehabilitating inmates is even more unacceptable.

Recovery and rehabilitation are clearly not services that prisons can offer to Native Americans without the help of those trained specifically in Native-oriented treatment. This is not, however, an attitude that correctional authorities share. They may recognize their lack of success with Native American clients, but they fail to see that their inability to attract Indians into therapy or deeply involve them once they get there is not a matter of plain stubbornness or resistance on the part of the Indian prisoners—it is a matter of perceived irrelevance to their lives. Indian inmates are seen by most mental health personnel as being like other minorities, suffering the same consequences of poor socioeconomic backgrounds experienced by other impoverished ethnic groups. While these similarities are certainly valid, the need to tailor intervention programs to make them culturally acceptable remains legitimate. As has been pointed out by every Indian-oriented treatment program, treating Native Americans requires intimate familiarity with the uniquely Indian cultural milieu—their family life, culture, kinship, religion, and tradition. Coupling Western approaches to psychotherapy with applicability to Indian culture may be the only acceptable approach for Native Americans.

Alcoholics Anonymous has had a demonstrable lack of success among Indian prisoners, so continuing to direct inmates to its meetings will continue to be fruitless. Indian inmates may attend AA to earn good time or to appear cooperative for the sake of their jackets or prospects of parole, but unless they relate to it, invest in it, and find it psychologically meaningful, such attendance will serve no useful purpose. Despite the overwhelming national success of AA, Nebraska Indian prisoners' rejection of it is not unique to them. Indians in others prisons throughout the nation share the same concerns and have the same hesitancies about its usefulness. The possibility of Indian-oriented AA programs is a very appealing option, and the dependence on them in urban Indian communities continues to grow, but restricting any therapy group to one particular ethnic type is incompatible with the objectives and approaches of prison rehabilitation. Be that as it may, unless there is an all-Indian group in which therapy can take place, it is simply not realistic to expect any genuine recovery in prison.

Prison mental health programs are defensive about their lack of success with Indian inmates in both the sex offender and the alcohol/drug programs. But when the suggestion is made that culturally relative programs may be a more feasible avenue, arguments are presented that such programs are neither philosophically desirable nor financially feasible. So we are back to square one.

This situation is not unlike the others faced by Native Americans and could be dealt with by correctional authorities in the same way: by being proactive, by designing a culturally acceptable program staffed by qualified Native Americans (even paraprofessionals), by inviting an Indian AA group into prison, and by incorporating the Native American inmates into the decision-making process. With culturally appropriate treatment, perhaps some hope of alcohol recovery exists. Of course, such a program represents an increased cost to the taxpayer. But the alternative—the cycle of release, reoffending, and reincarceration—is ultimately more expensive, both socially and economically.

## Treatment Programs and Parole Policies

If treatment avenues are perceived as closed by Indian prisoners, release from prison holds little hope for maintenance of sobriety. In fact, sobriety in prison is more often by default than by conscious intent. Release from prison may be accompanied by a parole agreement that requires abstinence from alcohol, disassociation with ex-offenders, and attendance at AA meetings, but without a prior psychological commitment to recovery and sobriety, such agreements are fraudulent. Coordination between prison mental health programs and parole planning does occur to an extent, but with such low success in the parolee treatment programs, parole plans can hardly be developed that reflect meaningful choices.

The obvious beginning point for parole development is communication between Native Americans and parole authorities. Organization of Native American efforts in prison could yield significant guidance and guidelines for the parole board, parole administrators, and officers in implementing culturally acceptable recommendations. This enlightened approach must occur on all fronts, however, for while the parole board makes the ultimate determinations, it is the parole officers who must enforce it and the parole administrators who must take action if plans are violated—and both of these groups are correctional employees, not parole board employees.

The greatest paradox is how any inmate can survive and actually remain free of the criminal justice system. In our parole and recidivism study, Jennifer Dam and I concluded:

> With a population of ex-offenders who have had little or no opportunity for therapy in prison, the risk of failure at treatment is greater. It is possible, then, that an Indian inmate who has been in prison for a decade will leave on parole or "jam" out . . . having had little or no therapy and no opportunity for working with a qualified therapist, and may not even have addressed the real nature of his or her offense or the social/environmental factors which contributed to it. It is not unlikely that an inmate will approach his or her final parole hearing at which he is being set for release without ever having worked through the offense he or she committed, its impact on society, and an understanding of how not to repeat history. (Grobsmith and Dam, 1990:423–424)

Another creative possibility is having a person—perhaps the religious coordinator—serve also in the capacity of a liaison with the board. This had in fact occurred, upon occasion, but had not been formalized or made permanent. No infrastructure supported the maintenance of such a liaison. Inmates who find difficulty in addressing the board (many find the experience overwhelmingly intimidating) could benefit from having a "cultural broker," advocate, or intermediary who understood their cultural and rehabilitative needs and could present them to the board. This strategy could only be effective, however, if the basic precepts about rehabilitative avenues were altered among all parole employees. With continuing turnover of parole board members, they too—like correctional employees—could profit from an ongoing training program.

All the parties involved in these issues—the Indian inmates, the parole board, the mental health staff, and the correctional authorities—have one thing in common: frustration. We know that whatever programs and provisions exist for Native American offenders are not being successful, yet state dollars continue to be expended. The Native Americans turn inward to look for solutions, but have not developed effective strategies for positive outcomes. The correctional authorities acknowledge that it is their responsibility to devise successful rehabilitative strategies, but they know too they have not been effective. Michael Kenney, superintendent of the Hastings Correctional Center, eloquently summarized the impasse: "I agree . . . it's not working—but what does? Faced with overcrowding, escapes, and violent disruptions, I *really believe* prison administrators are desperately seeking the 'key' that will change this self-destructive pattern in which literally everyone loses" (Kenney, 1990, personal communication).

Responsibility for change falls not only to inmates and their jailers, but to the academic scientific disciplines that study such phenomena. Criminal justice, sociology, counseling, anthropology, psychology—all have responsibility to bring scientific knowledge to bear on alleviation of society's concerns. Correctional authorities may argue that in fact it is their domain to inform correctional policy. "We need some very specific guidance, instruction, revelation," said Michael Kenney. "Interestingly, it seems to fall upon prison officials to 'correct' these human deficiencies—but why not the police or the judges? Wardens are no more responsible for antisocial behavior than police or judges, but it falls on us to 'fix' this problem, I suppose because we're the most recent custodians of their persons. Ironically, we look to the sciences—criminology, anthropology, sociology, psychology—to provide *us* with the 'key' to understanding, no, *changing* human behavior" (Kenney, 1990, personal communication).

The last century has seen the emergence of a new phenomenon: the disruption of American Indian families, the economically depressed conditions of Indigenous peoples, complete with disproportionately high rates of alcohol and drug addiction, delinquency, crime, and incarceration. Clearly an unacceptable situation such as this can be confronted only in one manner: on all fronts. Perhaps with all parties assuming responsibility for change, the next century may see a return of Native American youth to their communities, which drastically require their services, and to the greater society, which so greatly stands to profit from the contribution Native Americans make.

PART NINE

*Afterword*

# 36

*Hartford (Connecticut) Courant*

# A Justice System Develops, Based on Tribal Law

### BY HILARY WALDMAN

MASHANTUCKET—As a police officer in some of New York City's roughest neighborhoods, Clifford Sebastian routinely locked up drug offenders, only to watch them return to the streets as homeless, uneducated and unemployed as they were the day they were arrested.

In his new job, as assistant chief of the Mashantucket Pequot Tribal Police Department, Sebastian sometimes has to deal with drug abusers on the rural reservation, too.

But in the two years since its Foxwoods casino opened on Feb. 15, 1992, the tribe has made enough money to build a community infrastructure so complete that housing, education, work, drug treatment and almost any other service a person might need is available. Free.

*Hartford Courant*, "A Justice System Develops, Based on Tribal Law," Hilary Waldman, February 13, 1994: C9–C12. Reprinted with permission of the *Hartford Courant*.

Sebastian, who spent eight years patrolling the subways, buses and streets of Brooklyn, N.Y., as an officer with the New York City Transit Police, said the reservation could provide a laboratory for many social experiments—including how to build a legal system that actually has a chance to work.

Sebastian is the highest-ranking Mashantucket Pequot on a growing tribal police force that now includes eight sworn officers and four patrol sergeants. Tribal Police Chief William Hickey is a former state trooper who once was the state's top gambling regulator.

Within the next several months, the 310-member tribe expects to be running its own criminal court, where Native Americans arrested for minor offenses by the tribal police can be brought to justice.

The tribe has written its own criminal code which closely resembles Connecticut statutes. In the future, an appellate court will also be set up.

Under most scenarios, if a case is prosecuted on the reservation, there is no legal recourse in outside courts.

A civil tribunal, playfully dubbed the "slip-and-fall" court by tribal lawyers, has been operating for almost two years. There, gamblers hurt in accidents at Foxwoods can have their cases adjudicated.

The civil court is the only place on the reservation where non-Indian cases are handled. If visitors to the casino have a dispute with the tribe, it must be addressed within the tribal legal system.

Tribal leaders can now perform wedding ceremonies if at least one of the betrothed is Mashantucket Pequot, and may someday be able to finalize divorces for tribal members. Civil disputes among tribal members will soon be mediated in the traditional Indian way—by a Peacemakers Grievance Council. In the future, estates of deceased tribal members could be handled by a Mashantucket Pequot probate court.

The tribe has hired a San Francisco lawyer who is an expert in Indian law to help set up the probate court.

"You don't find a lot of Indian law on probate courts over the years because very few Indians have died with money," said Jackson King, one of two full-time lawyers for the Mashantucket Pequots.

The creation of a legal system is the strongest way for an Indian tribe to assert its status as a self-governing nation, said Henry J. Sockbeson, the other tribal lawyer.

Indian reservations have limited sovereignty under a U.S. Supreme Court ruling that in 1832 declared them "domestic dependent nations."

Although they are U.S. citizens, Indians on reservations are not covered by the U.S. Constitution, a circumstance that allows them to make their own laws and exempts them from such edicts as the separation of church and state.

Indian reservations are not bound by state or local zoning, fire or building codes, and are not subject to state taxes. Nor are they subject to many federal requirements, such as labor laws. Individual Indians pay federal income taxes, but tribal funds are not taxed.

Although all federally recognized Indian tribes have limited power to enforce their laws, many tribes are unable to do so fully, Sockbeson said. Without enough federal money to hire experienced police officers, lawyers and judges, laws often simply go unenforced, he said.

Sockbeson said the two-year-old casino provides the tribe with something no states and few other Indian reservations have: virtually unlimited resources. Combined with a small caseload, this has enabled the tribe to tailor its legal system to individual needs, as well as the greater good.

"It takes money to support an infrastructure," he said. "The casino is a means to an end, not an end in itself."

## BOUNDLESS OPPORTUNITIES

When a Wampanoag medicine man presided over the opening of Foxwoods High Stakes Bingo & Casino two years ago, tribal leaders and casino executives dreamed the gambling hall would yield $100 million a year in gross revenues.

Gross revenues are the amount of money the casino has after paying winnings, but before paying salaries, buying supplies and covering other expenses.

Since then, the one-building, table games–only casino has grown to include a second glittering game room, more than 3,000 slot machines, an eight-story hotel, a high-tech theater complex, four restaurants and a shopping concourse.

And its gross revenue this year from gambling alone is expected to total $600 million. Although financial information about Foxwoods is a closely guarded secret, financial experts confirm it will not be long before all tribal enterprises—including planned golf courses, a theme park and possibly a convention center—will be a $1 billion-a-year business.

While the casino has created almost boundless opportunities for the once-destitute Mashantucket Pequots, it has also created some problems common to other monied enclaves.

About a mile uphill from the casino, about 200 tribal members and their families live on the reservation. In the past year, new cars have appeared in the driveways. Construction workers are erecting additions that will double the size of some modest homes.

Along the twisting roads that run through the reservation are a child-care center where tribal children play and learn; a gymnasium with outdoor tennis courts; a ballfield; and the tribal firehouse.

So far, sightseeing has been among the most troublesome activities recorded on the reservation, said Sgt. Ronald Carter, a former Rhode Island municipal police chief and now a member of the tribal force.

But tribal police, driving new Ford Explorers and Crown Victorias, are on constant patrol, checking to ensure that children in the day-care center are safe and that homes are secure, he said.

"The tribe is worried about its children," said Sebastian, who refused to detail the nature of his concern, but said nothing has happened yet. "We have people coming up here at 3 a.m. Some are looking for teepees, some are curiosity-seekers."

In general, only crimes committed by Indians against Indians on the reservation are within the jurisdiction of the tribal police. State police typically get involved in motor vehicle accidents or robberies involving casino visitors.

While tribal police can ask non-Indians to leave the reservation, their only criminal jurisdiction is over Indians charged with minor crimes punishable by no more than one year in jail or a $5,000 fine or both.

But even that is the subject of some dispute. Last summer, a Superior Court judge in New London ruled that state authorities have the right to prosecute minor crimes that happen on the reservation. That case is being appealed and tribal police are proceeding under the assumption that the tribe will prevail.

If there were a major crime, such as a murder or a rape, federal authorities would investigate and any trial would be in federal court.

The limit on tribal jurisdiction was established by Congress in 1885, after a controversial case in which a member of the Sioux tribe, named Crow Dog, killed a fellow Sioux named Spotted Tail.

Crow Dog was tried on the reservation and sentenced to support Spotted Tail's widow and family. Outsiders who believed the sentence was too lenient took the case to a U.S. court, arguing that under federal law, Crow Dog should be hanged.

The court upheld the Sioux right to mete out justice. But two years later, Congress enacted the Major Crimes Act, taking responsibility for prosecuting major crimes out of Indian hands.

## PRE-TRIAL INTERVENTION

Since the Mashantucket Pequot tribal police began patrolling the reservation last August, they have made about a dozen arrests—one for breach of peace, one for a minor narcotics offense and several for infractions such as non-payment of child support, Sebastian said.

The suspects have been issued summonses, but few—if any—will ever appear before a judge or jury. Instead, the tribe is trying a system of pre-trial intervention loosely modeled after a program in New Jersey, Sockbeson said.

Before a case goes to trial, three senior citizens, known as tribal Elders, will be appointed to work with the defendant. With help from professional consultants and a court administrator, the Elders will determine if the defendant would be helped by drug treatment, counseling, or any other type of social or medical assistance.

The defendant could be sent to treatment for up to two years, and required to perform community service. If the person successfully completes the program, all charges would be dropped, Sockbeson said.

The tribe will also hire a part-time judge and a prosecutor, both of whom, Sockbeson said, will probably be Indian. Cases that go to trial would be heard by the judge and a jury of six tribal Elders.

Sebastian, the assistant police chief, said he's seen enough to know that throwing people in jail doesn't work. He said he's ready to put his faith in the new system.

"I think it's a good approach," he said. "I figure we can't do any worse."

If anyone needs to be locked up, the tribe is expected by summer to have plenty of space. Ground will be broken soon for a 55,000-square-foot public safety building that will house the tribe's police, fire and emergency medical services departments.

The building, designed to resemble a huge, old-fashioned carriage house, will also include an as-yet-undetermined number of jail cells for men, women and juveniles, a firing range and a staff exercise room.

Sockbeson said the busiest part of the legal system might be the Peacemakers Grievance Council, a place where tribal members can resolve disputes with their neighbors, and even family members.

The council will be modeled after a Navajo system of dispute resolution. Each of the Mashantuckets' eight traditional families, from which all tribal members trace their roots, will be asked to appoint two members to the council. One member from each family must be an Elder.

If a complaint is filed, three of the 16 members of the council will be assigned as peacemakers. They would investigate the case by visiting all of the parties involved. The peacemakers eventually would suggest a solution, which would be voted on by the full council and then be binding.

Sebastian said the idea behind all of the programs is to address the roots of problems, in the hope they will not recur. If the experiment works, he acknowledged, the need for a police department might diminish. But unfortunately, he said, it will never be obsolete.

"Wherever people are, they rub each other the wrong way," Sebastian said. "Whether it's in heaven or on the Indian reservation."

# 37

## MAJOR ISSUES IN
## NATIVE AMERICAN INVOLVEMENT IN
## THE CRIMINAL JUSTICE SYSTEM

MARIANNE O. NIELSEN

The historical involvement of Native peoples with the criminal justice system is a narrative of tragedy and injustice. The chapters of this book have each told a part of the story. For most non-Native readers, the story is unfamiliar and shocking; for most Native readers, it is all too familiar. There are hopeful indicators of change, however. In the United States Native crime rates may be declining, as Silverman points out, and in Canada they are relatively stable (Frideres, 1993:213). In both countries there are increasing numbers of innovative services to prevent crime and to assist Native offenders. Many of these are designed and operated by Native peoples.

A reminder of the differences between the United States and Canada must be repeated here: Because Native peoples are the largest minority group involved in the criminal justice system in Canada and the most impoverished group in the nation, Canadian Native peoples receive the kind of media and public attention that in the United States is reserved for African Americans and, more recently, Hispanics. Increased attention in both countries has worked to the benefit of Native peoples in that it has given them more political power, but it has also worked to their disadvantage in that many Native leaders now fear that the "quick fix" mentality that is currently ascendant in the dominant society will cause the public to lose sympathy for Native peoples because it is taking them "so long" (that is, more than twenty years) to remedy social problems that have taken centuries to develop.

Increasing the involvement of Native people as criminal justice service providers seems to be the main strategy for lowering the Native incarceration rate put forward not just by Native peoples but by scholars and dominant government bodies. This solution has important repercussions of many kinds, but it is also significant because of what gets left out: This solution focuses attention on Native offenders and diverts attention from primary prevention, that is, preventing Native people from becoming involved in the criminal justice system in the first place. Although increased numbers of Native service providers may well increase the effective and humane operation of the criminal justice system, it will not prevent crime.

The theme of increased involvement in service provision can be found running through many of the chapters in this book. This final chapter will highlight six main issues related to criminal justice services for and by Native peoples: sovereignty (self-determination), cultural revitalization, urbanization, developmental needs, and two related underlying themes—lack of political power and lack of legitimacy—that emerge out of the discussion of the other issues.

## SOVEREIGNTY

As was noted in Chapter 3, initiatives to establish Native-operated criminal justice services, such as police forces, peacemaker courts, alcohol- and drug-abuse treatment centers, and many other programs, are part of the efforts by Native peoples to reestablish more decision-making powers over their own communities as well as to decrease Native incarceration rates.

Sovereignty is the "inherent right or power to govern" (Canby, 1988:66), meaning that tribal governments may govern their internal affairs except where restricted from doing so by the federal government. Therefore, the drive toward increased "sovereignty," as the term is used in the Native political arena, is aimed at removing federal restrictions and regaining a greater degree of legal, political, and economic independence. Limited sovereignty is rooted in paternalistic ideologies that do not see Native peoples as capable of handling their own affairs. Some social scientists suggest that governments do not want Native peoples to govern their own affairs because of the economic threat this would pose to the current state of society (Boldt, 1993). Historically, struggling for sovereignty has meant resisting overt and covert assimilationist federal (and state) government policies that were and still are aimed at removing the legal and cultural distinctiveness of Native peoples and turning them into "ordinary citizens" with no special rights or benefits despite legal contracts (treaties) guaranteeing these (see Boldt, 1993).

Increased political power has been touted as the main solution to the socioeconomic inequalities of Native peoples. It is an attractive solution to many people, not only because it may decrease poverty (and therefore perhaps crime) but also because it increases the power of some Native politicians and provides non-Native politicians with a scapegoat if a "quick fix" does not occur. However, sovereignty may go against the interests of entrepreneurs who wish to develop Native lands, as well as against the interests of the Native factions working with them. Needless to say, sovereignty issues will not be resolved quickly.

Political sovereignty initiatives have helped to shape the development and operation of Native criminal justice services. The question of sovereignty influences which level of government (federal, state, or tribal) has the final power over the jurisdiction, mandate, and funding of the services and determines to whose model and standards the services will be held.

Perhaps the most important issue related to sovereignty is indigenization. Indigenization, in the long term, works against sovereignty. Indigenization refers to the employment of Native peoples within the dominant government's criminal justice system. It includes the creation of special criminal justice positions to be staffed by Native people only, the use of affirmative action to hire more Native peoples into standard job positions, and the "devolution" (by contract) of criminal justice functions to Native-operated and -staffed organizations. This concept has mainly been used to describe the establishment of Native police forces (Hagan, 1966; Havemann, 1985; Havemann et al., 1985), but it can be generalized to describe other criminal justice services as well.

Indigenized criminal services operate on the familiar dominant society model and are under the direct or indirect control of the dominant government. "Brown people in blue uniforms" do not play the same role as the traditional peacemakers of their own nation, however. Indigenized jobs are bound by the same job descriptions, standards, and principles as are the jobs held by any member of the dominant system. There are few efforts made (and few are even possible) to accommodate the cultural values and needs of the Native people who are the clients of the service or of the Native people staffing the jobs. As Dumont made very clear in Chapter 4, Native peoples' traditional justice values conflict with the values of European-based society. This is one reason that indigenization is not the most effective or satisfactory strategy for providing services.

A second reason is that, in keeping with the limited jurisdictions of Native governments in general (see Canby, 1988:72; Chapter 6 in this volume), indigenized criminal justice services that have been contracted to Native organizations have many limitations put on them. As mentioned in Chapter 3, these limits may have to do with jurisdiction and powers of arrest or sentencing, but they may also have to do with following non-Native ideals of organizational structure and operation (Nielsen and Redpath, 1994).

In the short term, indigenized services may assist self-determination in that they can be used to increase the legitimacy of Native people working in criminal justice administration (Nielsen, 1993). In the long term, however, indigenized services may hinder Native self-determination and may hurt the legitimacy of services based on traditional Native justice in that the successful operation of indigenized services could be used by assimilationists to argue that autonomous or semi-autonomous Native-operated criminal justice services are not needed. The result is that indigenization may serve to further assimilate Native peoples.

While indigenization is rooted in the need of the dominant government to acknowledge and at the same time control Native peoples, it is also related to prejudice. Many non-Native Americans and Canadians, including political decision-makers, feel that Native people should give up their traditions and assimilate into the dominant society. This mindset could be described as a contemporary version of Social Darwinism in that U.S. and Canadian culture and society, however they may be defined, are assumed to be more desirable and effective than Native cultures and societies.

A second issue related to sovereignty is that, as Dickson-Gilmore pointed out quite clearly in Chapter 33, the imposition of European values and criminal justice structures on Native communities has led to schisms within the communities. Government-imposed political structures invariably conflict with the traditional power structures. This means that divisions in the community develop between those who have political and economic power under the traditional structure and those who are given power under the imposed structure (see Boldt, 1993: 124–127). There are also political schisms rooted in the degree of acculturation of community members. One faction may support a new money-making venture, such as a casino or correctional institution, whereas another faction may feel it is against traditional values and refuse to support it.

In the development of a new criminal justice initiative, these schisms can have an impact on the degree of community support the project receives and on its eventual effectiveness. Several Canadian Native criminal justice service agencies refuse to have any political affiliations in order to minimize the impact of "Native politics" on the effective operation of their programs. This strategy works well for pan-Indian organizations, but it is more difficult to accomplish for reservation-based programs when the development of increased political power is a primary concern of their people.

## CULTURAL REVITALIZATION

Native communities across North America are reestablishing and in some cases rediscovering their cultures and traditions. It must be reemphasized that Native "culture" is not one culture. There are hundreds of Native cultures across North America, all different, all based on the unique history, ecology, and values of each group. Nor are Native cultures static, trapped somewhere in the eighteenth century. Native cultures, like all cultures, are dynamic. In fact, Native cultures, more than most cultures perhaps, are adaptive—how else would they have survived so many centuries of active repression and suppression? Native cultures as they exist now are taking the best of the old ways and the best of the new ways to develop a lifestyle for each group that best fits that group. Keeping this in mind, accusations that new programs are not really "traditional" are meaningless. Native peoples do not have to live up to the expectations of outside groups about what they should be like—this is the whole point of self-determination initiatives.

The cultural revitalization movement, actually a series of movements, has had a tremendous impact on the type of programs that were and still are being developed in the criminal justice field. Twenty years ago, when Native-operated services were first being started, the emphasis was on providing services that resembled those of the dominant society. While very little research has been done into why these models were chosen, there were probably two factors at play.

One was the need for Native peoples to develop legitimacy as criminal justice service providers. Because of the paternalistic and assimilationist policies of the dominant government and the lack of cultural sensitivity that was prevalent at the time among many White decisionmakers, it is likely that the Native groups proposing new services used a "foot in the door" approach; that is, they proposed services that were not very different from the government-operated services already in existence—indigenized services, in other words.

The second factor was that indigenized services were more familiar and comfortable for non-Native decisionmakers and also for some Native communities. There was already a history in the United States of the Bureau of Indian Affairs (and, to a lesser extent, in Canada of the Department of Indian Affairs and Northern Development) using Native people to police their own communities. In the United States in 1884, for example, there were Native police forces on forty-eight of sixty Indian agencies (Hagan, 1993:155; see also Peak, 1989). Furthermore, Courts of Indian Offenses operated on reservations beginning in 1883. The situation was not quite the same in Canada. Although Native police scouts were used by the Royal Canadian Mounted Police in the west, most policing and court adjudicating were carried out by non-Native members of the Mounted Police.

New Native-operated programs not only have to overcome the unwillingness of dominant governments to give up control, they also have to overcome the stereotypes of Native people that are held by European-based society. These stereotypes have historically fallen into three categories: the heathen savage Indian, the romantic childlike Indian, and the disadvantaged minority group member (Boldt, 1993:69–70; see also Trigger, 1985). These stereotypes grew out of the press representation of Indians during the early years of European exploration and later years of colonization, genocide and ethnocide, and resource exploitation. These images have been perpetuated by today's mass media and work against a realistic view of Native Americans' abilities to handle their own affairs. The mass media have also contributed to the deterioration of traditional Native values among younger generations of Native peoples.

Cultural revitalization is aimed at counteracting these negative stereotypes and at replacing indigenized services with more appropriate culturally based services. The wide range of Native cultures means that a wide range of criminal justice solutions are needed. With growing public awareness and increasing sympathy for multiculturalism, as well as supportive Court decisions in both countries, the door is being opened for more traditionally based programs. These programs are based on a model different from the adversarial, punishment-oriented European-based system. These models use respected community members as mediators and counselors, incorporate family members in the process, investigate underlying problems, use consensus building among all participants, and aim at healing for the offender, the victim, and the community (Nielsen, 1996).

On an individual psychological level, it has been suggested that the development of self-esteem among Native young people may be an important crime-prevention strategy, with the development of an appreciation for heritage and culture seen as a key step. Unfortunately, acculturation may mean that the young people who could benefit the most from increased self-esteem are the ones least likely to be interested in learning about Native cultures as a means of achieving it.

The development of feelings of kinship with other Native groups is also part of the process of cultural revitalization. It should be noted that pan-Indian activities such as powwows and arts and crafts exhibitions are not only ways of instilling pride in identity among Native peoples but also a means of developing increased awareness by the non-Native population.

## URBANIZATION

The number of Native people living in urban areas has increased dramatically since World War II. Native people migrate to cities because they are "pushed" or "pulled" away from their home communities. Push factors include government relocation policies, lack of employment opportunities, political factionalism, and violence related to drug and alcohol abuse. Pull factors include attending an educational institution, joining the military, finding work, and joining family members (Snipp, 1989:303, 84, 282). Adapting to an urban lifestyle can cause numerous problems: Not only must the person face poverty, a faster pace of living, and a lack of knowledge about places, laws, resources, and social expectations, but he or she may face active discrimination from potential employers, landlords, and the general public. They must also learn to survive without the extensive family and friend support networks that exist in their home communities. This disorientation and isolation may well contribute to the increase in the number of Native inmates who come from urban centers in Canada (LaPrairie, 1992:10–15) and in some American states (Grobsmith, 1994:37).

In the United States more than in Canada, Native people in urban areas are a forgotten minority group. There are few Native-specific criminal justice–related services in operation. If urban Native people need assistance, they must overcome the additional disadvantages they face (such as language barriers, lack of knowledge about urban life, and discrimination) in order to find it. Funding and policymaking are focused on reservations because of the federal governments' responsibility for reservations but not for Native people living outside them.

Thought needs to be given to adapting reservation-based initiatives so that they can operate effectively in urban environments. Since traditionally based service programs rely on social cohesion and their staff's' knowledge of the local Native community and its members for effective service provision (see Nielsen, 1993), more cohesive Native communities may need to be created within cities to encourage the development of traditionally based programs. In both countries there are urban organizations that serve as gathering places for Native people, such as recreational and social clubs. In Canada the Friendship Centers are an example; in the United States Indian Centers serve the same purpose. Furtaw (1993:30–38, 219–231) lists many such organizations in both countries. These urban organizations could form the core of the needed communities.

## DEVELOPMENTAL NEEDS

"Developmental needs" refers to the lack of resources that exist in Native communities and hinder the development of criminal justice services. Developmental needs are closely related to lack of sovereignty. Because Native peoples have been prevented from governing their own affairs and operating their own services until very recently, they have often not done well when experimental programs were thrust on them "from above," that is, by the federal government. Several centuries of economic dependency and social marginalization have meant that Native peoples need to learn more about European-based economic structures and bureaucratic operations in order to develop their own organizations and to gain legitimacy for their own developmental efforts. Furthermore, a hint of Social Darwinism remains in the insistence of the dominant governments that European-based ways are inherently better than Native ways. The common tendency of government bureaucracies to not give up control of any part of their mandate, in this case the mandates of the Bureau of Indian Affairs and Department of Indian and Northern Development, to control, as opposed to empower, their Native "wards" may contribute as well. It has also been suggested that "in the national interest" these departments have exploited Native peoples, often in partnership with major corporations (Boldt, 1993:68–72).

Because of these and other factors, the infrastructures of Native communities are not as developed as those of dominant society communities; that is, Native communities do not have the resources necessary to operate some criminal justice services. Developmental needs fall into four categories: lack of skilled staff, lack of financial resources, lack of facilities, and lack of service support networks.

Lack of skilled staff refers to a lack of community members skilled in areas of expertise that are needed to operate specialized programs such as sexual-abuse counseling or alcohol treatment. As problems come to light in Native communities, a wider range of skills need to be called upon. For example, in the community of Alkali Lake in northern British Columbia, Canada, the community developed its own very successful strategy for reducing the alcoholism rate in the community (from almost 100 percent to less than 5 percent). This strategy relied on community pressure and positive reinforcement for alcohol treatment. As the alcohol problem was dealt with, however, it became apparent that it had masked other equally severe social problems such as child sexual abuse and family vio-lence. Further strategies and resources were needed to deal with these issues. The Alkali Lake scenario is not unusual. It points to the complexity of needs and the wide range of services that are needed to support criminal justice services in a community.

The skills people need to develop depend on the needs of the community. In addition to lacking community members with specialized training, the commu-nity may also lack individuals skilled in traditional practices. Many communities are making strong efforts not only to encourage advanced education for their members but to teach traditional languages and practices to their young people. Until recently, Native American school dropout rates were well above the national average. In the last twenty years, there has been a distinct improvement in Native educational retention rates in both the United States and Canada, although the proportion of students completing a post-secondary degree has not increased quite as dramatically (Snipp, 1989:189; Frideres, 1993:180–193). In 1989, about 55 percent of Native Americans had completed twelve years of schooling, compared with 69 percent of Whites and 51 percent of Blacks (Snipp, 1989:189).

Lack of financial resources, the second developmental need, causes tremendous difficulties in developing new criminal justice services. The funding of reserva-tion-based Native peoples is controlled by the federal governments of Canada and the United States. Tribal governments cannot directly access funds without per-mission from the Bureau of Indian Affairs or the Department of Indian and Northern Development. This has led to incidents such as a recent case in which U.S. Public Law 101-630 authorized $90 million for the improvement of Native American child protection and family violence prevention but, because the Bureau of Indian Affairs did not request an appropriation, the Navajo Nation (or any other Indian Nation) could not get access to the money. Funding from other government departments, such as the Department of Justice, must be competed for, sometimes against other Native groups. Native peoples are caught within what Boldt (1993) calls a "culture of dependence."

A lack of facilities is closely related to a lack of financial resources. Native com-munities that would like to develop a youth crime-prevention program, for ex-ample, may find that they do not have a building to use as a drop-in center and cannot get permission to build one. Similarly the community may wish to start a drug- and alcohol-abuse treatment center but again, may not be able to get fund-ing.

Lack of service support networks is also a developmental problem in that there may not be the community resources needed, for example, to assist a mentally ill offender or to provide substance-abuse treatment for a gas-sniffing child. To send the person in need of treatment out of the community is often self-defeating in that the individual may fall into despair at being separated from family and com-munity, which instigates more problem behavior.

It should be noted that there may be resources available that are operated by the European-based system; however, many Native people are reluctant to use services that are culturally insensitive or inappropriate.

## UNDERLYING THEMES

Underlying these factors are two important themes: lack of political power and lack of legitimacy. Boldt (1993:72) argues that Native peoples do not have the political or economic power to overcome the interests of more influential segments of society, especially major corporations. Native peoples fall outside the "consciousness and concerns" of politicians. The recent history of Native peoples in both countries has been a recounting of attempts to influence the consciousness of the politicians and to become an unignorable part of their concerns. Native peoples are trying to remind politicians (and their electorate) of the intent of the treaties, which were legal contracts between nations, negotiated in good faith, at least in good faith on the part of the Native signatories. The intent of the treaties was that Native peoples should retain power over their own affairs (Boldt, 1993:41). Legal maneuverings and outright broken promises have removed this power.

Regaining control of criminal justice administration is a vital step in reestablishing political power. The criminal justice system is the enforcement arm of the non-Native society, and as such it enforces the values of the society and punishes wrongdoers. It is therefore a key branch of government for Native peoples to control if they wish Native values to be enforced and Native punishments to be used in their own communities.

The second underlying theme is that of establishing legitimacy. Native peoples have been considered inferior peoples for so long in U.S. and Canadian society that their ability to operate their own services is openly debated. This debate includes not only, justifiably, the developmental needs mentioned earlier but also, unjustifiably, the stereotypes of Native peoples as incapable of operating organizations or services (see, for example, Wuttunee, 1992).

Service programs need legitimacy to get the resources they need to operate: funding, clients, staff, and a mandate to offer services. The legitimacy of one program can be used as a resource to get the funding to develop a different and perhaps more "radical" traditionally based program (the "foot in the door"). This strategy has been used quite successfully in Canada by Native Counselling Services of Alberta, a Native-run agency that started out offering courtworker services in lower division courts and eventually increased their initiatives to include Native spirituality programs in correctional institutions, crime-prevention projects that focus on Native Elders interacting with young people, and youth justice committees that use Native Elders to recommend sentences to young offender (juvenile) courts.

Legitimacy is, however, not only something that is needed in dealing with the non-Native government decisionmakers; it is also needed in dealing with members of the Native community. In other words, because of the schisms caused by acculturation and conflicting authority structures, not all new programs will be accepted by all members of the community. If the new program is based on Native cultural practices, it may not be supported by assimilated community members. In order to gain legitimacy from these community members, new Native programs need to have the same kind of characteristics that earned them legitimacy with the non-Native government, such as having a bureaucratic organizational structure, following government-set standards of service, having a computerized client-information system, and having regular program reviews. It should be noted that these are not necessarily characteristics that do anything to contribute to the effectiveness of the service and, in fact, may actually detract from it (see Nielsen, 1993).

In order for the program to gain legitimacy with more traditional community members, the program must incorporate important Native values regarding justice, such as holistic and respectful treatment of clients, involvement of the family and community in the treatment of the individual, involvement of respected community members in the process, and consensus building (Nielsen, 1996).

## CONCLUSION

All of these issues—the impact of sovereignty, the impact of cultural revitalization, urbanization, developmental needs, lack of political power, and lack of legitimacy—will have to be addressed as Native peoples work to develop culturally appropriate and effective criminal justice services. The development of Native communities and the development of criminal justice services for Native peoples are intricately linked. They exist in a mutually influential balance: As one progresses, so will the other; as one is damaged, so is the other.

It must not be forgotten, as we discuss law, police, courts, and corrections, that the goal that Native peoples are working toward is to overcome the results of centuries of oppression and injustice. As mechanisms for addressing poverty, economic dependency, and marginalization are found, then so will be found the solutions to violence, suicide, substance abuse—and crime. Native people must not be alone in this struggle. Native crime and incarceration are not "Native problems," they are "societal problems." The cost in the waste of human life and potential is shared by us all.

# REFERENCES

Adair, James. 1930. *Adair's History of the American Indians*, ed. Samuel C. Williams, under the auspices of the National Society of the Colonial Dames of America, in Tennessee. Johnson City, Tenn: The Watauga Press.

Adams, K. C., and C. R. Cutshall. 1987. "Refusing to Prosecute Minor Offenses: The Relative Influence of Legal and Extralegal Factors." *Justice Quarterly* 4:595–630.

A. J. I. (Manitoba Public Inquiry into the Administration of Justice and Aboriginal People). 1991. *Report of the Aboriginal Justice Inquiry of Manitoba*. Vol. 1: *The Justice System and Aboriginal People*. Winnipeg: Province of Manitoba.

Alaska, Department of Public Safety. 1987. *The Village Public Safety Officer Program: A Conceptual Design to Improve Law Enforcement and Public Safety in the Rural Areas of Alaska*. Juneau: DPS.

Alaska Federation of Natives. 1988. "The AFN Report on the Status of Alaska Natives: A Call for Action." In U.S. Senate, 1989:424–502.

Alaska Police Standards Council. Various dates. *Minutes*. Juneau: APSC.

_____. 1982. *Regulations and Procedures Manual*. Revised January 1982. Juneau: Alaska, Department of Public Safety.

Albaugh, B., and P. Albaugh. 1979. "Alcoholism and Substance Sniffing among the Cheyenne and Arapaho Indians of Oklahoma." *International Journal of the Addictions* 14(7): 1001–1007.

Alland, Alexander. 1970. *Adaptation in Cultural Evolution: An Approach to Medical Anthropology*. New York: Columbia University Press.

Allen, Paula Gunn. 1986. *The Sacred Hoop: Recovering the Feminine in American Indian Traditions*. Boston: Beacon Press.

Alper, B. S., and L. T. Nichols. 1981. *Beyond the Courtroom*. Lexington, Ky.: Lexington Books.

Amerindian Police Council. 1979. *Organizational Analysis of the Amerindian Police and Recommendations*. Lac St. Jena, Quebec: Amerindian Police Council.

Anchorage Daily News. 1988. "A People in Peril: A Special Reprint." Anchorage: Anchorage Daily News.

Anders, Gary C. 1980. "Theories of Underdevelopment and the American Indian." *Journal of Economic Issues* 14(3): 681–701.

Anderson, Robert. 1991. "The Efficacy of Ethnomedicine: Research Methods in Trouble." *Medical Anthropology* 13(1–2): 1–17.

Angell, John E. 1978. *Alaska Village Police Training: An Assessment and Recommendations*. Anchorage: University of Alaska, Criminal Justice Center, December.

_____. 1981. *Public Safety and the Justice System in Alaskan Native Villages*. N.p.: Pilgrimage Inc.

_____. 1989. Interview, September.

Arizona Department of Corrections. 1990. *1990 Annual Report*. Phoenix: Planning Bureau.

Armstrong, T. L. N.d. "Restitution, an Alternative Sanction for the Tribal Courts: A Programming Strategy for Reducing Incarceration Among Native American Youth." Unpublished paper.

Austin, Raymond D. 1993. "Freedom, Responsibility, and Duty: ADR and the Navajo Peacemaker Court." *Judges' Journal* 32(2): 9–11, 47–48.

Bachman, J., J. Wallace, P. O'Malley, L. Johnston, C. Kurth, and H. Neighbors. 1991. "Racial/Ethnic Differences in Smoking, Drinking, and Illicit Drug Use Among American High School Seniors, 1976–1989." *American Journal of Public Health* 81:372–377.

Bachman, R. 1991a. "An Analysis of American Indian Homicide: A Test of Social Disorganization and Economic Deprivation at the Reservation County Level." *Journal of Research in Crime and Delinquency* 28(4):456–471.

_____. 1991b. "The Social Causes of American Indian Homicide as Revealed by the Life Experiences of Thirty Offenders." *American Indian Quarterly* 16:469–492.

_____. 1992. *Death and Violence on the Reservation: Homicide, Family Violence, and Suicide in American Indian Populations.* New York: Auburn House.

Bailey, Lynn K. 1978. *The Long Walk: A History of the Navajo Wars.* Los Angeles: Westernlore Press.

Bames, Barbara K. 1984. *Traditional Teachings.* Cornwall, Ontario: North American Indian Travelling College.

Banai, Edward Benton. 1979. *The Mishomis Book.* St. Paul, Minn.: Indian Country Press.

Barkun, M. 1968. *Law without Sanctions: Order in Primitive Societies and the World Community.* New Haven, Conn., and London: Yale University Press.

Basso, K. 1970. "To Give Up on Words: Silence in Western Apache Culture." *Southwestern Journal of Anthropology* 26(2):213–230.

Bayly, John A. 1988. "Entering Canadian Confederation: The Dene Experiment." In *Indigenous Law and the State,* ed. Bradford W. Morse and Gordon R. Woodman, 223–239. Dordrecht: Foris Publications.

Beauvais, F., E. R. Oetting, and R. W. Edwards. 1985. "Trends in the Use of Inhalants among American Indian Adolescents." *White Cloud Journal* 3(4):3–11.

Becker, H. 1963. *Outsiders: Studies in the Sociology of Deviance.* New York: Free Press.

Begay, Shirley M., and Charlotte Johnson Frisbie. 1983. *Kinaalda': A study of the Navaho Girl's Puberty Ceremony.* Middletown, Conn.: Wesleyan University Press.

Beiser, M., and C. L. Attneave. 1982. "Mental Disorders among Native American Children: Rates and Risk Periods for Entering Treatment." *American Journal of Psychiatry* 139(2).

Benderly, Beryl. 1974. "Rape-free or Rape-prone." In *Conformity and Conflict: Readings in Cultural Anthropology,* ed. James P. Spradley and David W. McCurdy. Boston: Little, Brown and Company.

Berger, Thomas. 1985. *Village Journey: The Report of the Alaska Native Review Commission.* New York: Wang and Hill.

Berkhofer, Robert F. 1978. *The White Man's Indian.* New York: Knopf.

Berstein, I., W. Kelly, and P. Doyle. 1977. "Societal Reaction to Deviants: The Case of Criminal Defendants." *American Sociological Review* 42:743–755.

Black, D. 1968. "Police Encounters and Social Organization: An Observational Study." Unpublished paper. Department of Sociology, University of Michigan, Ann Arbor.

_____. 1971. "The Social Organization of Arrest." *Stanford Law Review* 23:1087–1111.

_____. 1976. *The Behavior of Law.* New York: Academic Press.

_____. 1989. *Sociological Justice.* New York: Oxford University Press.

Black, D., and A. Reiss. 1970. "Police Control of Juveniles." *American Sociological Review* 35:63–77.

Black, T. E., and C. P. Smith. 1980. *A Preliminary Assessment of the Numbers and Characteristics of Native Americans under 18 Processed by Various Justice Systems.* Sacramento: National Juvenile Justice System Assessment Center, American Justice Institute.

Blackburn, Bob L. 1980. "From Blood Revenge to the Lighthorsemen: Evolution of Law Enforcement Institutions among the Five Civilized Tribes in 1861." *American Indian Law Journal* 8(1):49–63.

Bodley, John H. 1982. *Victims of Progress.* 2nd ed. Mountain View, Calif.: Mayfield Publishing Company.

Bohannon, P. 1965. "The Differing Realms of the Law." *American Anthropologist,* Part 2, 67(6) (December):33–37.

_____. 1967. *Law and Warfare: Studies in the Anthropology of Conflict.* New York: Natural History Press.

Boldt, Menno. 1993. *Surviving as Indians: The Challenge of Self-Government.* Toronto: University of Toronto Press.

Boldt, Menno, and J. Anthony Long. 1984. "Tribal Traditions and European-Western Political Ideologies: The Dilemma of Canada's Native Indians." *Canadian Journal of Political Science* 17(2):537–553.

_____. 1985. *The Quest for Justice.* Toronto: University of Toronto Press.

Bonta, J. 1989. "Native Inmates: Institutional Response, Risk, and Needs." *Canadian Journal of Criminology* 29:49–62.

Brantingham, P., S. Mu, and A. Verma. 1995. "Patterns of Crime." In *Canadian Criminology: Perspectives on Crime and Criminality,* 2nd ed., ed. M. Jackson and C. Griffith. Toronto: Harcourt, Brace and Company.

Brown, Joseph Epes. 1982. *The Spiritual Legacy of the American Indian.* New York: Crossroad Publishing.

Bryde, John R. 1971. *Modern Indian Psychology.* Vermillion: Institute of Indian Studies, University of South Dakota.

Bureau of Indian Affairs. 1974. *The American Indian.* U.S. Department of the Interior, Washington, D.C.: U.S. Government Printing Office.

_____. 1978. *Indian Court and the Future: Report of the National American Indian Court Judges Association's Long-Range Planning Project.* U.S. Department of the Interior, Washington, D.C.: U.S. Government Printing Office.

Bureau of Justice Statistics. 1993. *Report to the Nation on Crime and Justice.* Washington, D.C.: U.S. Department of Justice.

Burke, P., and A. Turk. 1975. "Factors Affecting Post-Arrest Dispositions: A Model for Analysis." *Social Problems* 22:313–332.

Bynum, T. 1981. "Parole Decision Making and Native Americans." In *Race, Crime, and Criminal Justice,* ed. R. L. McNeely and C. E. Pope. Beverly Hills, Calif.: Sage.

_____. 1982. "Release on Recognizance: Substantive or Superficial Reform?" *Criminology* 20:67–82.

Bynum, T. S., and R. Paternoster. 1984. "Discrimination Revisited: An Exploration of Frontstage and Backstage Criminal Justice Decision Making." *Sociology and Social Research* 69:90–108.

Camp, G., and C. Camp. 1992. *The Corrections Yearbook—Juvenile Corrections.* South Salem, Mass.: Criminal Justice Institute.

Canada, Department of Justice. 1991. *Aboriginal People and Justice Administration: A Discussion Paper.* Ottawa: Canadian Department of Justice. September.

Canada, Solicitor General, Ministry Secretariat. 1988a. *Correctional Issues Affecting Native Peoples.* Correctional Law Review Working Paper no. 7, February 1988. Canada: Solicitor General.

_____. 1988b. *Final Report.* Task Force on Aboriginal Peoples in Federal Corrections. Ottawa: Supply and Services.

Canada, Special Committee on Indian Self-Government. 1983. *Indian Self-Government in Canada.* Report of the Special Committee. Ottawa: Queen's Printer.

Canby, W., Jr. 1988. *American Indian Law.* 2nd ed. St. Paul, Minn.: West Publishing Co.

Carpenter, E. 1959. "Alcohol in the Iroquois Dream Quest." *American Journal of Psychiatry* 116:148–151.

Carroll, L., and M. Mondrick. 1976. "Racial Bias in the Decision to Grant Parole." *Law and Society Review* 11:93–107.

Case, David S. 1978. *The Special Relationship of Alaska Natives to the Federal Government: A Historical and Legal Analysis.* Anchorage: The Alaska Native Foundation.

_____. 1984. *Alaska Natives and American Laws.* Fairbanks: University of Alaska Press.

Cawsey, R. A. 1991. *Justice on Trial: Task Force on the Criminal Justice System and Its Impact on the Indian and Metis People of Alberta.* 3 vols. Edmonton: The Task Force.

Chambliss, W. 1969. *Crime and the Legal Process.* New York: McGraw-Hill.

Chambliss, W. J., and R. D. Seidman. 1971. *Law, Order, and Power.* Reading, Mass.: Addison-Wesley.

Chiricos, T., P. Jackson, and G. Waldo. 1972. "Inequality in the Imposition of a Criminal Label." *Social Problems* 19:533–572.

Chiricos, T., and G. Waldo. 1975. "Socioeconomic Status and Criminal Sentencing: An Empirical Assessment of a Conflict Proposition." *American Sociological Review* 40:753–772.

Chisholm, James S. 1983. *Navaho Infancy: An Ethnological Study of Child Development.* New York: Aldine.

Clinton, Robert N. 1976. "Criminal Jurisdiction over Indian Lands: A Journey through a Jurisdictional Maze." *Arizona Law Review* 18(3):503–583.

Cockerham, W., M. Forslund, and R. Raboin. 1976. "Drug Use among White and American Indian High School Youth." *International Journal of the Addictions* 2:209–220.

Coffee, J. 1978. "The Repressed Issues of Sentencing: Accountability, Predictability, and Equality in the Era of the Sentencing Commission." *Georgetown Law Review* 66:976–1107.

Cohen, F. 1982. *Handbook of Federal Indian Law.* Charlottesville, Va.: Mitchie: Bobbs-Merrill.

Cohen, L., and J. Kluegel. 1978. "Determinants of Juvenile Court Dispositions: Ascriptive and Achieved Factors in Two Metropolitan Courts." *American Sociological Review* 43:162–179.

Cohen, Stanley. 1985. *Visions of Social Control.* Oxford: Polity Press.

Collins, R. 1975. *Conflict Sociology: Toward an Explanatory Science.* New York: Academic Press.

Conn, Stephen. 1985. "Alaskan Bush Justice: Legal Centralism Confronts Social Science Research and Village Alaska." In *People's Law and State Law,* ed. Anthony Allott and Gordon R. Woodman, 299–320. The Bellagio Papers, Dordrecht: Foris Publications.

———. 1988. "Smooth the Dying Pillow: Alaska Natives and Their Destruction." Paper delivered at the 12th International Congress of the IUAES, Zagreb, August.

Conn, Stephen, and Bart K. Garber. 1989. "State Enforcement of Alaska Native Tribal Law: The Congressional Mandate of the Alaska National Interest Lands Conservation Act." Paper presented at the Harvard Indian Law Symposium, October 27 and 28, Cambridge.

Conn, Stephen, and Antonia Moras. 1986. *No Need of Gold—Alcohol Control Laws and the Alaska Native Population: From the Russians through the Early Years of Statehood.* Anchorage: University of Alaska-Anchorage, School of Justice, Alaska Historical Commission Studies in History #226.

Cornwall, Peter, and Jerry McBeath, eds. 1982. *Alaska's Rural Development.* Boulder, Colo.: Westview.

Coser, L. 1956. *The Foundations of Social Conflict.* London: Free Press.

Couture, Joseph E. 1978. "Philosophy and Psychology of Native Education." In *One Century Later,* ed. Ian Getty and Donald Smith, 126–131. Vancouver: University of British Columbia Press.

———. 1985. "Traditional Native Thinking, Feeling, and Learning." *Multicultural Education Journal* 3(2):4–16.

———. 1992. "Traditional Aboriginal Spirituality and Religious Practice in Prison." In *Aboriginal Peoples and Canadian Criminal Justice,* ed. R. Silverman and M. Nielsen, 199–203. Toronto: Butterworths.

Coyle, Michael. 1986. "Traditional Indian Justice in Ontario: A Role for the Present." Paper prepared for the Indian Commission of Ontario, Chair Mr. Justice E. P. Hart.

Cross, Phyllis Old Dog. 1982. "Sexual Abuse: A New Threat to the Native American Woman. An Overview." *Listening Post: A Periodical of the Mental Health Programs of Indian Health Services.* 6(1/2).

Crutchfield, R. D., G. S. Bridges, and S. R. Pitchford. 1994. "Analytical and Aggregation Biases in Analyses of Imprisonment: Reconciling Discrepancies in Studies of Racial Disparity." *Journal of Research in Crime and Delinquency* 31(2):166–182.

Dahrendorf, R. 1957. *Class and Class Conflict in Industrial Society.* Stanford, Calif.: Stanford University Press.

D'Allessio, S. J., and L. Stolzenberg. 1993. "Socioeconomic Status and the Sentencing of the Traditional Offender." *Journal of Criminal Justice* 21:61–77.

Davis, L. Burton. 1989. "A History of Law Enforcement on the North Slope." Mimeograph. Barrow: North Slope Department of Public Safety.

Deloria, Vine, Jr., and Clifford, M. Lytle. 1983. *American Indians, American Justice.* Austin: University of Texas Press.

———. 1984. *The Nations Within.* New York: Pantheon Books.

Department of the Interior, Office of Indian Affairs. 1892. *Sixty-First Annual Report of the Commissioner of Indian Affairs.*

Depew, R. 1986. *Native Policing in Canada: A Review of Current Issues.* Working paper no. 46. Ottawa: Ministry of the Solicitor General.

Dickson-Gilmore, Elizabeth J. 1991. *La renaissance de la Grande Loi de la paix: Conceptions traditionnelles de la justice au sein de la nation Mohawk de Kahnawake.* Montreal: Recherches Amerindiennes au Quebec.

Dorris, Michael. 1987. "Indians on the Shelf." In *The American Indian and the Problem of History,* ed. Calvin Martin, 98–105. New York: Oxford University Press.

Dozier, Edward P. 1966. "Problem Drinking among American Indians: The Role of Sociocultural Deprivation." *Quarterly Journal of Studies on Alcohol* 27:72–87.

Driver, H. E. 1969. *Indians of North America.* Chicago: University of Chicago Press.

Dryzek, John S. 1989. "Policy Sciences of Democracy." *Polity* 22(1):97–118.

Dryzek, John S., and Oran Young. 1985. "Internal Colonialism and the Circumpolar North: The Case of Alaska." *Development and Change* 16:123–145.

Dumont, James. 1985. "Aboriginal Government." Research document prepared for the Roseau River Tribal Council, Manitoba.

_____. 1990. "Justice and Aboriginal People." Paper prepared for the Manitoba Aboriginal Justice Inquiry, Winnipeg, September. Also published in *Aboriginal Peoples and the Justice System,* ed. Royal Commission on Aboriginal Peoples. Ottawa: Ministries of Supply and Services, 1993.

Duncan, B. 1983. *Amerindian Police Program Evaluation: Executive Summary.* Ottawa: Department of Indian and Northern Affairs.

Ellanna, Linda J. 1991. *Nuvendalton Quht' ana: The People of Nondalton.* Washington, D.C.: Smithsonian Institute Press.

Etheridge, David. 1977. "Law Enforcement on Indian Reservations." *The Police Chief* April: 74–77.

Farella, J. 1984. *The Main Stalk: A Synthesis of Navajo Philosophy.* Tucson: University of Arizona Press.

Farnworth, M., and P. Horan. 1980. "Separate Justice: An Analysis of Race Differences in Court Processes." *Social Science Research* 9:381–399.

Federal Bureau of Investigation. 1990. *Uniform Crime Reports of the United States: Crime in the United States.* Washington D.C.: U.S. Government Printing Office.

Feimer, S., F. Pommersheim, and S. Wise. 1990. "Marking Time: Does Race Make a Difference? A Study of Disparate Sentencing in South Dakota." *Journal of Crime and Justice* 13:86–102.

Ferguson, F. N. 1968. "Navajo Drinking: Some Tentative Hypotheses." *Human Organization* 27:159–167.

Fienup-Riordan, Anne. 1990. *Eskimo Essays.* New Brunswick, N.J.: Rutgers University Press.

Fletcher, Alice C. 1907, 1910. In *Handbook of the American Indians North of Mexico,* ed. F. W. Hodge. Smithsonian Institution, Bureau of American Ethnology, bulletin no. 30, Wash., D.C.

Flowers, R. Barri. 1990. "Native American Criminality." In *Minorities and Criminality,* ed. R. Barri Flowers, 105–118. Contributions to Criminology and Penology, no. 21. New York: Praeger.

Forslund, M. and Meyers, R. 1974. "Delinquency among Wind River Indians Reservation Youth." *Criminology* 23(1).

Foster, George, and Barbara Anderson. 1978. *Medical Anthropology.* New York: Wiley and Sons.

Franciscan Fathers, Saint Michael, Arizona. 1929. *An Ethnologic Dictionary of the Navaho Language.* Leipzig: M. Breslauer.

Frazier, C. E., D. M. Bishop, and J. C. Henretta. 1992. "The Social Context of Race Differentials in Juvenile Justice Dispositions." *The Sociological Quarterly* 33(3):447–458.

French, L. 1982. *Indians and Criminal Justice.* Totowa, N.J.: Allanheld, Osmun.

French, L., and J. Hornbuckle. 1982. "Indian Alcoholism." In French, 1982:165–177.

Frideres, James S. 1988. *Native Peoples in Canada: Contemporary Conflicts.* 3rd. ed. Scarborough: Prentice-Hall.

_____. 1993. *Native Peoples in Canada: Contemporary Conflicts.* 4th Ed. Scarborough: Prentice-Hall.

Frisbie, Charlotte Johnson. 1967. "Kinaalda: A Study of the Navaho Girl's Puberty Ceremony."

_____. 1982. "Traditional Navajo Women: Ethnographic and Life History Portrayals." *American Indian Quarterly* 6(1–2).

Furtaw, Julia C., ed. 1993. *Native Americans, Information Directory.* 1st ed. Detroit, Mich.: Gale Research, Inc.

Geffner, Robert, and Mildred D. Pagelow, 1990. "Mediation and Child Custody Issues in Abusive Relationships."*Behavioral Sciences and the Law* 8:151, 155–157.

Gerber, Linda. 1980. "The Development of Canadian Indian Communities: A Two-Dimensional Typology Reflecting Strategies of Adaptation to the Modern World." *Canadian Review of Sociology and Anthropology* 16(4):126–134.

Gill, Sam. 1983. *Native American Traditions: Sources and Interpretations.* Belmont, Calif.: Wadsworth.

Goffman, E. 1959. *The Presentation of Self in Everyday Life.* Garden City, N.Y.: Doubleday.

Goldberg, J. 1975. "Public Law 83-280: The Limits of State Jurisdiction over Reservation Indians." *UCLA Law Review* 22.

Goldstein, H. 1987. "Toward Community-Oriented Policing: Potential, Basic Requirements, and Threshold Questions." *Crime and Delinquency* 33(1) (January):6–30.

Gordon, D. 1973. "Capitalism, Class and Crime in America." *Crime and Delinquency* 19:163–186.

Graves, T. D. 1967. "Acculturation, Access, and Alcohol in a Tri-Ethnic Community." *American Anthropologist* 69.

Gray, Susan H. 1983. *No-Frills Statistics: A Guide for the First-Year Student.* Totowa, N.J.: Rowman and Allanheld.

Green, D. E. 1991. "American Indian Criminality: What Do We Really Know?" In *American Indians: Social Justice and Public Policy*, ed. D. E. Green and T. V. Tonneson, 222–270. Milwaukee: University of Wisconsin System Institute on Race and Ethnicity.

_____. 1993. "The Contextual Nature of American Indian Criminality." *American Indian Culture and Research Journal* 17(2):99–119.

Green, E. 1964. "Inter- and Intra-Racial Crime Relative to Sentencing." *Journal of Criminal Law, Criminology, and Police Science* 55:348–358.

Greene, Jack R., and Stephen D. Mastrofski, eds. 1988. *Community Policing: Rhetoric or Reality?* New York: Praeger.

Greuning, Ernest. 1954. *The State of Alaska.* New York: Random House.

Griego, Tina. 1994. "Urban Refuge." *Albuquerque Tribune* July 6: B6.

Griffen, Joyce. 1982. "Life Is Harder Here: The Case of the Urban Navajo Woman." *New Mexico History Review* 59(3).

Griffiths, C. T. 1988. "Native Indians and the Police: The Canadian Experience." *Police Studies* 11(4) (Winter):155–160.

Griffiths, C. T., and J. C. Yerbury. 1984. "Natives and Criminal Justice Policy: The Case of Native Policing." *Canadian Journal of Criminology* 26:147–160.

Griffiths, C. T., J. C. Yerbury, and L. F. Weaver. 1987. "Canadian Natives: Victims of Socio-Structural Deprivation." *Human Organization* 46(3):277–282.

Grobsmith, Elizabeth S. 1989. "The Impact of Litigation on the Religious Revitalization of Native American Inmates in the Nebraska Department of Corrections." *Plains Anthropologist* 34(1):135–147.

_____. 1994. *Indians in Prison: Incarcerated Native Americans in Nebraska.* Lincoln: University of Nebraska Press.

Grobsmith, Elizabeth S., and Jennifer Dam. 1990. "The Revolving Door: Substance Abuse Treatment and Criminal Sanctions for Native American Offenders." *Journal of Substance Abuse* 2:405–425.

Guilfoyle, K., and M. Guilfoyle. 1995. "Research of Native American Delinquency in Idaho; Context of Incident and Juvenile Crime on Reservation." Unpublished final report, Idaho Juvenile Justice Commission.

Guilfoyle, M. 1988. "Indians and Criminal Justice Administration: The Failure of the Criminal Justice System for the American Indian." Unpublished master's thesis, University of Arizona, Tucson.

Hagan, J. 1975. "Parameters of Criminal Prosecution: An Application of Path Analysis to a Problem of Criminal Justice." *Journal of Criminal Law and Criminology* 65:536–544.

Hagan, J., J. Hewitt, and D. Alwin. 1979. "Ceremonial Justice: Crime and Punishment in a Loosely Coupled System." *Social Forces* 58:506–527.

Hagan, William T. 1966. *Indian Police and Judges.* Lincoln: University of Nebraska Press.

_____. 1993. *American Indians.* 3rd ed. Chicago: University of Chicago Press.

Haile, Berard. 1968. *Property Concepts of the Navaho Indians.* St. Michael's, Ariz.: St. Michael's Press.

_____. 1981. *Women versus Men: A Conflict of Navajo Emergence.* Lincoln: University of Nebraska Press.

Hale, Horatio. 1881. *The Iroquois Book of Rites.* Philadelphia: D. G. Brinton.

Hall, E. L., and A. A. Simkus. 1975. "Inequality in the Types of Sentences Received by Native Americans and Whites." *Criminology* 13:199–222.

Hall, G. 1980. *Federal-Indian Trust Responsibility Filmstrip.* Washington, D.C.: Institute for the Development of Indian Law.

Hamamsy, Leila Shukry. 1957. "The Role of Women in a Changing Navaho Society." *American Anthropologist* 49(1):101–111.

Hamilton, A. C., and C. M. Sinclair. 1991. *The Justice System and Aboriginal People: Report of the Aboriginal Justice Inquiry of Manitoba*. Winnipeg: Province of Manitoba, Queen's Printer.

Hanson, J. R., and L. P. Rouse. 1987. "Dimensions of Native American Stereotyping." *American Indian Culture and Research Journal* 11(4):22–30.

———. 1990. "Racial and Ethnic Stereotyping: Facts, Feelings, and Followings." Paper presented at the annual meeting of the American Sociological Association, Washington, D.C., August.

Hanushek, E., and J. Jackson. 1977. *Statistical Methods for Social Scientists*. New York: Academic Press.

Harring, S. 1982. "Native American Crime in the United States." In French, 1982:93–108.

Harris, David. 1994. "The 1990 Census Count of American Indians: What Do the Numbers Really Mean?" *Social Science Quarterly* 75(3):580–593.

Harris, F. R., and L. Harris. 1981. "Native Americans and Tribal Governments in New Mexico." In *New Mexico Government*. Albuquerque: University of New Mexico Press.

Hauswald, L. 1988. "Child Abuse and Child Neglect: Navajo Families in Crisis." *Dine Be'iina': Journal of Navajo Life*. 1(2).

Havemann, Paul. 1985. "The Over-Representation of Indigenous People within the Criminal Justice System: Questions about 'Problem-Solving.'" In *Justice Programs for Aboriginal and Other Indigenous Communities*, ed. Kayleen M. Hazlehurst, 121–140. Canberra: Australian Institute of Criminology.

———. 1988. "The Indigenization of Social Control in Canada." In *Indigenous Law and State Law*, ed. Bradford W. Morse and Gordon R. Woodman, 71–99. Dordrecht: Foris Publications.

Havemann, Paul, Keith Couse, Lori Foster, and Rae Matonovich. 1985. *Law and Order for Canada's Indigenous People*. Regina, Saskatchewan: Prairie Justice Research, University of Regina.

Hawkin, R., and G. Tiedeman. 1975. *The Creation of Deviance*. Columbus, Ohio: Merrill.

Hawkins, Darnell F. 1986. "Devalued Lives and Racial Stereotypes: Ideological Barriers to the Prevention of Family Violence among Blacks." In *Violence in the Black Family*, ed. R.L. Hampton. Lexington, Ky: Lexington Books.

———. 1987. "Beyond Anomalies: Rethinking the Conflict Perspective on Race and Criminal Punishment." *Social Forces* 65(3):719–745.

Hawkins, K. 1971. "Parole Selection: The American Experience." Ph.D. dissertation, University of Cambridge, Cambridge, England.

Hayner, N. S. 1942. "Variability in the Criminal Behavior of American Indians." *American Journal of Sociology* 36:602–613.

Hendry, Charles E. 1969. *Beyond Traplines*. Toronto: Ryerson Press.

Hepburn, J. 1978. "Race and the Decision to Arrest: An Analysis of Warrants Issued." *Journal of Research in Crime and Deliquency* 15:573.

Hills, S. 1971. *Crime, Power, and Morality*. Scranton, Pa.: Chandler.

Hippler, Arthur E. 1982. "Final Report to the Commissioner of the Department of Public Safety on the Village Public Safety Officer Program (VPSO)." Anchorage: University of Alaska, Institute of Social and Economic Research.

Hippler, Arthur E., and Stephen Conn. 1973. *Northern Eskimo Law Ways and Their Relationship to Contemporary Problems of 'Bush Justice.'* Fairbanks: University of Alaska, Institute of Social, Economic, and Government Research, Occasional papers no. 10.

———. 1975. "The Village Council and Its Offspring: A Reform for Bush Justice." *UCLA-Alaska Law Review* 5(1):22–57.

Hobsbawm, Eric. 1983. "Introduction: Inventing Traditions." In Hobsbawm and Ranger, 1983.

Hobsbawm, Eric, and Terence Ranger, eds. 1983. *The Invention of Tradition*. Cambridge, Eng.: Cambridge University Press.

Hoebel, E. Adamson. 1936. "Associations and the State in the Plains." *American Anthropologist* 38:433–438.

———. 1954. *The Law of Primitive Man: A Study in Comparative Legal Dynamics*. Cambridge, Mass.: Harvard University Press.

———. 1960. *The Cheyennes: Indians of the Great Plains*. New York: Holt, Rinehart and Winston.

———. 1969. "Keresan Pueblo Law." In *Law in Culture and Society*, ed. L. Nader. Chicago: Aldine.

Horetski, Gayle. 1984. "Memorandum: The Authority of the Alaska Police Standards Council to Establish Minimum Standards for Village Public Safety Officers (VPSOs) and Village Police Officers (VPOs)." Report to James F. Mayer, Director, APSC, April 3, Juneau.

Humphrey, Norman D. 1942. "Police and Tribal Welfare in Plains Indian Cultures." *Journal of Criminal Law and Criminology* 33:2(July–August):147–161.

Hunt, William R. 1987. *Distant Justice: Policing the Alaska Frontier.* Norman: University of Oklahoma Press.

Hutton, C., Frank Pommersheim, and Steve Feimer. 1989. " 'I Fought the Law and the Law Won': A Report on Women and Disparate Sentencing in South Dakota." *Criminal and Civil Confinement* 15(2):177–201.

Indian Bureau. 1884. Regulations of the Indian Department.

Iverson, Peter. 1981. *The Navajo Nation.* Westport, Conn.: Greenwood Press.

Ivy, S., C. Moelsworth, H. Stuler, and D. K. Hunter. 1981. *Crime in Indian Country: Final Report.* Washington, D.C.: SRI International.

Jackson, Michael. 1988. "Locking Up Natives in Canada: A Report of the Committee of the Canadian Bar Association on Imprisonment and Release." Vancouver: University of British Columbia.

Jayewardene, C. H. S. 1971. "Violence among the Eskimos." *Canadian Journal of Corrections* 13:24–42.

_____. 1979/1980. "Policing the Indian." *Crime and/et Justice* 7/8(1):42–47.

Jensen, G., J. Stauss, and V. W. Harris. 1977. "Crime, Delinquency, and the American Indian." *Human Organization* 36(3):252–257.

Jilek, Wolfgang. 1982. *Indian Healing.* Surrey, B.C.: Hancock House.

Jilek, Wolfgang, and Chunibal Roy. 1976. "Homicide Committed by Canadian Indians and Non-Indians." *International Journal of Offender Therapy and Comparative Criminology* 20(3):201–216.

Johnson, W. B. 1990. "Navajo Peacemaker Court: Impact and Efficacy of Traditional Dispute Resolution in the Modern Setting." Thesis submitted to the University of New Mexico School of Law.

Johnston, L., P. O'Malley, and J. Bachman. 1989. *Drug Use, Drinking, and Smoking: National Survey Results from High School, College, and Young Adult Populations, 1975–1989.* Rockville, Md.: National Institute on Drug Abuse.

Jorgensen, Joseph G., Richard McCleary, and Steven McNabb. 1985. "Social Indicators in Native Village Alaska." *Human Organization* 44(1):2–17.

Kanowitz, Leo. 1969. *Women and the Law: The Unfinished Revolution.* Albuquerque: University of New Mexico Press.

Kaplan, B., and D. Johnson. 1964. "The Social Meaning of Navaho Psychopathology." In *Magic, Faith, and Healing: Studies in Primitive Psychiatry Today,* ed. A. Kiev, 203–229. New York: The Free Press.

Kaplan, M., S. Gans, and H. Kahn. 1968. "The Development Potential of the Pine Ridge Reservation." In Indian Education Subcommittee Hearing, 96th Congress, First and Second Sessions, Part 4.

Kaufman, A. 1973. "Gasoline Sniffing among Children in a Pueblo Indian Village." *Pediatrics* 51:1060–1064.

Kidwell, Clara Sue. 1978. "The Power of Women in Three American Indian Societies." *Journal of Ethnic Studies* 6(3):113–121.

Kiev, Ari. 1973. "Magic, Faith, and Healing in Modern Psychiatry." In *Religious Systems and Psychotherapy,* ed. Richard H. Cox. Springfield, Ill.: Charles Thomas.

Kleck, G. 1981. "Racial Discrimination in Criminal Sentencing: A Critical Evaluation of the Evidence with Additional Evidence on the Death Penalty." *American Sociological Review* 46(4):783–795.

Kleinman, A., and E. Sung. 1979. "Why Do Indigenous Practitioners Successfully Heal?" *Social Science and Medicine* 13B:7–26.

Kluckhohn, Clyde. 1962. "Navaho Morals." In *Culture and Behavior,* ed. Richard Kluckhohn. New York: Free Press.

Kluckhohn, Clyde, and Dorothea Leighton. 1962. *The Navaho.* Garden City, N.Y.: Natural History Library.

_____. 1974. *The Navaho.* Rev. Ed.

Kroeber, A. 1925. "Principles of Yurok Law." *Handbook of the Indians of California.* Washington, D.C.: Bureau of American Ethnology, bulletin 78.

Kruse, John A., Judith Kleinfeld, and Robert Davis. 1982. "Energy Development on Alaska's North Slope: Effects on the Inupiat Population." *Human Organization* 41(2):97–106.

Kynell, Kermit Syppli. 1981. "A Different Frontier: Alaskan Criminal Justice, 1935–65." Ph.D. dissertation, Carnegie-Mellon University, Pittsburgh, Pa.

LaFree, G. D. 1985. "Official Reactions to Hispanic Defendants in the Southwest." *Journal of Research in Crime and Delinquency* 22:213–237.

Lamphere, Louise. 1977. *To Run After Them: Cultural and Social Bases of Cooperation in a Navajo Community*. Tucson: University of Arizona Press.

LaPrairie, Carol Pitcher. 1984. "Selected Criminal Justice and Socio-Demographic Data on Native Women." *Canadian Journal of Criminology* 26(2):161–170.

_____. 1988. "Community Types, Crime, and Police Services on Canadian Indian Reservations." *Journal of Research in Crime and Delinquency* 25(4):375–391.

_____. 1992. *Dimensions of Aboriginal Over-Representation in Correctional Institutions and Implications for Crime Prevention*. Ottawa: Supply and Services Canada, catalogue no. JS5-/4–1992.

Latham, G. I. 1985. "The Educational Status of Federally Recognized Indian Students." *Journal of American Indian Education* 25(1).

Law Reform Commission. 1991. *Aboriginal Peoples and Criminal Justice*. Ottawa: Law Reform Commission of Canada.

Leiber, M. J. 1994. "A Comparison of Juvenile Court Outcomes for Native Americans, African Americans and Whites." *Justice Quarterly* 11(2):257–279.

Leighton, Dorothea, and Clyde Kluckhohn. 1948. *Children of the People: The Navaho Individual and His Development*. Cambridge, Mass.: Harvard University Press.

Lengyel, Linda B. 1990. "Survey of State Domestic Violence Legislation." *Legal Reference Services Quarterly* 10.

Lerman, Lisa G. 1984. "Mediation of Wife Abuse Cases: The Adverse Impact of Informal Dispute Resolution on Women." *Harvard Women's Law Journal* 7:52, 72, 92.

Levy, J., and S. Kunitz. 1971. "Indian Reservations, Anomie, and Social Pathologies." *Southwestern Journal of Anthropology* 27:97–128.

_____. 1974. *Indian Drinking, Navajo Practices and Anglo-American Theories*. New York: Wiley.

Levy, J. E., S. J. Kunitz, and M. Everett. 1969. "Navajo Criminal Homicide." *Southwestern Journal of Anthropology*. 25:124–152.

Levy, Jerrold E., et al. 1989. "The Effects of Regional Variation and Temporal Change on Matrilineal Elements of Navajo Social Organization." *Journal of Anthropological Research* 45.

Liban, C., and R. Smart. 1982. "Drinking and Drug Use among Ontario Indian Students." *Drug and Alcohol Dependence* 9:161–171.

Linn, Patricia. 1992. *Report of the Saskatchewan Indian Justice Review Committee*. Regina, Saskatchewan: Government of Saskatchewan and Government of Canada.

Liska, A., and M. Tausig. 1979. "Theoretical Interpretations of Social Class and Racial Differentials in Legal Decision-Making for Juveniles." *Sociological Quarterly* 20:197–207.

Lizotte, A. 1977. "Extra-Legal Factors in Chicago's Criminal Courts: Testing the Conflict Model of Criminal Justice." *Social Problems* 25:564–580.

Llewellyn, Karl N., and E. Hoebel. 1941. *The Cheyenne Way: Conflict and Case Law in Primitive Jurisprudence*. Norman: University of Oklahoma Press.

Lobb, M., and T. Watts. 1989. *Native American Youth and Alcohol: An Annotated Bibliography*. New York: Greenwood Press.

Lofland, J. 1920. *Primitive Society*. New York: Boni and Liveright.

_____. 1969. *Deviance and Identity*. Englewood Cliffs, N.J.: Prentice-Hall.

Longclaws, L., E. Barnes, L. Grieve, and R. Dumoff. 1980. "Alcohol and Drug Use among the Brokenhead Ojibwa." *Journal of Studies on Alcohol* 41:21–36.

Loree, D. J. 1985. *Policing Native Communities*. Paper prepared for the Canadian Police College, Ottawa.

Loree, Donald, and Chris Murphy, eds. 1986. *Community Policing in the 1980's: Recent Advances in Police Programs*. Ottawa: Solicitor General of Canada.

Lowie, Robert H. 1920. *Primitive Society*. New York: Boni and Liveright.

Lundman, R. 1974. "Routine Police Arrest Practices: A Commonwealth Perspective." *Social Problems* 22:127–141.

Lundman, R., R. Sykes, and J. Clark. 1978. "Police Control of Juveniles: A Replication." *Journal of Research in Crime and Delinquency* 15:74–91.

Lynch, M. J., and E. B. Patterson. 1991. *Race and Criminal Justice.* New York: Harrow and Heston.

MacLead, W. C. 1932. "Aspects of the Earlier Development of Law and Punishment." *Journal of the American Institute of Criminal Law and Criminology* 23.

_____. 1934. "Law, Procedure, and Punishment in Early Bureaucracies." *Journal of the American Institute of Criminal Law and Criminology* 25.

_____. 1937. "Police and Punishment among Native Americans of the Plains." *Journal of the American Institute of Criminal Law and Criminology* 28.

MacLean, B., and D. Milovanovic. 1990. *Racism, Empiricism, and Criminal Justice.* Vancouver: Collective Press.

Mail, P., and D. McDonald. 1980. *Tulapai to Tokay.* New Haven, Conn.: HRAF Press.

Mann, C. R. 1993. *Unequal Justice: A Question of Color.* Bloomington: Indiana University Press.

Marenin, Otwin. 1990. "The Difficulties of Policing: Perceptions of the Role of the Village Public Safety Officer (VPSO) in Alaskan Native Villages." Paper presented to the American Society of Criminology, Baltimore, Md.

_____. 1992. "Exploring Patterns of Crime in the Native Villages of Alaska." *Canadian Journal of Criminology* 34.

Marenin, Otwin, and Gary Copus. 1991. "Policing Rural Alaska: The Village Public Safety Officer (VPSO) Program." *American Journal of Police* 10(4):1–26.

Maure, M. 1992. *Americans Behind Bars: One Year Later.* Washington, D.C.: The Sentencing Project.

McBeath, Gerald A., and Thomas A. Morehouse, eds. 1987. *Alaska: State Government and Politics.* Fairbanks: University of Alaska Press.

McBride, D., and J. B. Page. 1980. "Adolescent Indian Substance Abuse: Ecological and Sociological Factors." *Youth and Society* 11(4).

McClintock, Walter. 1910. *The Old North Trail: Or, Life, Legends and Religion of the Blackfeet Indians.* London: Macmillan.

McKanna, Clare, Jr. 1993. "Murderers All: The Treatment of Indian Defendants in Arizona Territory, 1880–1912." *American Indian Quarterly* 17(3):359–369.

McKenzie, Evan. N.d. *The Report of the Third Bush Justice Conference Held in Kenai, Alaska, October 7, 8, and 9, 1976.* Anchorage: Alaska Federation of Natives.

McNickle, D'Arcy. 1973. *Native American Tribalism: Indian Survivals and Renewals.* New York: Oxford University Press.

Melton, A. 1989. "Traditional and Contemporary Tribal Law Enforcement: A Comparative Analysis." Paper presented at the Western Social Science Association Albuquerque, New Mexico.

Messick, James. 1989. Interview, September.

Miethe, T. D. 1987. "Stereotypical Conceptions and Criminal Processing: The Case of the Victim-Offender Relationship." *Justice Quarterly* 4(4):571–593.

Miethe, T. D., and C. A. Moore. 1986. "Racial Differences in Criminal Processing: The Consequences of Model Selection on Conclusion about Differential Treatment." *Sociological Quarterly* 27:217–237.

Miller, George. 1979. "Native Values and Attitudes." Mimeograph.

Miller, J. R. 1989. *Skyscrapers Hide the Heavens: A History of Indian-White Relations in Canada.* Rev. ed. Toronto: University of Toronto Press.

Minnis, M. S. 1963. "The Relationship of the Social Structure of an Indian Community to Adult and Juvenile Delinquency." *Social Forces* 41.

Mitzak, M. J. 1991. "The Concepts of Police and Community-Based Policing: The Canadian Perspective." Paper presented at the Annual Meetings of the American Society of Criminology, San Francisco, November.

Morehouse, Thomas A. 1989. "Rebuilding the Political Economics of Alaska Native Villages." ISER Occasional Paper no. 21. Anchorage: University of Alaska at Anchorage.

Morehouse, Thomas A., Gerald A. McBeath, and Linda Leask. 1984. *Alaska's Urban and Rural Governments.* Lanham, Md.: University Press of America.

Morgan, Lewis H. 1851. *League of the Ho-De-No-Sau-Nee, or Iroquois.* 3 vols. Rochester, N.Y.: Sage and Brothers.

Morrison, W. R. 1975. "The North-West Mounted Police and the Klondike Gold Rush." In *Police Forces in History,* ed. George F. Mosse, 263–275. Beverly Hills, Calif.: Sage.

Morse, Bradford W. 1985. *Aboriginal Peoples and the Law: Indian, Metis, and Inuit Rights in Canada.* Ottawa: Carleton University Press.

Mudd, J. E. 1972. "Indian Juveniles and Legislative Delinquency in Montana." *Montana Law Review* 33(2).

Murton, Thomas O'Rhelius. 1965. *The Administration of Criminal Justice in Alaska 1867 to 1902.* Master's thesis, University of California, Berkeley.

Nader, L., and E. Combs-Schilling. 1977. "Restitution in Cross-Cultural Perspective." In *Restitution in Criminal Justice,* ed. J. Hudson and B. Galaway. Lexington, Ky: Lexington Books.

Nagel, Joanne. 1995. "American Indian Ethnic Renewal: Politics and the Resurgence of Identity." *American Sociological Review* 60:947–965.

Naske, Claus-M. 1985. *A History of Alaska Statehood.* Lanham, Md.: University Press of America.

_____. 1988. "Steps Leading to the Establishment of the Territorial Police in Alaska." Unpublished paper.

National Clearinghouse on Alcohol Information. 1985. *Alcohol and Native Americans.* Rockville, Md. U.S. Government Printing Office.

National Household Survey Press Package. 1990. Rockville, Md.: National Institute on Drug Abuse, document no. D00008.

National Task Force on Juvenile Justice for Native Americans and Alaska Natives. 1987. *A Report to Congress with Recommendations Regarding the Reauthorization of the JJDP Act.* Senate Judiciary Committee Hearings, U.S. Congress.

Navajo Nation Department of Law Enforcement. 1991. *Navajo Division of Public Safety, Narrative Report on Domestic Violence.* October.

Navajo Supreme Court. 1990. *Kuwanhyoima v. Kuwanhyoima,* no. TC-CV–334–84 (Tuba City District Court, April 9, 1990) and no. A-CV–13–90 (Navajo Nation Supreme Court, December 5, 1990).

Ness, Robert C. 1980. "The Impact of Indigenous Healing Activity: An Empirical Study of Two Fundamentalist Churches." *Social Science and Medicine* 14B:167–180.

Nettler, Gwynne. 1989. *Criminology Lessons.* Cincinnati, Ohio: Anderson.

Newcomb, F. J. 1966. *Navaho Neighbors.* Norman: University of Oklahoma Press.

Nielsen, Marianne O. 1993. "Surviving In-Between: A Case Study of a Canadian Aboriginal-Operated Criminal Justice Organization." Unpublished Ph.D dissertation, University of Alberta, Edmonton.

_____. 1996. "A Comparison of Developmental Ideologies: Navajo Nation Peacemaker Courts and Canadian Native Justice Committees." In *Restorative Justice,* ed. Burt Galaway and Joe Hudson. Monsey, N.Y.: Criminal Justice Press.

Nielsen, Marianne O., and Lindsay Redpath. 1994. "New Management and Aboriginal Organizations: A Comparison of New Management Ideology and Management Practices in an Aboriginal-Operated Criminal Justice Organization." Paper presented at the Canadian Sociology and Anthropology Association Meetings, Calgary, Alberta, June 1994.

Nix, William. 1989. Interview, September.

Normandeau, A., and B. Leighton. 1990. "A Vision of the Future of Policing in Canada: Police-Challenge 2000." Background document for police and security branch, Ministry Secretariat, Solicitor General Canada. Ottawa: Minister of Supply and Services Canada. October.

Northwest Intertribal Court System. N.d. "Summary Report: Traditional and Informal Dispute Resolution Processes in Tribes of the Puget Sound-Olympia Peninsula Region."

O'Brien, M. 1977. "Indian Juveniles in the State and Tribal Courts of Oregon." *American Indian Law Review* 5.

O'Brien, S. 1989. *American Indian Tribal Governments.* Norman: University of Oklahoma Press.

O'Callaghan, Edmund B., ed. 1853–1887. *Documents Relative to the Colonial History of New York, Procured in Holland, England, and France by John R. Brodhead.* 15 vols. Albany, N.Y.: Weed, Parsons.

Oetting, E., and F. Beauvais. 1983. "A Typology of Adolescent Drug Use: A Practical Classification System for Describing Drug Use Patterns." *Academic Psychology Bulletin* 5:55–69.

_____. 1990. "Adolescent Drug Use: Findings of National and Local Surveys." *Journal of Clinical and Consulting Psychology* 58:385–394.

Oetting, E. R., and G. C. Goldstein. 1979. "Drug Use among Native American Adolescents." In *Youth Drug Abuse: Problems, Issues, and Treatment,* ed. G. M. Beschner and A. S. Friedman, 409–441. Lexington, Ky.: Lexington Press.

Office of Juvenile Justice and Delinquency Prevention. 1978. *Program Announcement, Restitution by Juvenile Offenders: An Alternative to Incarceration.* Washington, D.C.: U.S. Department of Justice.

Ogburn, M. J. 1971. "Constitutional Implications of an Indian Defendant's Rights to a Lesser Included Offense Instruction." *South Dakota Law Review* 16.

Ontario, Ministry of the Solicitor General. 1991. *Community Policing: Shaping the Future.* Toronto: Government of Ontario.

Otis, Delos S. 1973. *The Dawes Act and the Allotment of Indian Lands.* Norman: University of Oklahoma Press.

Otto, Laurie. 1986. "A Search for Control: The Effect of Alcohol on Public Rights and Private Wrongs." Report to the Legislature, Joint Committee on Local Option Laws, Juneau.

Palmer, J., and P. Carlson. 1976. "Problems in the Use of Regression Analysis in Prediction Studies." *Journal of Research in Crime and Delinquency* 13:64–81.

Parker, Arthur C. 1916. *The Constitution of the Five Nations: Or, the Iroquois Book of the Great Law.* New York State Museum, bulletin 184.

Parnas, 1991. "The American Bar Foundation Survey of Administration of Criminal Justice and Past, Present, and Future Responses to Domestic Violence." *Washington University Law Quarterly* 107.

Passel, J. S. 1976. "Provisional Evaluation of the 1970 Census Count of American Indians." *Demography* 13(3):397–409.

Passel, J. S., and P. A. Berman. 1986. "Quality of 1980 Census Data for American Indians." *Social Biology* 33(3/4):163–182.

Patterson, J. R. 1972. "Education, Jurisdiction, and Inadequate Facilities as Causes of Juvenile Delinquency among Indians." *North Dakota Law Review* 48(4).

Pattison, E. Mansell. 1973. "Foreword." In *Religious Systems and Psychotherapy,* ed. Richard H. Cox. Springfield, Ill.: Charles Thomas.

Peak, K. 1989. "Criminal Justice, Law, and Policy in Indian Country: A Historical Perspective." *Journal of Criminal Justice* 17:393–407.

Peak, K., and J. Spencer. 1987. "Crime in Indian Country: Another Trail of Tears." *Journal of Criminal Justice* 15:485–494.

Penner, Keith, Chairperson. 1983. "Indian Self-Government." Minutes of the Proceedings of the Special Committee on Indian Self-Government. House of Commons, issue no. 40, Ottawa.

Pete, J. 1982. *National Indian Police Survey.* Ottawa: National Indian Brotherhood, Ottawa.

Petersilia, J. 1983. *Racial Disparities in the Criminal Justice System.* Santa Monica, Calif.: Rand.

Peterson, D., and P. Friday. 1975. "Early Release from Incarceration: Race as a Factor in the Use of Shock Probation." *Journal of Criminal Law and Criminology* 66 (March): 79–87.

PHS Community Mental Health. 1968. *Pine Ridge Research Bulletin.* In Indian Education Subcommittee Hearings, 90th Congress, First and Second Session, Part 4.

Piliavin, I., and S. Briar. 1964. "Police Encounters with Juveniles." *American Journal of Sociology* 70:206–214.

Pinto, L. 1973. "Alcohol and Drug Abuse among Native American Youth on Reservations: A Growing Crisis." In *Drug Use in America: Problems in Perspective,* vol. 1. ed. U.S. Commission on Marihuana and Drug Abuse, Appendix. Washington, D.C.: U.S. Government Printing Office, 1157–1178, document no. 5266–00004.

Pommersheim, F. 1995. *Braid of Feathers: American Indian Law and Contemporary Tribal Life.* Berkeley and Los Angeles: University of California Press.

Pommersheim, F., and S. Wise. 1987. "Going to the Penitentiary: A Study of Disparate Sentencing in South Dakota." *South Dakota Barrister* 19(July–Aug).

_____. 1989. "Going to the Penitentiary. A Study of Disparate Sentencing in South Dakota." *Criminal Justice and Behavior* 16:155–165.

Price, M. 1973. *Law and the American Indian.* Indianapolis, Ind.: Bobbs-Merrill.

Prucha, F. P. 1973. *Americanizing the American Indians: Writings by the "Friends of the Indian," 1880–1900.* Cambridge, Mass.: Harvard University Press.

_____. 1984. *The Great Father: The United States Government and the American Indians.* Vols. 1 and 2. Lincoln: University of Nebraska Press.

_____. 1985. *The Indians in American Society.* Berkeley and Los Angeles: University of California Press.

Public Inquiry into the Administration of Justice. Aboriginal Justice Inquiry of Manitoba. 1991. *Report of the Aboriginal Justice Inquiry of Manitoba.* Vol. 1: *The Justice System and Aboriginal People.* Winnipeg: The Inquiry.

Quinney, R. 1970. *The Social Reality of Crime.* Boston: Little, Brown.

———. 1977. *Class, State, and Crime.* New York: McKay.

Reasons, C. 1972. "Crime and the American Indian." In *Native Americans Today: Sociological Perspectives,* ed. H. M. Bahr, B. A. Chadwick, and R. C. Day, 319–326. New York: Harper and Row.

Reaves, B. 1992. *State and Local Police Departments, 1990.* Washington, D.C.: Bureau of Justice Statistics.

Reddy, M. A. 1993. *Statistical Record of Native North Americans.* Detroit, Mich.: Gale Research.

Reese, H. 1975. "Obstacles to the Development of American Indian Children." *Family Law Quarterly* 573.

Reid, John P. 1970. *A Law of Blood: The Primitive Law of the Cherokee Nation.* New York: New York University Press.

———. 1971. "The Cherokee Thought: An Apparatus of Primitive Law." *New York University Law Review* 46(2) (April): 281–302.

Reuters. 1995. "High Court to Decide Case on 1990 Census Adjustments." clari.net.news.usa.law, Wed. September 27.

Riley, 1984. "Some European [Mis]Perceptions of American Indian Women." *New Mexico History Review* 59(3).

Robbins, Lynn Arnold, and Steven McNabb. 1987. "Oil Developments and Community Responses in Norton Sound, Alaska." *Human Organization* 46(1):10–17.

Robbins, S. 1985. "Commitment, Belief, and Native American Delinquency." *Human Organization* 44(1):57–62.

Roessel, Ruth. 1981. *Women in Navaho Society.* Rough Rock, Ariz.: Navajo Resource Center, Rough Rock Demonstration School.

Ross, Rupert. 1989. "Leaving Our White Eyes Behind." *Canadian Native Law Reporter* 3:1–15.

Sanders, D. 1985. *Aboriginal Self-Government in the United States.* Background paper no. 5. Kingston: Institute of Intergovernmental Relations, Queen's University.

Saslow, H. L., and M. L. Harrover. 1968. "Research on Psychosocial Adjustment of Indian Youth." *American Journal of Psychiatry* 125(2).

Schoolcraft, Henry R. 1846. *Notes on the Iroquois: Or, Contributions to the Statistics, Aboriginal History, Antiquities and General Ethnology of Western New York.* New York: Bartlett and Welford.

Schur, E. 1971. *Labeling Deviant Behavior: Its Sociological Implications.* New York: Random House.

Sellin, John A. 1981. *Village Public Safety Officer Program. First Annual Evaluation.* Juneau: Alaska, Department of Public Safety.

Shattuck, P., and J. Norgren. 1991. *Partial Justice: Federal Indian Law in a Liberal Constitutional System.* New York: Berg.

Shepardson, Mary. 1963. *Navajo Ways in Government: A Study in Political Process.* Washington, D.C.: American Anthropological Association.

———. 1982. "The Status of Navajo Women." *American Indian Quarterly* 149:161–162.

Shepardson, Mary, and Blodwen Hammond. 1970. *The Navajo Mountain Community: Social Organization and Kinship Terminology.* Berkeley and Los Angeles: University of California Press.

Shinkwin, Anne D., and Mary C. Pete. 1983. *Homes in Disruption: Spouse Abuse in Yupik Eskimo Society.* Fairbanks: University of Alaska at Fairbanks.

Silverman, Robert A. 1980. "Measuring Crime: More Problems." *Journal of Police Science and Administration* 8(3) (September): 265–274.

Silverman, Robert A., and Leslie Kennedy. 1995. "Unsolved Homicides in the United States and Canada." Paper presented to the Homicide Researchers Workshop Group, June, Ottawa. Published in the Proceedings of the Workshop (Marc Riedel, editor).

Silverman, Robert A., and Marianne O. Nielsen, eds. 1992. *Aboriginal Peoples and Canadian Criminal Justice.* Toronto: Butterworths.

Simmons, J. 1969. *Deviants.* Berkeley, Calif.: Glendessary Press.

Skinner, Alanson. 1915. "Societies of the Iowa, Kansa, and Ponca Indians." *Anthropological Papers of the American Museum of Natural History (APAMNH),* 13:679–801.

Skogan, Wesley. 1984. "Reporting Crime to the Police: The Status of World Research." *Journal of Research in Crime and Delinquency* 21:113–137.

Skolnick, J. H. 1966. *Justice Without Trial.* 2nd ed. New York: Wiley.

Skolnick, Jerome H., and David H. Bayley. 1986. *The New Blue Line: Police Innovation in Six American Cities.* New York: Free Press.

Skoog, D. M., and Barker, I. 1989. *Effects of Contact with Police among Aboriginals in Manitoba.* Paper prepared for the Manitoba Aboriginal Justice Inquiry, Winnipeg, July.

Skoog, D., L. W. Roberts, and E. D. Boldt. 1980. "Native Attitudes towards the Police." *Canadian Journal of Criminology* 22:354–359.

Skultans, Vieda. 1976. "Empathy and Healing: Aspects of Spiritualist Ritual." In *Social Anthropology and Medicine,* ed. J. E. Loudon, London: Academic Press.

Smith, D. 1984. "The Organizational Context of Legal Control." *Criminology* 22:19–38.

Smith, Watson, and John M. Roberts. 1973. *Zuni Law: A Field of Values.* With an appendix by Stanley Newman. Millwood, N.Y.: Kraus Reprints.

Snipp, C. Matthew. 1986. "The Changing Political and Economic Status of the American Indians: From Captive Nations to Internal Colonies." *American Journal of Economics and Sociology* 45:145–157.

_____. 1989. *American Indians: The First of This Land.* New York: Russell Sage.

Social Policy Research Associates/The Evaluation Group. 1983. *National Evaluation Overview of Indian Policing: Executive Summary and Main Report.* Ottawa: Department of Indian Affairs and Northern Development.

South Dakota Board of Charities and Corrections. 1987. *Analysis of Inmate Population: Calendar Year Report 1985–87.*

Spencer, Katherine. 1947. *Reflection of Social Life in the Navaho Origin Myth.* Albuquerque: University of New Mexico Press.

Spicer, George. 1927. *The Constitutional Status and Government of Alaska.* Baltimore: Johns Hopkins University Press.

Spitzer, S. 1975. "Toward Marxian Theory of Deviance." *Social Problems* 22:638–651.

Spohn, C., J. Gruhl, and S. Welch. 1987. "The Effect of Race on Sentencing: A Re-examination of an Unsettled Question." *Law and Society Review* 16:71–88.

Spohn, C., and S. Welch. 1987. "The Effect of Prior Record in Sentencing Research: An Examination of the Assumption That Any Measure Is Adequate." *Justice Quarterly* 4:287–307.

Stanley, D. 1976. *Prisoners among Us: The Problem of Parole.* Washington, D.C.: Brookings.

Statistics Canada. 1993. *Age and Sex (1991 Aboriginal Data).* Ottawa: Industry, Sciences, and Technology Canada.

Stewart, O. 1964. "Questions regarding American Indian Criminality." *Human Organization* 23(1):61–66.

Stratton, J. 1973. "Cops and Drunks: Police Attitudes and Actions in Dealing with Indian Drunks." *International Journal of Addictions* 8:613–621.

Strickland, R. 1975. *Fire and the Spirits: Cherokee Law from Clan to Court.* Norman: University of Oklahoma Press.

Strimbu, A., L. Schoenfeldt, and S. Southern. 1973. "Drug Usage of College Students as a Function of Racial Classification and Minority Group Status." *Research in Higher Education* 1:263–272.

Swafford, M. 1980. "Three Parametric Techniques for Contingency Table Analysis: A Non-Technical Commentary." *American Sociological Review* 45:664–690.

Swift, B., and G. Bickel. 1974. *Comparative Parole Treatment of American Indians and Non-Indians at United States Federal Prisons.* Washington, D.C.: Bureau of Social Science Research.

Swigert, V., and R. Farrell. 1977. "Normal Homicides and the Law." *American Sociological Review* 42:16–32.

Szasz, M. C. 1977. *Education and the American Indian: The Road to Self-Determination since 1928.* 2d ed. Albuquerque: University of New Mexico Press.

_____. 1990. "The Path to Self-Determination: American Indian Education, 1940–1990." In *One House, One Voice, One Heart: American Indian Education at the Santa Fe Indian School,* ed. Sally Hyer. Santa Fe: Museum of New Mexico Press.

Talbot, S. 1971. *American Indian Almanac.* New York: World Publishing Company.

_____. 1981. *Roots of Oppression: The American Indian Question.* New York: International Publishers.

Task Force on Indian Policing. 1990. *Indian Policing Policy Review: Task Force Report.* Ottawa: Department of Indian and Northern Affairs. January.

Taub, Nadine. 1980. "Equitable Relief in Cases of Adult Domestic Violence." *Women's Rights Law Reporter* 6:241.

Terrell, John U. 1971. *American Indian Almanac.* New York: World Publishing Company.

Terry, R. 1967. "The Screening of Juvenile Offenders." *Journal of Criminal Law, Criminology, and Police Science* 58(2):173–181.

Thomas, C., and R. Cage. 1977. "The Effects of Social Characteristics on Juvenile Court Dispositions." *Sociological Quarterly* 18:237–252.

Thompson, Joseph J. 1924. "Law amongst the Aborigines of the Mississippi Valley." *Illinois Law Quarterly* 6:204–233.

Thornberry, T. 1979. "Sentencing Disparities in the Juvenile Justice System." *Journal of Criminal Law and Criminology* 70:164–171.

Thwaites, Reuben G., ed. 1896–1901. *The Jesuit Relations and Allied Documents: Travels and Explorations of the Jesuit Missionaries in New France, 1610–1791.* The original French, Latin, and Italian texts, with English translations and notes. 73 vols. Cleveland, Ohio: The Burrows Brothers.

Timberlake, Henry. 1948. *Memoirs, 1756–1765.* Ed. Samuel C. Williams. Marietta, Ga.: Continental Book Co.

Torres, D., and T. Palmer. 1987. *Needs of Rural American Indian Youth in California: Offenders and Those at Risk of Offending.* Sacramento: California Department of the Youth Authority, Program Research and Review Division.

Trigger, Bruce G. 1976. *The Children of Aataensic: A History of the Huron People to 1660.* 2 vols. Montreal: McGill-Queen's University Press.

———. 1985. *Natives and Newcomers.* Kingston: McGill-Queen's University Press.

Traisman, Ken. 1981. "Native Law: Law and Order Among Eighteenth-Century Cherokee, Great Plains, Central Prairie, and Woodland Indians." *American Indian Law Review* 9:273–287.

Trojanowicz, Robert, and Bonnie Bucqueroux. 1990. *Community Policing: A Contemporary Perspective.* Cincinnati, Ohio: Anderson Publishing Co.

Trojanowicz, R., and D. Carter. 1988. *The Philosophy and Role of Community Policing.* Detroit: National Neighborhood Foot Patrol Center, Michigan State University.

Tso, Tom. 1986. "The Tribal Court Survives in America." *The Judges' Journal* 25(2):22–25 and 52–56.

———. 1989. "The Process of Decision Making in Tribal Courts." *Arizona Law Review* 31:225–235.

———. 1992. "Moral Principles, Traditions, and Fairness in the Navajo Nation Code of Judicial Conduct." *Judicature* 76(1).

Turk, A. 1969. *Criminality and Legal Order.* Chicago: Rand McNally.

Underhill, Ruth M. 1956. *The Navajos.* Norman: University of Oklahoma Press.

Unnever, J. 1982. "Direct and Organizational Discrimination in the Sentencing of Drug Offenders." *Social Problems* 30:212–225.

Unnever J., and Hembroff. 1988. "The Prediction of Racial/Ethnic Sentencing Disparities: An Expectation States Approach." *Journal of Research in Crime and Delinquency* 25:53.

U.S. Commission on Civil Rights. South Dakota Advisory Committee. 1977. *Liberty and Justice for All: A Report Prepared by the South Dakota Advisory Committee to the U.S. Commission on Civil Rights.* Washington: Commission on Civil Rights.

U.S. Department of Commerce. Bureau of Census. 1980. *Census of the Population. General Population Characteristics, South Dakota.* Washington, D.C.: U.S. Government Printing Office.

———. 1992. *1990 Census of Population and Housing.* Washington, D.C.: U.S. Government Printing Office.

U.S. Department of the Interior. Bureau of Indian Affairs. 1981. *BIA Profile: The Bureau of Indian Affairs and American Indians.* Washington, D.C.: Government Printing Office.

U.S. Department of Justice. Bureau of Justice Statistics. 1992. *Correctional Populations in the United States, 1990.* Washington, D.C.: U.S. Government Printing Office.

———. 1993. *Sourcebook of Criminal Justice Statistics, 1992.* Washington, D.C.: U.S. Government Printing Office.

U.S. Department of Justice. Federal Bureau of Investigation. 1992. *Uniform Crime Report, 1991.* Washington, D.C.: U.S. Government Printing Office.

U.S. Senate. 1989. "Report of the Alaska Federation of Natives on the Status of Alaska Natives: A Call for Action." *Hearings Before the Select Committee on Indian Affairs.* 100th Congress, first session.

U.S. Senate Committee on Interior and Insular Affairs. 1975. *Congressional Hearings, Subcommittee on Indian Affairs.* 94th Congress, second session.

U.S. Senate Subcommittee to Investigate Juvenile Delinquency. 1955. *Report to the U.S. Congress.* Washington D.C.: Senate Committee of the Judiciary.

Utter, Jack. 1993. *American Indians: Answers to Today's Questions.* Lake Ann, Mich.: National Woodlands Publishing.

Vallee, Frank G. 1978. "The Emerging Northern Mosaic." In *Modernization and the Canadian State,* ed. Daniel Glenday, Herbert Guindon, and Allan Turowetz, 317–334. Toronto: MacMillan.

Van Valkenburgh, R. F. 1938. "Navajo Common Law III: Etiquette-Hospitality-Justice." *Museum Notes Northern Arizona Museum* 10(12):39, 40.

Visher, C. 1983. "Gender, Police Arrest Decisions, and Notions of Chivalry." *Criminology* 21:5–28.

Von Hentig, H. 1945. "The Delinquency of the American Indian." *Journal of Criminal Law and Criminology* 36:75–84.

von Hirsch, A., and K. Hanrahan. 1979. *The Question of Parole: Retention, Reform, or Abolition?* Cambridge, Mass.: Ballinger.

Voris, Michael J. 1991. "Civil Orders of Protection: Do They Protect Children, the Tag-Along Victims of Domestic Violence?" *Ohio University Law Degree* 599.

Wachtel, David. 1980. "A Historical Look at BIA Police on the Reservations." *American Indian Journal* 6(May):13–18.

Waldman, Carl. N.d. *Atlas of the North American Indian, 200–201.* N.Y.: Facts on File.

Waldram, James B. 1990a. "The Persistence of Traditional Medicine in Urban Areas: The Case of Canada's Indians." *American Indian and Alaska Native Mental Health Research* 4(1):9–29.

_____. 1990b. "Access to Traditional Medicine in a Western Canadian City." *Medical Anthropology* 12:325–348.

Walker, J. 1982. *Lakota Society.* Lincoln: University of Nebraska Press.

Walker, James R. 1917. "The Sun Dance and Other Ceremonies of the Oglala Division of the Teton Dakota." *American Museum of Natural History Anthropological Papers* 16.

_____. 1993. "Aboriginal Spirituality: Symbolic Healing in Canadian Prisons." *Culture, Medicine, and Psychiatry* 17(3):345–362.

Walker, Samuel, and Molly Brown. 1995. "A Pale Reflection of Reality: The Neglect of Racial and Ethnic Minorities in Introductory Criminal Justice Textbooks." *Journal of Criminal Justice Education* 6(1):61–77.

Wallace, Paul A.W. 1946. *The White Roots of Peace.* Philadelphia: University of Pennsylvania Press.

Wax, R. 1967. "The Warrior Dropouts." *Transactions* 4:40–46.

Weibel-Orlando, Joan. 1984. "Substance Abuse among American Indian Youth: A Continuing Crisis." *Journal of Drug Issues* 14(2):313–335.

_____. 1989. "Hooked on Healing: Anthropologists, Alcohol, and Intervention." *Human Organization* 48(2):148–155.

Welch, S., J. Gruhl, and C. Spohn. 1984. "Sentencing: The Influence of Alternative Measures of Prior Record." *Criminology* 22:215–222.

Welch, S., and C. Spohn. 1986. "Evaluating the Impact of Prior Record on Judges' Sentencing Decisions: A Seven-City Comparison." *Justice Quarterly* 3:389–407.

Wilbanks, W. 1987. *The Myth of a Racist Criminal Justice System.* Monterey, Calif.: Brooks/Cole.

Williams, L. E. 1979. "Antecedents of Urban Indian Crime." Ph.D. dissertation, Brigham Young University, Provo, Utah.

Winfree, L., and C. Griffiths. 1983. "Youth at Risk: Marijuana Use among Native American and Caucasian Youth." *International Journal of the Addictions* 18:53–70.

Winfree, L. T., C. T. Griffiths, and C. Sellers. 1989. "Social Learning Theory, Drug Use, and American Indian Youths: A Cross-Cultural Test." *Justice Quarterly* 6(3):395–417.

*Winnipeg Free Press.* 1992. "McCrae using 'racist' tactics, natives charge." March 11:16.

Witherspoon, G. 1975. *Navajo Kinship and Marriage.* Chicago and London: University of Chicago Press.

Wolf, Eric R. 1988. "Inventing Society." *American Ethnologist* 15(4):752–761.

Wolfgang, Marvin E. 1963. "Uniform Crime Reports: A Critical Appraisal." *University of Pennsylvania Law Review* 3:708–738.

Wooden Leg. 1991. "Judge Wooden Leg Keeps One Wife." In *Native American Testimony: A Chronicle of Indian-White Relations from Prophecy to the Present, 1492–1992,* ed. Peter Nabokov, 229–231. N.Y.: Viking.

Wright, Lawrence. 1994. "One Drop of Blood." *The New Yorker* July 25:46–55.

Wright, Ronald C. 1992. *Stolen Continents: The "New World" through Indian Eyes.* Boston: Houghton Mifflin.

Wuttunee, Wanda A. 1992. *In Business for Ourselves: Northern Entrepreneurs.* Montreal: McGill-Queen's University Press.

Young, David, Grant Ingram, and Lise Swartz. 1989. *Cry of the Eagle: Encounters with a Cree Healer.* Toronto: University of Toronto Press.

Young, David, Janice Morse, Lise Swartz, and Grant Ingram. 1987. "The Psoriasis Research Project: An Overview." In *Health Care Issues in the Canadian North,* ed. David Young, University of Alberta occasional publication no 26. Edmonton: Boreal Institute for Northern Studies.

Zatz, M. S. 1984. "Race, Ethnicity, and Determinate Sentencing: A New Dimension to an Old Controversy." *Criminology* 22:147–171.

_____. 1985. "Pleas, Priors, and Prison: Racial/Ethnic Differences in Sentencing." *Social Science Research* 14:169–193.

_____. 1987. "The Changing Forms of Racial/Ethnic Biases in Sentencing." *Journal of Research in Crime and Delinquency* 24:69–92.

Zatz, M. S., C. C. Lujan, and Z. K. Snyder-Joy. 1991. "American Indians and Criminal Justice: Some Conceptual and Methodological Considerations." In *Race and Criminal Justice,* ed. M. J. Lynch and E. B. Patterson, 100–112. New York: Harrow and Heston.

Zion, James W. 1983. "The Navajo Peacemaker Court: Deference to the Old and Accommodation to the New." *American Indian Law Review* 11:89–109.

_____. 1992. "North American Indian Perspectives on Human Rights." In *Human Rights in Cross-Cultural Perspectives: A Quest for Consensus,* ed. Abdullahi Ahmed An-Na'im, 191, 196–197. Philadelphia: University of Pennsylvania Press.

Zion, James W., and Elsie B. Zion. 1993. "Hazho's Sokee'—Stay Together Nicely: Domestic Violence Under Navajo Common Law." *Arizona State Law Journal* 25(2):407–426.

# CASES CITED

*Cherokee Nation v. Georgia,* 30 U.S. (5 Pet.) 1 (1831)

*Duro v. Reina,* 110 S.Ct. 2053 (1990)

*Ex Parte Crow Dog,* 109 U.S. 556 (1883)

*Montana v. United States,* 450 U.S. 544 (1981)

*Oliphant v. Suquamish Indian Tribe,* 435 U.S. 191 (1978)

*Worcester v. Georgia,* 31 U.S. (6 Pet.) S7S (1832)

# About the Book
## and Editors

The historical involvement of Native peoples within the criminal justice system is a narrative of tragedy and injustice, yet Native American experience in this system has not been well studied. Despite disproportionate representation of Native Americans in the criminal justice system, far more time has been spent studying other minority groups.

*Native Americans, Crime, and Justice* is the first book in many years to provide students with a comprehensive overview of Native Americans and the unique challenges they face as justice is meted out, both in the United States and Canada.

Crossing disciplines, this important anthology, which includes the voices of both Native Americans and non–Native Americans, provides students in criminology, sociology, and Native American studies courses with articles ranging from the scholarly to the more humanistic. Also included are a number of news accounts that complement the other pieces with a sense of immediacy and timeliness about the involvement of Native Americans in the criminal justice system.

Students and general readers alike will come away from reading this collection with a better, more informed understanding of Native Americans, crime, and justice, whether they are learning about the unique problem of tribal versus federal jurisdiction on Indian lands, patterns of Native American crime, the process of decisionmaking in tribal courts, or Native American delinquency.

**Marianne O. Nielsen** is assistant professor in the Department of Criminal Justice at Northern Arizona University. (Please direct inquiries to Marianne Nielsen at N.A.U., e-mail: M.Nielsen@nau.edu.) **Robert A. Silverman** is dean of the Faculty of Arts and Science at Queen's University.

# About the Contributors

Alexander Alvarez, Department of Criminal Justice, Northern Arizona University
Troy L. Armstrong, Division of Anthropology, California State University, Sacramento
Ronet Bachman, Department of Sociology and Criminal Justice, University of Delaware
Fred Beauvais, Department of Psychology, Colorado State University
Philmer Bluehouse, Director, Peacemaker Project, Navajo Nation Judicial Branch
T. Bynum, School of Criminal Justice, Michigan State University
E. J. Dickson-Gilmore, Law School, Carleton University
James Dumont, Native Studies, University of Sudbury
S. Feimer, Government Research Bureau, University of South Dakota
E. Grobsmith, Department of Anthropology, University of Nebraska
Michael H. Guilfoyle, Native American Consultant, Genesee, Idaho
Maggie Hodgson, NECHI Institute, Edmonton, Alberta
C. Hutton, School of Law, University of South Dakota
Otwin Marenin, Department of Political Science, Criminal Justice Program, Washington
 State University
Ada Pecos Melton, Native American Consultant, Albuquerque, New Mexico
Marianne O. Nielsen, Department of Criminal Justice, Northern Arizona University
R. Paternoster, Department of Criminal Justice and Criminology, University of Maryland
Craig Perkins, Department of Justice, Bureau of Justice Statistics
F. Pommersheim, School of Law, University of South Dakota
Rupert Ross, Assistant Crown Attorney, District of Kenora (Ontario)
Robert A. Silverman, Faculty of Arts and Science, Queen's University
Douglas M. Skoog, Department of Sociology, University of Winnipeg
Zoann K. Snyder-Joy, Department of Sociology, Western Michigan University
Tom Tso, Chief Justice Emeritus, Navajo Nation, Judicial Branch
J. B. Waldram, Native Studies Department, University of Saskatchewan
Elsie B. Zion (Redbird), Women Studies Department, University of New Mexico
James Zion, Solicitor, Judicial Branch, Navajo Nation